The Global Lincoln

The Global Lincoln

Edited by Richard Carwardine

and

Jay Sexton

An Oxford University/Rothermere American Institute Book

OXFORD
UNIVERSITY PRESS

OXFORD
UNIVERSITY PRESS

Oxford University Press, Inc., publishes works that further
Oxford University's objective of excellence
in research, scholarship, and education.

Oxford New York

Auckland   Cape Town   Dar es Salaam   Hong Kong   Karachi
Kuala Lumpur   Madrid   Melbourne   Mexico City   Nairobi
New Delhi   Shanghai   Taipei   Toronto

With offices in

Argentina   Austria   Brazil   Chile   Czech   Republic France   Greece
Guatemala   Hungary   Italy   Japan   Poland   Portugal   Singapore
South Korea   Switzerland   Thailand   Turkey   Ukraine   Vietnam

Copyright © 2011 by Oxford University Press, Inc.

Published by Oxford University Press, Inc.
198 Madison Avenue, New York, NY 10016

www.oup.com

Oxford is a registered trademark of Oxford University Press

Library of Congress Cataloging-in-Publication Data
The global Lincoln / edited by Richard Carwardine and Jay Sexton.
p.   cm.
Includes bibliographical references and index.
ISBN 978-0-19-537911-2
1. Lincoln, Abraham, 1809–1865—Foreign public opinion.
2. Lincoln, Abraham, 1809–1865—Influence.
3. United States—History—Civil War, 1861–1865—Foreign public opinion.
4. United States—Politics and government—1861–1865—Foreign public opinion.
I. Carwardine, Richard. II. Sexton, Jay, 1978–
E457.8.G53   2011
973.7092—dc22   2011006172

1 3 5 7 9 8 6 4 2

Printed in the United States of America
on acid-free paper

To our Oxford colleagues
who illuminate the past with what Lincoln called "the calm light of history"

{ CONTENTS }

{ PREFACE }

More than any other American historical figure, Abraham Lincoln towers over the global landscape, a leader who spoke—and continues to speak—to statesmen and ordinary people alike. This book is an exploration of what we call the "Global Lincoln"—that is, the Lincoln that was imagined, debated, and appropriated by peoples around the world, from Lincoln's own lifetime to the present. The contributors to this volume show that the heart of Lincoln's global celebrity lies in his status as the archetypal self-made man, his record of successful leadership in wartime, his resolute defense of popular government and free labor, and the inspirational role he has played in the era of democratic, liberal nationalism. Yet Lincoln has also been a malleable and protean figure, one who is forever being redefined to meet the needs of those who invoke him.

Lincoln's worldwide impact during his lifetime and since has remained, some admirable pioneering work apart, a largely untold story, not least because of the breadth of scholarly expertise required to reconstruct the web of Lincoln trails and to assess their local and wider meanings. That work of reconstruction is the purpose of this book. As such, it contributes to a burgeoning literature intent on "globalizing" the history of the United States. That enterprise, of course, runs the danger of a sort of historiographical imperialism or imbalance, in which the role of the United States is over-magnified by being the only lens. For that reason *The Global Lincoln* draws considerably on the scholarship of historians who are not primarily or exclusively interested in the history of the United States and who are best placed to interpret Lincoln's legacy in the many global, national, and local contexts in which the United States has been a peripheral actor, if one at all. Those who study Africa, China, England, France, Germany, India, Ireland, Italy, Japan, Latin America, Spain, and Wales here consider how over time Lincoln has been interpreted, appropriated, and reinterpreted in these countries and continents. Their narratives may say rather less about the "real" Lincoln than about the many different "constructed" Lincolns that met national or local purposes. Since the Global Lincoln was so often filtered through and projected out of Britain (a point explored in chapter 1), this book offers several essays on the British Isles. Lincoln's story there, from the moment he entered the presidency, became a plural narrative, one which merits separate investigations: of his reputation, while alive, in the most powerful nation of the day; of his subsequent celebration in England and the more radical culture of Wales; and of his extraordinarily versatile utility amongst the Irish.

Complementing these case studies are essays that explore Lincoln's understanding of the wider world and his nation's special responsibilities to it, and the attempts of American policy-makers to deploy him as a means of projecting the values and power of the United States abroad. Also included is an essay on the dualistic, even schizophrenic, reading of Lincoln in the states of the former Confederacy. For a book concerned with foreign perspectives on Lincoln this is not as paradoxical as it may appear. For four years the seceded states deemed themselves an independent power, alienated from the old Union of 1787. Conquered by force of arms, the post-Civil War white South continued to harbor a powerful sense of separateness marked by an unforgiving bitterness against Lincoln and the other political and military leaders of the wartime Union; even today that animosity has not entirely dissipated. Lincoln-haters, as this book's contributors make clear, have by no means been restricted to North America, but they have rarely been as vocal and never as persistent in their hostility as have Confederates and their ideological descendants, who provide a valuable perspective from one extreme of a gamut of worldwide views that extends to uncritical hero-worship at the other.

The pursuit of the Global Lincoln has been a collective enterprise. We have been blessed with a group of contributors whom we consider a "team of the unrivaled": distinguished historians whom we thank wholeheartedly for embracing the project, recognizing that a work of this kind requires more than token collaboration, and engaging creatively and generously with our frequent editorial interventions. These are not the only debts we have incurred between the book's conception and realization. We offer sincere thanks to all those mentioned below and the organizations they represent.

The book's origins lay in a proposal to the Abraham Lincoln Bicentennial Commission (ALBC) for a conference on the international legacy of Abraham Lincoln, designed as a joint venture with the Rothermere American Institute (RAI) at Oxford University. Thanks to the determination of the ALBC Commissioners Harold Holzer and Frank J. Williams, and the practical support first of Michael Bishop, the ALBC's executive director, and then of his successor Eileen R. Mackevich, that proposal became a reality at St Catherine's College, Oxford, over the Fourth of July weekend in 2009. Through the ALBC we also benefited from the good offices of Darrel E. Bigham, Gabor Boritt, Jennifer Rosenfeld, Venkitaraman Suresh, and the ever-imaginative Caroline Cracraft. The Abraham Lincoln Presidential Library and Museum gave an unprompted and generous lead in funding, for which Rick Beard, Thomas F. Schwartz, and T. Tolbert Chisum deserve a special tribute. We are equally indebted to the Chicago History Museum and the support of its President, Gary Johnson, and Chief Historian, Russell Lewis. The United States Embassy in London, though the Cultural Attaché, Lisa Davis, and Susan J. Wedlake of the Cultural Affairs Office, covered several speakers' travel costs. The ever-generous Lewis E. Lehrman and Richard Gilder smiled on the venture: their Gilder-Lehrman

Institute for American History (GLI) in New York made substantial grants to teachers and graduate students and ensured the filming of the conference. In particular we benefited from the imaginative support at GLI of its President, James G. Basker, and the Executive Director, Lesley Herrmann. Oxford University's John Fell Fund and Faculty of History gave essential financial support, as did the RAI, whose Director, Nigel Bowles, could not have done more to help make the conference a landmark event. Not least he provided the incomparable administrative and diplomatic skills of Lucy Dugmore. We also benefited from the professionalism of Tim Pottle, Zim Nwokora, and—at St Catherine's College—Caroline Carpenter.

Most of the essays in this book had their first airing at the Global Lincoln conference. There they benefited from the collegial criticism of a cadre of perceptive commentators: Richard Blackett, Patricia Clavin, Catherine Clinton, John Darwin, Rosemary Foot, Russell Lewis, Marc Mulholland, Jörg Nagler, Peter Onuf, Thomas F. Schwartz, Frank J. Williams, and Douglas L. Wilson. President Ellen Johnson-Sirleaf of Liberia, Roger Wilkins of George Mason University, and the broadcaster Gavin Esler helped bring significant contemporary political perspectives to bear. We received additional scholarly help from Bryon Andreason, Michelle Ganz, Isabel Holowaty, Robert C. Kenzer, Benjamin L. Kenzer, Angus Lincoln, Holger Nehring, Keith Robbins, George Scratcherd, Christopher Vanier, Mary Vincent, Jennifer Weber, and Naomi Wolf. Andrea Greengrass delivered the index with her customary professionalism. Finally, we take pleasure in acknowledging the energetic and formidable role in this project of our editor at Oxford University Press, who here deserves the last word: Susan Ferber.

Richard Carwardine and Jay Sexton
Corpus Christi College, Oxford
October 2010

The Global Lincoln

The Global Lincoln

Richard Carwardine and Jay Sexton

Abraham Lincoln often dwelt on death and the evanescence of human existence. The poem he most treasured was "Mortality," Alexander Knox's melancholy rumination on the transience of life, and as a writer himself, he tried his hand at verse that explored these themes. He had, it seems, no firm belief in a future state. "It isn't a pleasant thing to think that when we die that is the last of us," he reflected.[1] How, then, might he hope to avoid ending up, in Knox's words, "hidden and lost in the depths of the grave"? The individual's only hope of immortality, Lincoln believed, lay in achievements that lasted in public memory. His closest friend, Joshua Speed, described a conversation in 1841, at a time when Lincoln's "deep depression" prompted thoughts of suicide: "He said to me that he had done nothing to make any human being remember that he had lived—and that to connect his name with the events transpiring in his day & generation and so impress himself upon them as to link his name with something that would redound to the interest of his fellow man was what he desired to live for."[2]

Twenty years later, Lincoln had not only achieved national recognition as the successful presidential candidate of the new Republican party but the whole world looked on as he squared up to the fearful demands of his nation's existential conflict. He felt acutely the historic moment. Lincoln understood that the international significance of the American Union would give the Civil War a permanent place in the public memory of the world. He declared this most forcefully in the peroration of his annual message to Congress in December 1862: "Fellow-citizens, *we* cannot escape history. We of this Congress and this administration, will be remembered in spite of ourselves. No personal significance, or insignificance, can spare one or another of us. The fiery trial through which we pass, will light us down, in honor or dishonor, to the latest generation."[3] Exactly one month later he issued his Emancipation Proclamation, to declare free the slaves in areas still under Confederate control. Discussing this initiative with Speed, he alluded to their long-ago conversation of 1841 and, his friend recalled, "said with earnest emphasis—I believe that in this measure . . . my fondest hopes will be realized."[4]

Lincoln's edict certainly won him international attention, though not untainted glory, since many saw it as a last throw of the dice in a forlorn contest, an invitation to a slave uprising, and the prelude to interracial slaughter.[5] Still, the president could reflect upon the proclamation's far-flung impact and take pleasure in the eulogies it elicited, even if their grandiloquence was surely not to his taste. "Heir of the thought of Christ and of [John] Brown," wrote Giuseppe Garibaldi, Italian liberal and nationalist, "you will pass down to posterity under the name of *the Emancipator*! more enviable than any crown and any human treasure!"[6] A West Indian editor lauded him for a public career "entitling your name to a niche in the Temple of Fame."[7] From Constantinople the American consul wrote: "The proclamation of freedom & the declaration to the world of its immutability are destined to an immortality as luminous as the Declaration of Independence & the Farewell Address of Washington."[8] Workingmen and liberals in Britain—"the intelligent masses of the industrious population"— declared their hearty support in a common cause.[9] And from Oroomiah, Persia, Lincoln learnt that a Syriac-language paper carried the translated text of his "firman," by which "hundreds and perhaps thousands are learning to reverence your name, among the oppressed Nestorians of Persia and of Koordistan."[10]

It is doubtful, however, that Lincoln, even when Confederates laid down their arms in April 1865, appreciated just how far he had stirred the hearts and minds of sympathizers at home and abroad. He was sharply aware of the opprobrium and scorn of domestic critics throughout the war, and he knew that abroad much opinion was hostile. Foreign verdicts, when they were not driven by ideological aversion, were often marked by misunderstanding and ignorance. European conservatives caricatured him as a hypocrite and buffoon, while sympathetic progressives doubted his fitness for a historic task. Yet Lincoln's death, just days after the rebels' surrender at Appomattox, prompted not only an unprecedented outpouring of public grief throughout the loyal Union, but also a quite extraordinary explosion of mourning around the world. Lincoln's playful joking, about a vain politician who would have chosen to die years earlier had he known how big his funeral would be, took on a mournful irony.

"What a general consternation, what an immense grief all over Europe! Lincoln dead! Lincoln assassinated! That is . . . the universal cry, the all excluding topic in Court-Palaces and in the cabins of the poor." So wrote Henry Boernstein, the distraught United States Consul in Bremen, to Lincoln's former Postmaster General, Montgomery Blair. "I have witnessed in Europe the memorable epochs of 1830 and 1848, but never have I seen such a general commotion, such a deep consternation."[11] This was no sorrow-induced overstatement. In many different parts of the world John Wilkes Booth's murderous act precipitated widespread public grief and some of the largest popular gatherings of the era. Hundreds of messages from national and municipal governments engulfed American consulates and embassies, as did a blizzard of tributes from voluntary civic groups comprising churches, secular societies, working-men's improvement and mutual aid associations, democratic circles, ragged schools, anti-slavery and freedmen's societies, temperance leagues, Masonic lodges, ladies' societies, literary and reading groups, student clubs, gymnastic and choral unions, fire companies, chambers of commerce, and agricultural alliances. Published by the U.S. State Department, the compendium of foreign condolences ran to more than 800 pages. Tributes from the peoples of Great Britain and her dependencies not surprisingly dominate the publication (360 out of its 837 pages), but the text makes clear that admiration of Lincoln was not confined to the English-speaking world. European voices from Austria to Würtemburg, and Latin American ones from Argentina to Venezuela also were prominent in the volume, and those from China, Japan, and north and west Africa indicated that even before death Lincoln had become a truly global figure, known in every continent, and that well beyond courts, chancelleries, and parliaments he had touched and inspired the lives of common people.[12] From the U.S. legation in Paris, during the weeks after the assassination, John Bigelow confessed to Secretary of State William Henry Seward his sheer amazement—and gratification—at the grip that Lincoln had exerted over pop-ular opinion amongst "the masses of Europe": it was the common tribute that no man's death had previously "awakened such prompt and universal sympathy at once among his own country people and among foreign nations."[13]

This outpouring of appreciation proved to be the prelude to a much longer and more significant story. Lincoln's international standing would burgeon over the next two generations, well into the 1920s at least; indeed, he would continue to be widely invoked throughout the twentieth century, in different places, at different times, for sundry purposes. When in 1909 Canadian poet Edward William Thomson composed "We Talked of Lincoln," a poem that opens with persons of six different nationalities discussing Lincoln while on the frozen plains of Saskatchewan, he depicted a scene that had occurred not just in Canada but countless times in myriad settings around the globe.[14] Carl Jung scarcely exaggerated in 1938 when he deemed Lincoln to have been "removed to the timeless sphere of mythical existence."[15] Yet the story of the character, range, and significance of Lincoln's worldwide appeal and appropriation has remained—some admirable pioneering work apart—largely untold.[16]

Following Lincoln's ideological, cultural, and political tracks around the globe can be a challenge, not least because of his impact on overlooked or-dinary lives, but also because his influence was sometimes exerted indirectly. Further complicating matters, even the most commonly repeated instances of Lincoln's global reach may include those of murky provenance. Take Leo Tolstoy's conversation with a Circassian tribal chief in a remote region of the Caucasus, a meeting regularly cited as a dramatic example of the ubiquity of

Lincoln's name. The Caucasian hungered for information about Lincoln, whom he called "the greatest general and greatest ruler of the world," an unmatchable hero who "spoke with a voice like thunder; he laughed like the sunrise and his deeds were strong as the rock and as sweet as the fragrance of roses. The angels appeared to his mother and predicted that the son whom she would conceive would become the greatest the stars had ever seen." There is more in the same vein, and the tale has unsurprisingly become the stuff of Lincoln lore. But there is need for caution. Many authors rely on Carl Sandburg, yet he himself gave no citation for the episode. The account in fact appears in the New York newspaper *The World* five days before Lincoln's centenary birthday. Those authors who do provide a citation variously give the date as February 7 or 8 in either 1908 or 1909. One version places Tolstoy's conversation with the tribal leader in 1908. However, Tolstoy had not been in the Caucasus for many years, his visits occurring mostly before the Civil War. His complete works and correspondence—running to ninety-one volumes—make no mention of Lincoln. This is not evidence that the newspaper article was a hoax, but its author was not Tolstoy himself. Rather, a certain "Count S. Stakelberg" wrote the story "especially for *The World*," apparently after visiting the old man, then in his eighty-first year and in poor health, on his estate in Yasnaya. The circumstances suggest that Tolstoy was recalling a conversation that dated back forty years.[17]

As this example suggests, pursuing Lincoln globally raises significant questions of historical method and interpretation. What relation does the "Global Lincoln"—a figure whose versatility has helped him speak to a multitude of conditions—bear to the "real" Lincoln? Which elements of this global figure predominate? When and where do they do so? How does his reception relate to larger forces in the modern world: nationalism, liberalism, and democracy; imperialism and de-colonization; economic modernization; individualism and collectivism; and secularization? By what routes did Lincoln's name and reputation travel? Who were the carriers? What does Lincoln's celebrity tell us about transnational networks—political, economic, and cultural—and the processes and limits of global integration? How far has foreign understanding been influenced by shifts in views of Lincoln at home? How much depended on Lincoln's projection by American agencies, how much on a spontaneous appropriation by local admirers? How far has he acted as a surrogate for the United States and its multiple images abroad? How far as a weapon to be used against overweening American power? How far as a symbol of inclusivity and universal principles? What does his appropriation say about the cult of celebrity in the modern world? Where has he stood in the international pantheon of statesmen and thinkers? How does he compare to other American figures in this respect? How ultimately might we measure his influence? Did his projection and appropriation materially change anything?

Intractable though some of these questions are and incomplete as the answers offered here must be, they promise a more complete historical picture of Lincoln. The outpouring of Lincoln studies, by looking ever more micro-scopically at the life and character of the sixteenth president, has generally worked to celebrate his special qualities and uniqueness. His global reach, how-ever, suggests that in significant ways he was a representative man of his time, one who spoke to ideas and aspirations common to the many who considered their world to be on the threshold of a new and better era in human history.

That outside the United States Lincoln would become a protean symbol reflects in part the ambiguous and enigmatic elements of the man himself. This "most shut-mouthed" man, as his law partner William H. Herndon described him, revealed little of himself even to the closest of associates; his merited reputation for telling the truth did not mean he necessarily told the *whole* truth, and in po-litical communication he commonly chose to leave much unsaid. Consequently Lincoln's contemporaries, and generations of biographers and historians since, have disputed the underlying motor of his politics and statecraft. Some see a reluctant emancipator "forced into glory," others a disguised radical, and yet others a gradualist reformer. Some identify a corporate railway lawyer, others a friend of the workingman and a hard-handed son of toil. Portraits of a prag-matic party political schemer contend with those of a principled statesman. Those who extol his nationalism for its liberal values have to confront those who damn its coercive practice. These antitheses are overstated, and need not be mutually exclusive, but they highlight how hard it has been for Lincoln's American audiences to agree on his defining qualities.[18] Unsurprisingly, foreign assessments have been equally varied in what they have chosen to celebrate or revile.

Lincoln's international appeal reached its height during the last third of the nineteenth century and the early decades of the next, though he enjoyed further phases of visibility during the Cold War and in recent years, thanks in part to invocations of him by successive American presidents, George W. Bush and Barack Obama. During the heyday of his reputation, Lincoln's authority derived less from his role as emancipator than as the robust defender of the principles of liberal and democratic nationalism. Lincoln was widely cast as the heroic tribune of the people or democratic leading man whose defense of his nation's integrity was far removed from narrow chauvinism. Instead, he won the acclaim of radicals and nation-builders around the globe whose own lives were devoted to projects inspired by—and designed to advance—the same universal democratic principles. Lincoln cast American nationalism not in ethnic or racial terms but as a moral force for the improvement of humankind, a beacon of lib-erty to the world. This purposeful universalism or liberal nationalism spoke to a wide spectrum of political progressives abroad: socialists, radicals, and dem-ocrats, who combined nationalist aspirations with informal membership of a community dedicated to freeing the world from monarchical power, aristocratic privilege, and constrained popular rights. For them, the nation was not an end in itself, but the mechanism by which political freedom and individual rights might be universally achieved. Lincoln provided the model of how to transcend one's nation to become a symbol of the common people's universal struggle.

Thus in Spain, the *Progresistas* of the Revolutionary Sexennium of 1868–74 paid homage to Lincoln the democratic hero; Emilio Castelar, president of the First Spanish Republic, saw him as the apotheosis of a free political system that acted as "a school of liberty."[19] Garibaldi's Italian democrats saw in the combined force of emancipation and assassination Lincoln's potency as a champion of republican liberty. As a symbol of a new political order, he won admirers amongst German radicals and, following the Meiji restoration, Japanese modernizers. Cubans—above all the independence leader José Martí—extolled Lincoln as an uncorrupted natural man whose democratic wisdom derived from his authenticity as a man of the people; in Uruguay the commentator José Enrique Rodó likewise deployed the president's "natural" qualities to press the case for the interlocking of democracy and meritocracy.[20] Several leading German social democrats and anti-Nazis of the Weimar Republic found an ideological anchor in Lincoln. He inspired influential figures amongst the Slavic minorities of the Austro-Hungarian Empire: during the 1880s and 1890s Tomáš Masaryk—self-made scholar, intellectual, and first president of Czechoslovakia—pressed for progressive reform and Czech autonomy within the empire, but after 1914 invoked Lincoln's and Woodrow Wilson's democratic ideas in the pursuit of full independence, declaring "that these principles have been and ever will be the policy of my government and my life."[21]

Successive British campaigns for suffrage extension enlisted him in the cause. None was more eloquent than George Holyoake and fellow members of the Sheffield Secular Society. Holyoake—who had earlier informed Lincoln that no president since Washington had "won the esteem of the liberal portion of the English nation as you have"—deemed his assassination "a crime against . . . the liberties of the human race . . . [and] that great doctrine of democracy which regards the whole people as entitled to equal conditions of personal improvement of social prosperity and civil equality." Lincoln, he wrote, "not only rose from the people, but he exalted the people among whom he rose."[22] Lincoln's sublime exaltation of the people, the Gettysburg Address, became the credo of both separatist and consolidationist nationalists, each group invoking the democratic basis of the cause. The versatility and utility of that address is no better exemplified than in its adoption by both Irish Unionists and Irish republican nationalists. "I believe fundamentally in the right of the Irish people to govern themselves," republican Éamon de Valera declared in 1921. "I believe fundamentally in government of the people by the people and, if I may add the other part, for the people."[23] No less earnestly, Ulster Unionists years later swore an oath en masse "that this nation under God shall have a new birth of freedom, and that Government of the Ulster people, by the Ulster people, for the Ulster people, within the United Kingdom shall not perish from the earth."[24]

Indicative of the ecumenical applications of Lincoln's thought are the many ways in which he was invoked to qualify or complicate a simple celebration of the nation-state. His appropriation by exponents of pan-Americanism exemplifies the attempt to separate Lincoln from the nation and deploy him on behalf of an alternative, supranational structure that would contain and control the ambitions of a powerful nation like the United States. The co-option of Lincoln by British Liberals as part of a larger Anglo-Saxonism revealed how Lincoln could be embraced in a racialized transnational way that sat awkwardly with his own concept of the nation. What may have helped the perception of Lincoln as a generous internationalist or ecumenical nationalist was his relative silence on specific foreign issues, his noninterventionist principles, and his elevating moral and political example above military power.

Central to Lincoln's appeal abroad was his reputation as the archetypal self-made man. Audiences around the world have found inspiration in the story of his rise from obscure and humble origins, through self-education, enterprise, hard work, and the simple virtues of the natural man, in a fluid society whose political system nurtured "self-actualizing citizenship." The image of Lincoln the ax-wielding "rail-splitter" on the prairie is almost as widely encountered outside the United States as it is within. The self-made man theme harmonized with the democratic aspirations of many of Lincoln's foreign admirers. It also personified the miraculous economic growth of nineteenth-century America. What gave Lincoln special power was the way he served as an example of how the interests of the individual, self-improving laborer could be congruent with, indeed inseparable from, the larger development and modernization of a national economy. This view of Lincoln was most frequently articulated in places undergoing rapid economic development—late nineteenth century Argentina or Japan in the early twentieth century—where Lincoln served as hope or reassurance that the dislocating changes of economic modernization would benefit both the individual and the larger polity.

In the popular Lincoln narratives of this era, emancipation and racial liberation are more often than not a lesser theme, and in this they only mirrored the changes that had occurred in white Americans' own reading of their Civil War as Southern Reconstruction gave way to national reunification on the basis of Jim Crow.[25] During the war itself foreign radicals had questioned the president's approach to slavery. Lincoln's initiatives to colonize black Americans abroad rankled, his progress toward emancipation seemed sluggish, and when freedom was announced it looked limited in scope and effectiveness. Yet even the emancipationist Francis William Newman and other British critics—some of the sharpest of his detractors—recognized in Lincoln the best hope for the abolitionist cause, not least on account of his character and honesty of purpose.[26] After his death, Lincoln's presidential edict of emancipation meant he could be given the role of an anti-slavery champion—he would become an inspiration in South Asia to Dalit thinkers and activists engaged in the struggle to end caste slavery—but more often this aspect of his achievement served as an exemplary or symbolic element in the larger narrative of the hero of democratic freedom. When Irish separatists paid tribute to Lincoln for freeing the slaves it was to make a link with national liberation. German socialists, following the influential example of Karl Marx, tended to celebrate Lincoln, the slaves' liberator, for his emancipation of a class, not a race.[27]

The "Great Emancipator" view of Lincoln appears to have had the most purchase in Russia and Spain, which is not surprising given that both joined the United States in abolishing involuntary servitude in the second half of the nineteenth century. But even in these countries Lincoln's freeing of the slaves was viewed through the prism of political reform and economic modernization. Russian Emperor Alexander II—liberator of the serfs in 1861 and loyal ally of the Union during the Civil War—held his fellow emancipator and "Great and Good Friend" in high esteem.[28] Yet Alexander's abolition of serfdom, which was part of a portfolio of reforms undertaken in Russia in the 1860s, was more an attempt to preserve an obsolete and rickety social and political system through unavoidable reform than it was a result of Lincolnian opposition to involuntary servitude.[29] In Spain, Lincoln was venerated by abolitionist Progresistas acutely aware of the stain of their country's being the only continental power still to tolerate slavery (in its colonies of Puerto Rico and Cuba, where emancipation would not triumph until, respectively, 1873 and 1886). In this instance, as well, anti-slavery was only one dimension of the liberal reformers' larger project of modernizing the nation and extending civil and political rights to all Spaniards. In Cuba itself, as in independent Brazil (where emancipation would not occur until 1888), Lincoln certainly featured in debates over abolition, but his predominant image there appears to have been that of the nation-builder, not the emancipator. That was certainly the case in Juárez's Mexico and in Argentina, where his influential biographer Domingo Sarmiento, drawing on first-hand experience of the power of entrenched local interests to obstruct centralizing liberals, praised Lincoln's tenacity in the face of Southern disunionists and his harnessing of abolitionist energies in the cause of unity.

Lincoln's emancipationist record took on particular significance for what it revealed about his humanitarianism, humility, moral code, and religion, elements which led early twentieth-century Japanese biographer Ōson Sakurai to deem him "the kindest man among the great men, and the greatest man among the kind men."[30] The theologian Albert Schweitzer saw him as a fount of "the ideas of truest and highest brotherhood"; Sigmund Freud wrote that he had widened "the limits of humanity."[31] Imperial Russian diplomats made much of Lincoln's humility, though for them it was not a sign of strength, unlike Soviet-era historians, who praised him for it.[32] That Lincoln never in fact made a declaration of Christian belief—and that his celebration of reason made him the hero of secularists—was no barrier to his widespread representation as a man of faith. In Britain in particular, Lincoln the foe of slavery (as well as the abstainer from alcohol and tobacco) won a place in the hearts and minds of pious, reform-driven, Protestant churchgoers. Those of the predominating nonconformist Protestant traditions in Wales, many of whom would have read and reread *Uncle Tom's Cabin* in their native tongue, saluted Lincoln for his religious devotion. This was a reading strengthened by the circumstances of his death. Assassination alone is no guarantee of enduring influence—witness James Garfield and William McKinley—but a deep and persisting religious sense of loss accompanied Lincoln's end. Booth's bullet created a sacrificial figure, a martyr who died to bring an end to the suffering of others, a composite of Moses and the redemptive Christ, whose Good Friday Passion he shared.

This interpretation of Lincoln enjoyed widespread and continuing influence throughout his reputational heyday. If Tolstoy really did call him "a Christ in miniature" in 1909, he was only echoing what men and women had been saying for nearly half a century since the torrent of eulogies and lamentation that followed his death. For Emilio Castelar he was a "new Moses" removed "in the very moment of his victory, like Christ, like Socrates, like all redeemers." Garibaldi described him as "the new Redeemer of man." French Masons regarded him as "the sublimest martyr . . . who came into the world, like Jesus of Bethlehem, to take away its sins."[33] As such, he spoke directly to the Christianized modernizers of Meiji Japan.

For many, the humanitarian Lincoln was entirely consistent with his alter ego, the forceful, resolute defender of constitutionalism, and the strong-willed, unyielding nationalist. He spoke to the strong moral, often profoundly religious, elements within the forces of aspiring nationalism. But to uphold justice and the democratic principle, a leader might have to overcome his natural inclination for peace and learn the arts of war. Argentineans, Germans, Irish, Italians, Slavs: all these, and more, found in Lincoln a supreme model of strength in defending the principle of national unity. Indomitable, manly, physically and morally strong, Lincoln evinced a firmness of purpose that took him to the edge of constitutional legitimacy, but whose natural prudence and wisdom would let him travel no further. Conscription, the suspension of the writ of habeas corpus, and the American Union's other war measures had not spilled over into despotism; popular opinion had been respected. Lincoln became the epitome of the firm, prudent, and moderate war leader. No one expressed this better than one of his greatest admirers, David Lloyd George, the British prime minister during the First World War and its aftermath. Lincoln, like himself, had dealt with troublesome generals and politicians, mastered military strategy, pursued unconditional surrender in the supreme crisis of the nation, and finally, in victory, worked for clemency and reconciliation. With the fate of democracy uncertain in postwar Europe, Lloyd George invoked the heroic Lincoln in what he called the "fight against the wave of autocracy that is sweeping over our continent. Russia, an autocracy; Italy for the moment a dictatorship; Germany, slipping into dictatorship—most of Europe having abandoned confidence in the people. It is the hour of Lincoln's doctrine to be preached in the countries of Europe."[34]

Lloyd George's embrace of Lincoln reflected a broader British impulse in the early part of the twentieth century to join with the United States in exalting Anglo-Saxonism as the cure for the world's ills. The poet and playwright John Drinkwater cast Lincoln as the "World Emancipator," although the role he gave him—the exponent of the fundamental unity of America and Britain— was distinctly racialized and thus quite at odds with how Lincoln himself had seen his nation's mission.[35] Yet in emphasizing Lincoln's Anglo-Saxon qualities and his genealogical roots in rural Norfolk—"He belongs to the Race . . . as a man of pure English blood," claimed James Bryce in 1918—his English admirers constituted only one of many sets of claimants around the world.[36] In Wales he was called "our Welsh president," descended from medieval princes. Germans—finding a "Linkhorn" amongst his ancestors, and convinced that German immigrants played an essential role in securing the Republican party's electoral success in 1860—made him one of them; Friedrich Ebert, the first president of the Weimar Republic, became in death "the Abraham Lincoln of German history."[37] Latin Americans claimed him as a great *americanista* who counseled mutual respect in interstate relations, identified with the broad transnational interests of the region's modernizers, and sternly opposed the narrow self-interest of United States expansionists. Benito Juárez thus embraced the title of "the Mexican Lincoln." French Freemasons, erroneously convinced of his Masonic connections, claimed him as "one who had handled the hammer, the square, and compass, the living insignia of our immortal society," and saw in his life story a progression through degrees of Masonry.[38] In contemporary and near-contemporary graphic art his foreign portraits took on the social and ethnic features of the audiences for whom they were designed. At a later date, in Kenya, anti-colonial students said "I . . . Abraham Lincoln" when reciting the Emancipation Proclamation.[39] Such disparate appropriations reflect the universalist and adaptable dimensions of Lincoln's thought. They also reveal the perceived empowerment of claiming Lincoln's mantle.

Lincoln's impact on the world beyond his nation's borders would never again enjoy the range and force that it achieved during the half century or so after his death. Yet he would enjoy a new salience during the Second World War and the subsequent era of anti-colonialism and Cold War tensions. He took on renewed relevance in familiar settings: during the 1940s the British political class and wartime opinion-formers turned once more to his words, especially the Gettysburg Address, to give rhetorical and explicitly Anglo-American expression to the fight for democracy and humanity.[40] In Germany during the postwar era, West Berliners linked their cause to a narrative of United States history that deployed Lincoln as a symbol of anti-communism and self-determination. "The truths which Lincoln spoke . . . ," West Berlin Mayor Willy Brandt declared in 1959 of Lincoln's "house divided" speech a century before, "are perhaps even more applicable to the present situation of the German people than to the one which he faced."[41] He also came to be celebrated and deployed in parts of the globe where he had once been a less familiar presence. In the "new birth of freedom" that followed the fall of the Axis powers, the anti-colonialist movements to establish independent nations in Asia, Africa, and the Caribbean appropriated Lincoln as both an exemplar of freedom and a national unifier. In 1945, after the capitulation of Japan, the Indonesian leader Sukarno bedecked Jakarta with Lincoln's phrases to encourage Harry S. Truman's administration to oppose Dutch colonialism; in the 1960s, by contrast, he turned to Lincoln the national unifier to give consolidationist license for his ambitions in New Guinea, Borneo, and parts of the Malay peninsula. The ambiguities in the "real" Lincoln's historical actions, as both liberator and consolidator, allowed his deployment in these incongruent ways. Similarly, in the African transition from colonialism to independence, leaders of the freedom struggle might invoke both faces of Lincoln. Ghanaians were able to use him to legitimate liberation, yet the nation's first ruler, Kwame Nkrumah, would "read Lincoln's texts on national unity to those of his associates who worried about the massive force the new state used to defeat its internal enemies."[42]

This prompts a further reflection, on the authoritarian uses of the protean Lincoln. In the sixteenth president's energetic use of federal muscle—and his resort to what for the United States was unprecedented force to defend its constitution, laws, unity, and political continuity—ruling classes across the spectrum of the political right have discerned a valuable means of legitimating their own deployment of state power. From British conservatives' appreciation during the late Victorian and Edwardian ages of Lincoln's relevance as an instrument of stability, to the Japanese authorities' screening the democratic phrases of the Gettysburg Address from the public during the oligarchic period of Meiji rule, to President Pervez Musharraf's invocation of Lincoln in 2007 to defend the Pakistan government's iron fist, conservative-authoritarian forces have found a means of turning his popular appeal to their own advantage. The Lincoln story, as sponsored by the government of imperial Japan for the benefit of younger readers during the 1930s, not only sought to prepare the children for life within a military regime but also took the precaution of avoiding any allusion to the president's assassination.[43]

As the personification of a set of principles associated with—though not limited to—America, Lincoln's international celebrity cannot be entirely separated from the global rise of the United States in the decades after his assassination. In Latin America Lincoln assumed iconic status in the late nineteenth century, not coincidentally as the United States implemented a more proactive and interventionist foreign policy in the Western hemisphere. His fame grew in Britain and continental Europe at the turn of the century, as America entered the club of great powers and departed from its traditional policy of political nonentanglement in the Old World. The British "cult of Lincoln" coincided with American troops fighting on European soil and a sitting U.S. president crossing the Atlantic for the first time to construct a new international order at a European peace conference. And in Africa and other parts of the Third World, Lincoln took on salience in the years when Cold War rivalry and American foreign policy created new threats and opportunities for peoples breaking free from European colonialism.

From the moment of his assassination, some in the United States political elite saw Lincoln's value abroad as a matchless symbol of American republican and democratic ideals. John Bigelow, the American minister in Paris, liaised with Secretary of State Seward over efforts to channel the oppositionist homage spontaneously paid to the dead president. He was astonished to discover Lincoln's "hold upon the heart" of the Parisian youth: the feelings of students and others, he reported, "were so demonstrative in some instances as to provoke the intervention of the police, who would only allow them in very limited numbers through the streets," and who imprisoned some for "an intemperate expression" of republican sympathies.[44] Determined to encourage the radical-liberal enemies of the Lincoln-hating Napoleon III, Bigelow discreetly penned unattributed editorials and articles for a range of opposition newspapers. This was just one of many examples that impressed on the American establishment Lincoln's value as the embodiment of an idealized United States. The sentiment that prompted Lloyd George to declare after the Great War that the world needed "the America of Abraham Lincoln" explained why the Washington elite was so appalled by the prospect of George Barnard's statue of a rustic and seemingly flatulent Lincoln demeaning London's Parliament Square.

Not until the mid-twentieth century did the United States more systematically incorporate "public diplomacy" into its foreign policy apparatus, notably through the United States Information Agency (USIA), which used Lincoln's sesquicentennial in 1959 as a Cold War weapon of soft power. Although America had deployed the Gettysburg Address in the international arena during the First World War, the USIA distributed it widely and more systematically, in many translations, and even in comic-strip form in Vietnamese. Given the growing domestic salience of racial segregation as an issue in the 1950s, however, it was not Lincoln's language of equality but of freedom that U.S. opinion-formers emphasized.[45] The full Address resurfaced in the textbooks of American-occupied Japan after the Second World War. Between 1960 and 1965 millions of people worldwide received letters from America whose airmail stamp bore its ringing phrases. In the early twenty-first century George W. Bush sought to capitalize on Lincoln as a key symbol in his administration's foreign policy; his advisor Karen Hughes, whom he charged with improving the U.S. image abroad, opened "Lincoln Corners" in public libraries in South Asia. These formal projections of Lincoln politicized his image in new ways by associating it with the foreign policy objectives of an increasingly powerful, and often interventionist, United States.

The growth of American power has not consistently promoted Lincoln's standing. Foreign critiques of American influence have also worked to limit his appeal or remove him from view. For example, the often strained relations between the United States and Spain (their hemispheric rivalries compounded by differences of religion and political tradition), as well as the complexity of the internal divisions in Spanish society, have contributed to fluctuating responses to Lincoln as a progressive political symbol. In Wales, the cult of Lincoln lost its force between the world wars, when Nonconformist Liberalism gave way politically to a Labour Party whose heartland, working-class, constituency never made him their hero. The political left "increasingly saw in America not the last, best hope of democracy but the linchpin of capitalism."[46] In the explosion of anti-American feeling that accompanied the mass popular protest against the impending invasion of Iraq in 2003, the British authorities took the precaution of putting screens around the Lincoln statue in London's Parliament Square to prevent its defacement.

Yet Lincoln never became a punching bag for anti-Americans. Indeed, the absence of sustained and bare-knuckled foreign critiques of Lincoln is remarkable. Even Benjamin Franklin, arguably the American most admired and praised outside the United States before Lincoln, has not been immune to visceral criticism. But Lincoln seems to have attracted nothing as savage as D. H. Lawrence's scorn for Franklin. Fidel Castro quoted Lincoln approvingly and claimed that "Lincoln belongs to us." Given Karl Marx's reading of the American Civil War and his explicit admiration for Lincoln as a son of the working class, Marxist-Leninists in the Soviet Union and elsewhere have had no reason or need to make the sixteenth president a target in their critique of unrestrained Western capitalism. Indeed, the opposite may be true: Marxist readings abroad may mostly have been in line with the American Communist Party's interpretation of him as a proto-communist. A Soviet schoolbook from the 1960s, for example, praised Lincoln for heeding the calls of the working class to abolish slavery.[47] Ironically, the most savage assaults on Lincoln have probably emanated from domestic American critics viewing him from the disparate angles of black radicalism, white supremacy, and libertarianism.

Far more often, opponents of the United States have made Lincoln not their target but their ally. One measure of the association of Lincoln with U.S. power abroad is the frequency with which foreign critics have played back his image at an American audience to achieve their diplomatic or political goals. Like U.S. propagandists, foreign leaders and peoples have themselves used Lincoln as an instrument of public diplomacy. Spanish statesmen contended that the United States betrayed Lincoln's noninterventionist principles in the War of 1898; Latin American opponents of Theodore Roosevelt's actions in Panama in 1903 compared him unfavorably to his Republican predecessor in the White House;

Filipino nationalists quoted Lincoln in their campaign for independence from U.S. colonial rule; Japanese critics of the 1924 Asian Exclusion Act argued that it was a repudiation of Lincoln's principles; more recently, Chinese Communists pointed to Lincoln's suppression of a secessionist region as justification for an assertive policy in Taiwan. Accorded the role of the nation's conscience, Lincoln has been held up as a mirror to reflect to the United States the degeneration, even betrayal, of its founding ideals.

American power cannot alone explain the ubiquity of Lincoln's international presence, however. The man himself had already stirred imaginations around the world, and fed cultural and political appetites, well before the rise of the United States to a position of prominence on the global stage. The views formed during the 1860s, above all following the Union's victory and the president's assassination, shaped his subsequent legacy. Moreover, the transnational communications networks by which Lincoln's fame was spread and his meaning interpreted were not controlled solely or chiefly by the United States during the years of his most meaningful hold on the world's imagination. These networks might be powered by ideology, as in the case of the transatlantic interconnections amongst liberal-reformist-anti-slavery movements, or could be the products of religion, as with transnational networks of evangelical missionaries.

Lincoln could not have become a global figure without some form of what we now call "globalization." In the key period of his spread in the late nineteenth- and early twentieth-centuries, global integration owed much to British power. The "British world-system," as it recently has been called, connected the world as never before.[48] Its infrastructure consisted not only of the official outposts of the empire upon which the sun never set, but also its many noncolonial, or informal, networks: telegraph cables, shipping lines, missionary organizations, banking agencies, publishing houses, and political contacts. These circuits of the "British world-system" transmitted Lincoln around the globe. The British news agency Reuters, for example, broke the story in Europe of Lincoln's assassination in 1865. Many in India, East Asia, and Africa first learned of him through British media—schoolteachers, missionaries, colonial administrators, books, and ephemeral print. In other instances Americans used British networks to spread word of Lincoln. Influential American biographies of Lincoln from the late nineteenth century, for example, were reprinted by London publishers and then disseminated throughout the British world.[49] The central, if often indirect, role played by British power in Lincoln's emergence as a global figure illustrates in microcosm the broader story of how the structures of the British Empire served as the launching pad for America's rise to superpowerdom.

The power of the written word in the spread of Lincoln's name during the nineteenth century is hard to overstate. Foreign volunteers in the Federal armies reflected on the Union cause and its president in the torrents of letters home to Britain, Germany, France, Hungary, and elsewhere. More visible and even more potent was the medium of print. Whatever the sneers and barbs of conservative foreign presses during the Civil War, the response to Lincoln's death reveals the equal if not greater influence of sympathetic coverage in liberal newspapers and journals. The radical printing and publishing developments of the mid- and later nineteenth century—new technologies, commercial journalism, cheaper and illustrated newspapers—carried Lincoln's words and image geographically far and wide, and to all social classes, including the aspirational but disfranchised working poor.

No medium was more important than biography. By 1900, Lincoln's life had been published in (sequentially) German, French, Dutch, Italian, Portuguese, Greek, Spanish, Danish, Welsh, Latin, Hawaiian, Hebrew, Russian, Norwegian, Finnish, Turkish, Swedish, and Japanese; and over the next thirty years or so the list had extended to include Ukrainian, Yiddish, Polish, Chinese, Tamil, Czech, Icelandic, Arabic, Hungarian, Persian, Slovak, Armenian, Scottish Gaelic, Korean, Kannada, Burmese and Vietnamese.[50] Some works were translations from texts in English, many others were original. If the exercise was often an invitation to plagiarism, more significant were the distinctive lines of interpretations that foreign authors pursued in serving the needs of their domestic audiences. Sometimes, as in Spain, Lincoln's democratic life story of the self-made man might be deployed to counter socialist or anarchist agitation even as it challenged the social passivity inculcated by conservative Catholicism. Biographers commonly engaged in a form of civic education by illustrating a life that fused public and private virtue, and revealed "the extraordinariness of ordinary lives." Tamil biographies sought to prepare young people for perseverance, hard work, self-reliance combined with humility, and the triumph of the human spirit in the face of adversity. Vietnamese radicals of the 1920s used biographical studies of Lincoln to glorify the individual will and urge readers to follow in their heroic footsteps to overturn French colonialism. The French censors in Vietnam banned *Dong Tay Vi Nham: Lam-Khang* (*Great Men of Asia and Europe: Lincoln*), published in Saigon in 1929, alarmed by its unsettling didacticism. The author has Lincoln's father on his deathbed telling his son "to make every effort to work to be a good person like I taught you everyday: to respect and venerate God and your family." Lincoln, in fact, had notoriously declined to travel to see his dying father, but the detail went unacknowledged or unregistered in this rendition of the slaves' emancipator. What mattered was that young Vietnamese should acquire Lincolnian qualities and, personally transformed, secure their country's liberation from the slavery of French rule.[51]

The proliferation in these years of popular biography, in and beyond Europe, was a measure of a developing culture of political celebrity and hero-worship, especially of democratic figures whose moral integrity and strength of character stirred both the hearts and minds of common people. Lincoln was easily incorporated into this pantheon of great men, standing alongside Garibaldi,

This engraving provided the cover of the July 1, 1865, issue of *The British Workman and Friends of the Sons of Toil*, a monthly religious magazine whose declared purpose was "to promote the Health, Wealth and Happiness of the Working-classes." Its editor, Thomas Bywater Smithies, a well-connected Wesleyan Methodist, was a philanthropist, total abstainer, and tireless campaigner for good causes. With its message of social and self-improvement, and reputation for high-quality illustrations, the magazine reached a mass circulation of 250,000 by the mid-1860s.

Oliver Cromwell, and others celebrated as enemies of despotism and ascribed status. The quality of the best graphic art and engraving techniques, combined with Lincoln's distinctive features, helped make him a familiar and immediate presence. Lincoln statuary and other monuments gave him permanence. Poets and playwrights, notably Carolina Coronado and John Drinkwater, celebrated his character and achievements. Parents, in homage and in hope, named their sons after him: Carl Schurz and Garibaldi were amongst the first. The England and Wales census for 1901 shows almost three hundred males with the first name "Lincoln," about twice the number of 1871, which suggests a persisting admiration in Britain.[52]

The ubiquitous commercial exploitation of Lincoln and his name in the United States has had no match abroad, but foreign enterprises have illuminated and extended his global reach. During the British heyday of the Staffordshire ceramic figurine, a measure of Victorian popular taste during the second half of the nineteenth century, all subjects of the celebrity pottery portraits had to pass the test of commercial viability in the domestic British market. Few American figures merited the investment risk, but Lincoln joined the select ranks of Benjamin Franklin, George Washington, John Brown, and Uncle Tom.[53] About a hundred different foreign nations have commemorated him on their postage stamp issues, beginning with Cuba in 1937.[54] A cascade of foreign issues between 1959 and 1965 marked the sesquicentenary of his birth and the centenaries of the Emancipation Proclamation and the assassination. As with stamps, so with the production and distribution of books and other cultural commodities, which have a commercial purpose as well as aesthetic and political dimensions. Significant here have been the international reach and profitability of American films devoted to aspects of Lincoln's life, notably D. W. Griffith's homage of 1930, *Abraham Lincoln*, his first film in sound; John Ford's *Young Mr Lincoln* (1939); and John Cromwell's *Abe Lincoln in Illinois* (1940), based on Robert Sherwood's Pulitzer Prize–winning play.[55] These films romanticized his history even as they traded on the familiarity of his name.

At the same time, Lincoln has been protected against complete ideological neutering, or reduction to a vacuous symbol, thanks to the power and clarity of his words. The author of the Gettysburg Address and the second inaugural of 1865 bequeathed to the world potent and memorable oratory, words and phrases made all the more powerful by their simplicity and accessibility. Even more than his wit and humor (some authentically his, much apocryphal), his serious political dicta have become common currency in many and varied contexts.

In describing the multifarious routes by which Lincoln has traveled we should not lose sight of their intertwined complexity. Take the British example of a Victorian workingman from Shropshire, persecuted for promoting trade unionism and democratic rights. In 1908 he named his son "Lincoln." Sir Lincoln Ralphs, as the boy would become, was instrumental—as chief education officer for Norfolk—behind the founding of a liberal college at Wymondham

in 1950. Close to Hingham, the village from which Lincoln's ancestors emigrated in the mid-seventeenth century, the college opened a new boarding fa-
cility in 1958. They named it Lincoln Hall. So in some respects both the college
and the hall—designed to provide the education that Lincoln never had—are
the working out of his legacy. The story is further layered. The speaker at Lincoln Hall's opening was Dean Acheson, then U.S. secretary of state. The college stood near a cluster of American Air Force bases. The event was a Cold
War celebration of transatlantic partnership. Lincoln was a perfect symbol of
shared common values.[56]

What does this expansive story of the Global Lincoln—his projection and
appropriation—say about Lincoln himself and his place in world history?
Studying him across this broad canvas brings sharply into focus the complexity and challenge of the "globalization project" in historical writing, not
least in relation to the tenacity of local cultures. The transmission of his ideas
and deeds to new contexts did not empty them of all authenticity, but neither were they likely to retain their original balance, emphasis, and nuance
of meaning. Thus, for example, there has been little sign abroad of the acute
disagreement that Lincoln's views and policies on race have occasioned within
the United States.

Yet equally and strikingly plain is that the underlying "real" Lincoln, however enigmatic and elusive he remains, is of enormous significance to the
process by which he became and remained an international figure. Whatever
the misreading or tendentious representation of Lincoln for local, partisan purposes, the fact is that essential elements of his character, personal philosophy,
political vision, and presidential record have worked to inspire and activate
foreign leaders, opinion-formers, and their publics. Lincoln's ideological and
cultural authority at its most potent has given his claimants significant power in
their domestic sphere. The evidence suggests that Lincoln has been at his most
authentic and powerful in settings where he has been most divisive, above all
during the Civil War and the political generations that immediately followed.
Those who repudiated Lincoln's principles in the second half of the nineteenth
century and the early decades of the twentieth—for example, unreconstructed
Confederates in the American South, Napoleon III and French anti-repub-
licans, French colonial elites, counter-revolutionary Spanish Carlists, British
extreme traditionalists, and Nazi book-burners—serve as powerful reminders
that liberal, democratic, nationalist principles were deeply contested and that
invocations of Lincoln thus carried profound political meaning.[57] In many contexts these principles lost their capacity to polarize, as democratic processes and
values became the norm. In more recent times, he could still inspire democratic
forces in highly polarized contexts, as in Eastern Europe during the final years
of Soviet domination or in present day China, but in other places Lincoln's
capacity to inspire action evolved into an appetite for a gentler, less sharply

ideological veneration, which could even dwindle into vacuity, quaintness, and bathos (a "Lincoln Tea Shoppe" beckons in ancestral Hingham, England).

The routes and agencies of Lincoln's travels also reveal much about the processes of global integration and cultural exchange since the mid-nineteenth century. The dissemination of Lincoln's story at times tells us as much about networks of communication, transnational movements, and geopolitics as it does about the man himself. The examination of Lincoln's international legacy also prompts an essential sense of perspective and a guard against a blinkered filio-piety. Far from being the only figure of his time to take on an iconic status, Lincoln became part of an international pantheon of great statesmen, most of whom were not Americans; they included Garibaldi, Simon Bolívar, Camillo di Cavour, Otto von Bismarck, and William E. Gladstone. Biographies of Lincoln were often part of a general series of eminent people.[58] An additional perspective comes from placing Lincoln in a historical line of American figures who have achieved high standing abroad. Benjamin Franklin (rather than George Washington) may be seen as the precursor of the self-made, enterprising, modernizing, and anti-slavery hero. If so, the international view of Lincoln draws, at least in part, from a more generic image of an ideal American forged earlier. Likewise Lincoln himself may have helped shape the image of his successors: Woodrow Wilson and, later, John F. Kennedy and Martin Luther King Jr. Since 2008, the inverse question can be put: how far do international observers now see Lincoln through the lens of Barack Obama?

The hunt for the international Lincoln prompts a further word of caution: his absences should be as much a spur to investigation as his presence. Why, for example, is Lincoln marginal to the Indian story of decolonization yet important to the experience of Ghana's independence? Absences may simply be a result of Lincoln's story not reaching indigenous populations in non-English speaking regions. But they may also indicate a measure of cultural or political choice. This appears to have been the case in France during the 1860s, when after his death Lincoln was an inspiring symbol, but then "disappeared" during the immediate prelude to the Paris Commune—a signal of progressives' disenchantment with the United States as the Johnson and Grant administrations acquiesced in the "counter-revolution" of Reconstruction policy in the American South. In post-1945 Britain, Lincoln lost some of his previous standing, perhaps because Winston Churchill could better fill the role.

Plotting Lincoln's reception around the globe remains a work in progress. He merits many more case studies than have been ventured here. The Swiss Confederation, a federal state established in 1848 and inspired by the constitutional example of the United States, witnessed an extraordinary outpouring of tributes to the assassinated president in 1865–66. Lincoln and the Union he represented clearly spoke to the condition of those Swiss unifiers and self-styled modernizers who had triumphed in the brief civil war against secessionist cantons in 1847 (the *Sonderbundskreig*), but the particular political and cultural nerve that he struck, and the duration of his influence, remain an untold story. When Norwegians gathered around Lincoln's statue in Oslo every July 4th during the Nazi occupation, on what collective understanding were they drawing? Why is there a Lincoln Foundation in Albania? How typical of the South Seas more generally is the Hawaiian reverence for Lincoln? What explains the continuing Korean appetite for his life story? How might the apparent Soviet embrace of Lincoln be reconciled with its Cold War anti-Americanism? The mapping of Lincoln images and sites remains in its infancy, as does the research on population censuses to track his name. The hundreds of foreign biographies cry out for an analysis of their contents and disparate emphases, as well as who published and read them.

Despite these considerable lacunae, an overall picture is emerging. However difficult it is to move beyond a description of Lincoln's global reception to an assessment of his influence and significance, the evidence makes clear that he and his legacy have made a difference to the world beyond the United States. First, his intellectual and political example has inspired a range of political leaders and thinkers: Domingo Sarmiento, Karl Marx, David Lloyd George, José Martí, Emilio Castelar, Rafael María de Labra, Mohandas Gandhi, Bhimrao Ramji Ambedkar, Kwame Nkrumah, and Willy Brandt provide just some salient examples. Second, he has touched, often powerfully, countless ordinary lives. It is unlikely that many lived through anything to match the experience of a concentration camp internee, Henry Dubin, who described a visitation from a ghostly Lincoln whose words gave him the strength to survive his harrowing ordeal.[59] But the widespread use of "Lincoln" as a given name reveals at least a quiet influence on those who chose the name, those who bore it, and those whom they impressed. Third, invocations of Lincoln have had some hard, identifiable outcomes. For example, Lincoln's image at times mitigated Yankee-phobia in Latin America, and John Bigelow's appeals to French progressives in the name of the recently assassinated Lincoln helped to secure a remarkable coalition of the Second Empire's liberal and radical forces.

Above all, though Lincoln's influence on the larger global processes of the modern age cannot be precisely calibrated, he must be accorded a major inspirational role in the era of liberal and democratic nationalism. No historian of the United States would doubt that Lincoln is the central figure in the construction of the modern American nation, one premised not upon racial identity or state's rights, but upon a more inclusive idea of common peoples joined by democratic and civic principles. This, too, has constituted the core of his appeal abroad, combined as it has been with his standing as the premier self-made man of the age. Lincoln provided the perfect embodiment of the key features of "modernity": the entwined processes of economic development and self-improvement, signaled by the expansion of the capitalist market worldwide, the assault on ancestral privilege, and the widening of life-chances as individuals freed themselves from hierarchies of ascribed status. As a self-made man from humble origins, Lincoln stood for the dignity of labor; as statesman and war leader, he embraced the modernization of a national economy. Without these larger forces at work in the wider world it is doubtful that Lincoln would have had lasting impact beyond his own country. But America's interconnectedness with the broader currents of his time delivered that expansive arena of influence. In spare and memorable language fit for the modern age, he spoke directly during his own lifetime and beyond to those around the globe who saw themselves engaged in freeing the present from an ossified past and who looked, as Lincoln himself did, "to a vast future also."[60]

Notes

1. Douglas L. Wilson and Rodney O. Davis, eds., *Herndon's Informants: Letters Interviews, and Statements about Abraham Lincoln [HI]* (Urbana: University of Illinois Press, 1998), 88; Walter B. Stevens, *A Reporter's Lincoln*, ed. Michael Burlingame (Lincoln: University of Nebraska Press, 1998), 12. Cf. Lincoln to his step-brother, John Johnston, January 12, 1851, in Roy P. Basler et al., eds., *The Collected Works of Abraham Lincoln [CW]* 9 vols. (New Brunswick, NJ: Rutgers University Press, 1953–55), 1:96–97.

2. *HI*, 196–97; Robert V. Bruce, "The Riddle of Death" in Gabor Boritt, ed., *The Lincoln Enigma: The Changing Faces of an American Icon* (New York: Oxford University Press, 2001), 130–41, 144.

3. *CW*, 5:537.

4. *HI*, 196–97.

5. Richard Heckman, "British Press Reaction to the Emancipation Proclamation," *Lincoln Herald* 71 (Winter 1969), 150–53; Howard Jones, *Union in Peril: The Crisis over British Intervention in the Civil War* (Chapel Hill: University of North Carolina Press, 1992), 225–26.

6. Giuseppe Garibaldi, Menotti Garibaldi, and Ricciotti Garibaldi to Abraham Lincoln [AL], August 6, 1863, Abraham Lincoln Papers, Library of Congress [ALP].

7. James F. Reed to AL, March 12, 1864, ALP.

8. Charles W. Goddard to AL, October 19, 1863, ALP.

9. London [England] Workingmen to AL, December 31, 1862; Robert Adamson to AL, December 9, 1863; George Oakley to AL, January 7, 1865; James Robie to AL, March 3, 1865, ALP.

10. *Rays of Light*, May 13, 1863; Henry N. Cobb to AL, April 6, 1864, ALP.

11. H. Boernstein to M. Blair, April 30, 1865, Blair Family Papers, LC, quoted in *Abraham Lincoln: An Exhibition at the Library of Congress in Honor of the 150th Anniversary of His Birth* (Washington, DC: Library of Congress and the Lincoln Sesquicentennial Commission, 1959), 82.

12. United States, Department of State, *The Assassination of Abraham Lincoln and the attempted assassination of William H. Seward, secretary of state, and Frederick W. Seward, assistant secretary, on the evening of the 14th of April, 1865. Expressions of condolence and sympathy inspired by these events* (Washington, DC: Government Printing Office, 1866).

13. John Bigelow to William H. Seward, May 31, 1865, in Ibid., 86–87.

14. Edward William Thomson, "We Talked of Lincoln" in *The Many-Mansioned House and Other Poems* (Toronto: William Briggs, 1909): "We talked of Abraham Lincoln in the night, / Ten fur-coat men on North Saskatchewan's plain— / Pure zero cold, and all the prairie white— / Englishman, Scotchman, Scandinavian, Dane, / Two Irish, four Canadians."

15. C.G. Jung, statement, December 1938, Lincoln Memorial University Archives, Abraham Lincoln Library and Museum, Harrogate, Tennessee [LMUA]. Jung recalled that "when I was a little boy in school . . . [Lincoln] was pointed out . . . as the model of a citizen, who has devoted his life to the welfare of his country. . . . [He] has remained since my early days one of the shining stars in the assembly of immortal heroes."

16. Especially noteworthy is the conference convened by Gabor Boritt, Uwe Luebken, and Jörg Nagler at the German Historical Institute, Washington, DC, October 3–5, 2007. See Uwe Luebken, "A Humanitarian as Broad as the World: Abraham Lincoln's Legacy in International Context," *German Historical Institute Bulletin* 42 (Spring 2008), 133–38. See also, for example, Merrill D. Peterson, *Lincoln in American Memory* (New York: Oxford University Press, 1994), 185–86, 198–206, 367–68; Gabor Boritt, *The Gettysburg Gospel: The Lincoln Speech Nobody Knows* (New York: Simon & Schuster, 2006), 192, 201–5. Several of the themes and ideas of the present book enjoyed a beneficial first airing in "Interchange: The Global Lincoln," *Journal of American History* 96 (September 2009), 462–99, a venture generously encouraged by the journal's editor, Edward T. Linenthal. The story of the Global Lincoln contributes to a growing literature on the United States' entanglement in world history and the larger ideological and geopolitical significance of the American Civil War. Key works include Thomas Bender, *A Nation among Nations: America's Place in World History* (New York: Hill and Wang, 2006) and Ian Tyrrell, *Transnational Nation: United States History in Global Perspective since 1789* (London: Palgrave Macmillan, 2007). For the more specialized studies that have influenced this book, see David Armitage, *The Declaration of Independence: A Global History* (Cambridge, MA: Harvard University Press, 2007); Lewis Baldwin, *Toward the Beloved Community: Martin Luther King Jr. and South Africa* (Cleveland, OH: Pilgrim Press, 1995); Erez Manela, *The Wilsonian Moment: Self-Determination and the International Origins of Anticolonial Nationalism* (New York: Oxford University Press, 2007).

17. The editors are grateful to Norman Saul and Thomas Schwartz for pointing out these discrepancies. See *The World* (New York), February 7, 1909, 1–2 (quotations); "Abraham Lincoln, the Russian Empire, and the American Civil War: People, Events, and Retrospectives," unpublished paper delivered to "The Global Lincoln" conference, Oxford University, July 5, 2010; Carl Sandburg, *Abraham Lincoln: The War Years*, 4 vols. (New York: Harcourt, Brace & Company, ca. 1939), 4:375–78; Albert Alexander Woldman, *Lincoln and the Russians* (Cleveland: World Publishing Company, 1952), 272; Gabor S. Boritt, *Lincoln and the Economics of the American Dream* (Memphis: Memphis State University Press, 1978), 294, 361 (noting the absence of the interview in Tolstoy's complete works); Doris Kearns Goodwin, *Team of Rivals: The Political Genius of Abraham Lincoln* (New York: Simon & Schuster, 2005), 747–48, 878 (the 1908 misdating); Boritt, *The Gettysburg Gospel*, 202, 363.

18. For a recent overview of the vast scholarship on Lincoln, see Matthew Pinsker, "Lincoln Theme 2.0," *Journal of American History* 96 (September 2009), 417–40.

19. Carolyn P. Boyd, "A Man for All Seasons: Lincoln in Spain," see chapter 12.

20. Emeterio S. Santovenia, ed., *Lincoln in Martí: A Cuban View of Abraham Lincoln,* trans. Donald F. Fogelquist (Chapel Hill: University of North Carolina Press, 1953); see also Nicola Miller, "Images of Lincoln in Latin America," chapter 12.

21. Thomas D. Matijasic, "In the Footsteps of Lincoln: Wilson, Masaryk & Czechoslovak Independence," *Lincoln Herald* 96 (Winter 1995), 133–39.

22. G.J. Holyoake to AL, September 4, 1864, ALP; *The Assassination of Abraham Lincoln,* 445.

23. See Kevin Kenny, "Abraham Lincoln in Irish Political Discourse," chapter 9.

24. The occasion was the huge 1962 commemorative celebration of the 1912 Ulster Covenant. *Belfast Telegraph,* September 29, 1962.

25. David Blight, *Race and Reunion: The Civil War in American Memory* (Cambridge: Belknap Press of Harvard, 2001); Barry Schwartz, *Abraham Lincoln and the Forge of National Memory* (Chicago: University of Chicago Press, 2000).

26. Stacy Pratt McDermott, *The Lincoln Editor: The Quarterly Newsletter of the Abraham Lincoln Papers* 9 (April–June 2009), 5–6.

27. Bettina Hofmann, "The Lincoln Image and the German Labor Movement, 1861–1914," unpublished conference paper, "A Humanitarian as Broad as the World: Abraham Lincoln's Legacy in International Context," German Historical Institute, 2007.

28. Tanis Lovercheck-Saunders, "Peculiar Moral Power: Russian Images of Lincoln," unpublished conference paper, "A Humanitarian as Broad as the World: Abraham Lincoln's Legacy in International Context," German Historical Institute, 2007, 3. Alexander's admiration of Lincoln did not prevent him from later expressing his frustration that Lincoln's freeing of the American slaves received more global praise than his abolition of Russian serfdom.

29. For a comparative study of Russian serfdom and American slavery, see, Peter Kolchin, *Unfree Labor: American Slavery and Russian Serfdom* (Cambridge, MA: Harvard University Press, 1987).

30. Ōson Sakurai, *Tales of Lincoln* [in Japanese] (Tokyo: Teibi Press, 1913, 3rd ed.), quoted in De-min Tao, "A Standard of Our Thought and Action: Lincoln's Reception in East Asia," see chapter 13.

31. A. Schweitzer, statement, November 22, 1937; S. Freud, statement, April 8, 1937, LMUA.

32. Lovercheck-Saunders, "Peculiar Moral Power: Russian Images of Lincoln," 1–2.

33. Boyd, "A Man for All Seasons: Lincoln in Spain," chapter 11; Eugenio F. Biagini, "'The Principle of Humanity': Lincoln in Germany and Italy, 1859–1865," chapter 4; *The Assassination of Abraham Lincoln,* 104.

34. David Lloyd George, "Abraham Lincoln, the Inspirer of Democracy," October 18, 1923, in Waldo W. Braden, ed., *Building the Myth: Selected Speeches Memorializing Abraham Lincoln* (Urbana: University of Illinois Press, 1991), 206.

35. John Drinkwater, *Abraham Lincoln* (London: Sidgwick and Jackson, 1919); John Drinkwater, *Lincoln: The World Emancipator* (Boston: Houghton Mifflin, 1920).

36. Harry Brittain, *Happy Pilgrimage* (London: Hutchinson, 1949), 289.

37. See Kenneth O. Morgan, "Kentucky's 'Cottage-Bred Man': Lincoln and Wales," chapter 8; and Jörg Nagler, "National Unity and Liberty: Lincoln's Image and Reception in Germany, 1871–1989," chapter 14.

38. *The Assassination of Abraham Lincoln,* 90, 92, 98–99, 103–4.

39. Kevin Gaines, "From Colonization to Anti-colonialism: Lincoln in Africa," chapter 15.

40. Jake Campbell, "British Views of Abraham Lincoln," (M.St. dissertation, University of Oxford, 2009.)

41. Quoted in Thomas F. Schwartz, "Lincoln and the Cold War," *Abraham Lincoln Association Newsletter* 6:1 (Spring 2004).

42. "Interchange: The Global Lincoln," 467, 493 (Arne Westad).

43. Michael Mogilevsky, "What was Abe Lincoln Doing in Pre-War Japan?" *Lincoln Herald* 90 (Fall 1988), 87–90.

44. John Bigelow to William H. Seward, April 28, May 10 and 31, 1865, in *The Assassination of Abraham Lincoln*, 83–87.

45. Jared Peatman, "The Gettysburg Address as Foreign Policy," unpublished lecture, The American University of Paris, October 17, 2009.

46. See Morgan, "Kentucky's 'Cottage-Bred Man': Lincoln and Wales," chapter 8.

47. Lovercheck-Saunders, "Peculiar Moral Power: Russian Images of Abraham Lincoln."

48. John Darwin, *The Empire Project: The Rise and Fall of the British World-System, 1830–1970* (Cambridge: Cambridge University Press, 2009).

49. For example, a London publishing house reprinted an abridged version of Hay and Nicolay in 1902. See John G. Nicolay, *A Short Life of Abraham Lincoln* (London: T. Werner Laurie, Ltd., 1902).

50. This list draws on George Scratcherd's research in WorldCat and an analysis of Jay Monaghan, comp., *Lincoln Bibliography 1839–1939*, 2 vols. (Springfield: Illinois State Historical Library, 1943–45). See Scratcherd's appendix at the end of this book.

51. M. P. Bradley, *Imagining Vietnam and America: The Making of Postcolonial Vietnam, 1919–1950* (Chapel Hill: University of North Carolina Press, 2000), 30–32; *Dong Tay Vi Nham: Lam-Khang* (Great Men of Asia and Europe: Lincoln) (Saigon, 1929), 35; Hue-Tam Ho Tai, *Radicalism and the Origins of the Vietnamese Revolution* (Cambridge, MA: Harvard University Press, 1992), 246. The authors thank C. J. Jenner for drawing this example to their attention.

52. Robert C. and Benjamin L. Kenzer, "Living Monuments: Americans named in honor of Abraham Lincoln," 2008, unpublished paper. For evidence that under British colonial rule in Burma "Lincoln" became a given name amongst indigenous Karens, see www.washingtonpost.com/ accessed April 24, 2006.

53. Adele Kenny and Veronica Moriarty, *Staffordshire Figures: History in Earthenware 1740–1900* (Atglen, PA: Schiffer Publishing, 2004).

54. Andrew Lincoln, "Honest Abe," *Stamp Magazine* (March 2009), 82–85. Lincoln had already appeared on a Philippines issue in 1906, when the country was under U.S. administration.

55. Melvyn Stokes, "Abraham Lincoln, Screen Idol," paper presented at the British American Nineteenth Century History conference, Cambridge, October 16, 2009; Ichiro Takayoshi, "Globalizing the Civil War: Robert Sherwood's Abe Lincoln in Illinois and the U.S. Foreign Policy, 1938–1941," paper presented at the annual meeting of the American Studies Association, 2009, www.allacademic.com/meta/p.113483_index.html, accessed October 28, 2010.

56. Carwardine's conversation with Enid Ralphs (Lady Ralphs), January 15, 2009; "In Memoriam," *The Times* [London], October 24, 1978, 20; "College Heritage," *Wymondham College*, www.wymondhamcollege.org/about/College-Heritage-31, accessed October 28, 2010.

57. The English writer R.F. Delderfield, born in 1912, would have been christened "Abraham Lincoln Delderfield" had his Tory mother not forcefully over-ridden the wishes of his radical father. Sanford V. Sternlicht, *R. F. Delderfield* (Boston: Twayne Publishers, 1988), 3.

58. "Interchange: The Global Lincoln," 479 (Caroline Boyd).

59. Andrew Ferguson, *Land of Lincoln: Adventures in Abe's America* (New York: Atlantic Monthly Press, 2007), 270–74.

60. *CW*, 5:53.

2

Lincoln's Horizons

THE NATIONALIST AS UNIVERSALIST

Richard Carwardine

At the unveiling of Abraham Lincoln's statue in Parliament Square in 1920, the British Prime Minister, David Lloyd George, reflected that the sixteenth president of the United States was "one of those giant figures, of whom there are very few in history, who lose their nationality in death. They are no longer Greek or Hebrew, English or American; they belong to mankind."[1] He gave voice to a sentiment long expressed beyond the United States. "Abraham Lincoln was our brother," declared the French radical, Leon Richer, as news of his death reverberated around the world. The assassinated president, he wrote, was one of those "true representatives of God upon earth" whose achievement "exalts them so high that they cannot be termed citizens of any particular country, for they are citizens of all; and though one single nation may claim them, their name belongs to all humanity and their death becomes a universal mourning."[2] A century later and in similar vein, Willy Brandt—then mayor of Berlin—told an audience in Lincoln's Springfield that "this man does not belong to you alone, my friends."[3]

If Lincoln and his legacy comprise a global story, there is another side to Lloyd George's remark, namely the "nationality" lost in Lincoln's death. Lincoln had a good deal of "nationality" to lose. He was, after all, a proud American. How, then, do we square his profound devotion to his nation with the world's subsequent reading of him as a universal man for the ages, one who rose above parochialism and narrow chauvinism? This question prompts three linked inquiries. What constituted Lincoln's nationalism, his tenacious loyalty to the American Union? What shaped his perception of the world beyond the United States—and indeed how well-informed was he about foreign lands and international affairs? And how did he conceive of the United States' duties to the world?

I

Lincoln's tenacious attachment to the United States—what he called his "eternal fidelity to . . . the land of my life, my liberty and my love"—is a given. This was a loyalty that encouraged—and was cemented by—comparison. He called the Union "this favored land" in his first inaugural address—and, since favored, then by implication a land superior to others.[4] What made it such? What were the particular strands in the rope that bound him so resolutely to the Union?

Significant amongst these was his deep faith in the nation's material potential: its natural bounty, physical grandeur, and material advantages. Growing up in Kentucky and Indiana, and arriving as a young man in the infant Illinois, Lincoln shared the faith of the emerging Whig party in the unique natural resources of the undeveloped country and the possibilities they opened up for the nation's modernization. As he told his audience at the Young Men's Lyceum of Springfield in 1838, the American people possessed "the fairest portion of the earth, as regards extent of territory, fertility of soil, and salubrity of climate."[5] Shortly afterward he wrote of his adopted state, that it "surpasses every other spot of equal extent upon the face of the globe, in fertility of soil, and in the proportionable amount of the same which is sufficiently level for actual cultivation; and consequently that she is endowed by nature with the capacity of sustaining a greater amount of agricultural wealth and population than any other equal extent of territory in the world." Lincoln the "improver" watched with pleasure the Union's galloping economic progress, to which his political career in the 1830s and 1840s had been chiefly devoted.[6] Later he wrote with approval of the "aggregate grandeur" of the American experiment, as reflected in its industrious, burgeoning population. During the war the London *Times* correspondent William Howard Russell noted Lincoln's "quaint reflections" on the potential might of his country: "He calculates . . . that there are human beings now alive who may ere they die behold the United States peopled by 250 millions of souls. Talking of a high prairie, in Illinois, he remarked, 'that if all the nations of the earth were assembled there, a man standing on its top would see them all, for . . . the whole human race would fit on a space . . . about the extent of the plain.'" On what would be the last full day of his life Lincoln told Indiana congressman Schuyler Colfax: "I have very large ideas of the mineral wealth of our nation. I believe it practically inexhaustible. It abounds all over the western country from the Rocky Mountains to the Pacific, and its development has scarcely commenced." With the war ended, hundreds of thousands of immigrants would arrive annually "from overcrowded Europe. I intend to point them to the gold and silver that waits for them in the West. Tell the miners . . . I shall promote their interests . . . because their prosperity is the prosperity of the nation, and we shall prove in a very few years, that we are indeed the treasury of the world."[7] More than mere celebration of America's vast natural resources, such comments also reflected an economic conception of the nation premised upon the creation of an autonomous and integrated market, secure from persistent British neocolonialism.

Far more often, however, Lincoln's rhetoric addressed the ethical and political purpose of the Union: the physical grandeur and material endowments of the United States were secondary to the moral magnificence of the nation's free institutions. Lincoln's esteem for the nation's revolutionary leaders and Founding Fathers was reflected in his unshakeable respect for the cornerstones of the Republic: the Declaration of Independence, with its philosophical celebration of equality, and the federal Constitution, the guarantor of freedom. Thanks to these legacies of the Revolutionary generation, the United States enjoyed a unique and unprecedented liberty ("far exceeding that of any other of the nations of the earth"), whose distinctive features included self-government, or government by the consent of the governed (lauded by Lincoln as "absolutely and eternally right"); a bill of rights which guaranteed a variety of religious and civil freedoms beyond those "which the history of former times tells us"; a legal system capped by a Supreme Court he deemed "the most enlightened judicial tribunal in the world"; and a commitment to meritocracy through a government "whose leading object is, to elevate the condition of men— . . . to afford all, an unfettered start, and a fair chance, in the race of life."[8]

In all this there is a powerful conviction of American exceptionalism. "*Most governments,*" he reflected, "have been based, practically, on the denial of equal rights of men . . .; ours began, by *affirming* those rights. *They* said, some men are too *ignorant*, and *vicious*, to share in government. Possibly so, said we; and, by your system, you would always keep them ignorant, and vicious. We proposed to give *all* a chance; and we expected the weak to grow stronger, the ignorant, wiser; and all better, and happier together."[9]

Through these guarantees of freedom the nation would realize its moral potential. Of course, Lincoln's celebration of the Union as a matchless instrument of liberty and the guardian of the principle of the equality of men can appear inconsistent, even hypocritical, in the face of the harsh reality of American slaveholding. Lincoln resolved this conflict through his particular reading of history. The nation's fathers, he maintained, had never intended that slavery should be permanent. Though they had seen no way of immediately eliminating it in its entirety, the founders had taken steps to abolish the African slave trade and to prevent the extension of slavery into the Northwest Territory; they had sought, he argued, to place slavery where "all sensible men understood, it was in the course of ultimate extinction."[10] Lincoln's religious faith, unconventional and attenuated though it was, shared some of the optimistic millennialism of mainstream Protestantism. This shines through his remarks in 1842 on the advancing temperance reformation, which he yoked with the political emancipation of 1776 and, by implication, with an aspiration to freedom for the slaves: "And when the victory shall be complete—when there shall be neither a slave nor a drunkard on the earth—how proud the title of that *Land*, which may truly claim to be the birth-place and the cradle of both those revolutions, that shall have ended in that victory. How nobly distinguished that People, who shall have planted, and nurtured to maturity, both the political and moral freedom of their species."[11]

Lincoln also gloried in what he judged the future protection afforded the Union by both geography and the founders' vision. In his much-quoted Lyceum address, Lincoln asked: "Shall we expect some transatlantic military giant, to step the Ocean, and crush us at a blow? Never! All the armies of Europe, Asia and Africa combined, with all the treasure of the earth (our own excepted) in their military chest; with a Buonaparte for a commander, could not by force, take a drink from the Ohio, or make a track on the Blue Ridge, in a trial of a thousand years." The danger, "if it ever reach us, . . . cannot come from abroad. If destruction be our lot, we must ourselves be its author and finisher. As a nation of freemen, we must live through all time, or die by suicide."[12] An indestructible, perpetual Union had been the Founders' objective; they designed their Constitution "*to form a more perfect union.*"[13]

Ultimately, Lincoln's vision of the Union drew rather less on a calculation of practicalities, than on a romantic feeling allied to a sense of the nation's providential role, of Americans being—as he expressed it in a speech en route to Washington in early 1861—the Almighty's "almost chosen people." The peroration to his first inaugural, addressed to his "dissatisfied fellow countrymen," provides the clue: "We must not be enemies. Though passion may have strained, it must not break our bonds of affection. The mystic chords of memory, streching [*sic*] from every battle-field, and patriot grave, to every living heart and hearthstone, all over this broad land, will yet swell the chorus of the Union, when again touched, as surely they will be by the better angels of our nature." It was this romantic attachment to Union, based on far more than the *material* benefits of nationhood, which the Confederacy so seriously underestimated. It led Alexander Stephens, Lincoln's Whig associate from Georgia, and the vice president of the Confederacy, subsequently to reflect of Lincoln: "The Union with him in sentiment, rose to the sublimity of a religious mysticism."[14]

II

Lincoln's powerful sense of America's exceptional place in the world raises the question of just how well acquainted he was with the realities of foreign countries, and through what prisms he reached his understanding. Conversing with a Canadian visitor during the final summer of the war, the president reflected on his relatively sheltered experience: "It is very strange that I, a boy brought up in the woods, and seeing, as it were, but little of the world, should be drifted into the very apex of this great event."[15] Until his nineteenth year, when he took a flatboat to New Orleans, Lincoln had had experience only of the raw young communities of the upper South and Midwest. Not until he was thirty-eight did he travel east to the nation's capital. Though over the course of his adult life Lincoln spent time in London, Berlin, Athens, Paris, Versailles, Amsterdam, Florence, Naples, Cadiz, Geneva, Petersburg, and even Palestine, these were American towns and cities, mostly in the Midwest, which he visited on legal or political business. Unlike several of his predecessors as president—John Adams and John Quincy Adams, Thomas Jefferson, James Monroe, Martin Van Buren, Franklin Pierce, and James Buchanan—and unlike his two chief rivals for the executive office, Stephen A. Douglas and William Henry Seward, Lincoln never crossed the Atlantic. He perhaps crossed into Canada for a better view of Niagara Falls, but if so it was his only venture abroad. Yet he was no provincial hick. The furnishings of his Springfield home reveal something of his broad horizons. The correspondent of a Boston journal, visiting Lincoln in the month of his presidential nomination, reported: "I crossed the hall and entered the library. There were miscellaneous books on the shelves, [and] two globes, celestial and terrestrial, in the corners of the room."[16] Lincoln's premature death denied him the overseas travel that would almost certainly have taken him to Britain and the birthplaces of two of his favorite authors, Robert Burns and William Shakespeare.[17] Indeed, on the last full day of his life, he is reported to have told his wife that when he had served his second term their travels should take them to Jerusalem and the Holy Land.[18]

Lincoln was not uninformed about the world beyond the United States, but his perspective was necessarily shaped by others: the authors he read, the many foreign-born visitors and citizens he met, and his more cosmopolitan associates. His reading during his boyhood and youth was restricted to the Bible and the very few other books he could lay his hands on, but once he got to New Salem, according to Mentor Graham, "he devoted more time to reading the scripture, books on science and comments on law and to the acquisition of Knowledge of men and things" than any man he had ever known in forty-five years of teaching. From Mason L. Weems's *Life of George Washington*, and especially William Grimshaw's popular and Whiggish *History of the United States*, Lincoln acquired an understanding of the geopolitics that shaped the country's destined course to nationhood and its guardianship of Enlightenment principles. His reading of Scripture, Edward Gibbon's *Decline and Fall of the Roman Empire*, and Plutarch's *Lives* delivered something of the sweep of history of the Old World. The young Lincoln was almost certainly acquainted with John O'Neill's standard textbook, *A new and easy system of geography . . .: containing a description of all the empires, kingdoms, republics, states and colonies in the known world*. We can be sure he read Captain James Riley's best-selling "authentic narrative" of his shipwreck off the northwest coast of Africa and his ensuing enslavement by Moroccan Arabs, a work replete with cartography and exotic description.[19] Above all, from his youth

Lincoln was an inveterate reader of newspapers: this would be his key printed source for the description and analysis of contemporary foreign affairs. Both the *Sangamo Journal* and its successor, the *Illinois State Journal*, with whose editors Lincoln was on close terms, gave their Springfield readers a steady diet of foreign news and editorial comment.

Lincoln's reading gave him a keen sense of the United States' escape from the autocratic forces of the Old World. In this he was essentially a creature of his time: in the young Republic the experience of the revolutionary genera-tion shaped a persisting, if fading, collective American memory of the war of independence from tyrannical rule.[20] The ideological legacy of the Revolution would fuse with the defining foreign events of his own lifetime to give Lincoln an enhanced appreciation of his country's place in the world. Those events—above all, the independence movements within Spain's New World empire, the Greek war of independence, and the nationalist uprisings and movements of radical republican protest in Europe—were in part mediated for Lincoln through those of his political friends, acquaintances and heroes whose travels or dealings gave them first-hand authority.[21] During Lincoln's two-year con-gressional term the European revolutions of 1848–49 were debated, as was Irish relief from the famine. Springfield itself had a sizeable community of Portuguese refugees, militant Protestants fleeing violent persecution in Catho-lic Madeira, the earliest of whom arrived in 1849—welcomed by a reception committee headed by Lincoln's close ally Simeon Francis, the editor of the *Sangamo Journal*.[22] Collectively, it is unlikely that any immigrant influence was greater than that of the Germans with whom Lincoln was involved after 1854 in bolstering the nascent Republican party, several of them exiled revolution-ists of 1848, or—like George Schneider of Chicago and Gustave Koerner of Belleville—radicals who had fled Germany even earlier. As Koerner's memoirs reveal, these Germans remained deeply concerned for the political future of the land they had fled. Lincoln clearly understood the common democratic-repub-lican agenda they sought to advance on both sides of the Atlantic. His personal cultivation of the German vote in Illinois and beyond during the 1850s was manifestly driven by electoral arithmetic and advantage, but there was more to it than that. He also knew that these European liberals and progressives would put metal in the Republicans' ideological backbone.[23]

Lincoln boasted no special or particular expertise in respect to the internal affairs of other nations, and they were rarely the theme of his political discourse. This was hardly unusual in a state-level legislator, but even as president he mostly left the detail of foreign matters to his secretary of state, William H. Seward, who prepared presidential remarks when foreign ministers were presented.[24] In filling diplomatic posts after his inauguration Lincoln had no interest in altering the conventional priorities, driven by domestic politics: rewarding party loyal-ists with plum jobs took precedence over cultivating "friendly or social relations with other governments."[25] Thus Lincoln sought to make one of his recent rivals

for the presidential nomination, William L. Dayton, minister to Britain; it was
Seward who saw that Charles Francis Adams was incomparably more suitable,
given his European education and the diplomatic pedigree of his family. Lincoln
eventually yielded, and Dayton became minister to France, "notwithstanding
his ignorance of the French language." Lincoln showed similar lack of finesse
in supporting Carl Schurz's ambition to become minister to Italy. It was left
to Seward to explain "the unwisdom of sending . . . a former revolutionist in
Germany . . . to a European court in such critical times." Here, too, the president bowed to his secretary of state's advice. Lincoln's choice of Cassius Clay
for Russia elicited from the first secretary of the legation there this reflection
to Horace Greeley: "Between ourselves, he [Clay] is much better suited to the
meridian of Kentucky than of St Petersburg." Clay, however, appears a near
perfect fit when compared with the appointee to the Papal States, Alexander
Randall of Wisconsin, whom the American consul in Rome described as "a
mere party hack . . . [knowing] nothing of diplomacy or good manners, or of
any language but Western American."[26]

Of course, Lincoln, as he made these appointments, was under enormous
pressure as the threat of civil war loomed and as he was plagued by importunate
job seekers. Titian F. Coffey, an assistant attorney-general, told the story of a
delegation that called on Lincoln to ask for the appointment of a gentleman
as commissioner to the Sandwich Islands. They presented their case earnestly,
pressing on Lincoln not only their candidate's fitness for the post but also his
bad health, and reflecting that the balmy climate of the South Seas would be
a great boon to him. The president closed the interview discouragingly: "Gentlemen, I am sorry to say that there are eight other applicants for that place,
and they are all sicker than your man."[27] The verdict of the American consul in Rome, William J. Stillman, indicates that political demands of this kind
weighed much more with Lincoln than did diplomatic sensitivities: "with the
exception of Adams, at London, and [George Perkins] Marsh at Turin, we had
hardly a representative abroad . . . who was a credit to the country. As the war
continued, the importance of being respected in Europe became more evident,
and a change took place; but the few men of respectable standing who were in
foreign countries representing the United States of America were appointed on
account of political pressure, and not on their merits."[28]

Lincoln was undoubtedly aware of his own inexperience and personal short-
comings in respect to foreign affairs. On arriving in Washington in February
1861, he told Seward he would "leave almost entirely" in the hands of his secretary of state "the dealing with . . . foreign nations and their governments."[29]
According to Rudolph Schleiden, minister from the Hanseatic League of German States, the president-elect confided to him: "I don't know anything about
diplomacy. I will be very apt to make blunders."[30] He also confessed to Carl
Schurz "that he deplored having given so little attention to foreign affairs and
being so dependent upon other people's judgment": he would, he said, set about

"studying up" the subject as opportunity allowed.[31] He knew at first-hand how even gestures of friendship between governments required deft handling. When King Mongkut of Siam not only sent elephant tusks to the White House as a gift, but—learning that there were no such animals in North America—offered to dispatch several pairs of elephants, too, Lincoln signed a reply whose barely suppressed humor suggests that he was more than the nominal author of the letter. The tusks, he noted, were of such "length and magnitude . . . as [to] indicate that they could have belonged only to an animal which was a native of Siam." He thanked the king for the "tender of . . . a stock from which a supply of elephants might be raised on our own soil. This Government would not hesitate to avail itself of so generous an offer if the object were one which could be made practically useful in the present condition of the United States. Our political jurisdiction, however, does not reach a latitude so low as to favor the multiplication of the elephant, and steam on land, as well as on water, has been our best and most efficient agent of transportation in internal commerce."[32]

As time went on, Lincoln's acute political intelligence, grasp of strategic essentials, and shrewd understanding of human nature combined to prompt several well-judged presidential interventions in foreign affairs, most notably in relations with the most powerful nation of the day, Britain. The president had a jaundiced—or at least ambivalent—view of British power and liked to quote the Indian chief who, having been told by a proud English visitor that "the sun never sets on England," replied, "Humph! I suppose it's because God wouldn't trust them in the dark."[33] Considerations of this kind gave way to unvarnished pragmatism in the case of the *Trent* affair—the sharpest crisis in Anglo-American relations during wartime, prompted by the removal of Confederate envoys from a British mail packet—and the *Peterhoff* case eighteen months later, involving the seizure of British mail from a blockade runner. Avoiding war with Britain and France was an absolute. (When Orville Browning urged Lincoln not to acquiesce to British demands during the *Trent* crisis, saying he was sure England was only bluffing and would not dare to fight, Lincoln told of a vicious bulldog back in Springfield. Neighbors said it wasn't dangerous, but Lincoln recalled the words of a man who wasn't sure: "I know the bulldog will not bite. You know he will not bite, but does the bulldog know he will not bite?")[34] Lincoln was also sharply alert to the likely overseas impact of his Emancipation Proclamation and its broadly beneficial implications for American foreign relations.[35]

If Lincoln lacked expertise in many of the particulars of foreign matters, he did possess broad intellectual and political horizons, and a capacious view of the foibles and aspirations of humankind. He was above all alert to the truth revealed by "the history of the world . . . that men of ambition and talents will . . . continue to spring up amongst us. And, when they do, they will as naturally seek the gratification of their ruling passion, as others have *so* done before them." Constitutions could not restrain "an Alexander, a Caesar, or a Napoleon," nor shackle *"the family of the lion, or the tribe of the eagle."*[36] Lincoln's conception of what he considered universal traits of human psychology and ambition was endorsed—and quite probably shaped, too—by his reading of the Scriptures and Shakespeare. The dramatist's special appeal for Lincoln lay in his meditations on political power, its uses and abuses: *Hamlet, King Lear,* the histories and, especially, *Macbeth.* Lincoln knew by heart the introspections of flawed legitimate monarchs like Lear and Richard II, and the usurping rulers Richard III, Macbeth, and Claudius. Shakespeare's exploration of the perversion of power confirmed the ubiquity of the danger latent in corruption, whether in the Old World or the New.

III

In this universal struggle between liberty and tyranny, and between social progress and lethargy, Lincoln conferred on the United States an international responsibility. His "Lecture on Discoveries and Inventions" is explicit in declaring the nation's advantage in freeing the human mind from its shackles, for the benefit of all:

> It is a curious fact that a new country is most favorable—almost necessary—to the immancipation [*sic*] of thought, and the consequent advancement of civilization and the arts. The human family originated as is thought, somewhere in Asia, and have worked their way princip[al]ly Westward. Just now, in civilization, and the arts, the people of Asia are entirely behind those of Europe; those of the East of Europe behind those of the West of it; while we, here in America, *think* we discover, and invent, and improve, faster than any of them. *They* may think this is arrogance; but they can not deny that Russia has called on us to show her how to build steam-boats and railroads—while in the older parts of Asia, they scarcely know that such things as S.Bs & RR.s. exist. In anciently inhabited countries, the dust of ages—a real downright old-fogyism—seems to settle upon, and smother the intellects and energies of man. It is in this view that I have mentioned the discovery of America as an event greatly favoring and facilitating useful discoveries and inventions.[37]

Striking in this passage is Lincoln's Enlightenment-inspired belief that progress depended above all on the intellectual ferment, human imagination, and cultural energy which would accompany the world's emancipation from stultifying social and political tradition. There was probably a racial element in his understanding of "civilization"—this was, after all, the common, Eurocentric perspective of the Enlightenment—but, if so, it was surely of a piece with his cautious approach to issues of racial difference in the domestic sphere: a lack of dogmatism above all characterized his stated opinions on the capabilities and potential of African Americans. Likewise, when it came to addressing policy toward the Mexican people or to Native Americans, Lincoln chose not to pursue racialized lines of argument. The weight of evidence—exiguous though it is—suggests that Lincoln, in measuring human behavior and capability, placed a higher value on social context and culturally shaped expectations than on racial or ethnic traits.

What is incontestable is that Lincoln's horizons stretched across the nineteenth-century world. As he prepared for the presidential office he repeatedly addressed the theme of the nation's "great promise to all the people of the world."[38] When he declared (in December 1861) that "The struggle of today, is not altogether for today—it is for a vast future also," and when, a year later, he spoke of the Union as the "last, best hope of earth" he was expressing his conviction that the Civil War constituted something larger than simply an American crisis.[39] Lincoln's revision of his final words at Gettysburg in November 1863—changing *this government* to simple *government*—turned his readers' gaze outwards: "that government of the people, by the people, for the people, shall not perish from the earth."[40] In these declarations he was only giving renewed voice to a sentiment running consistently through his rhetoric for over a quarter of a century: that the world's progressive forces looked to the United States as an unequalled exemplar of liberty; that it was the nation's mission to act as the improver of humankind. As a young man he had described his country as "that fair fabric, which for the last half century, has been the fondest hope, of the lovers of freedom, throughout the world." Later, as a congressman, he would similarly invoke the patriots of 1776 to assert the right of any people "to rise up, and shake off the existing government, and form a new one that suits them better. This is a most valuable,—a most sacred right—a right, which we hope and believe, is to liberate the world."[41] Such sentiments nourished Lincoln's hostility to nativist restrictions on the rights of immigrants and his determination to preserve America's western territories as "an outlet for *free white people everywhere*, the world over—in which Hans and Baptiste and Patrick, and all other men from all the world, may find new homes and better their conditions in life."[42] He saw in the labor of common people, and the human aspiration that accompanied it, traits as admirable as they were universal; the American model of social and economic opportunity—real enough, in his experience—reflected the ambitions of unfettered humankind. It was this that led him to tell New York working-men, "The strongest bond of human sympathy, outside of the family relation, should be one uniting all working people, of all nations, and tongues, and kindreds."[43] Declaring his faith in the American "system of labor where the laborer can strike if he wants to!" Lincoln added: "I would to God that such a system prevailed all over the world."[44]

Sharing Henry Clay's view that the Union was "the world's best hope," Lincoln viewed the European nationalist and revolutionary movements of the mid-nineteenth century—above all in Hungary, Ireland, Germany, and France—as part of "the general cause of Republican liberty." In 1848, when congressman, he supported Irish relief and concurred in the Senate's congratulations to the French people on their "February revolution" to establish republican government (and would share in the outrage over Louis Napoleon's "usurpation" in 1851). In 1849 and again in 1852, he joined with other leading figures in Springfield publicly to identify with the Hungarians in their bloody struggle for independence from the Hapsburg empire; to express sympathy for Irish patriots; and to deem Britain as at best a doubtful partner in delivering continental Europe "from the yoke of despotism" and in fact more likely to join "in suppressing every effort of the people to establish free governments, based upon the principles of true religious and civil liberty."[45]

Lincoln's view of America's proper role was shaped by Whig precepts and a faith in moral power, not by those of the expansionist wing of the Democratic party, with its imperialist vision and stirring ideas of "manifest destiny." Lincoln saw his nation's role as one of example. He would not use the nationalist aspirations of others as a justification or pretext for intervention. He helped draft the "Resolutions on Behalf of Hungarian Freedom" that he presented to a public gathering at the Springfield courthouse in January 1852, and took the lead there in defending the doctrine of nonintervention. American principles, he declared, undergirded Louis Kossuth's liberationist cause: it was "the right of any people, sufficiently numerous for national independence, to throw off, to revolutionize, their existing form of government, and to establish such other in its stead as they may choose." It was equally, however, "the duty of our government to neither foment, nor assist, such revolutions in other governments." Nonintervention was "a sacred principle of the international law"; it should be breached only in cases of unwarrantable foreign interference by others determined to suppress the struggle for liberty. These were the cautious views of a man who had recently spoken out in Congress against the Mexican-American war as one of American aggression. They were too cautious for a minority of dissenters concerned not to establish a straitjacketing principle in foreign affairs and more confident (if less realistic) about the United States' military potency on the European stage.[46]

When the South Carolinians turned their guns on Fort Sumter in April 1861, they thus raised an issue which embraced, in Lincoln's own words, "more than the fate of these United States. It presents *to the whole family of man*, the question, whether a constitutional republic, or a democracy—a government of the people, by the same people—can, or cannot, maintain its territorial integrity, against its own domestic foes. It presents the question, whether discontented individuals, too few in numbers to control administration, . . . can always . . . arbitrarily . . . break up their Government, and thus practically put an end to free government upon earth."[47] Lincoln knew he had to suppress the rebellion to prove to the world that popular government could be maintained against internal attempts at overthrow, and to keep alive the hopes of republicans and democrats around the globe.

As European liberals, republicans, and nationalists lauded Lincoln's wartime administration they only strengthened his sense of America's worldwide significance. At the end of the first year of the conflict, Giuseppe Mazzini, Alexandre Ledru-Rollin, and Karl Blind—radical refugees from failed assaults on the political establishments of Italy, France, and Germany—wrote to Lincoln from their exile in London. "As republicans, we have felt too well that the rending asunder of your great Republic would furnish arms to all the despotisms of Europe. . . . There was a bond of unity between you and us from the beginning of this struggle. In serving the cause of liberty, *your* cause—we are serving our own."[48] From Italy, Giuseppe Garibaldi wrote grandiloquently to the president—"heir of the thought of Christ and [John] Brown"—after the Federals' battlefield triumphs of July 1863. "America, teacher of liberty to our Fathers, now opens the most solemn Era of human progress," he rejoiced, "and whilst she amazes the world by her gigantic boldness, makes us sadly reflect that this old Europe albeit agitated by the grand cause of freedom, does not understand, nor move forward to become equal to her. Whilst the epicurean upholders of Despotisms intone the bacchic ode which celebrates the decay of a free people, let the free, religiously celebrate the downfall of Slavery."[49] Another told Lincoln that "the true liberals of Europe" celebrated his re-election in 1864 as "a great fortune for humanity" and a vote for a "noble and christian enterprise."[50] Similar affirmations swelled the president's incoming foreign correspondence throughout the conflict.

Foreign enlistments provided Lincoln with a more concrete and practical expression of the Union's capacity to inspire progressive forces abroad. Though Garibaldi himself declined the offer of a commission as major-general—he would accept nothing less than overall command of Union forces that were openly emancipationist—the story of overseas recruitment reveals the broad magnetic field of American ideals. Possibly a third of Union recruits were foreign-born. These soldiers were mostly American citizens, but many who served in these ethnic regiments—French, German, Hungarian, Irish, Italian, Polish, and Scandinavian—were volunteers from abroad. Lincoln well understood their enthusiasm and readiness to suffer for a cause of global significance.[51] Take the case of an English boy, Thomas Wolfe of Brinklow, Warwickshire, whose parents stopped him from joining Garibaldi's forces in Italy, but who made his way to North America, joined Meade's army, fought at Gettysburg, was captured, imprisoned, paroled, and then returned to the front to fight with Grant in the Wilderness campaign. "I am not affraid to die," he wrote to his father. "I know it is gods will if I should fall under that starry banner which is liberty and freedom." Taken prisoner in Richmond, he suffered dire privation. His distraught father wrote to Lincoln, enclosing his son's loyal correspondence, and pleading for the president to intercede for a boy who had "volunteerd through principal . . . to fight for liberty and freedom."[52]

Abraham Lincoln's understanding of the American Union's unique place in world history was more remarkable for the striking language in which he expressed it than for the sentiments themselves. In conceiving of the United States as a special nation under providence, he was expressing an idea widely held by Americans of his era. Political leaders spoke easily of a worldwide struggle for "human liberty and human rights." Lincoln was almost certainly familiar with Daniel Webster's prayer that "the time [might] come when freedom, civil and religious, now fully enjoyed over all this portion of North America, may also be enjoyed in every country throughout the civilized world."[53] As Lincoln confronted the existential crisis of the Union from the winter of 1860–61 onward, political allies wrote—as did the Connecticut governor, William A. Buckingham—to steel him "under God . . . to guide us through this crisis" and maintain "the strongest most free and liberal government the world has ever known." Senator James Doolittle reminded him—unnecessarily—that "the hopes of constitutional liberty throughout the world & for all time depend upon us now. In such a struggle God the Almighty must be with us. And there is no attribute of His which can take part with rebels and traitors, whose sole purpose is to establish & perpetuate forever, the most stupendous & insolent of all the Tyrannies of the world."[54]

Sentiments of this kind extended well beyond the mainstream political class. Take the words not of one of Lincoln's political associates but of George F. Kelly, a religious eccentric in Washington who cast himself as God's messenger. Writing to Lincoln early in 1863, he revealed that "the Angels, Showed me how God would destroy . . . [the enemy's] power and Save the Nation" from ruin. Beseeching the president to let him "render Service unto our Government *Without price,*" he offered this prediction: "As the first Jesus was crucified as sure shall the Second (as Gods Servant) Save the 'world' through this Nation and with it go on to Glory." Lincoln read his eccentric correspondent's "wild" words with some bemusement, jotting on the envelope "a vision."[55] He saw no soul-mate in Kelly. Yet there were essential similarities in the two men's understanding of the United States' role in world history and of the universal significance of the nation's crisis. Lincoln was in his own way as much a visionary as his correspondent. His romantic nationalism and providentialist reading of American history fused with a conviction that the hope of all humankind lay in his country's republican principles and practice, its democratic faith in the dignity and rationality of the people, and its cherishing of a fluid social order in which "the weights should be lifted from the shoulders of all men, and that all should have an equal chance." Sustaining him throughout the Union's existential struggle was the shining vision of an American nation that, in tenaciously holding to its founding principles, would continue to hold out to the world the hope of liberty not only in the present but "for all future time."[56]

Notes

1. "Address of the Honorable David Lloyd George at the unveiling of the statue of Lincoln, July 28, 1920," *International Conciliation* 156 (November 1920), 498–99.

2. United States, Department of State, *The Assassination of Abraham Lincoln, late President of the United States and the attempted assassination of William H. Seward, secretary of state, and Frederick W. Seward, assistant secretary, on the evening of the 14th of April, 1865. Expressions of condolence and sympathy inspired by these events* (Washington, DC: Government Printing Office, 1867), 92.

3. Quoted in Jörg Nagler, "National Unity and Liberty: Lincoln's Image and Reception in Germany, 1871–1989," see chapter 14.

4. Roy P. Basler et al., eds., *The Collected Works of Abraham Lincoln* [*CW*] 9 vols. (New Brunswick, NJ: Rutgers University Press, 1953–55), 1:179 (December 26, 1839), 4:271 (March 4, 1861).

5. *CW*, 1:108 (January 27, 1838).

6. *CW*, 1:135 ("Report and Resolutions Introduced in Illinois Legislature in Relation to Purchase of Public Lands," January 17, 1839).

7. *CW*, 2:222 (April 1, 1854?); Jay Monaghan, *Diplomat in Carpet Slippers: Abraham Lincoln Deals with Foreign Affairs* (Indianapolis, IN: Bobbs-Merrill Co., 1945), 172; Don E. Fehrenbacher and Virginia Fehrenbacher, comps. and eds., *Recollected Words of Abraham Lincoln* [*RWAL*] (Stanford, CA: Stanford University Press, 1996), 113–14.

8. *CW*, 1:108 (February 22, 1838), 277 (February 22, 1842), 312 (March 4, 1843); 2:265 (October 16, 1854); 4:438 (July 4, 1861).

9. "Notes for a speech on slavery and American government, c.1857–58," in Douglas Wilson et al., *Great Lincoln Documents: Historians Present Treasures from the Gilder Lehrman Collection* (New York: The Gilder Lehrman Institute of American History, 2009), 20–21. See also Jean H. Baker, "Lincoln's Narrative of American Exceptionalism" in James M. McPherson, ed., *"We Cannot Escape History": Lincoln and the Last Best Hope of Earth* (Urbana: University of Illinois Press, 1995), 33–44.

10. *CW*, 3:276 (October 13, 1858).

11. *CW*, 1:279 (February 22, 1842).

12. *CW*, 1:109 (January 27, 1838).

13. *CW*, 4:265 (March 4, 1861).

14. *CW*, 4:271; Alexander Hamilton Stephens, *A Constitutional View of the Late War between the States; Its Causes, Character, Conduct and Results*, 2 vols. (Philadelphia: National Book Co., 1868), 2:448.

15. Lincoln to Josiah Blackburn, Canadian editor of the London (Canada West) *Free Press*, as printed in *New York Times*, August 1, 1864, *RWAL*, 31.

16. Allen Thorndike Rice, ed., *Reminiscences of Abraham Lincoln by Distinguished Men of His Time* (New York: North American Publishing Company, 1886), 170; *Frank Leslie's Illustrated Newspaper*, March 9, 1861, presented a "Drawing of the Rear Parlor of the Lincoln Home, as it appeared in late 1860 or early 1861." An identical globe, manufactured in Britain in 1812, can be viewed in the Lincoln Home: http://www.nps.gov/history/museum/exhibits/liho/exb/Home/LIHO2_Globe.html accessed October 29, 2010.

17. *RWAL*, 502 (James Grant Wilson).

18. *RWAL*, 297 (Noyes Miner).

19. M. L. Houser, *Lincoln's Education and Other Essays* (New York: Bookman Associates, 1957), 112; Fred Kaplan, *Lincoln: The Biography of a Writer* (New York: Harper, 2008), 25–27; Douglas L. Wilson and Rodney O. Davis, eds., *Herndon's Informants: Letters, Interviews, and Statements about Abraham Lincoln* (Urbana and Chicago: University of Illinois Press, 1998), 10; Donald J. Ratcliffe, "Selling Captain Riley, 1816–1859: Why was his Narrative So Well Known?" *Proceedings of the American Antiquarian Society* 117 (2007), 177–209.

20. The stirring events of the American Revolution "we hope . . . will be . . . recounted, so long as the bible shall be read;—but even . . . then, they cannot be so universally known, nor so vividly felt, as they were by the generation just gone to rest." *CW*, 1:115 (January 27, 1838).

21. Henry Clay, Lincoln's inspiration in domestic matters, also offered a manifesto on the United States' global role that Lincoln embraced as his own. His fellow Kentuckian, Lincoln reflected, "witnessed . . . the throes of the French Revolution . . . the rise and fall of Napoleon . . . [and] the contest with Great Britain. When Greece rose against the Turks . . . his name was mingled with the battle-cry of freedom. When South America threw off the thraldom of Spain, his speeches were read at the head of her armies by Bolivar. . . . He . . . burned with a zeal for [his country's] . . . advancement, prosperity and glory, because he saw in such, the advancement, prosperity and glory, of human liberty, human right and human nature." *CW*, 2:123–26, 129–30 (Eulogy on Henry Clay, July 6, 1852).

22. Their numbers grew to 350 by 1855. Paul M. Angle, *"Here I Have Lived": A History of Lincoln's Springfield* (Chicago: Abraham Lincoln's Book Shop, 1971), 142–43. During the 1850s German and Irish immigrants made up the majority of Springfield's foreign-born inhabitants; they constituted 50 percent of the city's population by 1860. Kenneth J. Winkle, *The Young Eagle: The Rise of Abraham Lincoln* (Dallas, TX: Taylor Trade Publishing, 2001), 272–73.

23. *Memoirs of Gustave Koerner 1809–1896: Life-sketches written at the suggestion of his children*, 2 vols. (Cedar Rapids, IA: The Torch Press, 1909), esp. 2:33, 46–51, 56–69, 109–16; F. I. Herriott, *The Premises and Significance of Abraham Lincoln's Letter to Theodore Canisius* (Chicago, 1915); F. I. Herriott, *The Conference of German-Republicans in the Deutsches Haus, Chicago, May 14–15, 1860* (Danville, IL, 1928).

24. Richard Carwardine, *Lincoln: A Life of Purpose and Power* (New York: Alfred A. Knopf, 2006), 261.

25. This was the complaint of Alabama congressman, Jabez L. Curry in a congressional debate in 1859. Quoted in Harry J. Carman and Reinhard H. Luthin, *Lincoln and the Patronage* (New York: Columbia University Press, 1943), 79.

26. Carman and Luthin, *Lincoln and the Patronage*, 80–81, 84–86.

27. Allen Thorndike Rice, ed., *Reminiscences of Abraham Lincoln by Distinguished Men of His Time* (New York: North American Publishing Company, 1886), 239–40.

28. Carman and Luthin, *Lincoln and the Patronage*, 107.

29. *RWAL*, 398.

30. Norman B. Ferris, "Lincoln and Seward in Civil War Diplomacy: Their Relationship at the Outset Reexamined," *Journal of the Abraham Lincoln Association* 12 (1991), 23.

31. *RWAL*, 392.

32. *CW*, 5:125–26 (February 3, 1862).

33. *RWAL*, 436.

34. Monaghan, *Diplomat in Carpet Slippers*, 187.

35. *RWAL*, 314, 451–52, 477.

36. *CW*, 1:113–14 (January 27, 1838).

37. *CW*, 3:363 ("Second Lecture on Discoveries and Inventions," February 11, 1859).

38. *CW*, 4:236 (February 21, 1861).

39. *CW*, 5:53, 537 (December 3, 1861, December 1, 1862).

40. Gabor Boritt, *The Gettysburg Gospel: The Lincoln that Nobody Knows* (New York: Simon & Schuster, 2006), 256–86.

41. *CW*, 1:112, 438 (January 27, 1838, January 12, 1848).

42. *CW*, 3:312 (October 15, 1858).

43. *CW*, 7:260 (March 21, 1864).

44. *CW*, 4:7 (March 5, 1860).

45. *CW*, 2:62 ("Resolutions of Sympathy with the Cause of Hungarian Freedom," September 6, 1849), 2:115–16 ("Resolutions in Behalf of Hungarian Freedom, January 9, 1852"); *Lincoln Log: A Daily Chronology of the Life of Abraham Lincoln*, April 10, 1848, http://www.thelincolnlog.org, accessed October 29, 2010; *Sangamo Journal*, September 12, 26, October 10, 1849; *Illinois State Journal*, January 14, 17, 19, 31, 1852; October 8, 1860.

46. *CW*, 2:115–16 ("Resolutions in Behalf of Hungarian Freedom January 9, 1852"); *Illinois State Journal*, January 6, 12, 29, 1852.

47. *CW*, 4:425 ("Message to Congress in Special Session," July 4, 1861).

48. K. Blind, J. Mazzini, and A. A. Ledru-Rollin to AL, April 24, 1862, Abraham Lincoln Papers, Library of Congress [ALP].

49. Giuseppe Garibaldi, Menotti Garibaldi, and Ricciotti Garibaldi to AL, August 6, 1863, ALP.

50. Angelo Paolini to AL, December 3, 1864, ALP.

51. Stephen Gál, *American Presidents through Hungarian Eyes* (Budapest: Society of the Hungarian Quarterly, 1941), 10–11.

52. Thomas Wolfe Jr. to Thomas Wolfe Sr., May 11, 1864; Thomas Wolfe Jr. to [L. A. Buck], June 2, 1864; Thomas Wolfe, Sr. to AL, November 28, 1864, ALP.

53. "Mr Webster's Speech," *Illinois Journal*, January 26, 1852.

54. William A. Buckingham to AL, December 28, 1860, James R. Doolittle to AL, April 18, 1861, ALP.

55. George F. Kelly to AL, February 24 and 25, 1863, ALP.

56. *CW*, 4:240 (February 22, 1861).

3

An American Hero in Prints Abroad
THE EUROPEAN IMAGE OF LINCOLN
Harold Holzer

In 1866, Abraham Lincoln's onetime assistant, White House secretary John M. Hay, now secretary at the *Légation des Etats Unis* in Paris, wrote home to a New York artist to inquire about his progress on a planned portrait of the late American president, and the artist's plans to convert the result into a popular print. "There is a great deal of interest exhibited in Europe in regard to his life and character," Hay reported to painter Francis B. Carpenter. Yet so far, that interest had not manifested itself into worthy pictures, at least in France. "Those sold in the shops are mere caricatures," Hay complained. The world, he added, still awaited a picture that would convey "the final idea of what Lincoln was."[1]

Whether or not Hay's hopes were ever realized in Europe remains a matter of debate and study. From the beginning of Lincoln's international fame, on through his globally acknowledged martyrdom, he remained a persistently elusive subject for the professional image makers across the Atlantic. In the first year of the American Civil War, a member of British Parliament named Alexander Beresford-Hope—a Confederate sympathizer best known for founding the *Saturday Review*—offered a revealing observation about America's two reigning, rival presidents: "Without relying too much on physiognomy, I appeal to the carte-de-visites of both Lincoln and Davis, and I think all who see them will agree that Jefferson Davis bears out one's idea of what an able administrator and calm statesman should look like better than Abraham Lincoln, great as he may be as a rail-splitter, bargee, and country attorney."[2]

As this quotation suggests, right from the start of America's war, the Lincoln image probably embarrassed his European supporters—and emboldened his enemies. What is ironic is that the very carte-de-visite photograph that so appalled Beresford-Hope is likely the very same pose that eventually came to inspire more European print portraits of Lincoln than any other. Why and how such images proliferated reflects a status well beyond the idea of pictures as mere illustration. At their best, prints could evoke a response that was emotional, and at times, almost sacred. The pictures that people bought and kept in their homes and made part of their daily lives became pictorial heirs, as historian Robert Philippe has suggested, to the religious pictures of old.[3]

At first, Lincoln suffered from what today's political spin doctors call an "image problem." Those who opposed him used his rugged image—an inspiring metaphor for American opportunity at home—against him abroad. Even his most ardent admirers on the American side of the Atlantic must have wished that Lincoln better suited the European ideal of gentlemanly refinement. So it is not surprising that separate-sheet Lincoln prints, published in England and on the Continent, both to commemorate his rise and later to acknowledge his martyrdom, softened the "rail-splitter's" rough-hewn looks to make him look more gentlemanly.

The degree to which Europe's printmakers focused on Lincoln varied from country to country. But from publishers in London, Paris, Berlin, Florence, and elsewhere came a variety of engravings and lithographs of this emerging symbol of the American Union, democracy, and opportunity. Nearly all of them seem to have been designed to show a "calm statesman" and "able administrator," to use Beresford-Hope's words, rather than an aging rail-splitter and bargee unequal to his refined-looking Confederate adversary—precisely the kind of log cabin-to-White House image that proliferated in America, not just to encourage education and hard work, but to emphasize Lincoln's virtues as a self-made man.

From the 1860 election onward, predictable curiosity arose overseas about the new American president. "We still remember," admitted the French writer Prévost-Paradol, "the uneasiness with which we awaited the first words of that President then unknown . . . whose advent to power might be dated the ruin or regeneration of his country. . . . Democratic societies are liable to errors which are fatal to them."[4] Was Lincoln such an "error?" From the earliest European portraits, one might easily draw this conclusion.

In early 1861, an American campaign print of Lincoln, adapted from a rather poorly received crayon drawing from life,[5] inspired what was probably the very first European image of Abraham Lincoln: a crude woodcut for *The Illustrated London News* (see page 46). One can only imagine it amusing Lincoln's British detractors. But this was a mere illustration—a page in a weekly journal sent to subscribers whether they wanted to see Lincoln or not. Purchasing a display print, a more expensive and consciously contrived work of art, meant to be displayed on the walls of one's home, required a more votive response. The separate-sheet print was an icon. Naturally, Lincoln held iconic appeal for far fewer Europeans than Americans. Consequently, far fewer Lincoln prints appeared abroad.

But other subtler forces were at work to further limit Lincoln print production in Europe. For one thing, American political culture encouraged

THE ILLUSTRATED LONDON NEWS

ABRAHAM LINCOLN, OF ILLINOIS, PRESIDENT ELECT OF THE UNITED STATES.—FROM A LITHOGRAPH PUBLISHED BY
G. W. NICHOLS, NEW YORK.

Unknown engraver after a lithograph by J. E. Baker based on Charles Alfred Barry's life portrait of Lincoln, 1860, published in *The Illustrated London News*, December 8, 1860. (Library of Congress)

political prints. European politics did not—even in England, where the engraving trade was hugely successful. The comprehensive British Museum print collection, for example, owned as of 1986 only seventeen period prints of Lord Palmerston, who served as prime minister when Lincoln was president; thirty-six of William Gladstone; and just twenty-one of Benjamin Disraeli, including cartoons. Why did even these native political celebrities inspire so few prints?

An explanation may lie in the right to vote, freedom of speech, the maturity of political parties, and the intensity and regularity of political campaigns—all of which tended to inspire the graphic arts. America boasted all to the greatest degree on earth—and in 1860 witnessed a particularly vibrant eruption of parades, street rallies, speech-making, publishing, and of course an outpouring of campaign prints successively introducing, roman- ticizing, and mocking Abraham Lincoln. The marketing opportunities were manifest in a country where 80 percent of eligible white males were destined to vote. While the British enjoyed freedom of speech, only one in five of its people was allowed to vote, elections were few and far between, and many races went uncontested.[6]

One inevitable result was smaller demand for prints of politicians. This is unfortunate, because the British graphics industry was one of the best in the world and produced a huge number of portraits of celebrities like its royal family. In fact, several British printmakers did produce portraits of Lincoln— but in America, and for Americans. They were among the boatloads of English who had emigrated to America from colonial times onward—tens of thousands in 1863 alone, right in the middle of a rebellion. The group included Alexander Hay Ritchie—trained as an engraver in Edinburgh—to whom belongs the dis- tinction of producing the most popular Lincoln print ever published, a copy of Francis B. Carpenter's famous history painting, *The First Reading of the Emancipation Proclamation.*[7]

Ritchie's commercial success should remind modern readers that print- making, on both sides of the Atlantic, was a mercenary rather than missionary endeavor, pursued for profit, not proselytizing, which is why surviving prints speak volumes about their subjects' popularity. This is especially so in cultures where such men were not standing for office in elections that might require widely distributed pictures for political headquarters or parades. Prints were a bellwether response to genuine public demand—because printmakers went where the business was—sometimes literally. Ritchie was not the only Scottish engraver to journey to America. In 1861, a Confederate blockade runner left Liverpool loaded with what it considered essential supplies: lithographic stones and inks, and twenty-five lithographers from Scotland, hired for the rebel Trea- sury Department. The ship made it safely back to port, and before long, its captain remembered, "the Scotch lithographers found abundant employment in Richmond . . . in the government 'paper mills'"—that is, the printers of currency. They obviously weren't the best in their field. As the ship captain later admitted, "the style of their work was not altogether faultless, for it was said that the counterfeit notes, made in the North, and extensively circulated through the South, could be easily detected by the superior execution of the engraving upon them."[8]

Back in Britain, Lincoln portraits remained a rarity, in large measure because of the country's complex, far from unanimous response to America's

Civil War. Despite Britain's anti-slavery tradition, the Northern cause evoked significant hostility there—an official neutrality fueled by an undercurrent of outright belligerence seemingly strongest amongst the upper classes, who were most likely to buy prints with which to decorate their homes.

On the eve of Lincoln's inauguration, a New York newspaper reported the prevailing belief that the House of Peers "was so solicitous for the dismemberment of the . . . United States that their influence and their means were at the service of any traitors who proposed to effect the result."[9] The hostility generated in Britain by the *Trent* affair in December 1861, when a Union ship seized Confederate emissaries aboard a British vessel bound for England, understandably did little to improve Lincoln's standing. A visiting English journalist reported that Lincoln "was unable to comprehend the causes which have alienated the sympathies of the mother country."[10]

One English engraver who did overcome these obstacles to produce Lincoln images for the meager British audience was D. J. Pound of London. Using as a model an influential, if somewhat outdated and beardless 1860 Mathew Brady photograph, the picture was made hours before Lincoln's Cooper Union address in New York and credited by many, including Lincoln himself, with helping to make him president.[11] Pound engraved an aristocratic-looking, rosy-cheeked American as a premium for the *London Illustrated News of the World*. The caption identifying its subject as "President" suggests it was issued in 1861, by which time Lincoln had grown a beard, a piece of news that evidently had not crossed the ocean. Pound nonetheless went on to issue several variations of his outdated image, including an imposing, nearly full-figure variant. All of them had something else in common beside clean-shaven cheeks: Pound consistently softened the harsh lines in Lincoln's weather-beaten face, abbreviated his generous mouth, and occasionally tinted his cheeks. The result was, one might say, almost English.[12]

A less distinguished but more typical remedy to Lincoln's image transformation came from another London artist, one J. T. Whatley. In 1865, he produced England's first known lithograph of Lincoln, also based on the old Cooper Union photograph, but with fluffy whiskers superimposed. During the war Lincoln had aged markedly, posing for more than fifty new photographs that vividly recorded his deterioration.[13] Yet for this memorial print, no doubt hastily prepared in the wake of Lincoln's unexpected death, Whatley turned to the outdated Brady model anyway. It is likely that few noticed just how inappropriate it had become—except perhaps for buyers of a rival English-made print, based on a more recent Brady photograph and published by London's Zorn & Company. Remarkably, these remain the only known British separate-sheet prints of Lincoln.

London's prolific newspaper cartoonists memorably filled this image gap with far edgier, if more ephemeral, works. For years they lampooned Lincoln

D. J. Pound, after Mathew Brady, *President Lincoln*. Engraving, London, ca. 1861.
(Harold Holzer Collection)

mercilessly but brilliantly on the pages of *Vanity Fair, London Fun*, and the
leading pictorial weekly, *Punch*, whose principal artist was John Tenniel.[14] It was
Punch that seemed to anticipate the coming war between not only the states,
but their living symbols—for this prescient cartoon of Southern and Northern
"Siamese Twins" fighting each other for dominance showed men who looked
astonishingly like Jefferson Davis and Abraham Lincoln (see page 50). And
yet it was published in 1856, a full five years before either man took office,

much less began leading the war against each other.[15] By 1861, Lincoln and Davis "officially" appeared as identifiable—still equal—but foolhardy gladiators, about whom, in the words of a poem accompanying the *Punch* image: "All mankind will jest and scoff / at people in the case / of him that hastily cut off / his nose to spite his face."[16]

PUNCH, OR THE LONDON CHARIVARI.—September 27, 1856.

THE AMERICAN TWINS, OR NORTH AND SOUTH.

Artist unknown, *The American Twins, North and South.* Woodcut engraving in *Punch, or the London Charivari*, September 27, 1856. (Library of Congress)

Over the next four years, many of *Punch*'s cartoons turned decidedly more hostile to Lincoln, like the famous 1862 effort depicting him as a bartender mixing a deceptive brew of bunkum, bosh, brag, soft sawder, and treacle. Unlike the statesmanlike Lincoln depicted by Pound, Whatley, and Zorn, this image was decidedly unflattering—and bore an uncanny resemblance to the British cartoon symbol for America, a forerunner of "Uncle Sam" known as "Brother Jonathan." Eventually, Lincoln's image became all but inseparable from that symbol. As British journalist Edward Dicey observed, the American in his "badly-fitting suit of black, creased, soiled, and puckered up at every salient point of the figure," was no gentleman, but rather a strange amalgamation of "dignity coupled with . . . grotesqueness." In short, Dicey said, "if you take the stock English caricature of the typical Yankee, you have the likeness of the President."[17] And that was the only Lincoln image to which most Englishmen were exposed: a caricature.

But the cartoons were certainly inspired: Lincoln celebrating victory at New Orleans, yet still overwhelmed by defeat and debt (Big Lincoln Horner / Up in a corner, / Thinking of Humble Pie. / Found under his thumb, a New Orleans plum, and said, "what a cute Yankee am I!"); facing up to his broken promise to subdue the rebels in ninety days; or coldly turning a deaf ear to the pleas of besieged blacks caught violently in the maelstrom of the New York draft riots. In "Holding a Candle to the Devil," Lincoln was portrayed not only making friendly overtures to the fearsome Russian bear but looking very much like Satan himself.[18]

John Tenniel's Lincoln, like Beresford-Hope's, was no Jefferson Davis. In fact, in his cartoon "The Great Cannon Game," Tenniel portrayed the Union president losing a symbolic billiard match to his Confederate counterpart—exclaiming, "darned if he ain't scored ag'in." By September 1864, *Punch* portrayed him less metaphorically: facing both the repudiation of voters and the contempt of the widows his war created. Despite his surprising victory two months later, Tenniel and *Punch* granted only that he was a national phoenix—rising from the ashes of ruined commerce and credit, and abandoned constitutional rights, free press, and state's rights. Not even emancipation or imminent military success tempered the artist's harsh judgment. On the eve of his reinauguration, *Punch* still saw Lincoln as a potential global aggressor—a Mars, the Roman God of fire, now searching for a new arena as a sleepy Britain sulkily ignores the threat and neglects to rearm (see page 52).[19]

Not until Lincoln's assassination did *Punch* do a dramatic turnabout in a justifiably famous Tenniel cartoon, "Britannia Sympathises with Columbia" (see page 52). The tender scene was accompanied by a poem, ironically enough, by Tom Taylor—the author of the play Lincoln was watching when he was shot—which seemed to offer what longtime U.S. ambassador to Great Britain Joseph H. Choate called "a magnanimous recantation of the spirit with which it had pursued him."[20]

John Tenniel, *Vulcan in the Sulks*. Woodcut engraving, in *Punch, or the London Charivari*, March 25, 1865. (Library of Congress)

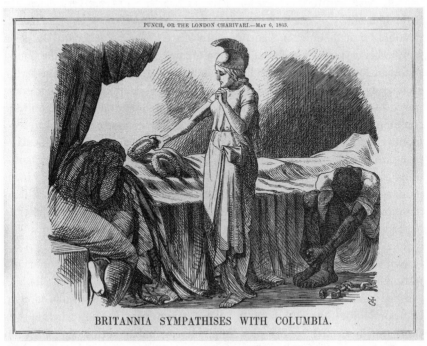

John Tenniel, *Britannia Sympathises with Columbia*. Woodcut engraving, in *Punch, or the London Charivari*, May 6, 1865. (The Lincoln Foundation Collection, courtesy of The Indiana State Museum)

Beside this corpse that beats for winding sheet
The stars and stripes he lived to rear anew,
Between the mourners at his head and feet
Say, scurrile jester, is there room for you!
. . . Yes, he had lived to shame me from my sneer
To lame my pencil and confute my pen—
To make me own this hind—of princes peer,
This rail-splitter—a true born king of men.[21]

As one *Punch* staff writer of the time observed, Tenniel and Taylor had "not only made Punch eat humble pie, but swallow dish and all."[22] Yet the turnabout did not inspire a flood of memorial tributes for home display. Apology notwithstanding, Britain's iconographic response to Lincoln, even in martyrdom, remained surprisingly sparse and narrow. And this for a man whose own family kept in its personal photo album cartes-de-visite of the Prince of Wales and the elegant British Ambassador, Lord Lyons—alongside images of rather cruder celebrities like the P. T. Barnum attraction Tom Thumb or the extravagantly bearded frontiersman Seth Kinsman.[23] As if in recognition of this aspiration to iconographic duality, the yearning for dignity leavened by the love of the informal, Americans chose a nickname for the American ruler's son, inspired by the future British king's recent visit to the west. After 1860, Robert T. Lincoln was known as the "Prince of Rails."[24]

No such affinity immediately manifested itself where French print makers and print buyers were concerned. The Lincoln family photograph album did include a carte-de-visite of a Washington social climber who called himself Prince Napoleon and certainly resembled his distant relative enough to make him a curiosity at White House parties. And *Mrs.* Lincoln, at least, loved European society, and spoke a bit of French herself, albeit with a Kentucky accent. But when Prince Napoleon met Lincoln at a White House reception in 1861, differences in language and origin apparently proved too much to make ordinary conversation—much less diplomatic relations—easy. While Lincoln droned on about the Washington weather, the prince remained all but silent, "polite but cold."[25]

Though no evidence exists that Lincoln was drawn to French culture, his image fared better in France, and for that matter throughout the Continent, than it did in Britain. Even under Napoleon III, whose government was far more overtly hostile to Lincoln and the Union cause, and where iconoclasm could be so violent that a few years after Lincoln's death, members of the Communard would topple a statue that the Second Empire had erected atop the colonnade in the Place Vendome, showing Napoleon Bonaparte in Roman costume.[26]

As Ambassador Jean-Jules Jusserand later admitted, while French liberals had their eyes on Lincoln when he unexpectedly became president, "the partisans of autocracy were loud in their assertion that a republic was well and good for a country without enemies or neighbors but that if a storm arose, it would be shattered. A storm arose, and the helm had been placed in the hands of that man almost unknown."[27]

So deep-rooted was the official hostility, so unyielding the censorship the government imposed, that when one Frenchman suggested two weeks after Lincoln's death that a Lincoln memorial medal be struck, financed by public subscription, many newspapers were afraid even to print the notice. But the plan succeeded. Some 40,000 subscribers eventually underwrote production of the bronze medal, including Victor Hugo, and no one was permitted to give more than two cents. "[D]edicated by the French democracy," the medal featured a neo-classical profile of Lincoln on the obverse, and on the reverse, between the images of the goddess of liberty and liberated slaves surmounted by an American eagle, the words: "Lincoln the Honest Man / Abolished Slavery / Re-established the Union / Saved the Republic without veiling the statue of Liberty."[28] Years later, the French government made the gift of a rather larger Statue of Liberty for New York Harbor. Transmitting a pure-gold copy to Mary Lincoln, a committee of liberal opponents of the dictator wrote: "If France had the freedom enjoyed by Republican America, not thousands, but millions among us would have been counted as admirers."[29]

Therein lies a powerful clue about the special nature of support for Lincoln in France. While America's Civil War must have seemed remote, and even primitive, to most Frenchmen, who shared neither a common language nor religious culture with Americans, as Britons did, Lincoln became a favorite among French liberal intellectuals. To them, pro-Lincoln sentiment usefully substituted for forbidden anti-Napoleon sentiment. And producing and purchasing Lincoln prints may have been a convenient avenue for expressing liberal opinions without running afoul of Napoleon's strict censors.

There was certainly no more affinity for Lincoln's style in France than in England. As French visitor Ernest Duvergier de Hauranne admitted, the American president was not "some splendid, decorative figure, wearing a white tie . . . like some sort of republican monarch. . . . What a stupid and egregious error to expect that . . . the former Mississippi boatman, could have the manners of a king or prince."[30]

But it should surprise no one that there were more French prints of Lincoln than English—despite the difference in language, culture, religion, even taste. On the subject of Gallic artistic taste, when Adolphe Compte de Chambrun, a relative of Lafayette by marriage, toured America in 1864, he could not disguise his contempt for the paintings on exhibit at the U.S. Capitol, including Francis Carpenter's original painting of the first reading of the Emancipation Proclamation. Chambrun confided that it was "beneath contempt," though he conceded that "neither painting nor camera" was capable of reproducing "the expression of his face," much less "suggesting his true psychology." But Chambrun confided a subtler observation about his country's attitudes toward such portrayals by adding that in France, no one would dream of placing portraits of living heroes "in an official building. Such things are usually left to posterity."[31] Yet from the beginning, French picture-makers did a robust industry in Lincoln images of far inferior quality and influence achieved by the engraving of the Carpenter in America. Nor did they fail to depict Lincoln's counterpart—for again, theirs was an industry largely fueled by commercial opportunity, not philosophy. In a grandiose group portrait of 1861 by Goupil & Company, Jefferson Davis was shown in uniform along with his early military family.[32] Though the portraits of men like Robert E. Lee and Stonewall Jackson were based on Mexican War-era photographs, hardly recognizable today, the magisterial group was clearly meant to inspire confidence in Confederate military might, with Davis, a Mexican War hero and former secretary of war, as implicitly the superior of the two American commanders-in-chief.

By contrast, Lincoln would be shown in France as a quintessential civilian—perhaps better for his image there in the long run, since the French were in no mood for military autocrats like Napoleon III. Thus Lincoln eventually won the image war waged in Paris. Using as a model Mathew Brady's pre-presidential Cooper Union photo, Goupil's leading competitor, the house of Lemercier, issued a well-detailed lithograph with a facsimile signature. E. D. Morin's adaptation (see page 56) was one of several woodcuts of lower quality, but no doubt greater circulation, that graced the French picture press, including a large front-page daub by an engraver named E. Parmentier, featuring a haphazard beard slapped onto the Cooper Union pose, but an acknowledgment that Lincoln was responsible for the *abolition de l'esclavage* (abolition of slavery).[33]

The French caricaturists weighed in as well—but far less often and less personally than the British, hardly surprising in a country where artist Honoré Daumier had once served six months in prison merely for lampooning the king. In one compelling but frustratingly vague example, Lincoln's re-election was recognized as *"le plus rude projectile qu'ait encore reçu le sud"*—but that is precisely how Lincoln was depicted, merely as a projectile, not a human.

While a period book-cover offered an opportunity for a handsome illustration, the result by the publishers Charlieu Frères et Huillery was but a crude daub of the memorial medallion, still instructive as a relic because it attempted to portray not Lincoln but an image of Lincoln in another medium (see page 57).[34]

Most French printmakers showed a strong preference for a photograph taken by Alexander Gardner when Lincoln first arrived in Washington for his inauguration (see page 58). The photo, quickly relegated to obscurity in America when Lincoln began trimming his hair and beard soon after entering office, became and remained the indisputable favorite model for European printmakers. Adaptations flowed off the presses by such artists as Emile Pierre Metzmacher for Goupil, who Europeanized Lincoln's appearance, substituting bee-stung lips for his pendulous mouth, and replacing his uncontrollable hair

M. LINCOLN, Président actuel de l'Amérique du Nord.

Dessins de MORIN et de B

E. D. Morin, after Mathew Brady, *M. Lincoln, President actuel de l'Amérique du Nord.*
Woodcut engraving, French, ca. 1861, publication unknown. (Harold Holzer Collection)

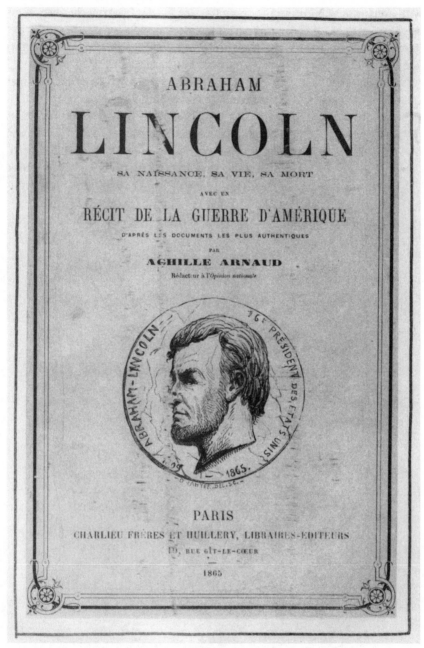

Jahyer (?), after the bronze medallion by Franky Magniadas titled *Dédié par la Démocratie Française à Lincoln*. . . . Woodcut engraving for title page of 1865 book, *Abraham Lincoln* by Achille Arnaud. (Harold Holzer Collection)

with a luxurious coif. Like all printmakers of his day, Metzmacher was interested in commercial success, not political propaganda, so he was not above issuing a companion print of Jefferson Davis as he negotiated the French marketplace in search of the broadest possible customer base.

An even more Gallic look characterized another adaptation of the Gardner photo by C. Bornemann, featuring an even more exaggerated pompadour and a refined tilt of the head (see page 60). Such prints not only made Lincoln look his part as a head of state, but suited the liberal cause beset by conservative criticism that democracy offered weak leadership and government instability. Lincoln could serve as a symbol in France—as long as he was cosmeticized by its artists.

Conversely, when they emphasized Lincoln's frontier naturalness, the printmakers could lapse into caricature. Engraver Charles Chardon's *Lincoln Recevant Les Indiens Comanches* may have reflected the French people's insatiable

Alexander Gardner, [Abraham Lincoln]. Photograph, Washington, D.C., February 24, 1861. (Library of Congress)

Emile Pierre Metzmacher, after Alexander Gardner, *Abraham Lincoln/(Président des Etats-Unis)*. Lithograph, printed and published by Goupil et Cie., Paris, and in New York by M. Knoedler, 1862. (The Lincoln Foundation Collection, courtesy of The Indiana State Museum)

interest in American Indians—enough to inspire a print of an event ignored by artists in the country where it took place—though it probably did little to enhance Lincoln's image in France (see page 61).

Unquestionably, the most extraordinary of all French—perhaps all European—prints was C. Schultz's *Fraternité Universelle*—which placed Lincoln within a symbolic pantheon populated by heroes from both history and mythology (see page 61). Among them was George Washington, a French favorite, shown here joining hands with Lincoln—common enough in American post-assassination prints—but unheard of in European ones. In its emphasis on work and freedom—Lincoln was also shown joining hands with a slave family—the American president becomes the overt symbol of liberalism. And with its liberal, if somewhat discordant, imposition of historic and metaphoric characters—Socrates (representing the integrity of philosophy) and Gutenberg

C. Bornemann, after Alexander Gardner, *Abraham Lincoln*. Published by Lemercier, Paris, ca. 1861–1862. (Photograph courtesy Harold Holzer)

(representing martyrdom to freedom of thought)—the print also demonstrated the comparatively provincial nature of American Lincoln prints. This extraordinary effort has never been equaled anywhere.

In other European capitals, Lincoln may have had even greater appeal as an icon. Italy and Germany were both embroiled in unification battles of their own in the 1860s. While preoccupied with internal matters, their liberals and nationalists had understandable interest in Lincoln's effort to preserve the American experiment in Union.

German printmakers probably produced more Lincoln prints than their Italian counterparts, but this is understandable for several reasons. For one thing, there were more German than Italian printmakers: Italy may have spawned the Renaissance, but Germany gave birth to lithography and incubated

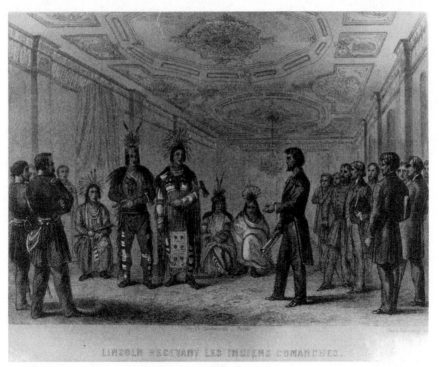

Ferdinand Delannoy, *Lincoln Recevant les Indiens Comanches*. Engraving, published by
Charles Chardon the elder, Paris, 1866. (Harold Holzer Collection)

C. Schultz, *Fraternité Universelle*. Lithograph, published by Lemercier, Paris, ca. 1865.
(Harold Holzer Collection)

a generation of specialists in that print form. But there was another factor: German immigration to America was high in the mid-nineteenth century, creating a common bond—and perhaps a second front in the fight for commercial pre-eminence. It is likely that German-made Lincoln prints found audiences not only there, but among German-Americans in cities like Cincinnati and St. Louis whom Republicans wooed as voters and soldiers. Judging from the number of these prints reposing in American collections, we can assume a vigorous international trade. Large-scale Italian immigration lay largely in the future, and Italian Lincoln prints are much rarer.

Rich as it was, the German printmakers' response to Lincoln might have been even greater had not so many German printmakers migrated to America after the revolutions of 1848—though they came armed with diverse political beliefs. Louis Prang of Breslau, a Lincoln admirer, was one of the first to adapt the handsome Gardner preinaugural photo favored by so many Europeans. But the pro-secessionist Maryland etcher Adalbert Volck, an émigré from Bavaria, saw Lincoln as an oppressor who drew ink from the devil's inkwell to write his Emancipation Proclamation. Lincoln's image might have been tarnished in Germany—indeed in America—had Volck not

Baumgartner, after Mathew Brady, *Abraham Lincoln*. Steel engraving, Leipzig, ca. 1861. (Harold Holzer Collection)

operated out of Union-controlled Baltimore, a city so violently anti-Lincoln that en route to his inauguration in 1861 he had snuck through town in the dead of the night to avoid a supposed murder plot. Volck etched that episode as well, suggesting that Lincoln was a coward, but like all his other pictorial attacks, it remained uncirculated until after the war. In America, geography trumped nationality. Prang, who later published a memorable suite of Civil War battle chromos, operated out of the Republican, abolitionist hotbed of Boston, where pro-Lincoln, pro-Union prints poured freely off local presses.

In Germany itself, pictorial response to Lincoln was swift, predictable, and positive. The pre-Civil War Cooper Union photograph inspired several early lithographs, including examples by P. W. M. Trapp and a lithographer named Baumgartner. An even earlier photo model, dating back to 1857, to which Mary Lincoln objected because of the "disordered condition," as she put it, of her husband's hair,[35] looked even more awkward in a print adaptation by W. Matthiesen, who imposed a slapdash beard—a favorite shortcut commonly

W. Matthiesen, after Alexander Hesler, *Abraham Lincoln*. Engraving, published by F. E. Bordings, Germany, ca. 1865. (Harold Holzer Collection)

Printmaker unknown, after C. S. German, *Abraham Lincoln/Präsident der Vereinigten Staaten von Amerika/Geb. D. February 12, 1809 Gest. D. April 15, 1865 ["]I regret nothing heretofore said as to slavery . . . I shall not attempt to retract or modify the Emancipation Proclamation["]. . . .* Lithograph, probably Berlin, ca. 1865. (Library of Congress)

practiced by American printmakers. With more pleasing results, the perennial
favorite European model, the Gardner pose, inspired several adaptations, including a richly colored chromolithograph by the printmaking firm of Berg &
Poersch, who produced it in a handsome frame backed by canvas so it resembled a painting.

A rarely adapted 1861 Lincoln photo, made before the president-elect left
his Illinois hometown for his inauguration, inspired the only German print
to celebrate emancipation, and, aside from *Fraternité Universelle*, the only
European print to do so—though many such tributes were manufactured in
America. In this unusual tribute, the German printmaker depicts Lincoln as if
he were delivering an oration—proudly announcing freedom. The grandeur of
the pose is at odds with the rather dull prose of the Proclamation itself, which
German Karl Marx, who granted that Lincoln was the "single-minded son of
the working class," condemned as resembling "the trite summonses that one
lawyer sends to an opposing lawyer."[36] So it comes as little surprise that when
the lithographer featured some words in defense of emancipation, he chose

THE LAST MOMENTS OF ABRAHAM LINCOLN PRESIDENT OF THE UNITED STATES.

Max Rosenthal, *The Last Moments of Abraham Lincoln President of the United States/
April 15th, 1865.* Lithograph, published by Joseph Hoover, Philadelphia, 1865.
(Harold Holzer Collection)

them not from the Proclamation itself, but from later Lincoln remarks defending it—curiously printed in English—even with the main caption in German—only adding to the suspicion that this image enjoyed distribution in America and Germany alike.

German artists achieved something else that no other Europeans did: they produced newsworthy separate-sheet prints of Lincoln's murder and deathbed. In Philadelphia, German-born lithographer Max Rosenthal created a fantastic view of the dying Lincoln being summoned to heaven by a band of winged angels surmounted by a portrait of George Washington appearing as a sunburst—a lavish brew of the secular and the religious (see page 65). But from Germany, pictures of Lincoln's assassination and last moments tended to be more realistic. The surprisingly modest and accurate lithograph by Gustave May of Frankfurt did pander a bit to popular taste by including Mrs. Lincoln in the scene. At least that is what the viewer is surely meant to infer from the sole woman in attendance, her back to the audience (probably because May had no model from which to work her portrait). In fact, Mary was not actually in the room when her husband breathed his last, nor was vice president Andrew Johnson, also included in the picture, most likely to suggest national continuity.

Gustave May, *Die Letzten Augenblicke des Prasidenten Lincoln (The Last Moments of President Lincoln)*. Lithograph, Frankfurt, 1865. (Harold Holzer Collection)

Despite these concessions to taste and propriety, Gustave May's print is still a work distinguished by accuracy and modesty.

On the other extreme is F. Hartwich's flamboyant and unrealistic *Lincoln in City Point,* which showed Lincoln arriving like a conqueror into the headquarters of the Union army at the end of the war. The print was almost surely the product of a misconception. While Lincoln indeed visited City Point a few days before Robert E. Lee surrendered his Confederate army at Appomattox, the president did not encounter anything resembling the kind of welcome Hartwich portrayed. The German printmaker probably confused the event with Lincoln's trip to Richmond a few days later. When Lincoln visited that nearby Union-occupied Confederate capital, he was greeted, according to a contemporary account, with "tropical exuberance," and "a wild delirium of joy," though only from its liberated African Americans.[37] Even so, Lincoln quietly walked onto Richmond's shores from an unprepossessing rowboat—he did not arrive on horseback, as the German-made scene suggested. Hartwich's City Point print not only got the details wrong, but more importantly, emphasized the kind of triumphalism Lincoln assiduously avoided.

F. Hartwich, after Gustave Bartsch, *Lincoln in City Point*. Lithograph, printed by J. Hesse, and published by Oswald Seehagen, Berlin, 1865. (Harold Holzer Collection)

Perhaps that is why Breslau publisher Edward Trewendt found it simpler—
and no doubt attracted an audience for it as well—to issue O. May's entirely
invented metaphorical portrait of Lincoln lolling rather languidly on some
unidentified shore. Precisely what he is supposed to be doing in the picture is

O. May, after a photograph by Mathew Brady, *Die Gefahr.* Engraving, published by Edu-
ard Trewendt, Breslau, ca. 1865. (Harold Holzer Collection)

rather hard to fathom. Is he facing the roiling waters of disunion? Watching calmly as the flood washes over the defeated South (palmetto trees are visible above the submerged farmhouse in the distance)? Or perhaps all of the above?

From Italy there came nothing so ambitious or daring. A Catholic region, it still lacked major emigration to the United States. But as early as 1862, Baron Ricasoli, the Italian prime minister, expressed his hope for "the success of the constitutional authorities in crushing the rebellion" in America.[38]

Again the popular 1861 Gardner photograph provided the source for most Italian prints, although the decline in artistic quality was as clear as their tendency to make Lincoln look Italian. Perhaps using a slightly later Mathew Brady studio photograph as an additional model, Buono e Borrani of Florence produced perhaps the most Mediterranean of all these Italian print

Buono e Borrani, after Alexander Gardner and Mathew Brady, *Abramo Lincoln/Presidente della Repubblica degli Stati Uniti.* Lithograph, Florence, 1861. (Abraham Lincoln Presidential Library and Museum, Springfield, Illinois)

portraits, another of which acknowledged Lincoln's martyrdom for unity by noting that he was *"morto assassinato 25 Aprile"*—mis-dating Lincoln's death by ten days.[39]

Perhaps the most perplexing of all these European prints was a group portrait of Lincoln, Jefferson Davis, and their Italian contemporary, Prime Minister Ricasoli. This may be the only separate-sheet print of Lincoln together with any foreign leader. The work of a Dutch lithographer named Desguerrois, it is difficult to know whether it was designed for audiences in Italy or Holland: other Italian prints called Lincoln "Abramo" and this one identified him "Abraham." But if the image was designed for the Dutch, why show Ricasoli at all? Had he achieved international fame as great as Lincoln's? Or was the print perhaps created simply to introduce three new world leaders to a curious Dutch public? Maybe it was designed to warn Italians of what would happen if their union, like America's, came unraveled: the result might be two presidents instead of one. It remains a mystery, but perhaps one suggesting that national boundaries did not automatically define or proscribe European representations of the American hero.

The Dutch otherwise seemed unconcerned about the American conflict. They remained doggedly neutral and their print industry produced only one other known Lincoln image—an effort by one P. Blommers whose beardless state suggests that it was published early to introduce, not celebrate, Lincoln. So remote did Lincoln remain to the Dutch that when their minister to the United States wrote home about the new American president, he dismissed him as a "railway worker"—his clumsy translation for the word he had no doubt been hearing around Washington: rail-splitter. But then, Karl Marx had done no better in describing the American president as a "stonecutter" and "mechanic"—though for him the terms were surely meant to be flattering. In Marx's world, the greater the toil, the greater the compliment.[40]

Even in Hungary, a country with a rich history of printmaking, along with a recent tradition of repression following the failed revolts of 1848 and 1849, Lincoln came to symbolize both liberalism and nationalism—particularly after he sacrificed his life for both. In the words of a Budapest news weekly, Lincoln became nothing less than "the greatest citizen of the world." The *Vasárnapi Ujság* predicted: "All will behold his portrait with reverence. It pictures a man who rose from being a simple railsplitter . . . solely through hard work and talent . . . to the highest rank."[41]

In time, Lincoln did become a hero in the European graphic arts. Yet the inescapable and ironic conclusion one must draw after examining this gallery is that the more repressive a society, the more its audiences seemed to use Lincoln as a symbol of freedom. Thus Palmerston's England had less need for the Lincoln image than Napoleon III's France, Bismarck's Germany, or an Italy roiling with unification battles—and this may explain why so many more prints of Lincoln were published in the latter countries.

There is no way to compare America's avalanche of Lincoln prints to Europe's far less frequent and rather specialized output. All we know is that the American long maligned or ignored in England evolved on the Continent into a symbol larger even than the symbol of America, Uncle Sam himself. So large, that in an 1873 French woodcut by Alfred Le Petit, Lincoln dwarfs the very symbol of America, looming so large he must view it through a magnifying glass.[42]

Alfred Le Petit after a photograph by Mathew Brady (February 9, 1864), [Abraham Lincoln with Uncle Sam]. Woodcut engraving, published in *Le Grelot*, Paris, November 23, 1872. (Harold Holzer Collection)

Viewing the European prints of Abraham Lincoln under equally close scrutiny invites two basic conclusions: First, that popular prints of the Lincoln image proliferated less often than we might have expected based alone on common language and heritage. And second, that the Lincoln image proliferated most where it seemed a useful symbol that crossed oceans, and trumped differences in language and religion by symbolizing freedom and nationalism.

Other countries have yet to be closely surveyed—but no doubt produced Lincoln images, too. For example, the outdated Cooper Union photograph inspired a mourning print, complete with a little sketch of his funeral procession, by Roca y Hermano in Barcelona. And a century later, another Spanish artist named Pablo Picasso collected thousands of Lincoln postcards, telling visitors that Lincoln's was "the real American elegance"—though sadly he never painted him.[43]

Ironically, the best-selling Lincoln image of the late twentieth century may well have been the work of yet another Spanish artist, Salvador Dali, whose trick 1975 painting, *Gala Contemplating the Mediterranean Sea—Which at 20 Meters Becomes a Portrait of Lincoln*, boasts encrypted homages to Mark Rothko, to previously painted works by Dali, and of course to the artist's wife's voluptuous buttocks. As a poster, perhaps representing as much enthusiasm for Mrs. Dali's appearance as it did for Mr. Lincoln's, it adorned shop windows and college dormitory rooms for a generation. Such audiences may not have realized that the Dali print was, in a way, only the most recent in a long and underappreciated tradition of European images of Abraham Lincoln.

Notes

The author gratefully acknowledges the years of research, writing, and lecturing conducted on the subject of iconography with colleagues professors Mark E. Neely, Jr. and Gabor Boritt. See in particular, Boritt, Neely, and Holzer, "The European Image of Abraham Lincoln," *Winterthur Portfolio* 21 (Summer/Autumn 1986): 153–83.

1. John M. Hay to Frank (Francis) B. Carpenter, January 22, 1866, Collection of Robert Todd Lincoln, Hildene, Manchester, Vermont. The author thanks David Quinlan for alerting him to this unknown letter.

2. Belle Becker Sideman and Lillian Friedman, eds., *Europe Looks at the Civil War* (New York: Orion Press, 1960), 33.

3. Robert Philippe, *Political Graphics: Art as a Weapon* (New York: Abbeville Press, 1980), 172.

4. Quoted in J. J. Jusserand, "Abraham Lincoln as France Regarded Him," *Addresses Delivered at the Memorial Exercises Held at Springfield, Illinois February 12, 1909* (Springfield: Illinois Centennial Commission, 1909), 19.

5. See *The Illustrated London News*, December 8, 1860. For the story of the original painting by Charles Alfred Barry and its domestic adaptation by Boston lithographer J. H. Bufford, see Harold Holzer, Gabor S. Boritt, and Mark E. Neely, Jr., *The Lincoln Image: Abraham Lincoln and the Popular Print* (New York: Charles Scribner's Sons, 1984), 50–56. Barry's reminiscences were republished in Rufus Rockwell Wilson, ed., *Intimate Memories of Lincoln* (Elmira, NY: Primavera Press, 1945), 308–10.

6. See, for example, Robert Worthington Smith, "Political Organization and Canvassing: Yorkshire Elections before the Reform Bill," *American Historical Review* 74 (June 1969): 1540; Boritt, Neely, and Holzer, "The European Image of Lincoln," 255n3.

7. Harold Holzer and Mark E. Neely, Jr., *Mine Eyes Have Seen the Glory: The Civil War in Art* (New York: Orion Books, 1993), 72–78; Harold Holzer, "Introduction," Francis B. Carpenter, *Six Months at the White House with Abraham Lincoln: The Story of a Picture*, orig. pub. 1866 (Washington, DC: White House Historical Association, 2008), 1–29.

8. John Wilkinson, *The Narrative of a Blockade-Runner* (New York: Sheldon & Co., 1877), 111, 130; Mark E. Neely, Jr., Harold Holzer, and Gabor S. Boritt, *The Confederate Image: Prints of the Lost Cause* (Chapel Hill: University of North Carolina Press, 1987), 6.

9. *Harper's Weekly*, March 1, 1861.

10. Edward Dicey, *Spectator of America*, ed. Herbert Mitgang (Chicago: Quadrangle Books, 1971), xiii.

11. Mathew Brady quoted in George Alfred Townsend, "Still Taking Pictures," *New York World*, April 12, 1891, in Mary Panzer, *Mathew Brady and the Image of History* (Washington, DC: Smithsonian Institution Press, 1997), 224.

12. Original in the author's collection.

13. See Charles Hamilton and Lloyd Ostendorf, *Lincoln in Photographs: An Album of Every Known Pose* (Norman: University of Oklahoma Press, 1963), esp. 386–403.

14. For an early history of its output, see *A Bowl of "Punch;" or, Selections from the London Charivari* (Philadelphia: G. B. Zieber & Co., 1844).

15. "The American Twins, North and South," *Punch*, September 27, 1856.

16. *Punch*, May 18, 1861. For a history of verse in the magazine, see Sir Francis C. Burnand, ed., *Poems from Punch* (London: George G. Harrap & Co., 1908).

17. Mitgang, *Spectator of America*, 91.

18. *Punch*, May 25, 1862 ("The New Orleans Plum"); September 27, 1862 ("The Overdue Bill"); August 8, 1863 ("'Rowdy' Notions of Emancipation"); November 7, 1863 ("Holding a Candle to the xxxxxxxx").

19. *Punch*, May 9, 1863 ("The Great 'Cannon Game'"); May 24, 1864 ("Mrs. North and Her Attorney"); December 3, 1864 ("The Federal Phoenix"); March 25, 1865 ("Vulcan in the Sulks").

20. Joseph H. Choate, *Abraham Lincoln and Other Addresses in England* (New York: The Century Co., 1910), 4.

21. *Punch*, May 6, 1865.

22. William Shirley Brooks, quoted in Samuel A. Goddard, "Extracts from Letters on the American Rebellion," *Magazine of History*, extra no., 19 (1912), 20.

23. Mark E. Neely, Jr. and Harold Holzer, *The Lincoln Family Album*, orig. pub. 1990 (Carbondale: Southern Illinois University Press, 2006), 70–73.

24. At first a reporter called Robert the "Yankee Prince of Wales." See Harold G. and Oswald Garrison Villard, eds., *Lincoln on the Eve of '61: A Journalist's Story by Henry Villard* (New York: Alfred A. Knopf, 1941). But writers could not resist the pun and Robert, son of the great American rail-splitter, was soon dubbed the "Prince of Rails." See David C. Mearns, *The Lincoln Papers: The Story of the Collection with Selections to July 4, 1861*, 2 vols. (Garden City, NY: Doubleday, 1948), 1:8.

25. Camille Ferri Pisani, *Prince Napoleon in America, 1861: Letters From His Aide de Camp* (Bloomington: Indiana University Press, 1959), 100.

26. A photograph showing the rubble of this toppled statue of Napoleon is in the collection of The Metropolitan Museum of Art.

27. Jusserand, "Abraham Lincoln as France Regarded Him," 16.

28. Boritt, Neely, and Holzer, "The European Image of Abraham Lincoln," 161–63.

29. Ibid., and Benjamin Gastineau, *Histoire de la souscription populaire à la médaille Lincoln* (Paris: Libraires Internationale A. Lacroix, 1865), 7, 10–13.

30. Ernest Duvergier de Hauranne, *A Frenchman in Lincoln's America: Huit Mois en Amérique: Lettres et Notes de Voyage, 1864–1865*, ed. Ralph H, Bowen, 2 vols. (Chicago: R. R. Donnelley & Sons, 1974–5), 2:351.

31. Marquis Adolphe de Chambrun, *Impressions of Lincoln and the Civil War: A Foreigner's Account*, translated and edited by Adalbert de Chambrun (New York: Random House, 1952), 15, 99.

32. See Neely, Holzer, and Boritt, *The Confederate Image*, xviii.

33. *Journal Historique Illustré*, September 10, 1865.

34. Engraving by O. Jahyer (?), for Achille Arnaud, *Abraham Lincoln: Sa Naissance, sa Vie, Sa Mort* (Paris: Charlieu Fréres et Huilery, 1865).

35. Abraham Lincoln to James F. Babcock, September 13, 1860, in Roy P. Basler, ed., *The Collected Works of Abraham Lincoln*, 9 vols. (New Brunswick, NJ: Rutgers University Press, 1953–55), 4:114.

36. Sideman and Friedman, *Europe Looks at the Civil War*, 299; Harold Holzer, ed., *The Lincoln Anthology* (New York: Library of America, 2009), 49.

37. Charles Carlton Coffin, in Allen Thorndike Rice, ed., *Reminiscences of Abraham Lincoln by Distinguished Men of His Time* (New York: North American Publishing, 1886), 181. (Note: this enormously influential book featured a gold-stamped version of the French memorial medal on its cover.) See also William C. Harris, *Lincoln's Last Months* (Cambridge, MA: Belknap Press, 2004), 205.

38. Quoted in Boritt, Neely, and Holzer, "The European Image of Lincoln," 174.

39. For the Buono & Borrani print's debt to an 1861 Lincoln photo by Brady, whose international circulation has otherwise not been proven, see Winfred Porter Truesdell, *Engraved and Lithographed Portraits of Abraham Lincoln*, Volume II [Volume I unpublished] (Champlain, NY: Troutsdale Press, 1993), 201. See also print by Watt after Gardner, *Abramo Lincoln/Presidente della Repubblica degli Stati Uniti d'America*, ca. 1865, (Alfred Whittal Stern Collection, Library of Congress).

40. Boritt, Neely, and Holzer, "The European Image of Lincoln," 177.

41. *Vasárnapi Ujság*, Pest, Hungary, May 21, 1865, in the collection of the Széchényi Konyvtár, Budapest, discovered there by historian Gabor Boritt in 1975.

42. *Le Grelot*, November 23, 1873.

43. Calvin Tomkins, *Living Well Is the Best Revenge*, orig. pub. 1962 (New York: Modern Library, 1998), 33–34.

4

"The Principle of Humanity"

LINCOLN IN GERMANY AND ITALY, 1859–1865

Eugenio F. Biagini

No other episode in American history, with the possible exception of the War of Independence, generated more interest and emotion in the Old World than the Civil War. The issues raised by the conflict—slavery, national unification, independence, and democracy—had immediate relevance in contemporary European politics. In Italy, Germany, Hungary, and Poland, patriots and revolutionaries were then striving to secure independence and national unification. The latter was achieved by the Italians in 1861 and by the Germans between 1866 and 1870, while the Poles rose up in arms in 1863. Although the Russians crushed their rebellion, the tsar emancipated the serfs in 1861, encouraging hopes that he would further modernize the country. Other empires were also liberalizing: the Austrians conceded parliamentary self-government to Hungary in 1866, and in 1867 London granted greater autonomy to Canada. In 1871 the French Empire was replaced by a Republic, and the United Kingdom saw a Fenian rebellion in Ireland and, in Britain, a renewal of the democratic agitation which led to enlargement of the parliamentary franchise in 1867. This was followed by a series of important social and political reforms, inspiring Victorian observers to write about the "Americanisation" of British politics. In short, throughout the Euro-Atlantic world, the 1860s was a decade of radical change, which in many respects reversed the failure of the revolutions of 1848–9. In this context it is not surprising that much of what was written about Lincoln and the Civil War had an eye on Old World priorities and concerns, with European observers projecting the American events onto the domestic scene.

Some historians have dismissed such a response as emotional and "naïve."[1] They have claimed that in their pro-Lincoln attitude, many Europeans seemed "unaware that American democracy was . . . a form of political organization which defended particular material interests, apart from the 'sacred' values of humanity."[2] It is certainly true that both the president and the Republican party stood for capitalism, which some socialists—such as Pierre-Joseph Proudhon—found as objectionable as slavery itself.[3] However, others were aware that at the time "bourgeois" democracy continued to be a revolutionary doctrine. And it is revealing that, while the antibourgeois rant of the French left was echoed and amplified by the monarchist and Jesuit presses,[4] Karl Marx— who was hardly naïve about the evils of capitalism—defended Lincoln, arguing that he was completing the "unfinished" revolution of 1775–83, with the aim of preserving his country as a land where labor was honored.[5] This view was widely shared by many other Germans and Italians, with a number of leading patriots seriously engaging with the politics of the Civil War. In the process they developed a perceptive understanding both of Lincoln and the United States, and indeed of democracy, which they began to regard as the global system of governance of the future.

Italy

In Italy, the outbreak of the U.S. Civil War coincided with national unification and the outbreak of peasant revolts in the south. Occupied as they were with domestic challenges, it has been argued, Italians showed "little interest" in the American crisis.[6] It is true that newspapers were hardly dominated by American headlines, but at the time most of the Italian press had a local or regional focus, and provided only limited coverage of international news.[7] However, the parochialism of the media was counterbalanced by the cosmopolitan outlook of the national leaders. Italian reformers had long been writing about America. The most perceptive analyst of its problems was Carlo Cattaneo. An economist, democrat, and supporter of federalism, Cattaneo took a distinctly pragmatic approach to the question of slavery, which he wished to see abolished by means of gradual economic reforms. Consequently, as early as 1833 he criticized militant abolitionism as "moralistic" and counterproductive.[8] Surprisingly, twenty years later, during the Civil War, he did not comment publicly on the war, although in 1863 he did ensure that Lincoln received a copy of Giuseppe Mazzini's writings.

Mazzini himself was more active, but—in contrast to Cattaneo—he adopted a purely moralistic and quasi-religious attitude to the American crisis, his abolitionism being partly informed by his Transcendentalist friends.[9] He had criticized slavery first in 1846 and subsequently in the aftermath of the publication of the Italian translation of Harriet Beecher Stowe's *Uncle Tom's Cabin*.[10] Although this novel was extraordinarily successful in Italy (where it remained a best-seller for the next century), it is not clear whether Mazzini's intervention had any impact on public opinion. In any case, at the outbreak of the Civil War, the pro-Lincoln front found its leader not in Mazzini, but in his colleague and sometime rival Giuseppe Garibaldi.

Remarkably, at the time Garibaldi was almost as popular in the United States as in Italy. To America's democratic imagination he symbolized the values of the Declaration of Independence, as suggested by a number of poetic lyrics. William C. Bryant, John G. Whittier, and Henry T. Tuckerman celebrated what they perceived as the universal significance of Garibaldi's campaigns, such as the defense of the 1849 Roman Republic and his single-handed liberation of Sicily and Naples in 1860. Their poems combined distinctly Protestant ideas (because of Garibaldi's hatred for the pope and his temporal power) with a perception of the Risorgimento as part of a global struggle for the emancipation of humanity from all forms of despotism.[11] While this had obvious relevance for the American opponents of slavery—including the Rev. Henry Ward Beecher and Senator Charles Sumner[12]—it also appealed to the libertarian supporters of state's rights. The Thousand—a citizens' army whose ranks were later swollen by Sicilian volunteers—overthrew one of the most infamous regimes in Europe, the Bourbons of Naples, defeating a large and well-equipped standing army. Their exploits had been closely followed by the American press, which commented with unbounded enthusiasm that "[n]o such feat is recorded in history, not even amongst the deeds of mythological heroes."[13] For the *New York Times*, Garibaldi's achievements "carried Americans back to the days of their own struggle for independence, and revived in the person of the patriotic general, their own heroic Washington."[14] Besides enthusing the press and the poets, Garibaldi also attracted substantial material help from America. Two fundraising committees, set up as early as November 1859, raised $100,000 toward the cost of the Sicilian campaign. Moreover, Colonel Colt made a substantial personal contribution, presenting the committees with a hundred of his famous cavalry carbines to equip Garibaldi's mounted "Guides."[15]

This was part of a wider pattern of American support for the Risorgimento. The United States was the first government to recognize the Kingdom of Italy in April 1860 (even before the official proclamation of the new state), in a motion introduced by Anson Burlingame, a Republican congressman from Massachusetts. On April 13, 1861, only two days after receiving official notification of the establishment of Italy as a united country, William H. Seward announced the appointment of George Perkins Marsh as U.S. Minister Plenipotentiary in Turin.[16] Marsh was an inspired choice. He was a great Italophile, emotionally closer to the aristocratic liberals of the Cavour administration than to the democrats in opposition, and was therefore *persona grata* in Italian diplomatic circles. His dispatches to Washington expressed his support for the count's commercial policy, which was favorable to American trade.[17] He was greatly impressed by the liberty now enjoyed by Protestants in Italy, which led to a gradual growth in their numbers and a proliferation of evangelical missions in the Peninsula, including representatives of the Methodist Episcopal Church and the Southern Baptist Convention.[18]

The U.S. diplomatic investment in the Cavour government paid the expected dividend.[19] Most of the Italian press likewise sided with the North, although in March 1865 Marsh complained to Garibaldi that "certain Turin journals have, for some time, manifested a malignant and unscrupulous hostility to the Federal Union."[20] Garibaldi responded that the newspapers which dared to attack the Union "were like the asses of the fable, who kicked the Lion believing that he was dead, but now that they see him rise again in all his majesty, they change their language." He added: "[t]he name of Lincoln, like that of Christ, marks the beginning of a glorious age in the history of Humanity and with pride I wish to perpetuate within my family, that name of the great Emancipator."[21] The allusion here was to a happy event in Garibaldi's family: his daughter had just given birth to a baby boy, who had been christened Lincoln. His arrival and the choice of his name were widely celebrated in democratic circles in Italy at the time.[22]

At this stage Italian opinion had already concluded that the Confederacy was "evil," but was as yet unconvinced that Lincoln was really against slavery. Such attitudes provide the background for the famous episode of Garibaldi's proposed commissioning as a major general in the U.S. Army. Soon after the outbreak of hostilities, in July 1861, Seward instructed Marsh to approach Garibaldi with the offer of a command of a Federal Army Corps.[23] The proposition was attractive both to the general and to Seward. On the one hand, Garibaldi was flattered, especially as he was feeling rejected and marginalized by the Italian government, following Turin's refusal to incorporate his Red Shirts into the regular army and to honor his commitment to pay their expenses and wages for the Sicilian campaign. On the other hand, Washington was desperately looking for competent generals, and Garibaldi was one of proven experience and popularity, and had demonstrated expertise in American-style guerrilla warfare.

Eventually Garibaldi turned down the offer when Seward was unable to satisfy his requests and conditions, namely the immediate abolition of slavery and that Garibaldi would be appointed commander-in-chief.[24] The Italian general was probably relieved: it is likely that he had deliberately come up with such extraordinary demands, which he knew Lincoln could not satisfy, because "his sights were still firmly set on Italy," and he was hoping that he would be able to raise another volunteer army and march on Rome.[25] He actually did so the following year, with the ill-fated expedition which was stopped at Aspromonte by the Italian government, who feared that his raid would provoke a French military intervention. In the aftermath, the Italian government imprisoned the disbanded Red Shirts, but Marsh tried to secure their liberation on the condition that they join the U.S. Army: "It might perhaps relieve the government of Italy . . . from embarrassment," he wrote to the Turin government in 1862, and "offer the prisoners an opportunity of usefulness to us without prejudice to the interests of Italy."[26]

Marsh again approached Garibaldi, this time with a copy of Lincoln's preliminary Proclamation of Emancipation (September 1862), trusting that "we shall soon have the aid both of your strong arm and of your immense moral power in the maintenance of our most righteous cause." On Seward's instructions, Marsh "[informed] the General that he and his friends will be welcomed with enthusiasm . . . and that a proper command will be assigned to him."[27] Garibaldi then negotiated the arming and equipping of 2,000 of his veterans. Ultimately, he was not able to take up the offer of a commission, largely because in the skirmish with the Italian army at Aspromonte he had been wounded and had not yet recovered, and partly because the Italian government was eager to appease the national hero and dissuade him from leaving the country.

In 1863 news of the Emancipation Proclamation created a further groundswell of enthusiasm for Lincoln. Congratulatory addresses to the president appeared in the press. One of the most significant and heartfelt was produced by Garibaldi. In his typically emphatic style, he praised Lincoln as "the emancipator, [a name] more covetable than any crown or human treasure. A whole race of men, yoked by egoism to the bondage of slavery is . . . restored to man's dignity, civilization and love . . . Hail, Abraham Lincoln, captain of liberty. . . . Hail to you, redeemed Hamitic race, Italy's free men kiss your chains' glorious marks on the ground."[28] The address was also signed by a number of leading democrats, including Mazzini, who, in a separate article, commented:

> The principle in whose name Garibaldi sends an address to Lincoln—the *principle* that God has placed as the *aim* of the American battles . . . is the principle of *humanity* . . . that says: God created not kings, masters and servants, but man . . . Whatever the colour the sun's ray may paint on human features, wherever a heart beats to love and a face smiles to Hope and lips whisper God's name, there we find an *I* whom no one can annihilate without crime . . . The freedom of the Whites . . . has neither reason to exist nor certainty of victory unless we go back to the principle which commands the freedom of the Blacks.[29]

Yet, in his attitude to Lincoln, Mazzini continued to be less enthusiastic than Garibaldi, or at any rate was hesitant about committing himself to the Northern cause. There were various reasons for this. First, he had tactical considerations in mind. Although he had condemned slavery as early as 1846, and despite having admirers in the abolitionist camp—including Henry Ward Beecher, Calvin Ellis Stowe (the husband of Harriet Beecher Stowe), William Lloyd Garrison and Sarah Parker Remond[30]—he also had friends in the Democratic party whom he was anxious not to alienate. In the past, they, and especially the "Young America" group, had shown some interest in his dream of a transatlantic revolutionary alliance. With a conservative monarchy in Italy and Napoleon III as firmly established on the French throne as ever, Mazzini saw such an alliance as his last hope.[31] Moreover, he felt isolated and bypassed both by Garibaldi and the Italian government, and was mystified by what he regarded as a change of heart among his American friends, who were happy to cooperate with Cavour, prioritizing "mere" commercial interests and the claims of Protestant missions above the "sacred" principles of international republicanism.[32]

A second explanation for Mazzini's comparative coolness toward Lincoln is probably to be found in the temperamental differences between the two leaders, which counterbalanced their ideological convergence. It was a rather complex relationship. They shared common views and attitudes, including a mystical commitment to republicanism. Indeed, both were influenced by Transcendentalism and German philosophical idealism, and both adopted a religious approach to democratic nationalism and values such as liberty.[33] One historian has gone so far as to argue that Lincoln, in his Gettysburg Address description of the Civil War as "a struggle over the . . . proposition that 'government of the people, by the people, for the people, shall not perish from the earth,'" consciously echoed Giuseppe Mazzini's 1833 statement that Young Italy sought revolution "in the name of the people, for the people, and by the people."[34] This may be difficult to establish. Although the Italian patriot is not listed in Wills' work on Lincoln's sources for his Gettysburg speech, we do know that in the winter of 1862 the president received from two Italian admirers a complimentary copy of the first volume of Mazzini's works and that he was appreciative of the gift.[35] This evidence is, admittedly, circumstantial and inconclusive, but not negligible.

Irrespective of any philosophical affinities or contacts, in matters of strategy and political priorities Mazzini differed profoundly from Lincoln. He was instead closer to John Brown.[36] The admiration may have been reciprocated: Brown's 1859 raid on Harpers Ferry was inspired by contemporary Italian theories of revolutionary guerrilla warfare.[37] It is remarkable that one year before Harpers Ferry, another revolutionary firebrand, the Mazzinian socialist Carlo Pisacane, attempted a similar expedition in the Kingdom of the Two Sicilies. Leading a small group of enthusiasts and preaching a gospel of social and economic emancipation, Pisacane tried to spark a peasant revolt in the Calabrian hills. Like Harpers Ferry, this raid ended in tragic failure: the rebellion failed to materialize and the republican guerrillas were surrounded and destroyed by the Neapolitan army.

The revolutionary strategy shared by Brown, Pisacane, and Mazzini depended on the assumption that the mass of the people were politically timid, but naturally aware of their patriotic duty and democratic destiny. What they needed was a prophet-martyr to initiate a war of liberation. That Mazzini entertained such a lofty vision of the people may explain his coolness toward the "prosaic" Lincoln. The latter, especially in 1861–63, seemed to embody what Mazzini most disliked about America, namely, the nation's fundamentally utilitarian, pragmatic, and individualistic mindset.[38] This may also explain his impatience toward Garibaldi, another pragmatic democrat. To Mazzini's dismay, there was much "calculating materialism" in Garibaldi's approach to revolution. Both Garibaldi and Lincoln saw the limits, as well as the potential, of democracy. Because of Lincoln's "pedestrian" attitude to politics, Mazzini suspected that he was waging the war only to preserve the Union, in the same way that Garibaldi had gone to Naples "merely" to bring about the unification of Italy, while ignoring the more ambitious aim of establishing a democratic republic.

Only when Lincoln produced his 1863 Proclamation did Mazzini come out unambiguously in favor of the North. Even then, however, he warned that slavery was "only one" of many forms of oppression, no worse than that of Hungary and Poland, and that a wider, "universal" republican program was necessary in order to emancipate humankind.[39] He was relieved that Garibaldi declined Seward's offer of a commission, because he wanted him to stay in Italy, expecting a new European revolutionary crisis to break out soon from the disintegration of either the Austrian or the Ottoman Empire under the pressure of the national aspirations of their oppressed subjects. If any such crisis materialized, Garibaldi was the man to lead the rebels. Moreover, because national self-determination remained a top priority for Mazzini, he dreaded Lincoln's commitment to full victory, which he believed would inevitably result in a prolonged Federal military occupation of the Confederate States. Instead, he hoped to see the war ended by a compromise peace, and the Union restored on the basis of some special deal for the Southern states, involving some return to "state's rights," although it is not clear how this could have been achieved without compromising the abolitionist and democratic agenda which he otherwise supported.[40]

Germany

There is a long history of German involvement in the transatlantic development of the plantation economy, especially through Hamburg and the other Baltic ports.[41] Yet, as late as 1848 public opinion was comparatively indifferent to American slavery, which was at best used as a metaphor for Eastern European serfdom.[42] Even in the run-up to and during the Civil War, German patriots seemed less responsive to slavery than to the question of U.S. national unity, which had direct relevance to contemporary Germany. The parallels between the ways the two countries secured or preserved their national unity in this decade have not gone unnoticed by modern historians.[43] At the time it was Heinrich von Treitschke who emerged as the most perceptive German nationalist commentator on the American crisis: he argued that Lincoln's victory in the war would transform U.S. federalism into a more unitary and dynamic system, with constitutional machinery adequate for the creation of a continental "empire."[44]

This was the voice of conservative nationalism. German democracy and socialism adopted a different, more idealistic approach, but were not for this reason naïve or ill-informed. On the contrary, the German radical perspective on the war was really sophisticated and nuanced, also thanks to the insight provided by the large and politically engaged German-American community.[45] The latter comprised a number of influential U.S. citizens, including the president's private secretary, the Bavarian John G. Nicolay.[46] He was obviously close to the heart of the war effort in ways not available to other Germans. However, even the most "utopian" among his fellow-German immigrants—such as the communist Fritz Annecke and the republican Gustav von Struve—were apparently well-integrated in U.S. society and happy to get involved in "the second struggle for American freedom."[47]

Partly because many had a revolutionary and Catholic background, the German-Americans originally displayed an instinctive sympathy for the Democrats and were suspicious of the Whigs and Republicans, who had links to anti-Catholic nativism. However, opposing the 1850 Fugitive Slave Law and the 1854 Kansas-Nebraska Act, which threatened to perpetuate and extend the slave system, they began to gravitate toward the Republican party. Thus, anti-slavery became the decisive issue in shaping their allegiances; although the "state's rights" battle cry had some appeal to these champions of national self-determination, most of them regarded emancipation as a categorical imperative.

Yet, in the run-up to the election of November 1860, the Germans were still divided between the candidates put forward by each party.[48] The situation was further complicated by the activism of the Republican radical left, who found Lincoln too conservative and championed John C. Frémont instead.[49] In the end, both in 1860 and 1864 the Germans supported Lincoln by a substantial majority, with one of their leaders, Carl Schurz, actually claiming that their vote was crucial to Lincoln's first election.[50] While this has recently been questioned by scholars, it is difficult to deny that—either as a real electoral bloc or as a perceived presence within the U.S. party system—the Germans were significant.[51] Lincoln himself valued their support, made the most of their "ethnic" leaders, and subsidized a German language newspaper.[52]

The German-American community included a broad cross-section of society, ranging from the established bourgeoisie to workers and small farmers.[53] It was influential partly because it was large, and especially because it was well organized, to such an extent that not only did German-Americans provide as many as 200,000 recruits for the Union forces, but also formed entire units, officered by émigrés with relevant military experience in the armies of Prussia, Baden, and Bavaria.[54] The community's leaders were veterans of "the '48," such as Friedrich Kapp, Caspar Butz, Carl Schurz, Franz Sigel, Friedrich Hecker, Emil Praetorius, and Theodor Olshausen. They had acquired significant acumen in the organization and management of democratic politics in their native lands during the revolution and were highly articulate in both German and English. They knew how to play the democratic game and were eager to get involved.[55]

Schurz is one of the best-studied and most widely celebrated representatives of the community.[56] Born in 1829, he grew up in a small village in the Rhineland, a predominantly Catholic region, which had been annexed by the Protestant Kingdom of Prussia in 1815. His uncle, a large tenant-farmer, was a member of the local Masonic Lodge, and his father, the schoolmaster, instilled in the young Carl a substantial amount of skepticism about the dogmas of the Church.[57] He was nineteen at the outbreak of the Revolution, which he perceived as being primarily about democracy and individual liberty, rather than German unification. After 1849 he became an exile, spending some time in England before emigrating to the United States. He became involved in American politics, partly because of his strong feelings against slavery. Opposition to the "peculiar institution" attracted him to the Republican party, turning him into an "avid supporter" of Seward.[58] Schurz was campaigning in Illinois when he first met Abraham Lincoln in 1858. He immediately became one of his admirers and supporters (he was to name his first-born son Carl Lincoln), and at the outbreak of the Civil War he was eager to secure a military command, which he eventually did with Lincoln's help.[59] He found himself in a unit with other German radical émigrés, such as Franz Sigel, Ernest Hoffman, and Karl Spraul (the latter two had served with Garibaldi in the Risorgimento campaigns).[60]

The abolitionist enthusiasm of these émigrés was matched by the interest and passion with which their fellow democrats and radicals back in Europe followed Lincoln's progress.[61] The president's name had such wide appeal that Ferdinand Lassalle began to style himself "the German Lincoln."[62] Lassalle's great rivals, Karl Marx and Friedrich Engels, were also mesmerized by the war: they perceived abolition as a step toward the fulfillment of the potential of bourgeois democracy in preparation for the eventual rise of the proletariat. From the beginning of the crisis, in his articles in the *New York Daily Tribune*, Karl Marx indicated that the conflict was primarily about slavery, not because of anything Lincoln said or did, but because the rebels had proclaimed that their secession was about slavery: "it was not the North, but the South, which undertook this war . . . by loudly proclaiming 'the peculiar institution' as the only and the main end of the rebellion."[63] Slavery—its morality or otherwise, its right to expand in the Western territories, and its place within the Constitution—was therefore the real cause of the war.

In contrast to Mazzini, Marx was prepared to assess American politics on its own terms, rather than as a function of some Eurocentric democratic strategy. Thus, he saw Lincoln's election not as a compromise, but as the confirmation that "the cause of the United States [was] . . . the cause of liberty . . . and that . . . the soil of the United States [was] the free soil of the landless millions of Europe . . . their land of promise, now to be defended sword in hand, from the sordid grasp of the slaveholder."[64] Later he disagreed with much of the European moderate-liberal press, which represented Lincoln as a tyrant in the making, and insisted that his decision to strengthen the executive had been forced on him by Confederate aggression.[65] As a result the secession crisis was inevitable. It had been brought about by the clash between the expansionist needs of the slave-powered cotton economy of the South and the rising tide of authentically democratic sentiment in the North and West, in the shape of the Republican party and its program. "The vitally important point in this platform was that not a foot of fresh terrain was conceded to slavery; rather it was to remain once and for all confined within the boundaries of the states where it already legally existed. Slavery was thus to be formally interned." This was, however, equivalent to a death sentence for the "peculiar institution," because extensive cultivation exhausted the fertility of the soil to such an extent that the states of the Old South had turned from the production and export of cotton and to-bacco, to the production of slaves, to be sold in the deep South and Southwest, until there as well the point of exhaustion was reached. "As soon as that point is reached, the acquisition of new territories becomes necessary, so that one sec-tion of the slaveholders with their slaves may occupy new fertile lands and that a new market for slave-raising, therefore for the sale of slaves, may be created for the remaining section."[66] Thus, "continual expansion of territory and con-tinual spread of slavery beyond its old limits is a law of life for the slave states of the Union."[67] Marx concluded by pointing out the wider implications of the war in terms of class struggle over the future of the Union, contrasting the will of "20 million free men of the North" with that of "300,000 slaveholders."[68]

A peaceful separation was not possible because North and South did not form two countries "like, for example, England and Hanover," and the South was no country at all, but merely "a battle cry." Marx concluded that "the foe's most vulner-able spot, the root of the evil—*slavery itself*" was bound to come up soon, irrespec-tive of Lincoln's "pusillanimity" in restraining the radical abolitionists.[69] However, unlike many German-Americans, he was not tempted to support Frémont: encour-aged by his daughter, he never wavered in his commitment to Lincoln.[70]

Like Mazzini, Marx was struck by Lincoln's "prosaic" style. While the Italian patriot was exasperated by the president's penchant for systematic un-derstatement, Marx interpreted it as device for disguising the full extent of his revolutionary intentions. He noted that, at a time when most public figures indulged in exaggerated rhetoric,

[he] gives his most important actions always the most commonplace form. Other people claim to be 'fighting for an idea,' when it is for them a matter of square feet of land. Lincoln, even when he is motivated by an idea, talks about 'square feet' . . . The most redoubtable decrees—which will always remain remarkable historical documents—flung by him at the enemy all look like, and are intended to look like, routine summonses sent by a lawyer to the lawyer of the opposing party.[71]

The president was like a revolutionary snowball, acquiring momentum and power as the war went on: "Should Lincoln succeed this time . . . it will be on a far more radical platform and in completely changed circumstances. Then the old man will, lawyer-fashion, find that more radical methods are compatible with his conscience."[72] To a relative, Marx confided: "*never* had such a gigantic revolution occurred with such rapidity. It will have a highly beneficial influence on the whole world."[73]

As is well known, it was Marx who penned the address with which the International Working Men's Association expressed their good wishes and support following Lincoln's re-election in November 1864.[74] In January 1865 the International received an official reply.[75] For Marx, the very fact that the president had taken the time and trouble to respond was "in fact, everything we could have asked for . . . the only answer [to European addresses] so far on the part of the old man that is more than a strictly formal one."[76] He felt that he had achieved what Mazzini had sought in vain to secure: U.S. endorsement for the cause of radical democracy in Europe.

The Assassination and the Aftermath

Marx was neither shaken nor confused by the news of Lincoln's murder. He felt instead that the assassination "was the most stupid act [the champions of the South] could have committed," because his removal would unleash the class-struggle dimension of the conflict, by empowering Andrew Johnson, who "as a former poor white has a deadly hatred of the oligarchy."[77] Moreover, in view of the popular response generated by the murder, he argued that, by making "such a colossal impact throughout the world," even in death Lincoln was striking a blow for democracy, to the chagrin of the European monarchs: "None of them has yet had such honour."[78]

If Marx really expected a democratic backlash in Europe, he was soon disappointed. There is little evidence that in Germany or Italy the establishment feared for its future. On the contrary, politicians and statesmen perceived the assassination as a threat to the principles of law and order on which bourgeois society operated. Moreover, many seemed genuinely moved. Not only were predictable official expressions of sympathy offered, but parliaments in various countries passed quasi-unanimous motions of condolence. The Italian and the Prussian chambers of deputies were the first two European legislative assemblies to vote an "address of sympathy" to the American people. The Prussian message was endorsed by all parties except the Conservatives and a few Catholic Ultramontanes.[79] Bismarck and the entire *corps diplomatique* attended a memorial service in the Dorothea Kirche.[80] The Italian Chamber passed a motion, moved by Francesco Crispi (who had been Garibaldi's deputy in Sicily in 1860 and was a spokesman for the Opposition), praising Lincoln as a man "who deserved so well of the cause of humanity and liberty" and ordering that the flag on the parliament building be draped with crape for three days in mourning.[81] On April 29, the lower chamber of the Austrian *Reichsrat* unanimously passed a motion praising both the late president and the Union for their fight for "the cause of freedom, civilization, and humanity," but also taking pleasure in Lincoln's recognition that the Austrian emperor sided with the North, as he was "the enemy of all rebellion."[82] This was ironic: Franz Joseph's identification of Lincoln with the cause of law and order was the exact opposite of Marx's claim that in life and death the president would be striking a blow for democracy.

In Italy it was Garibaldi—the "bourgeois democrat" hated and despised by both the Austrian kaiser and Karl Marx—who was most closely associated with the memory of the president. His public identification with Lincoln was such that he was perceived as the fit recipient of letters of condolence, almost as if he had been the assassinated president's brother.[83] It was typical of Garibaldi that the murder elicited no desire for revenge, but rather inspired him to support a petition to President Johnson for clemency on behalf of Jefferson Davis, and indeed asking for the abolition of capital punishment. His friend Karl Blind—whose activities spanned the world of radical democratic activism in three countries (Germany, Britain, and Italy)—by contrast wrote:

> As for us over here, all our German friends . . . we would really have wished to see an example made of the sole person of the Chief slave driver, of the *assassin* of so many good people who have suffered tortures just about incredible, but well authenticated, in the prisons of the South . . . The crime of high treason against the Republic is, for me, a crime which carries the capital punishment . . . I admire those who sentenced Charles Stuart, in the way I admire Brutus, Tell.[84]

Mazzini was apparently less stirred than either Garibaldi or Blind by Lincoln's murder, perhaps because he had always had reservations about him, but also because he felt that "martyrdom" was the fitting culmination of a republican hero's career.[85] His first response, in a private letter to his English friend Matilda Biggs, consisted of a rather unemotional analysis of the likely political consequences of the murder, which he regarded as "a mere act of revenge, a crime therefore and nothing else; it cannot help the South; it will incense the North and make the possible pacification more difficult."[86] Two days later he wrote to another friend: "Lincoln . . . died with the consciousness that the cause to which he had devoted himself was triumphant; and the thought must have soothed his last hours. Those are to be pitied who die doubting."[87]

By then he had realized the propaganda potential of the assassination and started to celebrate Lincoln as the fallen champion of republican liberty against despotism. Had he lived, Mazzini wrote, Lincoln would have sent the

U.S. Army against the Emperor Maximilian of Mexico—a prospect which he would have welcomed. He seemed sufficiently enthusiastic about America that he supported even the prospect of a U.S. invasion of Cuba.[88] Thus, in contrast to his attitude during the Civil War—when he had been concerned to protect Southern self-government from Washington's oppression—Mazzini was now a convert to "regime change" and republican imperialism. He was also a resolute supporter of the vote for blacks and of land redistribution in the former Confederate states, irrespective of whether this involved prolonged Federal military occupation or not. Perhaps the explanation for such a dramatic change is to be found in his hope that, if Washington were encouraged to become more assertive, "before long America will play an important role in European affairs."[89] In this spirit he tried to establish, in 1866, a Universal Republican Alliance, which he conceived as a counterbalance to the increasingly socialist International Working Men's Association.

By 1868 Mazzini linked Lincoln with "the real moral, intellectual, economic emancipation of the Whites" in Europe, as much as the blacks in America.[90] For him as well as for Marx, Lincoln was now the prophet of "positive" liberty and social entitlement, of a society based on economic and entrepreneurial freedom, but also committed to the opportunity of the common man, and devoted to the principle that property should be based on labor and should not degenerate into forms of monopoly.[91]

Garibaldi too was thinking along these lines. However, being less of a republican zealot, he thought that the United States and Britain would become partners in a future special relationship, working together for world *liberty*, rather than for republican *revolutions*.[92] Interestingly, while Mazzini operated on the assumption of Italy's superiority and its "special call" to lead the peoples of the world in their onward march, Garibaldi was prepared to admit that such primacy would eventually belong to a future Anglo-American alliance. Moreover, looking at the European Continent, he went so far as praising the Swiss Confederation (rather than Italy) as "the Guardian of the liberty of the old Continent" and the country which was best placed "to appreciate and express the joy and the sorrow of the Nation which emancipated the slaves," concluding that "the mourning of Switzerland is well worthy of Lincoln, the new Redeemer of man."[93]

In conclusion, throughout the Civil War Lincoln was "read" and appropriated by German and Italian political and social analysts and pressure groups, often, but not always, for purposes directly relevant to their own political and national priorities. Schurz, Mazzini, Marx, and Garibaldi stand out from the rest because of their understanding of the crisis and level of engagement with the contemporary American debate. Significantly, all of them had spent a substantial part of their life in exile in either England or America.[94] In fact, Schurz became an American citizen and Mazzini an advocate of American republican expansionism. Marx produced a sophisticated historical analysis of the war and, perhaps for the last time in his career, wrote as a champion of liberal democracy. Garibaldi was capable of genuine fellow-feeling for Lincoln, of which his contemporaries were somewhat aware. Like Lincoln, he knew his limits and had modest and realistic expectations of what democracy and internationalism could achieve.

Attitudes to both Lincoln and the United States changed over the twenty years following his assassination. By the late 1870s the American political system had come under intense scrutiny as its less attractive features—such as the working of Tammany Hall—became more widely known. In 1881 the Italian statesman and political analyst Marco Minghetti represented Lincoln as an honest man who had succumbed to the inexorable embrace of the party "machine," the ultimate example of the perverse effects of mass democracy on even the purest and most upright of patriots. Meanwhile, the democratic enthusiasm of the 1860s turned into the social imperialism of the 1890s, and in nationalist interpretations Lincoln became associated not so much with the cause of emancipation, but with militarism and the forcible suppression of secession and rebellion.[95]

Notes

1. Carlo Galli, "Introduzione. Ordine politico e guerra civile tra America ed Europa," in Tiziano Bonazzi and Carlo Galli, eds., *La Guerra civile americana vista dall'Europa* (Bologna: il Mulino, 2004), 18.

2. Ibid., 192.

3. James M. McPherson, *Battle Cry of Freedom: The Civil War Era* (New York: Oxford University Press, 1988), 24–25.

4. Giorgio Spini, "*Civiltà cattolica e Guerra civile*," *Rassegna storica toscana* 11 (1955), 153–65.

5. Jonathan Sperber, *Rhineland Radicals: The Democratic Movement and the Revolution of 1848–1849* (Princeton, NJ: Princeton University Press, 1991), 302.

6. Maria Laura Lanzillo, "Unità della nazione, libertà e indipendenza. Il Risorgimento italiano e la Guerra di secessione americana," in Bonazzi and Galli, *Guerra civile*, 189.

7. Valerio Castronovo and Nicola Tranfaglia, *La stampa italiana nell'età liberale* (Bari and Rome: Laterza, 1979), 25.

8. Carlo Cattaneo, "Notizia sulla questione delle tariffe daziarie negli Stati Uniti d'America desunte da documenti ufficiali," *Annali universali di statistica* 35 (1833), 133ff; Carlo Cattaneo, "Compenso ai coloni britannici per la liberazione dei negri," *Bollettino di notizie statistiche ed economiche, d'invensioni e scoperte italiane e straniere* 37 (1833), 384; Carlo Cattaneo, "Di alcuni stati moderni," *Il politecnico* (1842), fasc.28, 353. On Cattaneo's federalist priorities in his attitude to the United States, see J. Rossi, "Il mito americano nel pensiero politico del Risorgimento," in Agostino Lombardo et al., *Italia e Stati Uniti nell'età del Risorgimento e della Guerra civile. Atti del 2 Symposium di studi americani. Firenze, 27–29 maggio 1966* (Florence: La Nuova Italia, 1969), 246–48.

9. Eugenio F. Biagini, "Mazzini and Anticlericalism: The English Exile," in Christopher Alan Bayly and Eugenio F. Biagini, eds., *Giuseppe Mazzini and the Globalization of Democratic Nationalism 1830–1920* (Oxford: Oxford University Press, 2008), 145–66.

10. "Prière a Dieu pour les planteurs par un exilé," in Giuseppe Mazzini, *Scritti editi ed inediti* [hereafter cited as *SEI*] (Imola: P. Galeati, 1919), 29:283ff. About this "prayer" see Giorgio Spini, "I democratici e la Guerra civile americana," *Rassegna storica italiana* 9:1 (1965), 153 and "Le relazioni politiche fra Italia e Stati Uniti durante il Risorgimento e la Guerra Civile," in Lombardo et al., *Italia e Stati Uniti*, 165 n. Beecher Stowe's book went through seventeen editions and reprints in forty years, and the first edition was serialized in Cavour's newspaper, *Il Risorgimento*, in 1852. Ibid., 296, 298.

11. Aldo Celli, "Il Risorgimento nella poesia americana," in *Atti del I Congresso internazionale di storia Americana, Italia e Stati Uniti dall'indipendenza Americana ad oggi (1776–1976)* (Genoa: Tilgher, 1978), 35.

12. Howard R. Marraro, *American Opinion on the Unification of Italy, 1846–1861* (New York: Columbia University Press, 1932), 291.

13. *New York Herald*, September 21, 1860, cited in Marraro, *American Opinion*, 280.

14. Marraro, *American Opinion*, 280. Cf. *New York Times*, June 27, July 7, October 17, 1860. When Garibaldi retired to his island farm of Caprera, he was again compared with both George Washington and Cincinnatus, the ancient Roman republican hero: Marraro, *American Opinion*, 285; cf. *New York Times*, December 17, 1860.

15. Marraro, *American Opinion*, 287; Giorgio Spini, "Le relazioni politiche," 160. On Avezzana see Salvatore Candido, "Esuli italiani negli Stati Uniti d'America fra guerre e rivoluzioni (1820–1861). La Congrega della 'Giovine Italia' di New York," in *Atti del I Congresso internazionale di storia Americana*, 284, 287.

16. Marraro, *American Opinion*, 300.

17. Spini, "Le relazioni politiche," 129–30; Mary Philip Trauth, *Italo-American Diplomatic Relations, 1861–1882: The Mission of George Perkins March, First American Minister to the Kingdom of Italy* (Washington, DC: Catholic University of America Press, 1958), 103; Sexson E. Humphreys, "The attitude toward Moderate Liberalism expressed by United States envoys in Italy during the Risorgimento," in *Atti del XXXVIII Congresso di storia del Risorgimento italiano* (Rome: Istituto per la Storia del Risorgimento Italiano, 1960), 132–38.

18. Spini, "Le relazioni politiche," 157, 180.

19. David Lowenthal, *George Perkins Marsh: Prophet of Conservation* (Seattle: University of Washington Press, 2000), 236; Roland Sarti, "La democrazia radicale: uno sguardo reciproco tra Stati Uniti e Italia," in Maurizio Ridolfi, ed., *La democrazia radicale nell'Ottocento. Forme della politica, modelli culturali, riforme sociali, Annali Feltrinelli*, 39/2003 (Milan: Feltrinelli, 2005), 148. Cf. the two articles by Vincenzo Botta, "La questione americana," in *Rivista contemporanea* 26 (1861) and 29 (1862).

20. George Perkins Marsh to Giuseppe Garibaldi, March 20, 1865, in Giuseppe Garibaldi, *Epistolario, Vol. 10 (1865-marzo 1866)*, edited by Giuseppe Monsagrati (Rome: Istituto per la Storia del Risorgimento Italiano, 1997), 50.

21. Giuseppe Garibaldi to George Perkins Marsh, March 27, 1865, in Garibaldi, *Epistolario*, 10:50.

22. Giuseppe Garibaldi to the Associazione Generale degli Operai di Milano, Divisione Femminile, April 4, 1865, Ibid., 53.

23. Lowenthal, *George Perkins Marsh*, 239.

24. H. Nelson Gay, "Lincoln's Offer of a Command to Garibaldi: Light on a Disputed Point of History," *The Century Magazine* 75 (November 1907), 63ff.; Howard R. Marraro, "Lincoln's Offer of a Command to Garibaldi: Further Light on a Disputed Point of History," *Journal of the Illinois State Historical Society* 36:3 (September 1943), 237ff. Cf. Guiseppe Garibaldi to James W. Quiggle (June 27, 1861) and to H. Salford (August 31, 1861), in *Epistolario, 6, 1861–1862*, in *Edizione nazionale degli scritti di Giuseppe Garibaldi*, Vol. 12, ed. Sergio La Salvia (Rome: Istituto per la Storia del Risorgimento Italiano, 1983), 78, 151–52.

25. Christopher Duggan, *The Force of Destiny: A History of Italy since 1796* (London: Allen Lane, 2007), 244; Christopher Hibbert, *Garibaldi and His Enemies: The Clash of Arms and Personalities in the Making of Italy* (London: Penguin, 1987), 331.

26. Lowenthal, *George Perkins Marsh*, 240.

27. Ibid., 240–41.

28. *Il Dovere* (Genoa), August 14, 1863, 141–42.

29. Mazzini to the Editor of *Il Dovere*, August 18, 1863, *SEI*, 76:33–34.

30. Sarti, "La democrazia radicale," 147.

31. Ibid., 148.

32. Spini, "Le relazioni politiche," 158–59.

33. Garry Wills, *Lincoln at Gettysburg: The Words That Remade America* (New York: Simon & Schuster, 1992), 46, 104–8; For Transcendentalism's influence on Mazzini, see Eugenio F. Biagini, "Mazzini and Anticlericalism: The English Exile," cit.; Enzo Tagliacozzo, "Lincoln e il Risorgimento," in Lombardo et al., *Italia e Stati Uniti*, 318.

34. Timothy M. Roberts, "The Relevance of Giuseppe Mazzini's Ideas of Insurgency to the American Slavery Crisis of the 1850s," in Bayly and Biagini, eds., *Mazzini and the Globalization of Democratic Nationalism*, 322.

35. The volume was sent to the president by two Italian democrats, Gino Dealli and Alessandro Repetti. See their letter to Carlo Cattaneo, January 27, 1862, in *Epistolario di Carlo Cattaneo*, ed. Rinaldo Caddeo (Florence: G. Barbèra, 1956), 14–15; Lincoln replied and his note is preserved in the Archivio Repetti, Milan.

36. *SEI*, 61:66.

37. G. Schenone, "John Brown e il pensiero insurrezionale italiano," in *Atti del I Congresso internazionale di storia Americana, Italia e Stati Uniti dall'indipendenza Americana ad oggi (1776–1976)*, 357–66; Raimondo Luraghi, *La Guerra Civile Americana* (Bologna: Il Mulino, 1978), 132–36; and Roberts, "The Relevance of Giuseppe Mazzini's Ideas," 311–22.

38. *SEI*, 76:34, 77:147.

39. *SEI*, 52:177; 74:224; 69:73.

40. *SEI*, 80:126–27, 139–40.

41. Klaus Weber, "Deutschland, der atlantische Sklavernhandel und die Plantagenwirtschaft der Neuen Welt (15. bis 19. Jahrhundert)," *Journal of Modern European History* 7:1 (2009), 37–67.

42. Andreas Gestrich argued at a seminar at Sidney Sussex College, Cambridge, February 9, 2009, that in 1848 there was only one abolitionist society in Germany, and that it had published only one pamphlet.

43. Carl N. Degler, "The American Civil War and the German Wars of Unification: The Problem of Comparison," in Stig Förster and Jörg Nagler, eds., *On the Road to Total*

War: The American Civil War and the German Wars of Unification, 1861–1871 (New York: Cambridge University Press, 1997), 62–67, 71.

44. Heinrich von Treitschke, "Bundesstaat und Einheitsstaat" (first published 1864), in "Historische und politische Aufsätze," 4, vermehrte Aufl., Bd.2, *Die Einheitsbetrebungen zertheiler Völker* (Leipzig: Hirzel, 1871). More generally, on Prussian perceptions of America, see Enno Eimers, *Preussen und die USA 1850 bis 1867: Transatlantische Wechselwirkungen* (Berlin: Duncker & Humblot, 2004).

45. Walter D. Kamphoefner and Wolfgang Johannes Helbich, eds., *Germans in the Civil War: The Letters They Wrote Home* (Chapel Hill: University of North Carolina Press, 2006).

46. Michael Burlingame, ed., *Abraham Lincoln: The Observations of John G. Nicolay and John Hay* (Carbondale: Southern Illinois University Press, 2007), 35.

47. Fritz Annecke, *Die zweite Freiheitskampf der Vereinigten Staaten von Nordamerika* (Frankfurt a.M.: Sauerlander, 1861); Gustav von Struve, *Diesseits and Jenseits des Oceans* (Coburg: F. Streit, 1863).

48. Andreas V. Reichstein, *German Pioneers on the American Frontier. The Wagners in Texas and Illinois* (Denton: University of North Texas Press, 2001), 132.

49. Jörg Nagler, *Frémont contra Lincoln: Die deutsch-amerikanish Opposition in der Repblikanischen Partei während des amerikanisches Bürgerkriges* (Frankfurt: Peter Lang, 1984), 20–34, 111–12, 163–83.

50. William E. Dodd, "The Fight for the North West," *American Historical Review* 16:4 (July 1911), 774–88; Carl Wittke, *Refugees of Revolutions: The German Forty-Eighters in America* (Philadelphia: University of Pennsylvania Press, 1952), 203–20.

51. James M. Bergquist, "The Forty-Eighters and the Republican Convention of 1860," in Charlotte L. Brancaforte, *The German Forty-Eighters in the United States* (New York: Peter Lang, 1989), 141–56; Jörg Nagler, "The Lincoln-Frémont Debate and the Forty-Eighters," Ibid., 157–78; and Frederick C. Luebke, *Ethnic Voters and the Election of Lincoln* (Lincoln: University of Nebraska Press, 1971).

52. Hans L.Trefousse, "Unionism and Abolition: Political Mobilization in the North," in Förster and Nagler, eds., *On the Road to Total War*, 112; editor's note to the letter from Lincoln to Carl Schurz, November 10, 1862, in Roy P. Basler, ed., *Abraham Lincoln: His Speeches and Writings*, preface by Carl Sandburg (Cleveland: The World Publishing, 1946), 662.

53. Nagler, *Frémont contra Lincoln*, 18.

54. Sperber, *Rhineland Radicals*, 492; M.Trauth, *Italo-American diplomatic relations 1861–2*, 30–33; Spini, "Le relazioni politiche," 176; Nagler, *Frémont contra Lincoln*, 71–73.

55. Cleveland, Chicago, St. Louis, and Philadelphia included among their Republican "wire-pullers" men such as Nikolaus Schmitt, Jakob Müller and Georg Hillgärtner: Sperber, *Rhineland Radicals*, 491–92.

56. Clara Maria Lovett, *Carl Schurz, 1829–1906: A Biographical Essay and a Selective List of Reading Materials in English* (Washington, DC: Library of Congress, 1983); Rudolf Geiger, *Der deutsche Amerikaner: Carl Schurz; vom deutschen Revolutionar zum Amerikanischer Staatsmann* (Gernsbach: Katz, 2007); Frank Michael Schicketanz, *The "Lebenserinnerungen" of Carl Schurz: A Critical Reading* (Konstanz: Hartung Gorre-Verlag, 1987); Walter Kessler, *Carl Schurz: Kampf, Exil und Karriere* (Koln: Greven-Verl, 2006); James M. McPherson, *Abraham Lincoln and the Second American Revolution* (New York: Oxford University Press, 1990), 149–52. See also note to letter No. 3433, in *SEI*, 72:278.

57. Hans L.Trefousse, *Carl Schurz: A Biography* (Knoxville: University of Tennessee Press, 1982), 7–19 and 172.

58. Doris Kearns Goodwin, *Team of Rivals: The Political Genius of Abraham Lincoln* (New York: Simon & Schuster, 2005), 20.

59. Trefousse, *Carl Schurz*, 71, 195.

60. Ibid., 119.

61. Bruce C. Levine, *The Spirit of 1848: German Immigrants, Labor Conflict, and the Coming of the Civil War* (Urbana: University of Illinois Press, 1992).

62. "Lassalle-Lincoln," *Der Sozial-Demokrat*, No.15, January 29, 1865. Cf Karl Marx and Friedrich Engels, *Collected Works*, Vol. 42 (London: Lawrence & Wishart, 1987), 70.

63. Marx and Engels, *Collected Works*, 19:7: Marx in *The New York Daily Tribune*, October 21, 1861.

64. Marx and Engels, *Collected Works*, 19:29–30: Marx in *The New York Daily Tribune*, November 7, 1861.

65. Karl Marx, "The North American Civil War," in Marx and Engels, *Collected Works*, 19:34, originally published in *Die Presse* (Vienna), October 25, 1861. *Die Presse* was a liberal daily with about 30,000 subscribers. Marx's articles—fifty-two of them, which he wrote over a year—were published under the subheading "From our London correspondent" (see Marx and Engels, *Collected Works*, 19:373n.45).

66. Ibid., 39–40.

67. Ibid., 39.

68. Ibid., 42.

69. Karl Marx, "The Civil War in the United States," in Marx and Engels, *Collected Works*, 19:51, originally published in *Die Presse* (Vienna), November 7, 1861. Italics in the original.

70. Cf. Yvonne Kapp, *Eleanor Marx*, 2 vols. (London: Lawrence & Wishart, 1972), 1:34.

71. Marx and Engels, *Collected Works*, 19:250. This was the Emancipation Proclamation of September 22, 1862, declaring all slaves in rebel areas free as from January 1, 1863.

72. Karl Marx to Friedrich Engels, September 7, 1864, Ibid., 562; cf. Friedrich Engels to Hermann Engels, November 2, 1864, in Marx and Engels, *Collected Works*, 42:10.

73. Karl Marx to Ludwig Klugelmann, November 29, 1864, in Marx and Engels, *Collected Works*, 42:48. Emphasis in the original.

74. Karl Marx and Friedrich Engels, *Letters to Americans 1848–1895* (New York: International Publishers, 1953), 66.

75. "Mr Lincoln and the International Working Men's Association," *The Times*, February 6, 1865.

76. Karl Marx to Friedrich Engels, February 1, 1865, in Marx and Engels, *Collected Works*, 42:73; Karl Marx to Friedrich Engels, February 10, 1865, Ibid., 42:86.

77. Karl Marx to Friedrich Engels, May 1, 1865, in Marx and Engels, *Collected Works*, 42:150–51.

78. Karl Marx to Friedrich Engels, May 3, 1865, in Marx and Engels, *Collected Works*, 42:153.

79. This address is remarkable because of the emphasis on the Civil War as a struggle for "law and right" (rather than emancipation), and the Chamber expressed pride in the role played by the German-American community fighting in the Union army. *The Times*, May 2, 1865, 12.

80. *The Times*, May 6, 1865, 5.

81. Ibid., May 6, 1865, 5. The French *Corps Legislatif* passed its own motion of sympathy one day later: Ibid., May 3, 1865, 12.

82. Ibid., May 4, 1865, 14.

83. Garibaldi alla Loggia "Egeria" di Napoli, May 23, 1865, Ibid., 80.

84. Karl Blind to Garibaldi, November 10, 1865, Ibid., 20. Mazzini was also concerned for Jefferson Davis, feeling that if he was sentenced to death, this "would damp the enthusiasm of Europe for the North; and according to me would be absolutely unjust" (Mazzini to Matilde Biggs, June 1, 1865, *SEI*, 80:272).

85. *SEI*, 80:330.

86. Mazzini to Matilde Biggs, April 29, 1865, in *SEI*, 80:224.

87. Mazzini to Clementia Taylor, May 1, 1865, Ibid., 230.

88. Spini, "Le relazioni politiche," 152; Sarti, "La democrazia radicale," 150; *SEI*, 89:28–29. For the imperialist dimension of Young America, see McPherson, *Battle Cry of Freedom*, 48.

89. *SEI*, 71:230, 83:187–89; cf. Howard R. Marraro, "Mazzini on American Intervention in European Affairs," *Journal of Modern History* 21 (June 1949), 109–114.

90. Mazzini to the Masonic Lodge of Lodi (Lombardy) "Abraham Lincoln," on accepting the honorary presidency of that Lodge, June 3, 1868, *SEI*, 86:305.

91. Paolo Lingua, *Mazzini il riformista: Gli ultimi anni e la questione sociale* (Genoa: ECIG, 2005), 110–12; Enzo Tagliacozzo, "Lincoln e il Risorgimento," 322.

92. Garibaldi to the editor of the newspaper *La pubblica opinione* (April 1865, but written before the news of Lincoln's murder reached Italy; published in *Il Diritto* on May 28, 1865, and other newspapers on the following few days), in Lingua, *Mazzini il riformista*, 68.

93. To Mr Lombard, of the Geneva newspaper *Le Radical*, May 15, 1865, Ibid., 76.

94. Biagini, "Mazzini and Anticlericalism: The English Exile"; Lucy Riall, "Garibaldi esule nelle Americhe," in Michele Gottardi, ed., *Fuori d'Italia: Manin e l'esilio* (Venice: Ateneo Veneto, 2009), 347–72.

95. For one example of this nationalist interpretation, see the introduction by Ferdinando Martini (a deputy in the Italian Parliament) to H. Nelson Gay, *Abramo Lincoln liberatore-unificatore (1809–1865)* (Florence: R. Bemporad & Figlio, 1918).

{ 5 }

Liberté, Égalité, and Lincoln
FRENCH READINGS OF AN AMERICAN PRESIDENT
Michael Vorenberg

Abraham Lincoln had many admirers in France during the American Civil War. Napoleon III was not one of them. During and after the Civil War, "Louis Napoleon" did battle with Lincoln—not with the *person* of Lincoln, but with the *image* of Lincoln. For Napoleon's critics, both the liberal Orleanistes and the republican anti-Monarchists, Lincoln was a hero. In celebrating Lincoln, these opponents of Napoleon III could criticize the emperor—but safely, and without censorship. Abraham Lincoln, then, indirectly acted as a catalyst in the movement to unseat Napoleon. The role of Lincoln's reputation in giving ammunition to Napoleon's opponents was small and limited mostly to intellectuals in Paris, but it was these intellectuals who tended to control the newspapers and who would later write the paeans and pamphlets that would celebrate Lincoln as the great citizen, a man true to the spirit of *"liberté, égalité, fraternité"* as that spirit was weakening in France. There was an irony here, though. Lincoln may have been celebrated by the French as the great citizen, but he was a citizen in a mode that was distinctively American, not French. Nonetheless, his image among the French helped legitimize and publicize leftist thought in the late 1860s. Without adopting French radical thought, and without lifting a finger against the French emperor, Lincoln helped end France's Second Empire.

Arguing that Lincoln had anything to do with the end of the Second Empire, or that the French were great admirers of Lincoln, is unconventional. The dominant historical interpretation is that the French were more sympathetic to the Confederacy than to the Union during the American Civil War. Certainly that was the case for Napoleon III and his followers, who were many, especially after the emperor began his program of liberalization in the early 1860s. If the explicit cause of the Confederacy had been for the preservation of slavery, the French would have had difficulty supporting the South, as France had abolished slavery at home and in its colonies well before the outbreak of the American war. But because the ostensible cause of the Confederates was independence against the tyranny of Lincoln, their cause echoed the French Revolution, with President Lincoln playing the role of King Louis XVI. The excitement for the Southern cause and for the war in general was great from the beginning—so much so that Napoleon III had to prohibit army officers from visiting North America to observe the conflict. He worried that his army would be badly weakened if it lost its leaders to the American spectacle.[1]

Many in France—certainly those in power—saw a diplomatic advantage in supporting the South. The belief among many French leaders was that Britain was almost certain to become involved in the war, perhaps for the South but more likely for the North. The American distraction would spread British forces thin and weaken their power. And whatever was bad for the British, of course, was good for the French.[2] Moreover, when Napoleon III in 1862 unveiled his plans for an invasion of Mexico to be followed by the establishment of a French-backed government there, French supporters of the empire sympathized even more with the Confederate cause. A weakened United States would not be able to uphold the Monroe Doctrine and head off French intervention. Good relations between elite American Southerners and the French government suggested to the French people that the Confederate States of America would be friendlier than the United States as a northern neighbor to French-controlled Mexico.[3]

The major reason for support for the American South among the French, however, was economic. More than 90 percent of France's cotton for its textile industry came from the American South. Also, America represented crucial markets for French products, including silk and wine. Between Lincoln's blockade of the southern ports and Jefferson Davis's cotton embargo—a move of the Confederacy to try to force the French and English into an alliance with the South—the French economy was crippled, and the people in the countryside and the small towns, who were most hurt by the economic crisis, blamed Lincoln.[4] Prices of goods resumed their pre-Civil War levels by 1863, but many in the country never forgave Lincoln and the Union for the economic depression. When the Civil War ended, a group of liberals in the French legislature proposed a resolution congratulating the North on its victory. Only 24 deputies voted for it; 195 voted against it. The loudest cry on the floor of the assembly at the news was *"Tant Pis"*—essentially: "Too bad for the Americans."[5]

Embedded in elite French opposition to Lincoln and the Union was more than sixty years of French antagonism toward the forces of radical democracy, which had repeatedly disrupted their country. The liberal journalist Lucien Prévost-Paradol understood well this resentment. Prévost-Paradol was perhaps the best-known French liberal among American intellectuals. His writings on democracy, which praised the American political system, were widely published in the United States before the Civil War. Prevost-Paradol noted his countrymen's anti-American sentiment: "A large number of Frenchmen have contracted [after] four revolutions and so many deceptions, a general aversion to democracy, and for them the probable fall of the United States Republic gave some comfort." The procurator of Agen, France, echoed Prévost-Paradol's description, writing that the people in his region were "irritated" with the United States' pretensions to be the greatest republic, and also its "disdain for old Europe and its institutions." The Civil War was "just punishment" to such a country, the procurator wrote.[6]

If Lincoln and the Civil War united enemies of democracy in France, they also united the opponents of Napoleon III, providing a symbol that could be shared by the two main groups opposed to the monarchy. One group consisted of liberals like Prévost-Paradol, Francois Guizot, Edouard Laboulaye, the most famous French historian of the United States, and Adolphe Thiers, a one-time monarchist who, like his fellow liberals, now rejected the empire but believed in a strong central-state authority. The other group opposed to the empire, known as republicans, opposed a strong central state of any kind in favor of popular democracy. To Americans, the most famous republican was Victor Hugo, the author who remained in self-imposed exile from France during the American Civil War, but who watched the war with great interest, hoping that it would give inspiration to the old forces of republicanism which had gripped France during the uprisings in 1830 and 1848. The agents of the Union in France focused their efforts on getting liberals and republicans alike to publish editorials in the French papers in favor of Lincoln and the Union.[7]

Foremost among the Union agents attempting to influence the French public was John Bigelow, the United States consul in Paris. A former journalist, the New Yorker had contacts among leading writers in France and knew a bit about manipulating public opinion.[8] When Bigelow resigned in 1865, Secretary of State William Henry Seward chose John Hay, Lincoln's one-time personal secretary, as his replacement. Another experienced journalist, Hay had written many of the editorials in the *Missouri Democrat* during the Civil War in order to keep public opinion in that contested state on the Union side.[9] Historians like David Pinkney have criticized the efforts of Seward, Bigelow, and Hay as a form of propaganda. And maybe they are right. Bigelow for one was not above bribing journalists to write editorials favorable to the United States or simply writing the editorials himself and planting them in the French papers.[10]

Regardless of the intentions behind such efforts, the communications received by Bigelow represent some of the best sources available on French public opinion during the Civil War and Reconstruction. The hundreds of letters unsolicited and unedited by the diplomat reveal a deep, heartfelt support for Lincoln and the Union among French liberals and republicans. To give but one example: Bigelow was a regular visitor to the estate of François Guizot, who told the American consul that a defeat for the Union meant a defeat for the cause of popular democracy everywhere. This was the message of Lincoln's

Gettysburg Address, of course, but many French intellectuals like Guizot had the same idea even before Lincoln delivered his famous address. Guizot agreed with Bigelow that victory for the Union would carry a great signal to the world. According to Bigelow, he declared, "no monarch was ever strong enough to raise an army of 800,000 to put down a revolt of half his kingdom, and yet more than that number of soldiers have volunteered [for Lincoln and the Union]."[11]

Bigelow and other Americans with an eye on French popular opinion at first believed that they could build support for the Union in France by criticizing the venture of Napoleon III into Mexico. By early 1862, Napoleon had begun his intervention into Mexico over the protests of Spain and England, which at one time had seemed willing to support the venture. While Confederates hoped that Napoleon's invasion would lead to his lending of armed forces to the Southern cause, Northern newspapers were furious at the intervention. In unison they claimed that Napoleon was violating the principle of nonintervention in the Americas made famous by the Monroe Doctrine. American criticism of Napoleon's Mexican adventure was not well received in France. Supporters of Napoleon had an easy time in their editorials mocking the Union's hypocrisy: at the same time that the Lincoln government intervened against the Confederates' attempt to create a nation, it criticized the French emperor for acting similarly against the Mexicans. According to John Bigelow, reprints of American editorials against Napoleon's Mexican venture awakened popular enthusiasm for Napoleon. Without these editorials, Bigelow reported, the people were against the Mexico project. Bigelow asked his journalist friends in America to stop their criticism. "It would be a sad mistake to give the Emperor the support of his people in this Mexican business by an indiscriminate censure of the Nation [of France, by the United States]."[12] By mid-1862, French public opinion was mixed—not nearly as pro-Confederate as later historians would claim it was, and not nearly as pro-Unionist as Bigelow and others attempted to make it.

French public opinion became more clearly divided after Abraham Lincoln's preliminary Emancipation Proclamation of September 22, 1862. Behind the myth that persists today that the French, like the British, were generally anti-slavery and thus were solidly pro-Union after the Proclamation lies a different reality: the French, no less than the English, feared that emancipation might trigger slave revolts which would rock the political and economic systems of Europe. Of particular concern to the government of France was the phrase in the preliminary Proclamation in which Lincoln said that there would be "no act or acts to repress such persons"—meaning slaves—"in any efforts they may make for their actual freedom."[13] Many in Europe assumed that this was a call for slaves to rise up against their masters. Victor Hugo and other republicans frequently compared Lincoln's proclamation to John Brown's raid on Harpers Ferry, and they applauded both efforts. Napoleon III and his counselors no doubt made the same link but with a much more negative judgment.[14]

Lincoln, in fact, was very much against any stirring up of slave revolts, and he was no admirer of John Brown, but in the eyes of many in France, including the emperor, he intended to lead a racial rebellion not only in the South but in the whole Caribbean basin. A visitor from the French West Indies to the American consulate in Paris in late 1862 reported that his contacts in the islands were thrilled by the Proclamation and believed that it would lead to the islands breaking their imperial chains under the leadership of Afro-French rebels. In other words, in France and in the French-speaking Atlantic, Lincoln's Proclamation suggested to some that the American president meant to unleash a new version of the Haitian revolution. The French newspapers did not miss the fact that Abraham Lincoln was the first American president to recognize the independent Republic of Haiti. French interest in the impact of the Lincoln administration on the Caribbean was one of the factors leading Alexandre Dumas to plan a grand tour of the United States during this time. The writer was hugely popular in America. He was also a grandson of the French West Indies—his paternal grandparents met in Sainte Domingue, and his paternal grandmother was of African and French ancestry. Dumas saw the Proclamation as one of the signs that the time was right for a visit to North America.[15]

The belief that the Emancipation Proclamation inspired among many in the French-speaking world that race revolts in the Caribbean soon would be at hand may be an important and understudied context of Napoleon's diplomatic and military actions in late 1862 and afterward. In the wake of the preliminary Proclamation, Napoleon began exploring with Russia and Britain the possibility of mediating the American Civil War. Russia and Britain rejected Napoleon's plan, but the emperor went ahead and made the offer to Secretary of State Seward. Seward kindly and diplomatically refused the offer. From Paris Bigelow reported that the French regarded Napoleon's scheme as a direct reaction to Lincoln's Proclamation and the belief that it would lead to what many in Paris called a "servile war"—"the greatest of evils."[16]

Lincoln's Proclamation may also have accelerated Napoleon's intervention in Mexico. It was probably during the period between the preliminary and final Emancipation Proclamations (September 22, 1862–January 1, 1863) that Napoleon rejected a plan for a popularly elected government in Mexico in favor of the installation of the "emperor" Maximilian, though it would take more than a year until his plan came to fruition.[17] Indeed it is conceivable that the French monarch's move was in part a reaction to the prospect of a race war in the Caribbean—that is, an effort by Napoleon to establish a powerful base of operations on the western side of the Atlantic, from which he could maintain better control of the French colonies where those of African descent had a majority. In the end, of course, there was no massive race war—in the United States or the Caribbean. Indeed, Lincoln modified the language of the Emancipation Proclamation. The final Proclamation asked slaves to "abstain from all violence, unless in necessary self-defence" and suggested that "they labor faithfully for reasonable wages."[18]

Some French radicals were puzzled by the absence of a slave revolt in the American South. A Monsieur Bloncourt, a man of mixed race, reported his belief that people of mixed race in the United States, by contrast to those in the French-speaking Atlantic, were confined to the lowest ranks of society. He blamed the Christian tendencies of slaves—in his words, they were "reading the Bible too much and [had] the habit of dreaming and looking on high for help instead of helping themselves." He admitted to getting this view of African Americans from *Uncle Tom's Cabin*.[19] The more common—and more accurate—view among French people was that the Union government had channeled potential black rebelliousness into the military by coupling emancipation with military enlistment for African Americans. Colonel Chanal, who in 1864 viewed the maneuvers of black Union troops, returned to Paris and reported that they were, in his words, "as good as any French soldiers." He went on to add that "slaves will fight for [the] Confed[eracy] but only in small numbers—this was the French experience in Algeria."[20]

But the French also knew that white racism in the United States would make any great, immediate change in the status of former slaves unlikely. Alexandre Dumas eventually canceled his trip to the United States when he heard from many friends that he would likely be harassed and perhaps lose popularity if he showed his face in the country and people who did not know his racial makeup would begin to turn against him. As John Bigelow put it, Dumas was "in doubt [as to] . . . whether we had sufficiently conquered our Negrophobia to receive a person of mixed blood as he is accustomed to be received in France, . . . "[21] Dumas should have had doubts. White Northern lawmakers in the Midwest, for example, preserved many of the states' black laws until after the Civil War was over. And whites continued to harp on the dangers of race mixing and to use the example of race mixing in the French and Spanish colonies as a danger facing their country. Here on the subject is Francis P. Blair, Sr., one of Lincoln's elder advisers, from the slave state of Missouri: "[Our] Anglo-Saxon race cannot improvise Constitutions like the French and Mexicans—nor do they mix blood readily, like these swarthy Latins, with the darker castes. I prefer, therefore, to adopt that mode of a total deliverance from slavery which though slower, is surer, and which saves at once our political institutions intact and our blood unpolluted."[22] French republicans in particular were dismayed with such sentiments and especially with the racial violence that French newspaper correspondents had seen in the New York City draft riots of 1863.

For French liberals and republicans, however, the persistence of white racism did not keep them from seeing Abraham Lincoln not only as the great democrat but also as a racial egalitarian—especially after he was assassinated and became a martyr to the causes that French people chose to attribute to him. It was not the Emancipation Proclamation but rather Lincoln's assassination that turned the opinion of French liberals and republicans solidly behind the Union cause. Bigelow wrote privately after Lincoln's death:

> The feeling in France as you may have observed is very profound. Indeed I think Lincoln would gladly have sold his life to his assassin for the price his country will receive for it. The government cannot resist the popular feeling and is obliged to join in the general reaction. The universal reflection in all circles now is that we have accomplished with our democratic government, results that could never have been accomplished with any other. The Republicans are taking advantage of this to keep the subject before the people as much as possible. The death of Lincoln, I think, is destined to work a radical change in the Constitution of France.[23]

The death of Lincoln gave Napoleon's opponents an unforeseen opportunity to express their dissatisfaction with France in public letters and memorials ostensibly directed to a country thousands of miles away.

Democratic sentiment, sometimes radical in nature, ran fiercely through many of the messages of mourning for Lincoln that spilled from the pens of Napoleon's critics. Victor Hugo and other republicans began a fundraising drive to create some sort of gift for the widow Mary Lincoln. They collected ten centimes (roughly two cents) from 40,000 donors—despite the emperor's initial attempts to stop the effort—and created a bronze medallion for Mrs. Lincoln on which they had engraved: "If France had the freedom enjoyed by republican America, not thousands but millions among us would have been counted as admirers."[24] From Tours came a memorial signed by 208 "democrats." The cover letter explained:

> It was hard to obtain 208 signatures in a city where there is only one newspaper, where the press only speaks the official language of the prefecture, where liberty is limited by policemen and public functionaries, and where democracy's warmest partisans are among the common people.
>
> Our document will reach you after passing through the soiled hands of our hardy workmen, who cannot leave the sheet of paper spotless, whereon they have put their hearts with the signature of their hands to express their sympathy for your great republic.
>
> It is not you, a representative of a country where labor leads to the highest dignities of the nation, that will disdain our address because it carries the visible impress of hands devoted to work.
>
> These are the hands that will break, in this country, all the bonds and fetters that are put on liberty, under the specious pretext of measuring and regulating its gait; these are the hands that will shake most cordially those of your citizens.[25]

Lincoln, who already had been cast by some French radicals as an American Touissant Louverture, could just as easily be refashioned into a modern-day *sans-culotte*, an American Hébert or Chaumette. Had Lincoln not died so tragically and in such world-shaking circumstances—a renowned democratic republic nearly dissolved, and a massive slave population newly freed—the French liberals and republicans might not have crystallized into the powerful force that emerged against the emperor in the late 1860s.

Perhaps Lincoln, at least in his death, helped to set in motion the events leading to the Paris Commune of 1870–71. The possibility should not be over-stated, though. Napoleon's defeats in the Franco-Prussian war no doubt played the greatest role in turning public opinion against the emperor. But for a brief period—certainly from the time of the Emancipation Proclamation to the aftermath of his assassination—Lincoln became a powerful symbol to opposition groups in Paris.

The Lincoln image quickly faded from the French public view once the movement for the Paris Commune began, however. The steady stream of Lincoln biographies that flowed from French pens in the five years after his death dwindled to a trickle beginning in the 1870s.[26] One might have predicted from the outpouring of French democratic sentiment in the wake of the assassination that he would have been a great symbol during and after the Paris Commune, even among those who were displeased that the United States had refused to intervene on the French side in the Franco-Prussian war. Yet, in fact, once the movement for the Commune began, the power of the Lincoln symbol to unite the opponents of the Second Empire shriveled. Although French liberals who denounced the Commune sometimes invoked Lincoln, the Communards them-selves seem to have turned their backs on him.[27] Why did the Lincoln image lose its currency among the more radical members of the French opposition?

First, French intellectuals of the left could never put aside their awareness that American liberalism, in contrast to French liberalism, was based much more on a narrow band of historically specific economic-based rights than on universal, transhistorical ideas of "liberté, égalité, et fraternité." During the debates in the United States on the Thirteenth Amendment, the measure that abolished slavery, Senator Charles Sumner, a great student of French history, proposed alternative language drawn directly from the French Declaration of Rights. His proposal was quickly shot down, and a fellow senator mocked him, saying "I do not believe that we should turn to the French of all people for guidance on our Constitution." American lawmakers often repeated the joke of a French politician entering the store of a bookseller in Paris and asking for the Constitution of France; he was answered: "We do not deal in partisan pam-phlets." Well known as a champion of a stable constitutional order, Lincoln made a poor symbol for French citizens who still looked upon the stormy pe-riod of the French Revolution as a golden era.[28]

Second, as the Commune began to assume the character of an insurrection in the eyes not only of monarchists but of the French liberals led by Thiers, Lincoln's reputation as the enemy of rebellion eclipsed all other aspects of his image. Even before the Communards seized control of Paris, they looked with disdain at centralizing tendencies in the United States that they regarded as authoritarian. They knew, for example, as all readers of French newspapers knew, that Napoleon III supported President Andrew Johnson's attempts to undermine congressional Reconstruction. Then, when the U.S. Congress gained the upper hand and imposed military force on the South to effect Reconstruction, French republicans saw evidence of a conservative counterrevolution. Gustave Cluseret, the former Union general and future Communard, said that Americans had "spit on their fathers" and become "conservatives."[29] Such attitudes among the Communards must have seemed well founded once the Commune seized Paris, and Thiers called publicly for the army to suppress the radicals as Lincoln had suppressed the Southern secessionists.[30] For the Communards, Lincoln and the United States came to stand for autocracy. The leaders of the movement even attempted to expel from Paris the American ambassador, Elihu Washburne, a former U.S. congressman and an old friend of Lincoln's from Illinois. After conservative forces had triumphed over the Commune, the *Journal des Débats* praised the Thiers government and likened the moment to Lincoln's victory over the Confederacy. Lincoln had restored order not by authoritarianism, the newspaper claimed, but rather with constant fidelity to "*la figure de la Liberté*" and without suspending a single right ("*un seul droit*").[31] The image of Lincoln as the benign counterrevolutionary may have served the interests of the French anti-Communard liberals, but it did little to endear him to the more radical French republicans, who remained a powerful cohort among French intellectuals long after the Commune had fallen.

A final reason why Lincoln could never have retained much of a purchase on the imagination of French intellectuals has to do with a fundamental difference in the way that those intellectuals and Lincoln thought about citizenship. In the same way that Frederick Douglass remained skeptical about the president's commitment to equality—Douglass called Lincoln "the black man's president" immediately after the assassination in 1865 but then "the white man's president" in 1876—French republicans knew that Lincoln did not share their belief in the principle of universal citizenship. Much has been made of the fact that Lincoln paid for the burial of his friend and personal assistant, the African American William d'Fleurville, and had the single word "Citizen" inscribed on the headstone. But French intellectuals knew that Lincoln's idea of "citizen" was quite different from the "citoyen" of the French Revolution, especially when it came to black Americans. Consider the contrast in the way that he described foreign-born and African American soldiers for the Union. At the outbreak of the war, he authorized Secretary of War Simon Cameron to be favorable to a person who Lincoln called "a Polish gentleman, naturalized, [who] proposes raising a Regiment of our citizens of his nationality, to serve in our Army." Notice how he emphasized naturalization, an avenue toward citizenship not available for African Americans until 1870, and also how he spoke of "our" citizens, even though they were of "his"—the Pole's—nationality. Later that year, he made a similar endorsement, this time of a request for a Mexican-born Californian to raise a cavalry regiment of what Lincoln called "native Mexican citizens of California"—in other words, people born in Mexico, but now citizens of the United States, by way of California. Lincoln came to think at least as highly of the soldiering abilities of African Americans. He endorsed their service in the Emancipation Proclamation and came to praise it on many later occasions. But never did he use the word "citizens" to describe black soldiers, though he used precisely that word to describe foreign-born soldiers, and though these African American soldiers were citizens by law.[32]

To be sure, Lincoln was edged forward in his thinking about equal citizenship among races—in large part, it should be noted, by people of French descent. It was his meeting with two highly educated leaders of the black community in New Orleans that probably did more than anything else to convince him that some African Americans should be granted voting rights, a position that he expressed publicly just before he died. These men, Jean Baptiste Roudanez and Arnold Bertonneau, presented Lincoln on March 12, 1864, with a petition demanding black suffrage signed by over one thousand literate African Americans, many of them, like Roudanez and Bertonneau, of French descent. He sat down the next day to write his now famous private letter to Governor Michael Hahn, suggesting that intelligent blacks and black veterans be allowed to vote.[33]

French egalitarianism had some small effect on Lincoln, and perhaps Lincoln had an even greater effect on French democratic movements. But in the end, the radicalism of the Parisian intellectuals in general, and the establishment of the 1871 Commune in particular, was more than the Americans could tolerate, and the French knew it. Lincoln, their idealized citizen in 1865, had become by 1871, like the United States as a whole, a poor symbol of universal citizenship.

Notes

    1. David H. Pinkney, "France and the Civil War," in Harold Hyman, ed., *Heard Round the World: The Impact Abroad of the Civil War* (New York: Alfred A. Knopf, 1969), 97–106.
    2. Lynn M. Case and Warren F. Spencer, *The United States and France: Civil War Diplomacy* (Philadelphia: University of Pennsylvania Press, 1970).
    3. On the Mexican plan of Napoleon III and the Confederacy's reaction to it, see Howard Jones, *Blue and Gray Diplomacy: A History of Union and Confederate Foreign Relations* (Chapel Hill: University of North Carolina Press, 2010), 276–320; Michele Cunningham, *Mexico and the Foreign Policy of Napoleon III* (New York: Palgrave, 2001); and Alfred Jackson Hanna and Kathryn Abbey Hanna, *Napoleon III and Mexico: American Triumph over Monarchy* (Chapel Hill: University of North Carolina Press, 1971), 61–68.

4. Pinkney, "France and the Civil War," 120–37; Roger Price, *The French Second Empire: An Anatomy of Political Power* (Cambridge: Cambridge University Press, 2001), 248.

5. Pinkney, "France and the Civil War," 105.

6. Both quotations are cited in Pinkney, "France and the Civil War," 107.

7. Pinkney, "France and the Civil War," 108–12.

8. Margaret Clapp, *Forgotten First Citizen: John Bigelow* (Boston: Little, Brown, 1947), 146–87; John Bigelow, *Retrospections of an Active Life*, 5 vols. (Garden City, NY: Doubleday, 1909), 1:371–526.

9. Michael Burlingame, ed., *Lincoln's Journalist: John Hay's Anonymous Writings for the Press, 1860–1864* (Carbondale: Southern Illinois University Press, 2000).

10. Pinkney, "France and the Civil War," 111–12.

11. John Bigelow, Diary, Bigelow Papers, New York Public Library, Manuscripts Division, box 103 (typescripts), entry under July 27, 1863.

12. Bigelow to "Mr. Morgan," October 16, 1863, letterbooks, vol. 1, Bigelow Papers.

13. Roy P. Basler et al., eds., *The Collected Works of Abraham Lincoln*, 9 vols. (New-Brunswick, NJ: Rutgers University Press, 1953–55), 5:434 (hereafter cited as *CW*). See Mark E. Neely, Jr., *The Last Best Hope of Earth: Abraham Lincoln and the Promise of America* (Cambridge, MA: Harvard University Press, 1993), 110–12; Howard Jones, *Abraham Lincoln and a New Birth of Freedom: The Union and Slavery in the Diplomacy of the Civil War* (Lincoln: University of Nebraska Press, 1999), esp. 122–27; Howard Jones, *Union in Peril: The Crisis over British Intervention in the Civil War* (Chapel Hill: University of North Carolina Press, 1992), 162–97.

14. Victor Hugo, Notebook Entry, September-October 1865, reprinted in Harold Holzer, ed., *The Lincoln Anthology: Great Writers on His Life and Legacy from 1860 to Now* (New York: Library of America, 2009), 185; see also letter by A. Rey, May 1, 1865, and ode by Paul Thouzery, both in U.S. State Department, *Appendix to Diplomatic Correspondence of 1865. The Assassination of Abraham Lincoln . . . Expressions of Condolence and Sympathy Inspired by These Events* (Washington: Government Printing Office, 1866), 85, 94.

15. John Bigelow, Diary, Bigelow Papers, box 103 (typescripts), entry under "Thursday" (July 23, 1863); Bigelow to Thurlow Weed, October 6, 1864, letterbooks, vol. 1, Bigelow Papers.

16. Bigelow to William Cullen Bryant, November 14, 1862, Bigelow Papers.

17. Cunningham, *Mexico and the Foreign Policy of Napoleon III*, 108–31.

18. *CW*, 6:29–30.

19. John Bigelow, Diary, Bigelow Papers, box 103 (typescripts), entry under "Thursday" (July 23, 1863).

20. John Bigelow, Diary, Bigelow Papers, box 103 (typescripts), entry under January 1865.

21. Bigelow to Thurlow Weed, October 6, 1864, letterbooks vol. 1, John Bigelow Papers.

22. Francis P. Blair Sr. to Isaac Sherman, January 15, 1862, Isaac Sherman papers, Henry E. Huntington Library, San Marino, California.

23. Bigelow to William Cullen Bryant, May 16, 1865, letterbooks vol. 2, John Bigelow Papers.

24. Victor Hugo, Notebook Entry, September-October 1865, reprinted in Harold Holzer, ed., *The Lincoln Anthology*, 185.

25. Armand Riviere to Bigelow, May 17, 1865, reprinted in U.S. State Department, *Appendix to Diplomatic Correspondence of 1865. The Assassination of Abraham Lincoln*, 108–9.

26. See George Scratcherd, "Foreign Language Biographies of Lincoln," in the appendix of this book.

27. This claim is based on an extensive search of the pamphlets and periodicals of the Communards. For example, in a search of the pro-Commune newspapers for 1869–1871 in the "Gallica Bibliothèque Numérique" online database, Lincoln's name appears not at all— a sharp contrast to the many times his name appears in all the leading French newspapers in the period prior to 1869.

28. Michael Vorenberg, *Final Freedom: The Civil War, the Abolition of Slavery, and the Thirteenth Amendment* (Cambridge: Cambridge University Press, 2001), 57.

29. Cited in Philip M. Katz, *From Appomattox to Montmartre: Americans and the Paris Commune* (Cambridge, MA.: Harvard University Press, 1998), 12.

30. *Cassell's History of the War Between France and Germany, 1870–1871*, 2 vols. (London: Cassell, Petter & Galpin, 1871), 2:404.

31. *Journal des Débats*, December 7, 1870.

32. These citations and a fuller explication of the argument may be found in Michael Vorenberg, "Abraham Lincoln's 'Fellow Citizens'—Before and After Emancipation," in William A. Blair and Karen Fisher Younger, eds., *Lincoln's Proclamation: Emancipation Reconsidered* (Chapel Hill: University of North Carolina, 2009), 151–69.

33. See James M. McPherson, ed., *The Negro's Civil War* (Urbana: University of Illinois Press, 1982), 277–80.

6

"A Total Misconception"

LINCOLN, THE CIVIL WAR, AND
THE BRITISH, 1860–1865

Lawrence Goldman

British reactions to Abraham Lincoln during the American Civil War cannot be easily differentiated from British responses to the conflict itself. Lincoln's merits as a man and leader were bound up with, and often secondary to, British views of the war in general and the moral worth of the Northern cause. Lincoln was almost entirely unknown to the British upon his election, and the ends for which he worked, anti-slavery and the Union, were not always appreciated in their American context by a British audience. The British, like any people viewing a conflict in another nation, tended to regard the Civil War in terms of their own political interests and their own pre-existing ideological positions rather than in the terms that Americans themselves recognized and fought for. Beyond this, the British misunderstood Lincoln specifically because the president was reticent about many of the central issues of the Civil War, especially slavery. Many otherwise sympathetic British supporters of the Union's cause were suspicious of this reticence, failing to appreciate the complex political pressures which forced Lincoln to hide his ultimate intentions, or to work towards them only gradually. The debate over Lincoln in Britain during the Civil War was not just a product of the preexisting political and social divisions within Britain in the 1860s, which has been the usual treatment of British responses to the Civil War. It was also the result of fundamental misconstructions from every point on the British political spectrum of Lincoln's intentions and modus operandi.

That the British were divided in their approach to the Civil War was abundantly evident at the time and has been much debated ever since.[1] Many contemporaries in the 1860s and historians since then have taken the broad view that the British aristocracy and political conservatives took the side of the Confederacy, while the working class and its radical liberal sympathizers and leaders took the side of the North. British responses, in other words, were largely determined by social position and class consciousness. It is still widely believed in Britain that the cotton operatives working in the factories of Lancashire accepted the short-time and unemployment of the "cotton famine," caused by the Confederate policy of restricting exports of raw cotton, in the wider interests of Southern slaves and their emancipation. Their privations were a price worth paying for the eventual freedom of four million in the South. Yet against this, it has been argued that many of the cotton operatives were, in fact, pro-Confederate, and it has been accepted that some notable and vigorous leaders among the working class supported the South to spite the many liberal industrialists who favored the North.[2] Conflicting evidence has deterred historians from making simplistic judgments about British loyalties.[3] Recent work has presented British public opinion as largely neutral in regard to the conflict, often cynical about claims made by both sides, and, when focused on foreign affairs, far more likely to look to Europe and take inspiration from the struggles of Italian and Polish nationalists than to dwell upon the American situation.[4]

There have been equally fierce debates about the essential character and aims of Abraham Lincoln. If his stock as a politician and war leader is currently very high, it has not always been so. His status as the emancipator of the slaves has been questioned, the more so in recent times as emphasis has been placed on the self-emancipation of slaves who spontaneously absconded from plantations after 1861. The absence of high moral rhetoric in Lincoln's two Emancipation Proclamations has been held against him; so, too, the limits of emancipation as set out in these documents which freed slaves only in those states in rebellion.[5] Lincoln has been criticized for the generous terms he offered to rebellious states if they would return to the Union; for an unnecessary reverence for the letter of the Constitution in some contexts and his disregard of the law and civil rights in others; and for failing to think carefully about the problems that would face the freed people after a Union victory.

But with all judgments of Lincoln there is a problem: "how to distinguish the deeply held convictions of the man from the evasion and equivocation of the politician responding to public opinion."[6] There is no obvious answer to this problem except vigilance: to be constantly aware of the context, location, and background of Lincoln's pronouncements, weighing in different ways the evidence in a private letter written to a friend, a note for a speech jotted down for his own benefit, a public statement in Chicago, a response in small-town Illinois, a presidential proclamation.

Lincoln's personal views on slavery have never given historians much difficulty because the record is clear. His later recollections of his trip down the Mississippi in 1841 with Joshua Speed when he first encountered slavery, describing it as a "continual torment," set the tone for his private reflections on the injustice of slavery.[7] Whether it be the ironic notes on slavery that he drew up in 1856 to help in his speechmaking,[8] or the letter to Hodges of Kentucky in April 1864 in which he declared that "if slavery is not wrong, nothing is wrong,"[9] his private views have never been in doubt. But he was a moderate and, above all, a pragmatic exponent of anti-slavery rather than an unbending one. In early 1849, for example, he was set to introduce a bill into the House (though he never did so) that would have abolished slavery in the District of Columbia but would have required the city authorities to return all runaways to their masters in the South beforehand. A decade later in his debates with Douglas in Illinois in 1858, Lincoln disavowed racial equality[10] though this statement and other such declarations have usually been regarded as a "concession to anti-Negro feeling in an effort to win an anti-slavery victory."[11]

The contradiction between the public and private man was captured in the brilliant assessment of Lincoln by Frederick Douglass on the unveiling of the Freedmen's Memorial Monument in Lincoln Park in Washington on the eleventh anniversary of his assassination. According to Douglass in his carefully wrought oration of considered euphuisms:

> Viewed from the genuine abolition ground, Mr. Lincoln seemed tardy, cold, dull and indifferent; but measuring him by the sentiment of his country, a sentiment he was bound as a statesman to consult, he was swift, zealous, radical and determined.[12]

Douglass also recalled:

> In all my interviews with Mr. Lincoln I was impressed with his entire freedom from popular prejudice against the colored race. He was the first great man that I talked with in the United States freely, who in no single instance reminded me of the difference between himself and myself, of the difference of color.[13]

Yet Lincoln did not advertise his innate racial egalitarianism. This inscrutability, forced upon him by his situation, often evoking doubt and confusion among his supporters, made him difficult to judge, and all the more so in Britain. Lincoln proceeded with caution, often taking an indirect route, applying his influence away from the public's gaze. When he made public pronouncements, it was to make a case in terms that his audience could embrace, irrespective of his own thoughts or the merits of the argument.[14] Lincoln was prepared to dissemble or even perjure himself for the causes he favored, such as the fusion of the Illinois Know Nothings with the emerging state Republican party in the mid-1850s.[15] According to a noted commentator of today, Lincoln "dissembled, waffled, told racist stories and consorted with corrupt politicians" in the cause of freeing the slaves and saving the Union. Lincoln was "not admirable because he was 'Honest Abe' but *because* he was devious." His method involved "winding and flanking and circling back" but in the process he "never lost sight of his fixed goal."[16] This Lincoln brings to mind the recollections of a Chicago lawyer who knew Lincoln intimately before he became president:

> One great public mistake . . . generally received and acquiesced in, is that
> he is considered by the people of this country as a frank, guileless and
> unsophisticated man. There never was a greater mistake . . . He handled
> and moved men remotely as we do pieces on a chess-board.[17]

By dissembling, Lincoln constructed an image of himself, always so useful to American politicians of any age, "as a babe in the Washington wilderness." In this studied manipulation, Lincoln's sense of humor was a key advantage, another disarming tactic. Tall tales, lewd jokes, the slapping of backs and thighs, created a "smoke-screen of good humor" to lull and discompose suppli- cants, colleagues, and adversaries alike, behind which Lincoln advanced toward his goal.[18] As John Todd Stuart recalled, "He was an artful man and yet his art had all the appearance of simple-mindedness."[19]

There are some famous examples of this impenetrable and disingenuous style, not least Lincoln's reply to Horace Greeley's open letter in the *New York Tribune*—"the prayer of twenty millions"—in which he put the case for Union above that for freedom at a time when he had already drafted an Emancipation Proclamation and was awaiting the right moment—a Union victory—to unveil it. Earlier initiatives also illustrate the cautious and roundabout style. In March 1862 Lincoln sent Congress a special message asking for a joint resolution prom- ising financial aid for any state adopting gradual abolition. Yet he had already told Wendell Phillips that whatever the terms of the scheme, he meant slavery "should die" and saw this merely as an initiation of that process. In December 1862 in his annual message to Congress, he included the text of a constitutional amendment for compensated emancipation to the year 1900. At one level this was a distinctly cautious move, especially after the Preliminary Emancipation Proclamation of the preceding September. Yet one provision stated that all slaves "who shall enjoy actual freedom by the chances of war" would be "forever free"; and by another only loyal owners would be compensated. The fine print turned the plan into a more radical assault on the South. Or consider Lincoln's policy for Louisiana from its liberation in 1863 where he acted "in such a way as to keep an appearance of neutrality and of respect for the rights of white Louisianans to decide freely on the slave issue. But his objective and strategy was to get the state to end slavery by its own actions before admission."[20] He used the two Unionist congressmen, Benjamin Flanders and Michael Hahn, who were briefly seated in Congress in 1863, as conduits to encourage local unionist leaders to take an anti-slavery stance. He also used his powers of patronage; for example, by appointing a pro-slavery unionist as collector of the New Orleans Customs House on the understanding that his brother-in-law, an editor, would change the policy of his newspaper and come out in favor of black freedom. Throughout Lincoln's engagement with the restitution of Louisiana he applied pressure, sometimes publicly but usually behind the scenes, to secure a new state government that would recognize black political and civil rights.

Contradictions and obfuscations also feature in Lincoln's focus on the colonization of blacks outside the United States. In speeches from the 1840s and 1850s there is little doubt that Lincoln evinced sincere interest in colonization as one solution to the question of the black presence in American life. Supporters of colonization were not necessarily hostile to blacks but might have genuinely believed that relocation was in their interests. This is one way of interpreting Lincoln's careful words to the black delegation that visited him in the White House in August 1862 when he attempted to elicit support for colonization during the War. Lincoln was seeking their advantage because he genuinely did not think they could live on equal terms in the United States.[21]

Yet by then Lincoln was already determined on black emancipation, and in a matter of weeks. He had also asked for and received from Congress in 1862 two small grants of $100,000 and $500,000 to assist experimental colonies at Ile à Vache off Haiti and on the Panamanian isthmus. The grants were paltry in comparison to the size of the task, the relocation of potentially hundreds of thousands of former slaves. This prompts another interpretation of Lincoln's use of colonization at this stage: that in resurrecting the idea and trailing schemes through Congress, the black community, and the country at large, Lincoln was employing colonization not as an alternative to emancipation within the United States, but as a way of defusing criticism of emancipation.[22] It had once been an end in itself; now it had become a means toward another of Lincoln's ends, a tactic to assist an alternative strategy for blacks. Fearing disquiet in the North at a change of the war's aims and at the prospect of blacks coming to live in Northern cities, Lincoln transformed his genuine interest in colonization into an expedient gesture to reassure public opinion.[23] If this interpretation is correct, the ploy could hardly be explained to the people: it could only succeed if they believed that Lincoln's gambit of using colonization was, in fact, the beginning of a sincere program of black emigration. No wonder abolitionists on both sides of the Atlantic bridled at measures they interpreted as racist and discriminatory.

At the very least Lincoln was a pragmatist and "an experimentalist" who found different ways to advance chosen objectives. Whatever his public ambiguities, he displayed a consistency of purpose at a subterranean level, though a consistency that by its nature was difficult for onlookers to recognize. His statecraft was "an extraordinary combination of inflexible determination and flexible tactics."[24] We may also conclude that in the circumstances of a Civil War that required immense political sensitivity to prosecute, let alone win, Lincoln rightly judged that his purposes could be promoted as effectively by negotiation behind the scenes as grand rhetorical statesmanship from center-stage.[25] For Lincoln was constrained at many turns. He was bound to preserve the Union and uphold the Constitution. He needed to ensure that the slave-holding border states were not pushed by eager anti-slavery generals into the Confederacy. He had to keep power out of the hands of an opposition party in the North that might well make peace with the Confederacy and reconstruct the Union with slavery intact. He had to accept the racial views of many Northerners, who might have wanted to keep slavery out of the territories but had no sympathy for blacks, whether slave or free.[26] Any doubts we might hold about these constraints and the contending forces Lincoln faced should be dispelled by considering responses to emancipation. Unsurprisingly, Lincoln was execrated in the South. In the North his actions incited political opponents in the Democratic party to launch a movement for peace and reunion without abolition. There was disquiet (though short of mutiny) in the Union army, and unrest in several Northern cities.[27]

II

If many Republicans could not appreciate Lincoln's deeper policy, what hope had even the most well-informed Britons, three weeks' sailing time away, of understanding the man? Lincoln was almost entirely unknown in Britain before 1860, and many believed (as in the United States) that Seward would dominate the new administration.[28] When the manager of *The Times* in London, Mowbray Morris, wrote to the newspaper's New York correspondent in October 1860 he did not hide his ignorance:

> As to Lincoln's election I doubt whether I rightly understand its full significance. For the peace of the world, and especially for the advantage of Great Britain, it is advisable that the President of the US should be a man of sense and temper, uncommitted to any extreme party, and sufficiently independent to be able to exercise his own judgment in difficult emergencies. If Lincoln is such a man, we shall have four years of comparative quiet—if he is not, God knows what may happen.[29]

Lincoln was also underestimated in Britain, at his election and throughout his presidency. As Lord Lyons, British Minister in Washington, wrote to the Foreign Secretary, Lord John Russell, in April 1861:

> Mr Lincoln has not hitherto given proof of his possessing any natural talents to compensate for his ignorance of everything but Illinois village politics. He seems to be well meaning and conscientious, in the measure of his understanding, but not much more.[30]

The Times patronized Lincoln and Americans more generally:

> President Lincoln is, as the world says, a good tempered man, neither better nor worse than the mass of his kind—neither a fool nor a sage, neither a villain nor a saint, but a piece of that common useful clay out of which it delights the American democracy to make great Republican personages.[31]

Even Richard Cobden described Lincoln to his fellow British radical leader and passionate advocate of free trade, John Bright, in October 1862 as "intellectually inferior" and surrounded by "mediocre men."[32] Conservatives' criticism that Lincoln was undignified, vulgar, and uneducated, a symptom of the worst aspects of American democracy, could be expected.[33] But in Britain, as in the North, those liberals who supported the federal government nevertheless criticized Lincoln for raising unionism above abolitionism; for his reluctance to address the issue of black freedom from the very start of the war; for his suspension of habeas corpus, and the use of the courts to silence opponents.[34] Those papers that were not friendly, such as *The Times*, showed little understanding of the constitutional constraints that limited Lincoln and the Union's powers and actions. *The Times* had criticized Northern states before the Civil War for opposing the extension of slavery rather than promoting emancipation. The latter "would have strongly commended their cause to the sympathies of this country . . . but the North was never genuinely possessed of any such feeling."[35] Many in the North were committed to black freedom but were bound to respect the constitutional protections for private property, a point that *The Times* never seemed to understand.

Lincoln's reasons for reversing the proclamations of General John C. Frémont, commandant of the Department of Missouri, and of General David Hunter, when in control of South Carolina, Georgia, and Florida, that freed the slaves in these specific areas were not understood in Britain, or at least not by many. The Liberal MP and minister, W. E. Forster, famous for the Education Act of 1870 which brought elementary education to all the people, had the acumen to appreciate in October 1861 that "the President has forced General Fremont to lower the standard of freedom which he had hoisted, but military necessities might compel him to raise it again."[36] But Forster was an exceptional figure in British public life, a leading entrepreneur, politician, and intellectual all in one. In the discussions of the British press, there was precious little recognition of the sensitivity of the slave-holding border states, like Kentucky and Maryland, to these independent acts of emancipation, nor of the border states' strategic importance to the Union. Countermanding Frémont's decree in September 1861 was seen by *The Times* as a deliberate "undermining of the abolitionist argument."[37] Meanwhile, among those who followed such things, Lincoln's proposals for colonization were taken at face value as indicative of his latent racism rather than as a gambit to sugar the pill of the emancipation, which Lincoln knew was coming.

The greatest quantity of bile was reserved for the preliminary Emancipation Proclamation, which was criticized for its timidity and lack of moral grandeur. Many British supporters of the Union either didn't understand the constitutional protections of slavery and the consequent requirement that to attack the institution Lincoln had to work within the limits of his powers as commander-in-chief, or willfully ignored what they knew. Lincoln was forced to make the doctrine of "military necessity" the grounds for freedom because he had no other constitutional means of attacking slavery. There was no place for a moral justification of emancipation. It followed that a power based only on military necessity made it impossible to emancipate slaves in states not in rebellion and in lands occupied already by Union forces. The niceties of the situation escaped *The Spectator* which, though usually pro-Union, complained that "the principle asserted is not that a human being cannot own another, but that he cannot own him unless he is loyal to the United States."[38] According to *The Times*, "Where he has no power Mr Lincoln will set the negroes free; where he retains power he will consider them as slaves."[39] Even the voice of the organized working class in Britain, the newspaper *The Bee-Hive*, made similar points:

> Lincoln offers freedom to the negroes over whom he has no control, and keeps in slavery those other negroes within his power. Thus he associates his Government with slavery by making slaveholding the reward to the planters of rejoining the old Union.[40]

A year later the aged British anti-slavery hero from an earlier age, Lord Brougham, told a vast meeting of workingmen at the annual meeting of the Social Science Association in Edinburgh that the Emancipation Proclamation "was not for the sake of emancipating the slaves, but for the sake of beating the whites."[41]

The British had no difficulty understanding the *origins* of a sectional conflict which could be grasped (though at the risk of some distortion, for sure) in terms of their own recent history. They, too, had known a politics divided between the interests of the north and south of the country in the 1830s and 1840s. They, too, had experienced the political and economic tensions between a new industrial class and an aristocracy of the land. Arguments over tariffs between industrial and agricultural interests were central to British as well as American politics. The British had also grappled with the slave trade and slavery in the British Empire. They had reflected at length on the politics of nationalism and self-determination in Europe and the Americas since the Napoleonic era, such that some Britons placed the right of the South to create its own nation above the moral imperatives of anti-slavery. But the twists and turns of Lincoln's policies, and the reasons for presidential caution, were less comprehensible.

III

Why were the British so confused, and so often just plain wrong about the Civil War? Why, by extension, did they fail to grasp the essence of Lincoln's character and strategy? Historians have tended to advance variants of a sociological answer, contending that different groups reacted to the American situation in terms of their own interests, outlooks, and positions in British society. The argument of this essay is that the British were essentially ill-informed and

ignorant of American affairs; that they took positions based on incomplete
information and faulty understanding of the contest, its origins and its chief
protagonist, Lincoln himself.

This was the age when *The Times*, under the editorship of J. T. Delane, was
at its most influential and very largely shaped British public opinion and the
"official mind." More to the point, it shaped and led the opinions of provincial
newspapers serving the new Victorian cities, many of which had been founded
only very recently after the removal of the stamp taxes on newspapers and magazines in 1855. These papers were without foreign correspondents of their own
and tended to follow the line taken by *The Times*, which was generally believed
to have access to the most reliable sources. But over the course of the Civil War
that line was inconsistent and confused.

The Times was never in any doubt over the evils of American slavery, but it
made clear in its editorials during the 1850s that its removal required caution
and care. It was critical of the extremism (in its terms) of immediatist American
abolitionism.[42] But its initially sympathetic response to Lincoln's election in
which it hoped for a peaceful resolution of the secession crisis, gave way quickly
to the view that secession was inevitable and the Union irretrievable.[43] In particular, *The Times* began to see the conflict in terms of British interests, whether
those were matters of maritime law, the supply of cotton to Lancashire, or free
trade across the Atlantic. Perversely, it judged the North's policies in relation
to their inconvenience for British traders and merchants rather than in relation
to their efficacy in the causes of Union and emancipation. Thus the Morrill
Tariff of early 1861, which was used to pay for the war, was an immediate
and constant object of *The Times'* ire, judged an affront to the doctrines of
free trade and the economic interests of the British, rather than one of several
fiscal expedients forced on Lincoln as the price of national unity.[44] The narrow-
ness of *The Times'* view of the Civil War, which was so frequently dismissed
as unwinnable by the North and detrimental to long-term Anglo-American
relations, prevented it from understanding the conflict in specifically American
terms. Strategic realities and constitutional necessities were never explained to
its vast readership in Britain. These errors and weaknesses may have been the
result of the latitude that Delane gave his leader-writers. The editor decided the
subject of a particular editorial to appear on a specific day but left the author—
and there were several different leader-writers who wrote about America in the
1860s—to develop his own views, enjoying "thorough freedom for his work."[45]

IV

Discussion of the British press and its depiction of the Civil War has omitted
consideration of arguably the most interesting and critical of all British sources
on this issue, the long pamphlet published by the young Leslie Stephen at the

beginning of 1865 entitled *The "Times" on the American War: A Historical Study*. Stephen later found fame as a notable Victorian man-of-letters, father of Virginia Woolf, and the first editor of the *Dictionary of National Biography* on which he began work in 1882. In 1865 he had just resigned his fellowship at Trinity Hall, Cambridge and moved to London after a gilded youth as an undergraduate and college tutor. He came from one of the most notable anti-slavery dynasties in Britain—his grandfather had been a key figure in the "Clapham Sect" who had led British anti-slavery in the early nineteenth century, and his father, Sir James Stephen, as under-secretary for the colonies, had drafted the bill for the emancipation of slaves in the British empire in 1833. Stephen's politics did not differ from his forebearers on these matters; in Cambridge in the early 1860s where "the most exciting topic was the Civil War in America," he was a noisy partisan for the Union.[46] As he wrote later, "it struck me that I should gain new power to my elbow if I could say 'I have been on the spot.'"[47] In the summer of 1863 he undertook a visit to the United States (in their wartime form) to gather information and to compile a case against *The Times*.[48]

Stephen arrived in Boston on July 9, 1863 bearing letters of introduction from John Bright among others. He met there the American men-of-letters Oliver Wendell Holmes Sr., James Russell Lowell, and Charles Eliot Norton, and the abolitionists William Lloyd Garrison and Wendell Phillips. He visited New York, Chicago, St. Louis, Cincinnati, and Philadelphia. He journeyed to the Rappahannock to see General Meade's encampment. On his return to Massachusetts in October he went to Concord and met Longfellow, Emerson, and Hawthorne. In mid-September Stephen also visited Washington and was taken by Seward to the White House to meet Lincoln. He stayed "for half an hour or so till all the Cabinet were assembled and ready for business." His description of the president in a letter to his mother is further evidence of British underestimation:

> In appearance he is much better than I expected. He is more like a gentleman to look at than I should have given him credit for from his pictures, and, though tall and bony, has not that clumsy elephantine look the [characterizers?] . . . attribute to him.[49]

Stephen's letters are interesting for another reason: his consistent refrain, offered as an excuse to Americans who could not understand British hostility toward the North, "that we know nothing at all about them." He would have felt ashamed of his country, he explained, if "Englishmen had really understood the nature of the quarrel."[50] After Stephen had spoken at the Harvard Commencement Dinner he reported that his remarks there had been "to the effect that there were only about six men in England who yet understood this war (including J.S. Mill and myself) . . ."[51] The culprit was *The Times*: "Everything that the *Times* says is either a lie, a blunder, or a mystification."[52]

Writing for publication a year later, Stephen convicted *The Times* of digest-ing public prejudice and serving it up to readers as verified news and informed comment. It merely reflected back the common views of the British, whose attitudes toward the Civil War were uncertain and uncomprehending, rather than informing and educating its readership.[53] Beyond this, *The Times* was frequently in error. The newspaper took the strength of Unionist feeling and the unwillingness to employ extra-constitutional means to suppress slavery as evidence of the North's insincerity over the fate of the slaves. Because it mis-construed the centrality of slavery to the war it was always in "perplexity."[54] The basic facts of American demography—the relative populations of North and South—were mangled in its columns.[55] Its constant prophecies of South-ern victory looked "absurdly wrong" by the first weeks of 1865.[56] Again and again Stephen convicted *The Times* of ignorance. The paper was ignorant "of the great cause of [this] foreign convulsion"; it had "stumbled into mistakes"; it was guilty of "a total misconception of the conditions of the struggle"; of "an error, not merely in calculation, but in knowledge of the primary data"; it "looked on like an ignorant person at a game of whist, knowing nothing of the hands." Its "total ignorance" and "presumption" led "to its pouring out a ceaseless flood of scurrilous abuse."[57] All that could be said in its favor was the absence of malice: "The Times was, I believe, more honest than most per-sons suppose, because it was more ignorant than common readers can easily be persuaded to believe."[58] Stephen commented on "the virulence, persistence, and energy with which it repeated the assertion that Lincoln was a despot."[59] Indeed, according to *The Times* his despotism was all the more "insupport-able" because he was apparently a man of such low caliber.[60] *The Times* inter-preted Lincoln's re-election as "an avowed step towards the foundation of a military despotism."[61]

V

Stephen's pamphlet changed little in early 1865. It was not widely noticed in Britain, though it garnered him the praise and thanks of friends on both sides of the Atlantic. What did change *The Times'* presentation of the con-flict and the attitude of Britons was Lincoln's death. By April 14, 1865 the war was over, the North was victorious, secession had been vanquished, the slaves were free. By then the natural supporters of the Union in Britain could appreciate Lincoln's achievement, and even natural enemies could at least be respectful of a president in death who they had disparaged in life.[62] Tom Tay-lor, the notable mid-Victorian public servant and the author of the play *Our American Cousin*, which Lincoln was watching at Ford's Theatre when he was murdered, published a poem in *Punch* in early May 1865 about the former president. Illustrated with an image—by John Tenniel who had caricatured

Lincoln unmercifully for four years—of Britannia laying a wreath on Lincoln's shrouded corpse that was titled "Britannia Sympathises with Columbia," it referred to Lincoln as "This rail splitter a true born king of men." Taylor did not spare those who had previously lampooned the president in the pages of *Punch*:

> *You* lay a wreath on murdered Lincoln's bier,
> *You*, who with mocking pencil wont to trace,
> Broad for the self-complacent British sneer,
> His length of shambling limb, his furrowed face.[63]

Others began to appreciate for the first time both the deep structure of Lincoln's statecraft and the error of their own interpretations. The Unitarian minister, the Rev. John Page Hopps of Dukinfield, a town outside Manchester, spoke at a meeting at the end of April 1865, which had been called to mark the president's death. "Some of us may have been wrong in our estimate of the man throughout," he said.

> Perhaps, the thoughts, the aims, the aspirations, and the clear policy, which seem to us of later growth, were, in reality, his own from the first; perhaps we did not think sufficiently of the awful difficulties of his position; but history will be just where we have been hasty, and time will only serve to bring to light whatever was wise in the statesman, and whatever was virtuous in the man.[64]

The Times was shameless in its volte-face. On April 29 it told its readers that Lincoln "was as little a tyrant as any man who ever lived. He could have been a tyrant if he had liked but he never made so much as an ill-tempered speech."[65] Yet we may catch a hint of a dawning and genuine recognition of Lincoln's subtle and complex modus operandi in another of its editorials, notable now for a reflective, even chastened tone:

> The quality of Mr. Lincoln's administration which served . . . more than any other to enlist the sympathy of bystanders was its conservative progress. He felt his way gradually to his conclusions, and those who will compare the different stages of his career one with another will find that his mind was growing throughout the course of it.[66]

A week later a leader further contrasted favorably "his practical and tentative statesmanship," which had succeeded, "with the dogmatism of a more trained politician" who "might have erred."[67] If the paper was still condescending to an untrained leader, it was a recognition of sorts of Lincoln's tactical flexibility. Time was already doing its work, and has done so ever since: Lincoln after his death was appreciated in quite different ways from Lincoln in life. But if we are to understand the reactions to him in Britain while president we need to understand the man himself. And with Lincoln that isn't easy.

Historians frequently feel at a disadvantage when trying to recover a past that, they believe, would have been so much clearer and more comprehensible to those alive at the time. It is the burden of this essay that in trying to recover British attitudes to the Civil War in general and to Abraham Lincoln in particular, this is emphatically not the case. It is always difficult for the people of one nation to understand the politics of another, and as Stephen bemoaned, on "foreign politics . . . English ignorance in such matters is proverbial."[68] But when fed a diet of misinformation about a complex conflict, and when faced with a figure as impenetrable as Lincoln, it is no wonder that Britons divided, argued, and fell into error in the early 1860s. Americans did as well over their president, and some never understood a man with whom they had worked intimately for years. If to Billy Herndon, Lincoln's law partner, he remained "a profound mystery—an enigma—a sphinx—a riddle . . . incommunicative— silent—reticent—secretive—having profound policies—and well-laid—deeply studied plans . . .," how inscrutable must he have been to even his most ardent defenders in London and Lancashire?[69] In this particular case, the historian with the benefit of the sources and documents of the era is much better able to understand Lincoln and the ultimate direction of his policy, than Lincoln's contemporaries of any nationality.

Beyond this, the errors into which the British fell have implications for our understanding of British responses to the Civil War in general. Faced with the evidence of deep divisions in British reactions, for more than seventy years historians have attempted to explain these differences in terms of the interests and ideologies of different groups in British society. It has been a perfectly rational approach but has not resulted in a consensus because there are simply too many exceptions to any pattern of response grounded in domestic politics or sociology, and there is always too much contrary evidence to counter any generalization. Liberals may have tended to support the cause of the Union, though not all of them, and not all the time. We cannot say that all the working classes believed this, or that all the middle classes that, or that the aristocracy was naturally and consistently pro-Southern. It is the contention of this essay that few Britons really understood the intricacies of the conflict itself and the thinking of the man who led the "war for Union." In part this was because of the nature of Lincoln himself, whose instinct was to shield his thoughts and deepest impulses from others; in part it was also the result of his studied reaction to a political issue—the removal American slavery, in which honesty to his different electorates over the course of his career would almost certainly have undermined his efficacy. But it is also a contention of this essay that even if Lincoln had been an easier statesman to "read" and follow, the reporting of the Civil War in London was tainted by condescension, misunderstanding, ignorance, and narrowly conceived national interest. In such a situation it is hardly surprising that the British were confused and that their confusion led to cynicism. This is not to decry past attempts to explain British responses, or to deter future scholars from trying again to explain who in Britain supported North and South, and why. But when we reflect on the information available to contemporaries and on the problems they encountered trying to understand Abraham Lincoln, the only advice for anyone rash enough to return to this issue is to proceed with caution—as Lincoln did throughout his career.

Notes

1. E. D. Adams, *Great Britain and the American Civil War*, 2 vols. (New York: Longmans, Green and Co., 1925); Donaldson Jordan and Edwin J. Pratt, *Europe and the American Civil War* (New York: Houghton Mifflin Co., 1931).

2. Frank L. Owsley, *King Cotton Diplomacy: Foreign Relations of the Confederate States of America*, 2nd ed., (Chicago: University of Chicago Press, 1959); Mary Ellison, *Support for Secession: Lancashire and the American Civil War* (Chicago: University of Chicago Press, 1972); Royden Harrison, "British Labour and the Confederacy: A Note on the Southern Sympathies of Some British Working Class Journals and Leaders during the American Civil War," *International Review of Social History* 2 (1957), 78–105.

3. R. J. M. Blackett, *Divided Hearts: Britain and the American Civil War* (Baton Rouge: Louisiana State University Press, 2001).

4. Duncan Campbell, *English Public Opinion and the American Civil War* (London: Royal History Society, 2003).

5. Richard Hofstadter, *The American Political Tradition and the Men Who Made It* (1948; rpt. New York: Vintage, 1974), 169.

6. George M. Frederickson, "A Man but not a Brother: Abraham Lincoln and Racial Equality," *Journal of Southern History* 41 (February 1975), 40.

7. Lincoln to Joshua Speed, August 24, 1855, in Roy P. Basler et al., eds., *The Collected Works of Abraham Lincoln* [*CW*], 9 vols. (New Brunswick, NJ: Rutgers University Press, 1953–55), 2:320.

8. Stephen Oates, *With Malice Toward None: The Life of Abraham Lincoln* (New York: Harper & Row, 1977), 137–38.

9. Lincoln to Albert G. Hodges, April 4, 1864, *CW*, 7:281.

10. Lincoln-Douglas Debates, Ottawa, Ill., August 21, 1858.

11. Don E. Fehrenbacher, ed., *The Leadership of Abraham Lincoln* (New York: Wiley, 1970), 114.

12. Frederick Douglass, "Oration in Memory of Abraham Lincoln," April 14, 1876, in Philip S. Foner, ed., *The Voice of Black America* (New York: Simon & Schuster, 1972), 439.

13. Allen T. Rice, ed., *Reminiscences of Abraham Lincoln* (New York: North American Pub. Co., 1888), 193.

14. Lawanda Cox, *Lincoln and Black Freedom: A Study in Presidential Leadership* (Columbia: University of South Carolina Press, 1981).

15. Matthew Pinsker, "The Race of Ambition: Abraham Lincoln and the Republican Vocation" (unpublished D. Phil thesis, University of Oxford, 1995).

16. Garry Wills, "Dishonest Abe," *Time*, October 5, 1992, 45–46.

17. Quoted in David Donald, *Lincoln Reconsidered. Essays on the Civil War Era*, 2nd ed. (New York: Knopf, 1965), 67.

18. Ibid., 66.

19. Ibid., 68; Allen C. Guelzo, *Lincoln: A Very Short Introduction* (Oxford: Oxford University Press, 2009), 43.

20. Lawanda Cox, "Lincoln and Black Freedom" in Gabor S. Boritt, ed., *The Historian's Lincoln* (Urbana: University of Illinois Press, 1988), 179.

21. "Address on Colonization to a Deputation of Negroes," August 14, 1862, *CW*, 5:370–75.

22. Fehrenbacher, *The Leadership of Abraham Lincoln*, 114.

23. David Donald, *Lincoln* (New York: Simon & Schuster, 1995), 367.

24. J. R. Pole, *Abraham Lincoln and the American Commitment* (Cambridge: Cambridge University Press, 1966), 5, 34.

25. Fehrenbacher, *The Leadership Of Abraham Lincoln*, 114.

26. Hofstadter, *The American Political Tradition*, 164.

27. James M. McPherson, *Battle Cry of Freedom* (New York: Oxford University Press, 1988), 497–98.

28. Adams, *Great Britain and the American Civil War*, 1:79, 114–15.

29. Morris to John Chandler Bancroft Davis, October 30, 1860, quoted in Martin Crawford, *The Anglo-American Crisis of the Mid-Nineteenth Century. The Times and America 1850–1862* (Athens: University of Georgia Press, 1987), 79.

30. Lyons to Russell, April 9, 1861, in Adams, *Great Britain and the American Civil War*, 2:258.

31. *The Times*, October 7, 1862.

32. Cobden to Bright, October 7, 1862, quoted in Blackett, *Divided Hearts*, 226.

33. Adams, *Great Britain and the American Civil War*, 2:276. On the inferior caliber of American political leadership, Lincoln included, see the *Saturday Review*, December 6, 1862, 675: "It is the oligarchy of Caucuses and Conventions which has kept the real leaders of all the parties out of the highest place in the Commonwealth, and has handed the chair of Washington to Polk, Pierce, and Abraham Lincoln."

34. *Spectator*, September 20, 1862, 1043, quoted in Campbell, *English Public Opinion*, 105.

35. *The Times*, September 30, 1861.

36. Forster was speaking at the Mechanics' Institute, Bradford. *Reynolds Weekly*, October 6, 1861, 9, quoted in Campbell, *English Public Opinion*, 55.

37. *The Times*, September 30, 1861.

38. *The Spectator*, October 11, 1862, 1125.

39. *The Times*, October 7, 1862. This was one of the more considered responses to the Emancipation Proclamation on the part of *The Times*. On the previous day it had pictured Lincoln inciting race war: "He will appeal to the black blood of the African; he will whisper of the pleasures of spoil and of the gratification of yet fiercer instincts . . ." *The Times*, October 6, 1862. See also *The Times*, October 21, 1862.

40. *The Bee-Hive*, October 11, 1862.

41. *Reynolds Weekly*, October 18, 1863, 4; Lawrence Goldman, *Science Reform and Politics in Victorian Britain: The Social Science Association 1857–1886* (Cambridge: Cambridge University Press, 2002).

42. Crawford, *The Anglo-American Crisis of the Mid-Nineteenth Century*, 54–59.

43. Ibid., 84, 123.

44. Ibid., 89–96.

45. Dung-mauh Lin, "An Intellectual in Politics: The Educational and Political Ideas of George Charles Brodrick, 1831–1903" (unpublished M.Litt thesis, Faculty of History, University of Oxford, 2008), 13. This should be contrasted with Crawford's view that "Delane exercised strict supervision over his editorial staff" and "leading articles were expected to conform both in style and content to a generally prescribed pattern." Crawford, *The Anglo-American Crisis*, 20.

46. Leslie Stephen, *Life of Henry Fawcett* (London: Smith, Elder, 1885), 89.

47. Leslie Stephen, "Some Early Impressions," *The National Review* 13, no. 248 (October 1903), 221.

48. F. W. Maitland, *The Life and Letters of Leslie Stephen* (London: Duckworth, 1907), 108; Gillian Fenwick, *Leslie Stephen's Life in Letters: A Bibliographical Study* (Aldershot: Scolar, 1993), 160–64.

49. Maitland, *Life and Letters of Leslie Stephen*, 119–20. The best source for Stephen's American sojourn are the letters he sent his mother which were then passed to Stephen's close friend Henry Fawcett. The originals are not extant but extracts can be found in Maitland's biography of Stephen.

50. Maitland, *Life and Letters of Leslie Stephen*, 122.

51. Ibid., 114.

52. Ibid., 124.

53. Stephen, *The "Times" on the American War* (London: W. Ridgeway, 1865), 5–6.

54. Ibid., 21, 53.

55. Ibid., 17.

56. Ibid., 17, 81–89.

57. Ibid., 6, 7, 17, 18, 105.

58. Ibid., 53. See also 92.

59. Ibid., 65.

60. *The Times*, October 21, 1862.

61. *The Times*, November 22, 1864.

62. See, for example, the editorial in *The Times* on April 29, 1865.

63. *Punch*, May 6, 1865, 182.

64. Quoted in Blackett, *Divided Hearts*, 233. Blackett describes Hopps as a Confederate supporter but he was, in fact, "an advanced liberal" and may be better understood as a radical critic of Lincoln's timidity. R. K. Webb, "Hopps, John Page (1834–1911)," *Oxford Dictionary of National Biography* (Oxford: Oxford University Press, 2004) at http://www.oxforddnb.com/view/article/49458, accessed January 26, 2010.

65. *The Times*, April 29, 1865.

66. *The Times*, April 27, 1865.

67. *The Times*, May 2, 1865.

68. Stephen, *The "Times" on the American War*, 4.

69. Donald, *Lincoln Reconsidered*, 67.

7

"The Stuff Our Dreams Are Made Of"

LINCOLN IN THE ENGLISH IMAGINATION

Adam I. P. Smith

In 1941 the Ministry of Information released a film called *Words for Battle*, directed by Humphrey Jennings, a well-known pioneer of the documentary style. The film begins with images of England as a pastoral idyll; the camera soars over the white cliffs of Dover, rolling hills, sleepy villages, and magnificent cathedrals, to a soundtrack of the words of Milton, Browning, Blake, and Kipling read by Laurence Olivier. Gradually, the pace and intensity of the words and images increase, and, as Olivier reads from a speech by Winston Churchill, the camera comes down to ground level and the audience sees, for the first time, the people of England engaged in their daily business. The camera comes to rest on a statue of Abraham Lincoln in front of the Houses of Parliament and Olivier reads the final sentence of the Gettysburg Address with one small but significant alteration: "*this* nation" becomes the more universal "*the* nation." When he reaches the final line ("government of the people, by the people, and for the people, shall not perish from the earth") the film cuts to a shot of ordinary Londoners hurrying past the statue on their way to work as tanks and military vehicles roll by.[1] This final scene from a short but powerful film offers a glimpse of the place of Lincoln in the English imagination at this moment of national crisis. On one level, Lincoln's function in the film was to suggest to Americans that they shared the values Britain was defending in the struggle against fascism. Yet it was only possible for Humphrey Jennings to use Lincoln's image with such confidence in a film produced primarily to be shown in British cinemas because, over the preceding twenty years, the sixteenth American president had become a familiar figure in the English landscape. There was no apparent incongruity in applying words originally spoken of the meaning of the sacrifice at Gettysburg to the struggle against Hitler.

The interwar years were the high-water mark for Lincoln in England. He was not only a familiar but also a consensual figure, admired, albeit for slightly different reasons, across a wide social and political spectrum. That had not always

been true. Lincoln had a varied career in the English imagination in the century
or so after his death; the salience and political content of his image shifted
according to the context. The causes for which he was appropriated include
teetotalism, trade unionism, wartime conscription, and British military intervention to prevent the unilateral independence of Rhodesia. That Lincoln was,
for example, invoked by both the supporters and the opponents of Irish Home
Rule suggests how multifaceted his image was and reminds us that his image is
more revealing about the groups and individuals who used and responded to
his image than it is about Lincoln himself. To make some sense of this complexity, the image of Lincoln in the English imagination needs to be understood
in relation to the image of America and the language of democracy.

The United States, as an imagined place, has had great currency in the English cultural and political imagination over the past two centuries and more.[2]
Lincoln's image reflected, and also reinforced, familiar components of that
imagined America. The association of the idea of America with the frontier,
for example, was evoked by stories about Lincoln's humble birth, his wood-
cutting, his formidable physical strength, his "folk wisdom," and his lack of
formal education. Meanwhile, the image of America as a land of opportunity
was embodied by Lincoln's rise to the top, while the promise that democracy
meant a less corrupt and less financially profligate government was captured
by his reputation as "Honest Abe." At the same time, like the English image
of America more generally, Lincoln was constructed as simultaneously foreign
and "one of us," a familiar yet exotic figure. A quintessential embodiment of
America, Lincoln was nevertheless imaginatively rooted in English contexts,
quite literally so in the case of the Westminster statue. We can see this in *Words
for Battle* where Lincoln is both the symbol of America and the spokesman for
England's cause. Indeed, the prevalence of the idea of Anglo-American racial
kinship is crucial to understanding how Lincoln was seen in the century after
his death. The language of "Anglo-Saxon" racial unity became most prominent
in the Edwardian era, but was present, in one form or another, throughout
the century after Lincoln's death. In 1865, at a meeting in Newcastle-upon-
Tyne to express sympathy with the American people, one speaker explained
that "[Lincoln's] was not an assassination that had taken place in some foreign
country [but] in a land kindred to our own, speaking the same language, moved
by the same impulses, and animated by the same principles."[3] This perception
of Anglo-Americans as fundamentally one people goes a long way to explaining how Lincoln—"that knightly son of our blood," as *The Times* once called
him—came to be so embraced, especially in the first half of the twentieth century.[4] He had, as the *Manchester Guardian* put it in 1919, a "binding power
and significance for all who speak the English tongue."[5] This was also the view
of one the most influential shapers of the twentieth-century English image of
America, Winston Churchill, whose *History of the English Speaking Peoples*
devoted an inordinate amount of space to the American Civil War. Churchill's

mother had watched Lincoln's funeral procession pass her house when she was a little girl, and the figure of Lincoln seems to have loomed fairly large in Churchill's conception of the world. One of his childhood memories was his accidental discovery of a powerful cartoon in *Punch* of a weeping Britannia laying a wreath on the "cold marble" of Lincoln's tomb.[6]

Humphrey Jennings' film also hints at the second, and perhaps even more helpful, framework for understanding the place of Lincoln in English culture: the evolving language of democracy. If Blake and Milton evoked a tradition of English liberty, Kipling and Browning spoke of the English character, and Churchill offered defiance, it was the American Lincoln who expressed the idea that it was the ordinary man and woman—not rulers or landscape or beautiful buildings—who made England worth fighting for. Between 1865 and 1945 the word "democracy" was transformed from a radical aspiration into a mainstream means of legitimizing the political order. Over that time there were at least three different ways of imagining the relationship between Lincoln and democracy. The first, associated with nineteenth-century radicalism and, to a lesser extent, with the twentieth-century Labour movement, saw Lincoln as the champion of the working man, an embodiment of the radical challenge to the ascendancy in British politics of inherited wealth and privilege. The second image emphasized Lincoln's essential conservatism and saw in him reassurance that democracy could be reconciled with order and established institutions. *Words for Battle* encapsulated the third image: Lincoln as the emblem of a distinctive Anglo-American democratic community on which the future of freedom depended—an image brought to the fore by the world wars, which lingers in some quarters even today.

The Radical Lincoln

In his lifetime, Lincoln's image was almost as deeply enmeshed in partisanship in Britain as it was in the United States. The voice of the establishment, the London *Times*, had been one of the president's most dismissive critics, lampooning him as a buffoon and a hypocrite, while for liberals and radicals the struggle of the North against the slave-drivers of the South was one of the great radical cause célèbres of the nineteenth century.[7] John Bright, probably the most vocal of Lincoln's advocates in Britain, warned that if the Confederacy triumphed, "European democracy would be silenced and dumbfounded forever," a view that summed up what was widely perceived to be at stake.[8] Lincoln's assassination probably had a public impact in England as great as any other international event in the Victorian era. When the news reached Newcastle, the local paper reported "men in the public street reaching out their trembling hands each to the other trying to articulate some trembling words of comfort, the hot tears falling down their cheeks, and every manifestation given of the profoundest, most intense grief."[9] It was not only in the great centers of labor activism like London, Liverpool, Manchester, and Birmingham that public meetings were held to mark and mourn Lincoln's death but also in many smaller towns and cities.[10] While these meetings often claimed to be gatherings of the whole community, a radical political agenda was rarely far from the surface. The chairman of the Gateshead meeting told the crowd that "they must all feel interested in President Lincoln, as he sprung from the laboring classes, and had always shown his deep sympathy with them," while across the river in Newcastle, the guiding light behind the mass meeting on the Town Moor was the radical leader Joseph Cowen. The outpouring of public grief in England, one speaker explained, was because Lincoln was "not a man seated on the throne by Divine right or heredity prestige, but a man elected by a thousand voices—a man who had sprung from the people and who was part of the people."[11]

For the rest of the century "honest Abe, the rail-splitter, who piloted [the United States] through the hours of their greatest trial" was invoked frequently enough in the popular press to suggest that his image had substantial popular resonance.[12] Often, Lincoln was held up as the standard against which politicians should be measured. In the agitation which preceded the 1867 Reform Act, he was repeatedly invoked as an example of a leader who came from the people and who could "stand comparison with hereditary nobility of any country or age."[13] *Reynolds's Newspaper*, the most successful radical publication of the mid- to late nineteenth century, even carried the motto "government of the people, by the people, for the people" on its masthead.[14] There is also evidence of Lincoln's status as a democratic hero in the autobiographical writings of the generation of British radicals politicized by the American Civil War.[15] The Durham Miners' leader, John Wilson, dedicated his memoirs to "Stern, Indomitable 'Old Abe,'" for whom, Wilson wrote, "freedom was an eternal principle; to live in the White House was a temporary fleeting."[16] The affinity between Lincoln and the British left was to prove an enduring one. In the 1920s, Ramsay MacDonald, the first Labour prime minister, was still able to say that "the shadow of Abraham Lincoln should somehow or other be associated with those of us who represent the Labour Party," while as late as the 1960s, Prime Minister Harold Wilson found Lincoln a useful figure to invoke in speeches.[17]

This radical vision was inflected by religious ideas, especially for nonconformists, among whom admiration for Lincoln always ran deepest. Lincoln's martyrdom at the moment of his triumph intensified the romantic power of his image, making him an almost redemptive figure. In an 1873 lecture to the Turners' Burial and Sick Society of Longton, Staffordshire, a speaker stressed God's clear "election" of Lincoln in "His plan for the raising of the class he came from."[18] His martyrdom—on Good Friday—was widely seen as a sure sign of divine providence, and indeed Lincoln's life narratives paralleled Christ's more closely than that of any other modern figure. Without doubt, Lincoln's status as the "Great Emancipator" was an important component of this radical nonconformist image. The once-vibrant abolitionist tradition in

Britain was somewhat attenuated by the late 1860s, but, for those who kept the flame alight, Lincoln was hailed as a secular saint.[19] In 1866, the British and Foreign Freedmen's Aid Society published a book of extracts from speeches by Lincoln together with a commentary emphasizing Lincoln's lifelong dedication to the cause of black freedom.[20] Meanwhile, the congregation of the Surrey Chapel in Blackfriars Road, Lambeth, which had been a center of anti-slavery activism since the eighteenth century, raised funds in America for the erection of a new church, completed in 1876, whose spire was decorated with red stars and stripes and known as the "Lincoln tower."[21]

Emancipation, however, was never the most important explanation for Lincoln's appeal to late nineteenth-century English radicals. For most, it was Lincoln's journey from the "plough to the presidency" that mattered.[22] Nineteenth-century English narratives of Lincoln's life generally followed the same basic pattern. Dwelling on his childhood hardships, his humility, his godliness, his hard work, and his wisdom, they included versions of the same four stories: the distances he would walk to find books to read; his flat-boat trip down the Mississippi; his humility on becoming president; and his assassination.[23] Emancipation was generally a very minor theme in the transformation of Lincoln into an example of what historian Patrick Joyce calls "democratic leading men."[24] Liberal heroes like Bright, Gladstone, and Garibaldi were celebrated not just for their charisma, or for their achievements, but through the stories of their lives as champions of the people.[25] In this genre, Abraham Lincoln was the pre-eminent example of the man who never forgot his origins as he fought and won the greatest struggle of the century against slavery and despotism.[26] He was imagined as a "transnational" figure—waging a universal struggle on behalf of "the people" against privilege and despotism. Lincoln's radical image helped to shape the forms and narrative patterns of a distinctive genre of radical political celebrity culture, which was enabled by new printing technologies and cheaper newspapers, and the spread—in the years immediately preceding the American Civil War—of the new rapid engraving techniques pioneered by the *Illustrated London News*. The widely circulating temperance weekly *The British Workman* was only one of many newspapers to publish a print of the martyred president in 1865, in its case an image laden with allegory: Columbia and Britannia clasp hands and weep surrounded by the British and American flags and mourning drapes.[27] To hang such a print on the wall of one's front parlor was to broadcast radical political allegiance.

The Nation-Builder

This vision of Lincoln as the tribune of the people never entirely faded, but by the end of the nineteenth century it was countered by an alternative image of Lincoln, one which could be embraced by conservatives. Traditionally, the

British political establishment had viewed the upstart republic askance as a society without the anchor of established institutions. In the decades after the Civil War, however, this began to change, and with it came a reassessment of Lincoln.[28] Having survived the bloodiest war the Western world had seen since 1815, and with a newly self-confident bourgeois class making extraordinary fortunes from rapid industrialization, the United States could be reimagined as a model of how to contain democratic impulses within a fundamentally conservative structure. Searching for reassurance that the democratization of the British constitution would not undermine the foundations of political stability and respect for property, late nineteenth-century Liberals and Conservatives alike found in Lincoln an impressive determination to preserve the government at all costs. Lincoln, after all, had once called secession "the essence of anarchy," a sentiment shared by Unionists in Britain facing down calls for Irish Home Rule.[29] Unionist politicians frequently compared Lincoln to Cavour and Bismarck. "These great men will be famous for all time," said one Tory MP in the House of Commons in 1893, "for the glorious work of unity and consolidation which they had achieved for their own nations and their own race." In each instance they had succeeded "in destroying and wiping out the fatal principle of separation and dismemberment."[30] On the other side of the debate, supporters of Irish Home Rule had their own "Lincoln" but the willingness of Tories t use Lincoln in defense of the status quo was new.

In this conservative counter-image, Lincoln's humble origins were downplayed. Instead the focus was on the president's conduct of the war, especially his willingness to suspend habeas corpus and his determination to give no quarter to those, behind the lines as well as on the battlefield, who would weaken and destroy the nation. One strand of the conservative reappraisal made the Lincoln story compatible with long-standing Romantic notions about the inseparability of greatness of character from noble birth. This approach was developed most elaborately by the novelist and Tory imperialist John Buchan in *The Path of the King* (1921). The book is a series of fictionalized tales of great leaders through more than a thousand years of history all of whom, in Buchan's fantasy, were descended from a Viking king. Oliver Cromwell makes an appearance, but the culmination of the book is Lincoln's rise to greatness. He may be the "first American," Buchan suggests, but he is also "the last of the kings."[31] The fantasy that the only explanation for transcendent greatness was a noble lineage had deep folkloric roots, and, as always with such conceits, the effect was to separate Lincoln rhetorically from the mass of working men from which he came: just because Lincoln could rise from the bottom of society to the top, it did not mean that just anybody could.

At the same time, this new breed of conservative English Lincolnophiles suggested that Lincoln's legacy was to demonstrate that liberty and the law (at least English-derived Common Law) remained one and inseparable. Sometimes this only required a slight tweaking of the radical narrative of Lincoln's life.

Stories of his early thirst for learning were familiar; now it became significant that among his few books was a copy of Blackstone's *Commentaries.* Lincoln demonstrated how liberty and law could be reconciled and how the power of the state could be used effectively in pursuit of a greater good.[32] Prime Minister Lord Rosebery explained the "attraction and glamour" that Lincoln held for Englishmen as that peculiar combination of "unflinching principle" and "unflinching commonsense."[33]

This emerging reinvention of Lincoln reconstructed the old radical democratic image rather than attempting to invert it. Lincoln's democratic credentials were not denied but adapted. In the face of the rise of socialism, here was a statesman who had begun life as a manual laborer but to whom the language of class was quite alien. Democracy, Lincoln seemed to suggest, could be absorbed without destroying civilization, at least when practiced by Anglo-Saxons.

The Anglo-American Lincoln

The conservative reappraisal of Lincoln was a prerequisite for the final stage of his journey from radical hero to establishment figure. During the Great War, Lincoln came to symbolize the idea that liberty could be combined with military victory, indeed that each was inseparable from the other. Lincoln's 1864 letter to Mrs. Bixby, a woman who had apparently lost all five of her sons in the Union army, was an especially important document in the rising wartime Lincoln "cult." Several publications contrasted the humanity and moral purpose evident in Lincoln's words with a brusquely worded letter allegedly sent by the kaiser telling a German woman who had suffered a similar loss that he was "gratified" by her sacrifice.[34] Coupled with the frequently retold stories about Lincoln's willingness to pardon soldiers sentenced to death by court-martial, the Bixby letter was, one newspaper argued, evidence that democracy, freedom, and compassion went hand in hand.[35] *The Times* invoked Lincoln repeatedly through the war, to legitimize the introduction of conscription, calls for ever more troops, and, above all, the need to carry on the fight through to ultimate and unconditional victory. "The pacifists and optimists who think that there is a deal to be done with the evil of Prussianism echo the defeatists in the North in 1864," wrote a *Times* correspondent, "and Lincoln stood firm, and he was right to."[36]

Undoubtedly, much of the credit for the "cult of Lincoln" in England, as the playwright George Bernard Shaw put it, was due to the biography published in 1916 by Lord Charnwood, an Oxford-educated Liberal peer.[37] A life-long admirer of Lincoln, Charnwood believed that the sixteenth president of the United States served the needs of an English public battered by war and in need of spiritual anchorage.[38] He conceived of his biography, recalled his wife, as a "war service."[39] In some respects, Charnwood's Lincoln would have been instantly recognizable to the radicals and labor leaders who had admired him so fervently in the decades after his death. There was no doubting his hatred of privilege in all its forms or his authentic man-of-the-people credentials. In these ways he remained the quintessential democratic hero. Yet the core of Charnwood's interpretation was Lincoln's essential moderation. His sincere "disapprobation" of slavery was real enough, but did not make him an abolitionist, nor did it blind him to the realities (as Charnwood saw it) of racial difference and racial privilege. "He balanced the claims of quick and subversive, and of slow and constructive reform," Charnwood wrote, "[just as he also balanced] the manifest weakness of the negro and the rights in which he was the equal of the white." Charnwood emphasized Lincoln's "struggles in the last months of his life for liberality in the reconstruction of the South" and his efforts for compensated emancipation.[40] One of Charnwood's most telling descriptions of Lincoln—as "practical statesman"—was widely adopted. It was a coinage which captured the distinctively "Anglo-Saxon" balance of pragmatism and realism on the one hand, with moral purpose and the wider issues of right and wrong at stake in seemingly parochial conflicts. "Practical statesmanship" was juxtaposed against dogmatic, irrational leadership (whether of the left- or the right-wing variety) on the one hand, and cynical, unprincipled populism on the other. It became a synonym for what was imagined to be a very British style of pragmatic but principled leadership in the interwar years. Thus, when, at a meeting of the Primrose League in 1929, Stanley Baldwin was toasted as the leader who "in temperament, character, outlook and exposition . . . resembled Abraham Lincoln more closely than any other great statesman," the compliment implied this Charnwood-style blend of moderation and principle.[41]

After the Armistice, Lincoln's vision seemed more relevant than ever. George Bernard Shaw thought that Lincoln was perceived in England as "essentially a saint," a "man of genius of the kind that crosses frontiers and takes its vessel far above the common political categories into the region which belongs, like the sky, to all mankind."[42] The statue Jennings filmed—a copy of the one designed by Augustus Saint-Gaudens in Chicago—was unveiled in July 1920 at a grand ceremony in Parliament Square attended by the prime minister and numerous dignitaries. The moment which best summed up the spirit of the occasion was when one of the speakers, Lord Bryce, turned to the American ambassador on the platform and proclaimed: "he is ours, sir, almost as much as he is yours," provoking a hearty round of applause.[43] No doubt many of those who gathered to watch this unveiling would have "made the pilgrimage," as the author Arnold Bennett described it, to see John Drinkwater's immensely successful play, *Abraham Lincoln,* then running at the Lyric Hammersmith.[44] "Nobody can dine out in London today and admit without a blush that he has not seen 'Abraham Lincoln,'" wrote Bennett.[45] The play cast such a spell over its audience that night after night "the audience somehow cannot leave its seats and the thought of the worry of the journey home and last 'busses and trains is banished."[46] The extraordinary popularity of the play throughout the three decades or so after its first production was captured by a reviewer of a 1952 revival in Birmingham who commented that it was "hard to judge objectively" since it was "like some high summer pageant remembered from childhood."[47] In six episodic scenes, the play dramatizes some of the key dilemmas in Lincoln's public life: the challenge of how to respond to secession, the problem of how to end slavery, and the issue of how to deal with the defeated Confederates at the end of the war. It culminates in a scene in Ford's Theatre at which Lincoln delivers a digest of his most famous speeches to the audience before being shot. The hagiographic quality of the piece did not escape criticism from reviewers, but the doubters were drowned out by the praise heaped on the production.[48]

Notwithstanding the success of Charnwood's biography, Drinkwater's play probably reached more people and should, therefore, be considered the most effective popularizer of this distinctively Anglo-American Lincoln in the first half of the twentieth-century. With the hopes for a new Wilsonian world order that might be forged at the Versailles peace conference in mind, one reviewer concluded that the play resonated not because of the skill of the playwright so much as because Lincoln spoke to the historical moment as no other figure could. Lincoln "seemed to incarnate our purpose, our usefulness, our sacrifice. This nobility—was it not ours? . . . This man of government of the people, for the people and by the people—was this not the 'new order' promised by our politicians, nay, actually being made in Paris by the People's representatives? And so Lincoln became the stuff our dreams are made of."[49]

As this (mis)quotation suggests, Shakespeare was never far away in the English interwar vision of Lincoln.[50] A couple of years after his play was first performed, Drinkwater published a short book, *Lincoln: World Emancipator,* a romantic meditation, some of it in verse, that ends with an imagined conversation between Abe and Will in another world. When Lincoln observes that what he most wanted to do was to "bring a poet's understanding to the workaday government of a nation," Shakespeare tells him that sensibility is what he is giving England. And when Lincoln muses that "it was splendid wasn't it, trying to understand people instead of trying to dominate them?" Shakespeare sagely comments: "That's what England gave you." At root, what the two have in common, it turns out, is a shared democratic sensibility—a belief that "everybody had a chance."[51]

Despite the endorsement of Lincoln by the establishment, the older, radical—even in some ways subversive—image of Lincoln retained some hold. There were hints of this in the response to the unveiling in 1919, a year before the Westminster Lincoln appeared, of a very different Lincoln statue in Manchester.[52] By all accounts, this was a rather limp, oddly subdued occasion, almost entirely ignored by the national press and shunned by the political establishment; even the American ambassador equivocated until almost the last minute before accepting the invitation to attend. The statue, by the modernist sculptor George Gray Barnard, was of a shambling figure with apparently distended hands crossed in front of his abdomen, alarmingly large feet and strangely sloping shoulders. To George Bernard Shaw, the Manchester statue was "the image of a saint" and the "mirror of Lincoln's soul."[53] To others, it resembled nothing so much as a weak man troubled by severe indigestion; to Lord Charnwood, it looked "like a minor poet who had gone under."[54] Where the Saint-Gaudens Lincoln could be hailed as the embodiment of virtuous Anglo-Saxon liberal statesmanship, Barnard's was not the representation of a hero but the defiant celebration of the homely, ordinary man.[55] Lincoln's real significance, the Barnard statue suggested, was that, for all his achievements, he remained a member of the working class. The *Manchester Guardian* mounted a stout defense of this controversial monument, arguing that "London, in possessing the St Gaudens statue, will have Lincoln the President; Manchester has Lincoln the man."[56] Yet it was precisely this representation of Lincoln as Everyman which offended so many British Lincolnophiles. "It is claimed that [the Barnard statue] represents 'the man of the people,' and not the statesman," sniffed one of *The Times'* correspondents, but "it is the statesman who . . . gave freedom to the slaves; the statesman . . . who lives in history and . . . should be commemorated in this country, and not merely the awkward, shambling figure the sculptor has chosen to hand down to future generations."[57] Clearly, the "cult of Lincoln" encompassed multiple images of the man. It was what we might call the "Saint Gaudens Lincoln"—the war leader, the defender of the Constitution, of law, and of justice—who had been embraced by the establishment. Yet a "Barnard Lincoln"—the homely man of the people—retained a popular hold.

When war broke out in 1939 Lincoln again seemed to serve the needs of the hour. The John Ford film *Young Mr. Lincoln* starring Henry Fonda opened in England just as war began, a juxtaposition which the novelist Graham Greene found fortuitous. "There now seems an added value in this attempt to draw in the simplest of least rhetorical terms a man who cared passionately for justice," he wrote in the *Spectator*.[58] Two phrases from the Gettysburg Address—"the dead shall not have died in vain" and "new birth of freedom"—peppered wartime rhetoric.[59] During the Second World War, the BBC produced at least three different original dramas featuring Lincoln and on Lincoln's birthday in 1944 mounted an ambitious broadcast combining Vice President Henry A. Wallace's Lincoln Day Address from Springfield, Illinois, with a sermon on Lincoln's legacy by the Archbishop of Canterbury in Westminster Abbey, and, from beside the Lincoln statue in the square, a talk about Lincoln, democracy, and the cause of freedom by the young Tory MP Quintin Hogg.[60] Drinkwater's ubiquitous play was revived in the West End in 1940 and ran continuously through the Blitz till the end of the war.[61]

The Lincoln that remained in the postwar years was drained of political potency. A children's biography by Michael Gorham, published in 1959, placed so much emphasis on Lincoln's early childhood and the trials of frontier life that only about 20 of 190 pages are devoted to the presidency and many of those are about the Lincolns' son Tad's mischievousness.[62] As one reviewer observed sourly, "the chief lesson of Mr Gorham's book seems to be that you too can be president if you learn enough funny stories and get on well with your friends."[63] Lincoln still featured prominently in the early work of British scholars of American history and the early shaping of the discipline.[64] Nor did Lincoln disappear entirely from public life. The sesquicentennial of Lincoln's birth was marked in Britain by a wreath-laying ceremony at the Saint-Gaudens statue in Westminster during which Prime Minister Harold Macmillan told the audience that "Lincoln will always be remembered for putting into simple and noble language the fundamental aspirations of ordinary men."[65] The U.S. Information Service, determined to use the commemoration to "make clear the importance of Lincoln and his ideas in the development of democracy throughout the world," appointed a full-time "co-ordinator of Lincoln activities" and created two photographic exhibitions that toured the country.[66] The centenary of the Civil War in the early 1960s also prompted a brief revival of interest in Lincoln, including yet another revival of the Drinkwater play, and there was a flurry of articles about Lincoln in the wake of the Kennedy assassination.[67] Occasionally in these postwar years the old heroic image of Lincoln could still be glimpsed, even if in such discordant contexts as the composer Malcolm Williamson's "Josip Broz Tito: A Tribute in Music," which prompted dire reviews at the 1981 Aldeburgh festival. The piece is ostensibly, as the title suggests, a lament for the dead Yugoslav leader (a somewhat surprising choice of subject for the Master of the Queen's Music), but is in fact, according to the composer, a "tribute to a dead hero, whoever he may be" which uses the texts of Whitman poems to relate Tito to Lincoln.[68] Such esoteric references aside, however, Lincoln gradually faded from the visible place he had once had in British public life.

At root, the power of Lincoln's image was that, like America more generally, dreams, hopes, and fears could be invested in him. In Drinkwater's words, he was a figure to whom "all sorrows and ambitions may be brought, a touchstone by which every ideal of conduct may be tried, a witness for the encouragement of the forlornest hope."[69] As a man of the common people with primitive folk-wisdom and a simple Protestant faith, he spoke to an important radical dissenting tradition in English politics; as a lawyer who read Blackstone by candlelight as a young man, and as a pragmatist who subordinated his private passions to the greater interest of the community and of order, he seemed to embody the reformist and improving liberal tradition; as a war leader, he showed that determination and force were sometimes necessary to achieve or to secure freedom. Like America itself, Lincoln's place in the English political imagination was both a product of the tension between his familiarity (a man of "Anglo-Saxon stock" who embodied all that was best about his race) and his otherness (as a frontiersman who lived a life unimaginable to his English admirers). Lincoln was both a recognizable human being—with his crumpled clothes and his folksy ways—and a statesman who transcended time and place. Lincoln, wrote Drinkwater, was "intimately of the world, yet unsoiled by it; vividly in contact with every emotion of his fellows and aware always of the practical design of their lives; always lonely, brooding apart from it all, yet alienated from none."[70] In Lincoln, as in Shakespeare's plays, could be found the gamut of human qualities: the humor and the humbleness as well as the heroic.

If Lincoln's power to capture the English imagination on a mass scale has now faded, it is not because these things are any less true than they once were but because other figures serve the functions Lincoln once did. The radical political culture in which he was first celebrated has long since vanished, while the role played by the Lincoln of the Saint-Gaudens statue—the hero-statesman—has, in a sense, been inherited by Winston Churchill. Like Lincoln before him, Churchill became the embodiment of resolution and the democratic spirit in the postwar era. Most of all, perhaps, Lincoln's image has been diminished by the decline of the language of Anglo-Saxonism, the prism through which America and Lincoln were viewed by the English for so long. Yet if Lincoln's image in England is now faint, it has not altogether faded. He retains the power to capture the imagination, if only, in recent times, through the reflected light of Barack Obama.

Notes

1. Copies of the film are held by the National Archives and by the British Film Institute and can be viewed online at http://www.screenonline.org.uk/film/id/727923/; (accessed October 4, 2008). I am grateful to John Ramsden, Keith McClelland, and Robert Cook, as well as to the participants in the "Global Lincoln" conference at Oxford in July 2009, for their comments on an earlier draft of this essay.

2. On the idea of America as a "fictional space," see Malcolm Bradbury, *Dangerous Pilgrimages: Transatlantic Mythologies and the Novel* (New York: Viking, 1996); James Epstein, "'America' in the Victorian Cultural Imagination," in Fred M. Leventhal and Roland Quinault, eds., *Anglo-American Attitudes: From Revolution to Partnership* (Aldershot: Ashgate, 2000); Howard Temperley, "Anglo-American Images" in H. C. Allen and Roger Thompson, eds., *Contrast and Connection: Bicentennial Essays in Anglo-American History* (London: Bell, 1976), 321–47.

3. *Newcastle Daily Chronicle,* May 5, 1865.

4. *The Times,* April 23, 1918.

5. *Manchester Guardian*, September 16, 1919.

6. Winston Churchill, *History of the English Speaking Peoples: The Great Democracies* (London: Cassell, 1956); Martin Gilbert, *Churchill and America* (New York: Simon & Schuster, 2008), 4, 9.

7. Eugenio Biagini, *Liberty, Retrenchment and Reform: Popular Liberalism in the Age of Gladstone, 1860–1880* (Cambridge: Cambridge University Press, 1992); R. J. M. Blackett, *Divided Hearts: Britain and the American Civil War* (Baton Rouge: Louisiana State University Press, 2001); Duncan Campbell, *English Public Opinion and the American Civil War* (Woodbridge: Boydell, 2003).

8. John Bright, *Speeches on Questions of Public Policy,* ed. James E. Thorold Rogers, 2 vols. (London: Macmillan, 1868), 1:225.

9. *Newcastle Daily Chronicle,* May 5, 1865.

10. See, for example, *Carlisle Express,* April 29, 1865; *Preston Guardian,* May 6, 1865; *Leeds Mercury,* May 6, 1865 (for report of the meeting in Huddersfield).

11. *Newcastle Daily Chronicle,* May 5, 8, 1865.

12. *Lloyd's Weekly,* January 20, 1886.

13. George Lorimer, speech in the Music Hall, Edinburgh, *The Caledonian Mercury,* June 28, 1865. See also report of the meeting of the National Reform Union, *Reynolds's Newspaper,* May 19, 1867; speech of William Lloyd Garrison in the Victoria Hall in Leeds, *Leeds Mercury,* October 22, 1867. On the idea of America in the debates leading up the 1867 Reform Act see also, Keith McClelland, "England's Greatness: The Working Man" in Catherine Hall, Keith McClelland, and Jane Rendell, *Defining the Victorian Nation: Class, Race, Gender and the Reform Act of 1867* (Cambridge: Cambridge University Press, 2000), 90.

14. The quotation from the Gettysburg Address was incorporated into the masthead of *Reynolds's Newspaper* from April 5, 1885.

15. See, for example, George N. Barnes, *From Workshop to War Cabinet* (London: Herbert Jenkins, 1924), 1.

16. John Wilson, *Memories of a Labour Leader: The Autobiography of John Wilson, J. P., M.P.* (London: T. F. Unwin, 1910), 173–74.

17. *The Times,* November 9, 1929. On Wilson's use of Lincoln, see John Grigg, "Lesson of Fort Sumter," *The Guardian,* November 29, 1965.

18. Quoted in Eugenio Biagini, *Liberty, Retrenchment and Reform: Popular Liberalism in the Age of Gladstone* (Cambridge: Cambridge University Press, 1992), 79.

19. Christine Bolt, *The Anti-slavery Movement and Reconstruction: A Study in Anglo-American Co-operation, 1833–77* (Oxford: Oxford University Press, 1969); Howard Temperley, *British Antislavery, 1833–1870* (London: Longman, 1972).

20. John Malcolm Ludlow, *President Lincoln: Self-Portrayed* (London: Alfred W.Bennett, 1866).

21. *Reynolds's Newspaper,* July 12, 1874.

22. *Reynolds's Newspaper,* October 2, 1881.

23. For example, "Abraham Lincoln," *The British Workman and Friend of the Sons of Toil,* July 1, 1865.

24. Patrick Joyce, *Democratic Subjects: The Self and the Social in Nineteenth-century England* (Cambridge: Cambridge University Press, 1994), esp. 136–46.

25. On the cult of Gladstone's leadership, see Biagini, *Liberty, Retrenchment and Reform,* 369–425; on Bright, see Joyce, *Democratic Subjects,* 85–146; on Garibaldi, see Lucy Riall, *Garibaldi: Invention of a Hero* (New Haven, CT: Yale University Press, 2007), 114.

26. President Garfield's assassination in 1881 spurred a similar construction of a "log cabin to White House" narrative which echoed faithfully the democratic fantasy invented

for Lincoln, but Garfield's image was, figuratively speaking, superimposed onto the Lincolnian template. On British responses to Garfield's assassination, see Mike Sewell, "'All the English-Speaking Race is in Mourning': The Assassination of President Garfield and Anglo-American Relations," *Historical Journal* 34 (September 1991): 665–86.

27. *The British Workman,* July 1, 1865. For this image, see above, p. 18.

28. H. A. Tulloch, "Changing British Attitudes towards the United States in the 1880s," *Historical Journal* 29:4 (1977), 825–40.

29. *The Times,* August 10, 1891.

30. HC Deb April 11, 1893, vol. 11, cc29–116.

31. John Buchan, *The Path of the King* (London: Nelson, 1921), 283.

32. For an extended treatment of this theme, albeit at a later date, see Isaac Foot, "The Lawyer Outside his Profession," a speech to the Law Association Conference in 1956, reprinted in Michael Foot and Alison Highet, *Isaac Foot: A Westcountry Boy—Apostle of England* (London: Politico's, 2006), especially 318–19.

33. *Leeds Mercury,* November 14, 1900.

34. *The Times,* February 12, 1917; Barry Schwartz, *Abraham Lincoln and the Forge of National Memory* (Chicago: University of Chicago Press, 2000), 241.

35. *The Times,* July 28, 1920.

36. *The Times,* August 27, 1917.

37. George Bernard Shaw to Judd Stewart, January 11, 1918, Lincoln Memorial University Letters (responses to request for signed photographs for the Holograph Room), Abraham Lincoln Library and Museum, Harrogate, Tennessee.

38. Charnwood's was not the first full-length biography of Lincoln by an Englishman. In 1907, Henry Bryan Binns published *Abraham Lincoln* (London: Everyman Library, 1927 ed.). Imitators of Charnwood include: J. Alfred Sharpe, *Abraham Lincoln* (London: The Epworth Press, 1919); Herbert R. Allport, *Abraham Lincoln* (London: privately published, 1923); John Drinkwater, *Lincoln: The World Emancipator* (Boston: Houghton Mifflin, 1920).

39. Lord Charnwood, *Abraham Lincoln* (London: Constable, 1916). Lady Charnwood is quoted in Merrill D. Peterson, *Lincoln in American Memory* (New York: Oxford University Press, 1994), 200. In 1947 Benjamin P. Thomas called Charnwood's biography "the best one-volume life of Lincoln ever written." Thomas, *Portrait for Posterity: Lincoln and his Biographers* (New Brunswick, NJ: Rutgers University Press, 1947), 208.

40. Lord Charnwood, "Abraham Lincoln: A Reading of his Character: The Plain Man in Politics," *The Times,* July 28, 1920.

41. *The Times,* April 9, 1929. After the war, however, when Baldwin's reputation was lower, the comparison was on occasion introduced to make a negative comparison. "It was precisely on the central test of leadership [over re-armament against the dictators] that the comparison founders." *The Times,* November 14, 1952.

42. Shaw to Stewart, January 11, 1918.

43. The American guests were as forthright in their efforts to define Lincoln in Anglo-American terms as were the British Lincolnophiles. Former Secretary of State Elihu Root prophesied that English school children would look at the Westminster Lincoln statue with a glow of pride and rejoice that "of such stuff are English people made." *The Times,* July 29, 1920.

44. *The Times,* July 29, 1920; Arnold Bennett, "Introduction," to John Drinkwater, *Abraham Lincoln* (London: Sidgwick and Jackson, 1919), iv.

45. *New York Times,* December 21, 1919.

46. Bennett, "Introduction," iv.

47. *Manchester Guardian,* October 2, 1952. Review of the revival of *Abraham Lincoln* at the Birmingham Repertory Theatre.

48. *Birmingham Gazette,* October 14, 1918. The play was continually revived by provincial repertory companies, amateur dramatic societies, and, on several occasions, in the West End. Many of the leading actors of the period appeared in the play: Arnold Ridley was in the original production, while the revival at the Old Vic and then at Sadler's Wells in 1931–32 starred Harcourt Williams as Lincoln and Ralph Richardson as General Grant. Alistair Sim appeared in blackface in the part of a thinly veiled Frederick Douglass. *Birmingham Post,* October 14, 1918, Arnold Ridley clippings file, Theatre Collection, Bristol University Library; "Abraham Lincoln," Programme (1931–2), Theatre Collection, Bristol University Library.

49. "The Success of Abraham Lincoln," *The English Review* 30 (February 1920): 186–88. On the success of *Abraham Lincoln,* see Herbert Farjeon, "Abraham Lincoln," *Time and Tide,* 1943; *Manchester Guardian,* October 2, 1952.

50. The correct quote is "we are such stuff/as dreams are made on" (Prospero), *The Tempest,* Act IV, scene 1. For other comparisons of Lincoln and Shakespeare, see Lord Curzon, speech on "Modern Eloquence," *The Times,* November 7, 1913; also, a book by the Anglo-American spiritualist Francis Grierson, *Abraham Lincoln: The Practical Mystic* (London: John Lane, 1919), 33.

51. Drinkwater, *Lincoln: The World Emancipator,* 114–15.

52. The Barnard statue had, for a while, been destined for London before opposition to it was mobilized in the United States and the Saint-Gaudens statue sent to Westminster instead. Lincoln's only surviving son, Robert Todd Lincoln, was at the forefront of the opposition, warning that if Barnard's *Lincoln* was sent to London it would amount to an "international calamity." (Robert Todd Lincoln is quoted in British Ambassador to Washington, Cecil Spring Rice to A. J. Balfour, November 29, 1917, WORK 20/106, National Archives.) The fullest account of this bizarre controversy is Frederick C. Moffatt, *Errant Bronzes: George Grey Barnard's Statues of Abraham Lincoln* (London: Associated University Presses, 1998), especially 108–20.

53. Shaw to Stewart, January 11, 1918.

54. Lord Charnwood to Charles Moore, May 1, 1920, Charles Moore Papers, Library of Congress, quoted in Moffatt, *Errant Bronzes,* 117.

55. Moffatt, *Errant Bronzes,* 8.

56. *Manchester Guardian,* September 16, 1919.

57. Letter to the editor from F. C. De Sumichrast, *The Times,* October 2, 1917.

58. *Spectator,* September 22, 1939, "Young Mr Lincoln" clippings file, British Film Institute Library.

59. For the use of the Gettysburg Address in British wartime propaganda see, for example, *Manchester Guardian,* August 5, 1940.

60. *Manchester Guardian,* February 14, 1944; *The Times,* February 14, 1944.

61. It was simultaneously performed at the Bristol Old Vic (with Herbert Lomas, who later found fame in horror movies, in the lead role) and at the Liverpool Playhouse, and a third production toured in rep between 1943 and 1945. Bristol Old Vic, programmes file, Theatre Collection, Bristol University Library; *Manchester Guardian,* April 18, 1940, February 6, 1943.

62. Michael Gorham, *The Real Book of Abraham Lincoln* (London: Dennis Dobson, 1959).

63. *The Guardian,* December 4, 1959.

64. In what Michael Heale has described as the "take off" period for the British study of American history, Denis Brogan, W. R. Brock, J. R. Pole, and their slightly younger contemporary Peter J. Parish all wrote influential books about Lincoln and the Civil War. Michael Heale, "The British Discovery of American History," *Journal of American Studies* 39 (2005): 357–69; Denis Brogan, *Abraham Lincoln* (London: Duckworth, 1935); W. R. Brock, *The Character of American History* (London: St Martin's Press, 1960); Peter J. Parish, *The American Civil War* (London: Eyre Methuen, 1975). One of the leading figures in the immediate postwar effort to interpret American history for British audiences was Denis Brogan, who, according to his son, Hugh, found in "Lincoln's extraordinary blend of personal virtues and public virtue . . . the exemplar of the democratic citizen." Hugh Brogan, "Preface" to the 1974 edition of Denis Brogan, *Abraham Lincoln* (London: Duckworth, 1974), xiii.

65. *The Times,* February 13, 1959.

66. U.S. Information Agency Report R6148, "Records of the Lincoln Sesquicentennial Commission," Box 14, "Foreign Countries General," National Archives II. There is some evidence that the touring exhibitions were popular. The *Nottingham Evening Post* reported that people "poured into the exhibition right after the opening. And many hours later, even after the shopping crowds had thinned, they were still filing in to look at the collection of pictures and extracts from letters and speeches." *Nottingham Evening Post,* February 14, 1959. J. R. Pole, a young lecturer in American history at UCL, published a pamphlet, *Abraham Lincoln and the Working Classes of Britain,* with an introduction by the Chairman of the Trades Union Congress, thirty-thousand copies of which were distributed by the English Speaking Union. J. R. Pole, *Abraham Lincoln and the Working Classes of Britain* (London: English Speaking Union, 1959).

67. John Grigg, "Lincoln and Kennedy," *The Guardian,* September 5, 1963; *The Economist,* November 30, 1963.

68. *The Guardian,* June 23, 1981.

69. Drinkwater, *World Emancipator,* 1–2.

70. Drinkwater, *World Emancipator,* 1–2.

{ 8 }

Kentucky's "Cottage-Bred Man"

ABRAHAM LINCOLN AND WALES

Kenneth O. Morgan

The Welsh, like other small nations, delight in praising famous men (famous women far less often). In 2009 three particular heroes had key anniversaries commemorated—President Lincoln, Mr. Gladstone, and George Frideric Handel. Handel may be left to messianic celebration elsewhere. Gladstone's celebrity resulted from the overwhelming Liberal ascendancy in Wales from the 1868 general election onward. After all, he married a Welsh woman and lived in Hawarden Castle in Flintshire.[1] Abraham Lincoln, born and bred in the American Midwest, is a more surprising hero, but perhaps the most emblematic of them all. Long before his assassination, he had become an iconic figure for many in Wales. For nonconformists, he was the very embodiment of their libertarian values. After his death, *ein Lincoln* (our Lincoln) was close to being sanctified.[2] Both Old and New Testaments were seen as offering parallels as he was variously depicted as another Moses leading his people toward the promised land and a second Christ at Gethsemane. The man and his gospel seemed indivisible. For the chapel-going, male, Liberal-voting majority in Wales down to the First World War, he symbolized their ideological and moral creed. For two generations, he was created and re-created in their image.

The Welsh had been closely involved with American liberal ideas long before Lincoln's time. Radical Welsh groups of nonconformists had been drawn there by the excitement of the American Revolution. One such was the Baptist Jacobin radical, Morgan John Rhŷs, who migrated to the new American republic in the 1790s and briefly set up a Welsh *gwladfa* (settlement) in Beula in western Pennsylvania in 1794.[3] Others followed at Paddy's Run in Ohio and near Utica in New York state. In the first half of the nineteenth century, as elsewhere in Britain, a steady stream of Welsh people crossed the Atlantic in search of a better world. Many of the first settlers were from rural areas; increasingly, others were miners and ironworkers. They settled in the anthracite coalfield of western Pennsylvania in the Schuykill and Susquehanna valleys, and in the bituminous field of that same state, and in Ohio, Indiana, and Illinois. A Welshman, David Thomas, set up the first American hot-blast furnace in Pennsylvania in 1839.[4] The historian Bill Jones has finely described the largest Welsh settlement of all, in Scranton and Wilkes-Barre in northeast Pennsylvania.[5] But many, too, found new homes in rural America, from Utica, where the first Welsh newspaper, *Y Drych* (*The Mirror*), moved in 1860,[6] down to scattered prairie towns like New Cambria in Missouri, and Arvonia and Bala in Kansas in the 1850s, as gravestones still bear witness today.[7] By the 1850 census, there were almost 30,000 Welsh-born residents of the United States, making an impact beyond their numbers through their skills and presence within an older English-speaking migration. Many more were to follow: indeed during the years of the Civil War Welsh emigration to America increased. There were said to be 384 Welsh-language chapels in America in 1872. The 1890 census recorded the Welsh-American population as 90,000.

They were from the first politically and ideologically active, above all through the nonconformist chapels. Strong links developed between chapels in Wales and America on behalf of such themes as temperance, land tenure reform, and cutting down the privileges of the established church. The political awakening of the Welsh chapels in the 1840s made the United States ever more appealing. Radical journalists like "Gwilym Hiraethog," editor of the newspaper *Yr Amserau* (*The Times*), drew simplistic parallels between the "feudal" dominance of landlords in the Welsh countryside and the power of the plantation owners in the American South. A natural kindred transatlantic theme was the anti-slavery movement. In Wales, as in England, it had lost some impetus after the achievement of the abolition of slavery in the empire in 1833, but the progress of abolitionism in the U.S. in the 1840s gave it new life. Welsh emigrants like the family of the Rev. Benjamin Chidlaw in Ohio played their own aggressive part.[8] It was a natural transition for Lincoln to provide a spearhead for this kind of passion later on.

No novel made a greater impact on Welsh-speaking Wales than did *Uncle Tom's Cabin*. Much was made of the Welsh great-grandmother of Harriet Beecher Stowe herself. It was, of course, a huge publishing success in England with 1,500,000 copies in circulation. Less well-known is its importance in kindling political passions in Wales. It was, in fact, the first novel translated into Welsh, even ahead of Dickens himself. A version of it, much adapted and relocated to a Welsh setting, appeared in *Yr Amserau* from September 1852, around the time of its publication in England, under the title *Aelwyd f'Ewythr Robert* (*Uncle Robert's Hearth*). Published as a book in Denbigh in 1853, it had a huge and enduring impact. I read it myself as a child in Aberdyfi Sunday school in the 1940s. Several other Welsh translations followed around this time: with its strong moral tone, Stowe's work helped to weaken the resistance of Welsh nonconformists to the novel as an art form. *Uncle Tom's Cabin* appeared at a key moment in Welsh public sensibility, soon after the uproar caused by the report of the Education Commissioners in 1847 which had traduced the culture, religion, and moral standards of the Welsh, the so-called "Treason of the Blue Books."[9] All the chapels, the Calvinistic Methodists last of all, now moved into forceful political mode. This followed the pattern of similar movements in England, but the starker class division in Wales and the cultural-nationalist overtones made Welsh radicalism always distinct in nature, as the later career of David Lloyd George was to indicate.

A key figure in Wales at this time was "Gwilym Hiraethog," the Rev. William Rees, born in a remote farm on the Denbighshire moors, auto-didact, preacher-poet, crusading editor, and above all, powerful journalist whose columns "Llythyrau 'Rhen Ffarmwr" (The Old Farmer's Letters) were widely read and discussed.[10] He had a major impact in stimulating the new democratic radicalism of a part of the United Kingdom hitherto, according to another preacher-politician, Henry Richard, sunk in "feudalism," with "clansmen struggling for their chieftain." Hiraethog had strong views on most topics. He advocated universal suffrage, the vote for women, temperance, disestablishment of the Church, penal reform, and an end of landlordism; he flirted with republicanism. He is perhaps most notable in Welsh history for his strong international sense. He met and corresponded with the celebrated Italian nationalist Giuseppe Mazzini during his time in Britain and lauded the exploits of Garibaldi and Kossuth. He had strong personal links with American abolitionists, and in 1844 launched a powerful "Address to the Welsh in America," published in most Welsh-American newspapers, which condemned slavery as a sinful offense against American ideals of liberty. He masterminded the publicizing of *Uncle Tom's Cabin* in Wales. In public lectures, he became the most passionate of Lincoln's champions and inspired the movements that made him a unique Welsh hero.

Lincoln's eminence in Wales was, naturally, a product of the Civil War. The Welsh were at first uncertain about the strength of his commitment to ending slavery. But, after the Emancipation Proclamation his stature was assured. Most of the Welsh-language newspapers formed at this time—the monthlies *Dysgedydd* (1821) and *Diwygiwr* (1835, both Independent), the *Drysorfa* (Calvinistic Methodist) and *Yr Eurgrawn Wesleyaidd* (Wesleyan), the bimonthly *Seren Gomer* (Baptist), the nondenominational weekly *Herald Gymraeg* and, most important *Baner ac Amserau Cymru* the major weekly founded and edited by Thomas Gee at Denbigh in 1859—gave him full and favorable coverage. English-language newspapers were less ecstatic. From the start, Lincoln was claimed to embody Welsh values, such as social mobility, and the free ethic of the democratic-republican ideal. He exemplified the later words of the nationalistic Liberal MP Tom Ellis that "the day of the cottage-bred man has dawned." He was, more dubiously, also hailed for his devotion to religious principle. His flirting with Unitarianism and the fact that he was said not to be "technically a Christian at all" was not revealed, and indeed would have dented his image more than somewhat in relentlessly orthodox Protestant Wales.[11] Here and elsewhere, he is a classic example of what has been called "reputational entrepreneurship" where a former leader, such as Churchill, is subsequently used to strengthen communal solidarity.[12] Lincoln was not just a Welsh hero. Amongst filio-pietistic sentimentalists, it was claimed that he was actually Welsh. Through his mother, Nancy Hanks, it was believed that he could claim descent from medieval Welsh princes. His maternal grandmother was said to have come from Yspytty Ifan on the Caernarfonshire/Denbighshire border. The Scranton Welsh in 1909 referred hopefully to "our Welsh president." There were also claims that Mary Todd Lincoln was of Welsh descent, but the evidence for this appears to be speculative and is not accepted by genealogical scholars.[13]

Lincoln's standing was sustained by overwhelmingly strong Welsh support for the Union cause. This was wholly predictable. Of the 45,763 Welsh-born in the United States, over 90 percent lived in the northern states.[14] There was a strong new settlement in the new territory of Wisconsin which materially helped the Union armies. Perhaps 10,000 Welsh-born men served in the Union armies in such regiments as the 5th Wisconsin and the 56th Ohio. There were Welshmen in the 5th Wisconsin when they finally stormed the Confederate defenses at Petersburg in April 1865. Ministers like the Rev. Benjamin Chidlaw became recruiting sergeants for the Union armies. *Y Drych,* like the Welsh-American community generally, was zealous on behalf of the Union cause and fierce in its condemnation of defeatists or Copperheads. After the war was over, it sponsored *Hanes y Gwrthryfel Mawr* (*History of the Great Civil War*) in 1866, a book that set the great conflict against the background of earlier U.S. history in highly partisan terms.[15] Hardly any Welsh were to be found in the Confederate armies. One remarkable exception was John Rowlands, born in the workhouse at Denbigh, who was captured at Shiloh in 1862 and then turned his coat and fought for the Union cause instead. He seems to have no principled view and to have been little more than a mercenary. He was to follow a similar course later in life in his travel around Africa under his adopted English name, Henry Morton Stanley.[16]

A rare Welsh backer of the South was the famous radical journalist, S.R. – Samuel Roberts of Llanbrynmair in Montgomeryshire.[17] He had unwisely set up Brynffynnon, a Welsh settlement in Tennessee, as a refuge from landlord rule in Wales, in 1856. His previous views (including pacifism) had been impeccably radical. When the war began in 1861, Roberts became a stout defender of the Southern cause. Beyond his pacifism, he defended the right of the Confederate states to secede and defend themselves, and condemned Northern aggression. Worse still for S.R., his brother J.R., in his own newspaper *Y Cronicl*, kept up a stream of aggressive invective directed against the North and of insults directed against Lincoln in particular, whom he accused of unconstitutional, tyrannical rule, and of poor mental and moral qualities. Lincoln's re-election in 1864 was greeted by J.R. with a mixture of incredulity and derision.[18] His eccentric stance did his brother no favors. When S.R. returned to Wales after the Civil War, he seemed a broken man, discredited, his influence destroyed. Unwisely, a volume of his lectures and sermons published just after Appomattox included much harsher invective against Lincoln. His hostility to the Great Emancipator ruined his career. His attempted settlement in Tennessee was widely condemned as a treacherous beachhead on alien soil. By total contrast, *Y Wladfa*, the later Welsh settlement in Patagonia in 1865, inspired by the radical nationalist the Rev. Michael Daniel Jones, has always been seen as embodying the noblest of Welsh virtues.

Lincoln's reputation built up as the war took its course. At first, his apparent caution and anxiety to distance himself from the abolitionists somewhat lessened his reputation in Welsh political circles. Even at the time of his nomination in 1860, *Baner ac Amserau Cymru* had speculated whether Seward or even Sumner might not have been a more effective candidate.[19] There were three particular causes for doubt about Lincoln. The preliminary Emancipation Proclamation in September 1862 was received less than ecstatically. It was seen as a military stratagem to put pressure on the cotton plantations of the South rather than a moral gesture: as things stood, not a slave would gain his freedom in areas where Federal troops were in occupation. Lincoln, it was said, was unduly swayed by his origins as a product of a slave-holding state and his own resultant sensitivity to border states such as Delaware, Kentucky, and Missouri. Much attention focused on his response to the famous editor, Horace Greeley, that his object was to save the Union, rather than either save or destroy slavery as such.[20] Second, his use of executive power to make inroads into traditional civil liberties such as freedom of the press met with much criticism.[21] Most significantly, there was what seemed to be American aggression in the *Trent* case. Here, the taking of the Southern envoys Mason and Slidell by Wilkes's *San Jacinto* while they were traveling on the British steamer, the *Trent*, was condemned by many in Wales. The Welsh, after all, were British, and had their meed of sympathy with the jingoism of Prime Minister Palmerston.[22] Throughout the century down to 1914, the attitude of the Welsh and the Irish toward union and empire were sharply divergent. Something of a wedge appeared between the Welsh community in America and sentiment in the mother country over the *Trent* affair. In the end, Lincoln's role as a pacifying element in preventing any outbreak of war (as he did again with the depredations of the British-built *Alabama* on Northern shipping during the war) was said to redound greatly to his credit.

The coming of emancipation at the start of 1863 turned the tide. From then on, for almost all Welsh political and religious leaders, the Union cause had an unquestioned moral integrity. Newspapers like *Baner ac Amserau Cymru* and *Yr Herald Cymraeg* hailed Lincoln's wisdom and idealism in giving full effect to the process of emancipation.[23] Nonconformist ministers addressed meetings around Wales strongly supporting his unequivocal approach. All earlier reservations about the president were dispelled. His re-election as president in 1864 was almost universally hailed in the Welsh press and pulpit as a powerful blow for the ideals of liberty.[24] He was now seen as embodying, in his own person as a country lawyer of humble origins, the democratic principles which Welsh reform movements now celebrated. He symbolized the triumph of the legendary *gwerin*, the Welsh common folk. In this, Welsh radical and Liberal opinion mirrored that of England, with the huge surge in support among the Reform League and, indeed, the nascent trade unions, for Lincoln and the Union cause. In England, the popular hero the Quaker John Bright, a friend of Charles Sumner, had passionately defended Lincoln throughout.[25] His close associate in Wales, Henry Richard, who wrote powerful articles on behalf of parliamentary reform in the *Morning and Evening Star*, had as a pacifist taken a somewhat similar stand toward the war as the unpopular S. R. Henry Richard, justifying the South's right to secede but, interestingly, his reputation remained untarnished. In 1868 he was to be triumphantly returned as a radical member for Merthyr Tydfil.[26]

One feature of press coverage is the almost universal enthusiasm for Lincoln among Welsh-language newspapers. By contrast the English-language daily, the *Cambria Daily Leader*, founded in Swansea in 1861, was consistently sour. It denounced the Emancipation Proclamation in starkly reactionary terms: "Unrestricted liberty, in the hands of those who do not understand the privilege, may be found inconvenient, if not dangerous; and a legion of uneducated slaves, with a guiding intelligence little above the brute, is not the sort of thing to be let loose upon society, without proper provision being made for its reception."[27]

It was cold in its judgment on Lincoln after his assassination. He had been intolerant and oppressive toward the press. "America could probably have found a better President."[28] A similarly harsh view had been sent to a prominent Welsh landowner-politician, Sir George Cornewall Lewis of Harpton Court, Radnorshire, Home Secretary in Palmerston's Cabinet. He had been given absurdly one-sided comparisons of Jefferson Davis and his vice president, with Lincoln. The latter, Lewis was told in 1861, was "destined to great and inevitable degradation."[29] Like *The Times*', his grief at Lincoln's death was somewhat muted. This patrician detachment contrasts sharply with the anguish and sorrow of almost all the Welsh-language journals after the tragedy. A similar phenomenon may be found as in the South African War in 1899–1902 when the Welsh-language press was overwhelmingly anti-war and "pro-Boer" whereas English-language newspapers (including, again, the *Cambria Daily Leader*), whether Liberal or Conservative, were mostly imperialist and jingo.[30] No doubt the imperatives of Welsh nonconformity offer one major explanation. More generally perhaps, the rhetoric and emotional thrust of Welsh-language publication and thought seemed then, as earlier, a more natural outlet for the immemorial grievances of a marginalized small nation.

After the war, Lincoln's "martyrdom" had powerful emotional impact. The passing of "Our Lincoln" was viewed as another crucifixion.[31] The cult of Lincoln grew steadily. He became regarded as perhaps the very greatest of all American presidents, with the exception of George Washington, and venerated by the Welsh community in America. More than most immigrant groups, the Welsh in America identified totally with the values of post-bellum society; since 1856 they had voted solidly Republican, with much effect in newer Midwest states like Wisconsin and Iowa. Industrial Scranton and Wilkes-Barre, Pennsylvania, with their vigorous chapel life, local *eisteddfodau* (cultural festivals), and *cymanfaoedd canu* (singing festivals) were very epitomes of all-American Welsh republican values.[32] William Allen White, a shrewd critic of the excesses of the Gilded Age, viewed from his editorial offices in Emporia, Kansas, noted that the Welsh seemed to him very models of that sober, honest, industrious civic involvement which American democracy most needed.[33] A Welsh-American like Samuel "Golden Rule" Jones, the Mayor of Toledo, embodied this spirit as the executive instrument of progressive municipal reform.[34]

After the 1868 election, Wales moved into a long period of Liberal hegemony that lasted until the end of the First World War, when David Lloyd George was prime minister. It made an impact on the British political scene as never before. Its middle-class, mainly professional spokesman naturally revered Lincoln as an inspirational model. Not all looked immediately to him. An important Welshman like Tom Ellis, chief whip in 1894–95, a man perhaps more nationalist than Liberal, found his inspiration in the patriotic gospel preached by Mazzini and the Irish nationalist of the 1840s, Thomas Davis, rather than in movements across the Atlantic.[35] But, otherwise, Lincoln was a dominant figure. Ellis' close friend, D. R. Daniel, wrote a glowing essay on Lincoln as "the first American." The emancipation of "the American negro" he saw as "the downfall of the most accursed and degrading system of human bondage that ever dishonoured the name of a nation."[36] By the 1870s, Lincoln's portrait was hanging in many of the humbler Welsh homes, often next to another popular hero, Gladstone, "the people's William" proudly alongside "Honest Abe," for all Gladstone's illiberal and effectively pro-Southern views during the earlier part of the Civil War. There were plays about Lincoln, and eisteddfodic prizes awarded for compositions about him. He provided a subject for a drama competition in the Pontypool eisteddfod as late as 1925.[37] Lincoln became a recognized Welsh Christian name, as with the steelworkers' leader Sir Lincoln Evans, and the Cardiff politician, Sir Lincoln Hallinan. One especial enthusiast for Lincoln was William Williams, "Carw Coch" (1808–72), bard and man of letters, an Aberdare Unitarian who owned the Stag Hotel in that town and hosted *eisteddfodau* there. His passion for Lincoln knew no bounds. His hotel had a map of the United States on its wall where supporters of Lincoln would gather to discuss the latest developments in the war. Williams received a large portrait of Lincoln (allegedly from the United States), which was hung "in the most honourable place in the house." Of all devotees of the Lincoln cult, Carw Coch was the most fanatical.[38]

One exotic visitor to Welsh political life had seen the great man at closer quarters. This was Major Evan R. Jones, a Cardiganshire man elected Liberal MP for Carmarthen Boroughs in 1892.[39] He had emigrated and set up a dry goods store in Milwaukee before the war. Then he fought bravely in the 5th Wisconsin in the Army of the Potomac for four years, distinguishing himself at the battle of White Oak Swamp in 1862, the siege of Petersburg, and the battle of the Wilderness generally in 1864. He served at Gettysburg and was wounded at Spotsylvania, but later returned to front-line duties. He was made captain in February 1864 and later rose to Major. He returned to Britain as the U.S. consul in Newcastle before entering Liberal politics. Among his four books were a handbook of advice for would-be emigrants, his own war diary *Four Years in the Army of the Potomac*, and a volume of three historical sketches on Lincoln, Edwin M. Stanton, and General Ulysses Grant. Jones expresses a conventional admiration for Lincoln. His more interesting essay on Stanton, Lincoln's angular secretary of war, whom Jones regarded as unjustly neglected, paid warm tribute to his services "for the salvation of the country and the overthrow of slavery for ever." Jones's political career soon ended and he died a forgotten figure in 1920, but he was a courageous man and a link to Lincoln's heyday who deserves better of posterity.[40]

The Welsh links with Lincoln and his reputation continued to flourish. The Lincoln centenary in 1909 saw much reverent celebration of the hero, as in a long analysis in *Baner ac Amserau Cymru* in which he was hailed as a unique pioneer of human equality. It also drew the contrast between Lincoln's selfless ideals and the segregation and "lynch law" currently operating in the post-bellum South.[41] The Welsh devotion to Lincoln extended to the United States itself. There was the case of the Rev. Jenkin Lloyd Jones, a Unitarian minister who had fought in the war, published his war diary in 1913 and in his retirement founded the Abraham Lincoln Center, near Louisville, Kentucky, Lincoln's birthplace. Jones' son, Robert, was much involved in saving the famous log cabin for the nation.[42] Welsh-Americans participated in the huge commemoration in July 1913 to mark the fiftieth anniversary of Gettysburg, seen by President Wilson as part of a nationwide movement of reconciliation and harmony.[43] Whether the Welsh, however, responded so cordially to the Southerner Wilson's declaration of the effective moral equivalence of North and South in "a quarrel forgotten" is another question. For Welsh-Americans, waving the bloody shirt was a tradition not easily set aside.

By far the most important Welsh champion of Lincoln, however, was Woodrow Wilson's close wartime collaborator, the most famous Welsh politician of them all, David Lloyd George. From the very start of his career, when he read about the recently fought Civil War battles in the *Examiner* and lapped up tales of Grant, Robert E. Lee, and Stonewall Jackson, all heroes of his, Lloyd

George was Lincoln's most passionate and eloquent champion.[44] He was an ardent worshipper of great men—Gustavus Adolphus, Oliver Cromwell, and Napoleon were amongst his favorites. But Abraham Lincoln was unique, a life-long hero with qualities all his own. Years later, his secretary-mistress Frances Stevenson and his daughter Megan would become resigned to hearing yet another eulogy of the great American's qualities.[45] This passion began almost at birth, since Lincoln was venerated also by his shoemaker uncle and mentor, "Uncle Lloyd." To this day, the portrait of Lincoln may be seen on the wall of the parlor of "Highgate," the shoemaker's home in the village of Llanystumdwy where Lloyd George was brought up. It was Lincoln the democrat rather than Lincoln the emancipator that he chose to emphasize. As a small-town lawyer of limited education, who conquered the high political world through his own talents, Lincoln had obvious resemblances to "the little Welsh attorney" that could be usefully exploited. J. Hugh Edwards, an early biographer of Lloyd George's, titled his volume *From Village Green to Downing Street*, an obvious "log cabin to president" evocation of another populist leader.[46] His subject liked to refer to Lincoln as a combatant in the age-long contest between the common rights of humanity and the divine right of kings.[47] Lloyd George himself was not averse to pointing out parallels of a more personal kind. He referred to Lincoln's difficult marriage on more than one occasion, and also his alleged attraction to pretty women. He quoted Lincoln when comparing his love of women with his love of gingerbread—"I like it very much but I never get any."[48] Throughout Lloyd George always placed particular emphasis on Lincoln's humanity as a man of the people. He was "the biggest man thrown up by the United States—far bigger than Washington who was always so correct that he was uninteresting. He never did anything wrong!"[49]

If Lincoln was a background influence for Lloyd George in his career as a democratic radical before 1914, the First World War added enormously to the relevance of his career as a Liberal leader in war. This, of course, became a more powerful influence still when Lloyd George himself became leader of the nation in December 1916. He proclaimed Lincoln as a great British icon, a revered name with "its amplitude and equality of opportunity for all those who toiled and wrought intelligently." He wrote in June 1918 to the organizers of the Lincoln memorial at New Salem, Illinois: "It is perhaps only since the great world war began that people have come to realize how much Lincoln's work for the United States has meant to the cause of human freedom in all nations." Less heroically, perhaps, the check he enclosed was for just one pound.[50] Several aspects of Lincoln's greatness appear in Lloyd George's conversations and speeches at the time, and in his *War Memoirs*, and later *The Truth about the Peace Treaties* published in the 1930s. First, there is Lincoln the uncompromising defender of the Union against secession (Lloyd George could use this analogy to justify his own resistance to Irish nationalist republicanism during the "troubles" in 1921).[51] Second, Lincoln is praised as a civilian with no personal knowledge of warfare who involved himself to great effect in the running of the war. This was obviously a helpful argument for Lloyd George in justifying his own position in disputes with his generals in 1917–18. He cites Lincoln's wise judgment in removing McClellan and then Meade from command, the latter after the victory at Gettysburg, and then retaining Grant despite much criticism. In 1922, Lloyd George was to tell his aide Thomas Jones, "When Lincoln found a general in Grant he had no desire to interfere. When I found Foch I had no desire to interfere." The *Memoirs* emphasize how often Lincoln was proved right. Lloyd George's own prolonged contests with Generals Douglas Haig and William Robertson over strategic decisions on the western front are naturally brought into the account, with the implication that here was another Lincoln at the helm. Haig he later compared most unfavorably with Stonewall Jackson. His men always followed Jackson devotedly because he never gave them an impossible task. Unlike Haig at the Somme and Passchendaele, he never ordered an attack until he was convinced that the object was attainable.[52] Third, Lincoln is commended for being uncompromising in his fight for victory. His policy in adopting conscription and restrictions on civil liberties and freedom of the press were proved right, just as Lloyd George believed his own policies were in the use of the Defence of the Realm Act and in his stern treatment of dissenters. Lincoln in 1864–65, like Lloyd George in 1917–18, is seen as the symbol of unconditional surrender, doing what had to be done in a supreme crisis.[53] Finally and crucially for Lloyd George's vision of his own postwar role, Lincoln is praised as the great magnanimous reconciler, who rejected a settlement based on vengeance, but who wanted to bring the defeated South back into a more perfect union. His statesmanlike approach is contrasted with the bigoted partisanship of radical republicans, anxious to wreak vengeance on the South in 1865, the equivalent of those in 1918 who wanted a punitive peace and squeezing the defeated Germans until the pips squeaked.

There is, fascinatingly, one Lincoln whom Lloyd George does not mention. This is the Great Emancipator. Lloyd George's account conforms fully to the historian David W. Blight's "reconciliationist" view of the Civil War, seeing moral equivalence between North and South, and setting aside the ideals of racial equality and multicultural citizenship which had inspired the abolitionists prior to 1861.[54] Lloyd George's emphasis on the need for reconciliation in 1865, steering clear of ideological extremes, in effect saw the attempt to turn the war into a crusade for civic equality as misguided. Lloyd George, for all his liberalism, would not have embarked on any reconstruction of the South; he would have bound up the nation's wounds without attending to the social evils that had led to war coming about. He was a supreme democrat, but not a crusader for racial equality. He had opposed the Boer War because of the evil deeds of the men who had caused it and had some sympathy for Protestant Boer farmers, not because he aspired to an equal future for the black majority in South Africa. Indeed, the settlement of the Union of South Africa introduced by the prewar Liberal government and brought into effect in 1910, actually made the status of black people in Natal and Cape Colony far worse by dragging them down to the same level of powerlessness as those in the Boer republics of Transvaal and the Orange Free State.[55] In this, Lloyd George was thus all too typical of the politics of his time. It is a significant, if surprising, lacuna in his outlook.

Lincoln and his message hovered above the three major peacemakers at the Paris peace conference in 1919. On one memorable occasion, Lloyd George, Wilson, and Georges Clemenceau, the French premier, had a private discussion of Lincoln and his career. Wilson, a Southern Democrat who held conservative views on race issues, and Clemenceau who first went to America in 1865 shortly after Lincoln's funeral and married an American woman, had different perspectives. In their distinct ways, they all hugely admired Lincoln. But Wilson was dogmatic on race questions. He introduced segregation into the social arrangements of the White House as president, while as an academic historian he had significantly altered his historical writings on the Civil War so as not to offend southern readers. Lloyd George, as noted above, was not passionate on the issue of slavery. Perhaps, therefore, it was Georges Clemenceau, the old French "tiger" who had backed Andrew Johnson's impeachment, and not the "Anglo-Saxon" who was closest in sympathy to the old president.[56]

Lincoln was always a factor in Lloyd George's lack of confidence in, or regard for, Woodrow Wilson. A more recent personal comparison was with Theodore Roosevelt, the great exponent of the "New Nationalism" against Wilson's "New Freedom" in the famous 1912 presidential election. Lloyd George and T.R. much admired each other: they met briefly in 1910 when Roosevelt was en route to shoot lions in Africa. Roosevelt's Bismarck-style blend of social reform and a strong foreign policy was closer to Lloyd George's own vision of political leadership.[57] In *The Truth about the Peace Treaties*, Lloyd George described his own shock and anger when Wilson responded unemotionally to the news of Roosevelt's death. "I was aghast at the outburst of acrid detestation which flowed from Wilson's lips. . . . There is the story of a famous American politician who, on being asked whether he proposed to attend the funeral of a rival whom he cordially detested, replied, 'No, but I thoroughly approve of it.'"[58] But there was also the historical comparison of Wilson with Lincoln. *The Truth about the Peace Treaties'* comparison of the two is wholly in favor of Lincoln. He was "a man of genius who had the practical common sense of a son of the soil." Like many of Lloyd George's heroes, he embodied the wisdom of the common man rather than the arid learning of the scholar. Lincoln was also far more human whereas Wilson "completely lacked the human touch. The hand was too frigid. It gave you the impression that Wilson's philanthropy was purely intellectual, whereas Lincoln's came straight from the heart."[59] Lincoln was not only much the greater man, but also the more effective president. Wilson dithered about throwing all his energies into battle, whereas Lincoln never hesitated about using all legitimate methods to win the war, and showed far better judgment than his generals in so doing. By these standards, Wilson was mediocre.

Lloyd George had one great opportunity to proclaim Lincoln's qualities to the world during his premiership. He unveiled Lincoln's statue in Parliament Square in 1920. The ceremony had been preceded by a bitter argument about which statue to have, a debate in which Lloyd George took no part. The original statue by Barnard, which was thought "uncouth" and demeaning to Lincoln, was sent to Manchester instead. Augustus Saint-Gaudens' more dignified, if more conventional, sculpture was erected in Westminster. But Lloyd George's address on Lincoln, delivered in pouring rain on July 28, 1920, added nobility to the occasion. "He is one of those giant figures, of whom there are very few in history, who lose their nationality in death. They are no longer Greek or Hebrew, English or American; they belonged to mankind." These remarks were greeted with "loud and prolonged cheering." Lloyd George's rhetorical passion was never more memorably deployed.[60]

Lloyd George's love affair with Lincoln reached its climax after his premiership had come to an end. In October 1923 he paid his one visit to the New World, including a journey to Springfield, Illinois, to speak on Lincoln.[61] In a sense, Lincoln's ideals, as interpreted by Lloyd George, provided the very core of his speeches on his lengthy, 6,000-mile tour across eastern Canada and the United States. It was largely arranged by the new Welsh-American "Gorsedd," notably through a newspaper, *The Druid*, in Pittsburgh.[62] He told Frances Stevenson that it was "one triumphant procession." By any standards it was a grueling experience for a man in his sixties, and he came close to losing his voice toward the end. Mrs. Lloyd George had to deputize for him at Chicago on October 16 when her husband had a "slight fever."[63] He was greeted everywhere by huge crowds and journalists were respectful. One asked Lloyd George what it felt like to be the most famous man in the world. The reply was "it makes me very shy."

Despite meetings with eminences such as President Calvin Coolidge, Secretary of State Charles Evans Hughes (a fellow Welshman), and Charlie Chaplin, there was still plenty of time for Lloyd George's Civil War enthusiasms. He had already been given a biography of Lincoln (probably that by Nicolay and Hay) when re-entering the United States at Niagara Falls. He later visited Gettysburg on October 27, Chancellorsville the next day (when he spoke about Stonewall Jackson who met his death there), and Richmond to see the site of the Seven Days Battle and meet some Confederate veterans.[64] But the highlight, and fulcrum of the entire tour, was the focus on Abraham Lincoln. He went to see Lincoln's birthplace in Kentucky, walked around the log cabin several times, and knelt to drink at a nearby stream. It was, he declared, "a glorious day." He then visited Lincoln's home in Springfield and saw his tomb. Here he laid a wreath with the inscription, "A humble and reverent homage to one of the world's greatest men." He also met Abraham Lincoln's elderly son, Robert, "a man fragile and worn with a faint resemblance to his father."[65] He had had a notable career himself, serving as minister to England during the presidency of Benjamin Harrison in 1889–93. Lloyd George's daughter, Megan, who accompanied him, wrote how "Father was overcome with joy to meet the son of the man he has always hero worshipped." He was greatly moved by discussing his father's personal qualities with Robert and told him how a civil war was far more harrowing than even his own wartime experiences.[66]

Then at Springfield, Illinois, on October 18, Lloyd George spoke movingly, under the modest auspices of the Mid-day Luncheon Club there, about Lincoln's ageless qualities. "He was one of those rare men whom you do not associate with any particular creed, or party . . . not even with any country, for he belongs to mankind in every race, in every clime and in every age." Lincoln was a great man of all time for all parties, for all lands. He was the choice and champion of a party, but "his lofty soul could see over and beyond party walls the unlimited terrain beyond." He was "misrepresented, misunderstood, maligned, derided, thwarted in every good impulse, thought or deed." But he triumphed in the end. He was "the finest product in the realm of statesmanship of the Christian civilization, and the wise counsel he gave his own people in the day of their triumph he gives today to the people of Europe in the hour of their victory over the forces that menace their liberties."[67]

Lincoln, in Lloyd George's view, had a vivid message for the present time. Lincoln stood, he argued, for two great principles. One was "clemency in the hour of triumph." Lincoln's doctrine was "Reconcile the vanquished." The second was "Trust the Common People." He believed in their sincerity, their common sense, their inherent belief in justice. Thus the two great conclusions that Lloyd George drew from the Great War he linked to Lincoln's ideas— reconciliation and reconstruction of a shattered continent, and faith in democracy. A time would come "when the principles of Abraham Lincoln will have to be fought for again."[68] One stated implication was that the United States should modify its isolationist stance toward Europe to help give them effect. At the Biltmore hotel in New York, in his final speech on November 1, he drove the point home. Lincoln in 1865 had called for reconciliation, in opposition to "vindictive men after the war who wanted to trample on the defeated South." This was "the Lincoln touch, a policy of conciliation not of vengeance." He urged moderation in dealing with reparations and German frontiers, refraining from imposing humiliating terms, working for European reconstruction.[69] Lincoln's approach was the very converse of the belligerent French prime minister, Raymond Poincaré, currently sending in troops to occupy the Ruhr.[70] The Lincoln touch, therefore, magnanimity in the hour of victory, was precisely the answer to mankind's problems at the present time. In a series of well-publicized (and very well paid) newspaper articles, Lloyd George, the champion of reconciliation and a fundamental revision of the peace treaties in a way that finally commanded the approval of John Maynard Keynes, underlined Lincoln's message. His American visit was to be long remembered and would later be recalled by Franklin Roosevelt and John F. Kennedy.

Lloyd George's passionate evocation of Lincoln and his ideals, however, was perhaps the final chapter in this story. Lincoln's fame in Wales really amounted to a cult status among the Liberal nonconformist forces which had dominated the nation since the 1868 election. The Welsh working class, which emerged as increasingly powerful in the Labour Party after 1918, never shared the same passion. They did not respond to the views of the early German Social Democrats who saw Lincoln, as Marx had done, as a kind of working-class hero.[71] The Left in Wales, as elsewhere in Britain, increasingly saw in America not the last, best hope of democracy but the linchpin of capitalism. Aneurin Bevan, left-wing socialist and founder of the great National Health Service, illustrates this precisely: Lincoln never featured in his oratory. I noted this when writing on Bevan's biographer, Michael Foot. His father, Isaac Foot, a Liberal MP, regarded Lincoln as supreme among statesmen and among human beings. In a lecture before the Royal Society of Literature in London in April 1944, he compared Lincoln with Oliver Cromwell as a colossus in both peace and war—and for Isaac, founding father of the Cromwell Association, there could no higher standard of comparison.[72] Isaac Foot was not only a huge admirer of Lincoln but also of the United States, partly nurtured by his strong sense of the history of his native Plymouth, whence the Pilgrim fathers had famously set sail to the New World. His socialist son, Michael, by contrast, for all his devoted loyalty to his father, had no especial regard for Lincoln whom he saw as a conservative figure. His American heroes were Thomas Jefferson, friend of Tom Paine and enlightened architect of revolution, and the novelist, Ernest Hemingway.[73] In a similar vein, the black American singer, Paul Robeson, became a cult figure among the Welsh miners, especially after taking part in the radical film *Proud Valley* (1939) about the Welsh mining valleys. He sang in Ebbw Vale, Bevan's constituency, during the *eisteddfod* in 1958.[74] But his fame there may have been because of his Marxist socialism rather than his symbolizing emancipation. So the new era of Labour dominance in Welsh political and social life from the 1920s saw Lincoln retreat from center stage, perhaps only re-emerging during commemoration of the abolition of the slave trade in the bicentenary year of 2007.

Still, it is right that Wales should be represented here. Modern Welsh politics from the 1860s differed in substance and style from those of England. There was, therefore, a distinctive perspective on Lincoln. He towered over the Welsh democracy in its most formative period. The Welsh, like free citizens the world over, could claim him as one of their own, and many of us still do.

Notes

I am much indebted to the research assistance of Mr. Rhodri Glyn, Aberystwyth, and to John Graham Jones of the National Library for advice on sources.

1. Kenneth O. Morgan, "Liberals, Nationalists and Mr. Gladstone" in *Modern Wales: Politics, Places and People* (Cardiff: University of Wales Press, 1995), 322–38.

2. Jerry Hunter, *Sons of Arthur, Children of Lincoln: Welsh Writing from the American Civil War* (Cardiff: University of Wales Press, 2007), 484 ff.

3. See Gwyn A. Williams, *The Search for Beulah Land* (Oxford: Croom Helm, 1980).

4. Rowland T. Berthoff, *British Immigrants in Industrial America* (Cambridge, MA: Harvard University Press, 1954), 62ff.

5. William D. Jones, *The Welsh in America: Scranton and the Welsh, 1860–1920* (Cardiff: University of Wales Press, 1993).

6. For *Y Drych*, see Aled Jones and Bill Jones, *Welsh Reflections: Y Drych and America 1851–2001* (Cardiff: University of Wales Press, 2001).

7. The author confirmed this while exploring cemeteries in Emporia, Kansas, in 1999.

8. Chidlaw served as chaplain to the 39th Ohio. See his autobiography, *The Story of My Life* (Philadelphia, 1890).

9. See Prys Morgan, *Brad y Llyfrau Gleision* (Llandysul: Gwasg Gomer, 1991).

10. His biography, T. Roberts and D. Roberts, *Cofiant y Parch. William Rees* (Dolgellau: W. Hughes, 1893) is useless on these matters. There is an excellent discussion of Robert Everett and other Welsh anti-slavery figures in Jerry Hunter, *Sons of Arthur, Children of Lincoln*, 49ff. I am greatly indebted to Dr. Hunter for advice in this area.

11. Richard J. Carwardine, *Lincoln* (Harlow: Pearson, 2003), 35ff. This description comes from Mary Todd Lincoln.

12. Richard Toye, "The Churchill Syndrome: Reputation, Entrepreneurship and the Rhetoric of Foreign Policy since 1945," *British Journal of Politics and International Relations* 10:3 (August 2008), 364–78.

13. See William E. Barton, *The Lineage of Abraham Lincoln* (New York: Bobbs-Merrill, 1929). I am grateful for information from Mr. Tom Schwarz and Professor Richard Carwardine here. Also cf. letters of Thomas Jones (National Library of Wales, Aberystwyth, MS 11004C) on Lincoln's alleged Welsh ancestry. More precisely linked Welsh-American presidents are Thomas Jefferson (who seems to have read Welsh) and alas! Richard Nixon.

14. Alan Conway, *The Welsh in America* (Cardiff: University of Wales Press, 1961), 283–89.

15. Hunter, *Sons of Arthur, Children of Lincoln*, 24–25.

16. See Dorothy Stanley, ed., *The Autobiography of Sir Henry Morton Stanley* (London: Sampson Low, Morton, 1909), for a veiled account.

17. See Glanmor Williams, *Samuel Roberts, Llanbrynmair* (Cardiff: University of Wales Press, 1950).

18. *Y Cronicl* (1863), 78–86, (1865), 27, 168.

19. *Baner ac Amserau Cymru*, November 28, 1860.

20. Ibid., September 17, 15 October 1862.

21. *Y Dysgedydd*, 43 (1864), 341; *Y Traethodydd*, 20 (1865), 478 ff.

22. Robert Huw Griffith, "The Welsh and the American Civil War, c. 1840–1865" (University of Wales unpublished Ph.D. thesis, 2004), 143ff; Dean B. Mahin, *One War at a*

Time: The International Dimensions of the American Civil War (Washington, DC: Brassey's, 1999), 58ff.

23. *Baner ac Amserau Cymru*, January 21, 1863; *Yr Herald Cymraeg*, October 11, 18, 1862.

24. *Baner ac Amserau Cymru*, December 7, 1864.

25. James G. Randall, *Lincoln. The Liberal Statesman* (New York: Dodd Mead, 1947), 135–50, indicates the way in which the image of Lincoln, as interpreted by Bright, helped promote the cause of parliamentary democracy in Britain during the 1860s.

26. His biography by C. S. Miall (1889) omitted any discussion of Richard's views on the Civil War.

27. *Cambria Daily Leader*, October 7, 1862.

28. Ibid., April 27, 1865.

29. Sir Edmund Walker Head to Sir George Cornewall Lewis, February 24, 1861, March 25, 1861, National Library of Wales, Aberystwyth, C1555, 1556.

30. Kenneth O. Morgan, "Wales and the Boer War," *Modern Wales*, 46–58.

31. Hunter, *Sons of Arthur, Children of Lincoln*, 474ff.

32. Jones, *The Welsh in America*, chaps. III and IV.

33. Walter Johnson, *William Allen White's America* (New York: Henry Holt, 1947), 235.

34. For Samuel Milton ("Golden Rule") Jones see Russell B. Nye, *Midwestern Progressive Politics* (Ann Arbor: University of Michigan Press, 1959), 175–78. Jones, a Christian socialist, was a brilliant mayor of Toledo after 1897. He was born in Caernarfonshire and it is curious that he is always ignored among the accounts of the American Welsh.

35. See Neville Masterman, *The Forerunner* (Llandybie: Christopher Davies, 1972).

36. "Essay on the First American," D. R. Daniel Papers, National Library of Wales, 591.

37. *Y Dysgedydd*, 104 (1925), 160.

38. See his entry in the *Dictionary of Welsh Biography* (Oxford, 1959), 1083. "Carw Coch" is the Welsh for stag.

39. For a sketch of him, see T. Marchant Williams, *The Welsh Members of Parliament* (Cardiff: Daniel Owen, 1894), 17–18.

40. E. R. Jones, *Lincoln, Stanton and Grant: Historical Sketches* (Frederick Warne, 1875), 130ff. Jones was a poor parliamentarian and had a serious drinking problem: Lloyd George wrote derisively of him as "the little major." Cf. Kenneth O. Morgan, ed., *Lloyd George: Family Letters, c. 1885–1936* (Oxford: Oxford University Press and Cardiff: University of Wales Press, 1973), 69–73. Unfortunately for Jones, while a link with America might have been popular in 1892, by the time of the next general election in 1895, the United States was associated with the catastrophic effects of the McKinley Tariff on the local tinplate industry. "The curse of McKinley" was fatal not least because McKinley was a Republican, the party which Jones had supported. He lost his seat to a Liberal Unionist, a local tinplate employer, in 1895, and his brief political career was over. On this election, see Kenneth O. Morgan, *Wales in British Politics 1868–1922* (Cardiff: University of Wales Press, 1963), 159.

41. *Baner ac Amserau Cymru*, February 17, 1909.

42. Merrill D. Peterson, *Lincoln in American Memory* (New York: Oxford University Press, 1994), 178–80.

43. David W. Blight, *Race and Reunion: the Civil War in American Memory* (Cambridge, MA: Harvard University Press, 2001), 11 ff.

44. W. R. P. George, *The Making of Lloyd George* (London: Faber, 1976), 179–80.

45. For example, A. J. P. Taylor, ed., *Lloyd George: A Diary by Frances Stevenson* (London: Hutchinson, 1971), 252 (entry of February 12, 1934).

46. J. Hugh Edwards, *From Village Green to Downing Street* (London: Newnes, 1908). The same author's *David Lloyd George*, 2 vols. (London: Waverley, 1929), 1:45–49 explicitly compares the two leaders and their humble backgrounds.

47. Edwards, *David Lloyd George*, 1:393.

48. Colin Cross, ed., *A.J. Sylvester, Life with Lloyd George* (London: Macmillan, 1975), 82–83 (entry of November 10, 1932).

49. Lord Riddell, *Intimate Diary of the Peace Conference and After* (London: Gollancz, 1933), 226.

50. David Lloyd George, *War Memoirs*, 2 vols. (London: Odhams, 1938 ed.), 1:999; Lloyd George to Thomas P. Reep, June 22, 1918, Abraham Lincoln Presidential Library; *Petersburg Observer*, July 19, 1918. I am much indebted to Professor Richard Carwardine on this matter.

51. Keith Middlemas, ed., *Thomas Jones. Whitehall Diary*, 3 vols. (Oxford: Oxford University Press, 1969–71), 3:60 (entry of April 27, 1921).

52. Middlemas, ed., *Thomas Jones. Whitehall Diary*, 1:203 (entry of June 13, 1922); Lloyd George, *War Memoirs*, 2:2014–15.

53. Lloyd George, *War Memoirs*, 1:232–33.

54. Blight, *Race and Reunion*.

55. Kenneth O. Morgan, *Keir Hardie* (London: Weidenfeld and Nicolson, 1975), 198. Hardie was one of the very few to criticize the Union of South Africa bill.

56. Peterson, *Lincoln in American Memory*, 199.

57. See Morgan, ed., *Lloyd George Family Letters*, 164 (Lloyd George to Mrs. Lloyd George, October 16, 1912).

58. David Lloyd George, *The Truth about the Peace Treaties*, 2 vols. (London: Gollancz, 1938), 1:232.

59. Lloyd George, *War Memoirs*, 1:233.

60. *The Times*, July 29, 1920; F. Lauriston Bullard, *Lincoln in Marble and Bronze* (New Brunswick, NJ: Rutgers University Press, 1952), 85; National Archives, WORK 20/106 for government correspondence on the statue.

61. There is a file on this visit in the Lloyd George of Dwyfor Papers, Parliamentary Archives, House of Lords, Box G/165.

62. Jones, *The Welsh in America*, 184ff; *The Druid*, October 15, 1923 (Lloyd George Papers, G/259).

63. *The Times*, October 17, 1923; Lloyd George to Frances Stevenson, October 22, 1923, in A. J. P. Taylor, ed., *My Darling Pussy* (London: Weidenfeld and Nicolson, 1975), 72.

64. Lloyd George Papers, Box G/165.

65. *The Times*, October 31, 1923.

66. Notes by Megan Lloyd George, National Library of Wales, MS 23265D, 93.

67. Text of speech in Lloyd George Papers. Box G/165.

68. Ibid.

69. *The Times*, November 3, 1923.

70. Ibid. Philip Kerr had urged Lloyd George not to be too abusive about France in his speeches (Kerr to Lloyd George, September 1, 1923, Lloyd George Papers, Box G/259).

71. "A Humanitarian as broad as the World: Abraham Lincoln's legacy in International Context," *German Historical Institute Bulletin* 42 (Spring 2008), 135.

72. Isaac Foot, *Oliver Cromwell and Abraham Lincoln* (London: Royal Society of Literature, 1944), inscribed copy in the author's possession.

73. Conversations with Michael Foot, 2002 onwards.

74. David Berry, *Wales and Cinema: The First Hundred Years* (Cardiff: University of Wales Press, 1995), 166–70. Robeson had first come into contact with the Welsh miners when singing in Wales to raise money for the Popular Front government in Spain: see Hywel Francis, *Miners against Fascism. Wales and the Spanish Civil War* (London: Lawrence and Wishart, 1984), 249. The Bevan Foundation takes a close interest in the Paul Robeson archive trust.

9

"Freedom and Unity"

LINCOLN IN IRISH POLITICAL DISCOURSE

Kevin Kenny

"Lincoln, more than any other American, and more than most great men of any country," the *Irish Times* remarked on July 29, 1920, "is an international character." The occasion was the unveiling of a statue of the American president in Westminster, a copy of the magnificent original in Chicago by the Irish-born sculptor August St.-Gaudens. David Lloyd George, who accepted the statue on behalf of the British government, was a well-known admirer of Abraham Lincoln. Éamon de Valera, Lloyd George's great antagonist in the struggle for Irish independence, admired Lincoln with equal fervor, but for quite different reasons. Whereas the British prime minister celebrated Lincoln as a great wartime executive who had preserved freedom by prevailing over the forces of reaction, de Valera admired him primarily for preventing the permanent partition of the United States. Lloyd George invoked Lincoln to defend the Union of Britain and Ireland but de Valera did so in an effort to destroy that union and replace it with a united Ireland whose legitimacy, he believed, transcended all attempts to limit national sovereignty.[1]

Lincoln's posthumous image took shape in Ireland in a context defined by Union, a constitutional arrangement that existed in varying forms on both sides of the English-speaking Atlantic world. Lincoln's purpose when he went to war was to preserve the Union of the American states. Ireland too was part of a Union; the entire island between 1801 and 1921, and six northern counties thereafter, belonged to a United Kingdom that included England, Scotland, and Wales. Some Irishmen were prepared to fight to maintain the British-Irish Union, which they regarded as the foundation of their identity, while others gave up their lives in an effort to destroy it. Irish Unionists cited Lincoln in their effort to preserve the United Kingdom, denying that Irish nationalists had the right to local autonomy, let alone independence. Irish nationalists, by contrast, turned to Lincoln to justify their belief in a free and united Ireland from which Protestant Ulster would have no right to secede. Most nationalists regarded the Union as artificial and coerced. The dominant, moderate faction called for legislative autonomy, or Home Rule, under the crown and within the empire. A radical republican minority, including de Valera, wanted a full-fledged united Irish republic, achieved through force of arms if necessary. All sides to the "Irish Question"—from British government officials and Unionists to moderate nationalists and hard-line republicans—found occasion to invoke Abraham Lincoln, demonstrating that utility rather than consistency is the hallmark of politically effective historical memory. The Irish image of Lincoln can be judged in part against the documented record of the president's life, but its full significance lies in what it tells us about the political history of modern Ireland.

Modern Irish political history featured variations on some fundamental questions that preoccupied Lincoln throughout his career. These included the nature of national sovereignty, the idea of Union, the legitimacy of secession, the qualities of political leadership during times of crisis, and the brutal realities of civil war. Noticeably absent from this list was slavery. Irish contemporaries did pay tribute to Lincoln in 1865 for freeing the slaves but, while subsequent leaders, including de Valera, sometimes associated national liberation with emancipation in this sense, the link was always tenuous, even on a rhetorical level. Lincoln freed the slaves in order to keep a nation free, not to liberate a nation from colonial rule. Much more important than slavery in determining the Irish image of Lincoln were questions concerning national freedom and unity, partition, and civil war, especially in the period of political upheaval that began in the 1880s and subsided in the 1920s.

I

In Ireland, as in many other countries, Lincoln's assassination was met with an extraordinary outpouring of grief. "The feeling with which the intelligence was received when the first vague sense of incredulity had passed away was one of overpowering sorrow," the Dublin *Daily Express* noted on April 29, 1865. "It was as though there were some great danger impending, some great personal bereavement to be endured, some vague and indefeasible horror to be undergone." The municipal councils of Dublin, Belfast, Cork, Limerick, Galway, Sligo, and other Irish towns and cities gathered to pass resolutions expressing their sympathy with the American people. So too did the Wesleyan ministers of the Dublin district, the ministers of the Northern Presbytery of Co. Antrim, the Grand Lodge of Irish Freemasons, and "a meeting of the democratic classes of Dublin, held in the Mechanics' Institute."[2]

As well as expressing sorrow, sympathy, and indignation, Irish people of many backgrounds responded to Lincoln's assassination by emphasizing the enduring power of American republican democracy. "The loss of the President of the United States is great," the *Ulster Observer* explained, "but the

Constitution can repair it." Republics were "free from the perils" besetting countries where "power is centred in an individual or a dynasty." The Dublin *Daily Express*, likewise, suggested that if the emperor of France were assassinated there would be a revolution and a change of dynasty, whereas the United States would survive Lincoln's death by electing a new president from among the people. "In the one case," the *Express* explained, "the nation is the creature of the man, in the other the man was the creature of the nation." According to the meeting at the Mechanics' Institute, the assassination would "have no other effect than to hasten the completion of Lincoln's glorious work, the restoration of the Union, the extinction of slavery, and the establishment of a solid and durable peace." Lincoln might be gone, the *Ulster Observer* noted, but his life had been "long enough for its purpose." He had accomplished his goals—preserving the Union and eliminating slavery—before his untimely death. And his victory was now secure.[3]

Comparisons between the American and the British-Irish unions first came to the fore during the Home Rule crisis of the 1880s. Invariably they were designed to defend the United Kingdom and the British Empire against the perceived threat of Irish nationalism, with Abraham Lincoln cast in the role of savior of the Union. These comparisons were often somewhat strained, given that the American Union was federal in structure and the British-Irish Union was a centralized unitary state. The American states, moreover, had joined their Union voluntarily, while most Irish nationalists believed that Ireland had not. Supporters of Home Rule insisted that modifying the Union by giving legislative autonomy to Ireland posed no threat to British or imperial unity: the Irish would manage domestic affairs, but Westminster would continue to control finance, taxation, and defense. Their Unionist opponents, who included an influential segment of the British and Irish ruling classes, saw Home Rule as a direct threat to the Union and the empire. In their decades-long campaign to prevent Irish autonomy, and later independence, the Unionists turned repeatedly to Abraham Lincoln and the American Civil War.[4]

Analogies between the United Kingdom and Lincoln's United States emerged forcefully in 1886 when Prime Minister William Gladstone declared his support for Irish Home Rule. Pointing to Gladstone's initial support for the Confederacy, his critics argued that Irish autonomy would be a precursor to secession. The prime minister's foremost opponent within the Liberal Party, Joseph Chamberlain, declared in the House of Commons that Gladstone had once "counselled the disintegration of the United States" and predicted that the inevitable outcome of Home Rule would be separation, followed by a civil war within the United Kingdom. "I say to Ireland what the Liberals or Republicans of the North said to the Southern States of America," Chamberlain announced. "The Union Must be preserved." This was the principle Lincoln had stood for above all else. Convinced that Ireland's geographical and strategic proximity to England ruled out any possibility of Home Rule, Chamberlain and his followers justified their position by insisting that the Irish were unfit for self-rule. As the Liberal Unionist Goldwin Smith put it in a letter to an American friend in 1886, "You fought for your Union against Slavery; we are fighting for ours against Savagery and Superstition."[5]

As positions hardened on Irish Home Rule in the coming decades, the American Union became a flexible metaphor for the British Union, despite the differences between the two, and Lincoln's actions during the Civil War became a potential model for preserving the United Kingdom against the threat of Irish nationalism. Celebrating Lincoln's centenary in 1909, the leading southern Irish Unionist newspaper, the *Irish Times*, quoted the London *Times* that "maintenance of the Union" was his "governing passion." He was determined to maintain it "by peace if that were any way possible; but, if not, then by war, which he abhorred, and which wrung every fibre of a gentle and compassionate nature." Clearly, the Union that both newspapers had in mind was not just the American one that Lincoln had saved but also, by extension, the United Kingdom of Great Britain and Ireland. From this perspective, Irish nationalists had no right to dictate terms to Protestant Ulster, which belonged to an indissoluble British Union.[6]

When another, more protracted Home Rule crisis began in 1910, enduring for more than a decade, the image of Abraham Lincoln began to assume its most prominent form in Irish history. On December 26 the *Irish Times* enthusiastically endorsed "An Appeal to Ulster" recently published in the *Spectator* magazine. Seeking to counter republican nationalist claims that Ireland was "an indivisible unit, and cannot in any circumstances be separated," the "Appeal" had quoted a well-known passage from Lincoln. By what right, Lincoln had demanded to know, did a state presume to "to rule all which is *less* than itself, and ruin all which is larger than itself." What "mysterious right to play a tyrant is conferred on a district of a country," he asked, "by merely calling it a State"? These questions, according to the *Irish Times*, "contain Ulster's case in a nutshell." An Irish Home Rule state, the newspaper predicted, would seek on the one hand to absorb the smaller entity of Ulster and, on the other hand, to disrupt the larger entity of which it was but one integral part, the United Kingdom.[7]

Ronald McNeill, the Unionist MP for East Kent, cited Lincoln's example along similar lines at a "Magnificent Dublin Meeting" in the Theatre Royal on November 28, 1913. McNeill attacked Prime Minister Herbert Asquith for insisting that further refusal to grant autonomy to Ireland, after so many "General Election majorities in Ireland in favor of Home Rule," would be a negation of democratic government. Turning to Lincoln and the American Civil War to refute the idea that a given region within a Union could leave of its own volition, McNeill declared that this "was not the opinion of one of the greatest democratic statesmen that ever lived, and it was not the opinion of the greatest democratic nation that ever existed. It was not the opinion of Abraham

Lincoln, and it was not the opinion of the people of America." Lincoln had been prepared "to fight to the last in the greatest civil war the world has ever known rather than concede the demand put forward" by a large and unanimous minority of his countrymen. He was "willing, rather than to allow secession or disunion, to face civil war." Asquith, by contrast, was "willing to run the risk of civil war in our country not to prevent disunion, but to force it upon those who do not want it."[8]

Questioning the analogies between Anglo-Irish and American history increasingly in vogue among his fellow Unionists, McNeill contrasted the position of Lincoln as president of the United States with that of the Ulster Unionist leader a half century later, who, in defending the United Kingdom against Irish nationalists and their appeasers in the British government, stood at the head of a loyal but extra-legal movement. The latter, he noted, must always be "confronted by certain difficulties from which Abraham Lincoln was free." Like Lincoln, the Unionist leader was prepared to use force to counter the threat of secession. But Lincoln had the law "at his back," whereas Unionists were "called upon to resist technically legal authority"—i.e., British law—in the name of the higher good of preserving the United Kingdom. In this respect, McNeill believed that the Ulster "rebellion" was historically unique, for it "had in it no subversive element" and was the first rebellion intended "to maintain the status quo." The Ulster "rebellion," McNeill continued, was based on "resistance to the transfer of a people's allegiance without their consent; to their forcible expulsion from a Constitution with which they were content and their forcible inclusion in a Constitution which they detested." Thus, "whereas Lincoln took up arms to resist secession," Ulster Unionists did so "to resist expulsion." Critically, however, the purpose in both cases was to "preserve union."[9]

II

On December 23, 1920 the British Parliament passed the Government of Ireland Act, establishing two separate Irish parliaments, one for six heavily Protestant counties in Ulster and the other for the remaining twenty-six counties on the island. Ulster Unionists, who had initially resisted Home Rule in any form, accepted their own locally autonomous legislature as a counterweight to the body that was supposed to meet in Dublin. The Parliament of Northern Ireland duly came into being in June 1921, but the representatives elected in the other twenty-six counties constituted themselves, not as an autonomous legislature within the United Kingdom, but as the second Dáil Éireann—successor to the sovereign but unrecognized parliament of the Irish republic declared by armed force during the Easter 1916 rebellion and democratically elected in 1918. Home Rule came too late for Southern Ireland; by the time it was offered the self-constituted Irish republic, presided over by Éamon de Valera, was engaged in a guerilla war against Britain to secure its independence. During the critical period of violence, negotiation, and political definition between 1916 and 1923, with de Valera and Lloyd George as the dominant figures on the Anglo-Irish stage, Abraham Lincoln loomed larger than ever before or since in Irish history.

When either de Valera or Lloyd George talked about Lincoln, he was inevitably talking to a large extent about himself. At Westminster in July 1920 the British prime minister had listed Lincoln's chief characteristics as courage, fortitude, patience, humanity, and clemency. "Resolute in war, he was moderate in victory," the prime minister declared. "Misrepresented, misunderstood, underestimated, he was patient to the last." De Valera, for his part, reflecting in 1933 on the political carnage in Ireland a decade earlier, praised in Lincoln not only "the love of truth which through all the vicissitudes of life inspired him" but also "the confidence in the ultimate triumph of right which upheld him in the darkest years of the Civil War." Born in New York City in 1882, de Valera made a crucial visit to the United States as head of the de facto Irish republic in 1919–20 and always identified closely with the American political tradition. According to an American secret service agent who visited him when he was serving as Taoiseach (Irish prime minister) during World War II, "a large reproduction of the Lincoln Memorial statue of Lincoln and framed reproductions of the Declaration of Independence dominate[d] the reception room next to his office." De Valera also reportedly kept a bust of Lincoln on his desk.[10]

In July 1921, when the British offered Southern Ireland the status of a self-governing dominion subject to external control over Irish defense, trade, and finance, de Valera rejected the offer in a manner that turned Lloyd George's understanding of Lincoln on its head. Under de Valera's idea of "external association," an independent Ireland might associate with the British Commonwealth, but only on a strictly voluntary basis. Citing Lincoln, Lloyd George insisted that no British government could acknowledge Ireland's right "to secede from her allegiance to the King." De Valera, however, had a strong counter-argument: Ireland, he insisted, had no such allegiance to yield. "We are not claiming any right to secede," the Irish leader declared on August 17, 1921, " . . . there never can be in the case of Ireland a question of secession because there never has been a union."[11]

The Dublin *Freeman's Journal*, though traditionally more moderate than de Valera and the republicans, made a similar argument. "Mr. Lloyd George reiterates the analogy he has so frequently drawn between Ireland and the Southern States of America during the Civil War," the newspaper noted. But Ireland had never agreed to a union with Great Britain: the union was imposed, not chosen, and hence it was invalid. There could be "no question of secession from a position never occupied." The Confederate states, by contrast, had "voluntarily accepted and acquiesced in the Union of the American States" and hence "the word 'secession' may rightly be applied to their case." Like Lincoln and the *Freeman's Journal*, de Valera saw secession as constitutionally impossible; but while the American president used this argument to preserve one political Union, Irish republicans used it not only to support their belief in an eternally united Ireland but also to hasten the demise of another Union, that between Ireland and Great Britain, which they regarded as a fictive entity. It followed that the true secessionists in the Irish case, as the *Freeman's Journal* noted, were not the Irish nationalists but the Unionist residents of North-East Ulster who wished "to secede from the Irish nation." They had no more right to do so than American Southerners had in 1861.[12]

Responding to de Valera that his government was "profoundly disappointed" by this characterization of the British-Irish Union, Lloyd George quoted Lincoln's first inaugural address to support his case. "I cannot better express the British standpoint in this respect," he wrote on August 26, 1921, "than in the words used of the Northern and Southern States by Abraham Lincoln in the first inaugural address. They were spoken by him on the brink of the American Civil War, which he was striving to avert." "Physically speaking," Lincoln had told the South, "we cannot separate. We cannot remove our respective sections from each other, nor build an impassable wall between them." Lincoln warned Southerners that "you cannot fight always; and when, after much loss on both sides, and no gain on either, you cease fighting, the identical old questions, as to terms of intercourse, are again upon you." It could not "be reasonably contended," Lloyd George insisted, "that the relations of Great Britain and Ireland are in any different case." Britain would "discuss no settlement which involves a refusal on the part of Ireland to accept our invitation to free, equal, and loyal partnership in the British Commonwealth, under one Sovereign." Exchanging diplomatic notes was no longer sufficient, Lloyd George warned. Immediate progress was necessary if the truce was to be maintained; otherwise, like Lincoln in 1861, he would unleash war on the secessionists.[13]

III

When representatives of the Irish and British governments signed the Articles of Agreement for a Treaty on December 6, 1921, the nationalist government in Ireland split. The Treaty gave Southern Ireland the equivalent of self-governing dominion status within the Commonwealth but it required members of the Irish parliament to swear an oath of allegiance not just to the Irish Free State but also to the British monarch and it endorsed the partition of Ireland (while making vague provisions for a Boundary Commission to review the borders between the two Irish states). Although many seasoned republicans, including

Michael Collins, urged that the Treaty be accepted on pragmatic grounds, de Valera balked at the requirement that Irish elected officials swear an oath of allegiance to the British crown. He continued to insist, first, that Ireland would associate with the Commonwealth only on a voluntary basis, as a sovereign independent state, and second, that no part of Ireland could exclude itself from the national territory. When Dáil Éireann met to vote on the Treaty in the first week of January 1922, de Valera quoted from the Gettysburg Address in clarifying his position. "Now, I stand here as one who believes in ordered government," the president of the Irish Republic began. "I believe fundamentally in the right of the Irish people to govern themselves. I believe fundamentally in government of the people by the people and, if I may add the other part, for the people. That is my fundamental creed."[14]

Supporters of the Treaty sharply criticized the limitations of de Valera's democratic creed, quoting Lincoln in an impassioned defense of the Treaty and the principle of democratic majority rule. "If representative government is going to remain on the earth, then a representative must voice the opinion of his constituents," the founder of Sinn Féin, Arthur Griffith, declared in the Dáil, "if his conscience will not let him do that he has only one way out and that is to resign and refuse to misrepresent them." For a T.D. (member of the Dáil) to vote against the Treaty when his constituents supported it, Griffith insisted, "is the negation of all democratic right; it is the negation of all freedom." Tactics of this sort, he warned, would kill Irish democracy at birth. When de Valera visited America in 1919–20, Griffith continued, he had "honoured the memory of Abraham Lincoln; and Abraham Lincoln was one of the greatest men of the last century—he was one of the men who upheld the rights of the people—and Abraham Lincoln's words are words I recommend to you now." During an election campaign in 1836, Griffith explained, Lincoln had promised, "If elected, I shall consider the whole people of Sagamon [sic] my constituents, as well as those who oppose me as those who support me. While acting as their representative I shall be governed by their will on all such subjects on which I have the means of knowing what that will is." Irish T.D.s ought to adopt the same principle, Griffith concluded, and if they did so, none could "go down to his constituency and stand on a platform before his people and say he is against this Treaty." But Griffith dodged the question of what a T.D.'s democratic duty would be in a constituency where most voters opposed the Treaty.[15]

Griffith's overall point that majority rule was essential to the functioning of democracy, though not entirely persuasive in its formulation, came close to the heart of Lincoln's political vision. As early as 1861 Lincoln told his secretary, John Hay, that "the central idea" in the Civil War was to prove "that popular government is not an absurdity." Americans must settle the question "whether in a free government the minority have the right to break up the government whenever they choose. If we fail it will go far to prove the incapability of the people to govern themselves." Griffith made the same point in May 1922, with Ireland on the brink of civil war. There was "nothing more insolent in the history of this country, or in the history of modern civilization," he declared, "than the claim that any body of men, or any minority of this country, should tell the Irish people that they have no right to decide upon an issue which affects their whole future and affects the destiny of the country."[16]

Among the most uncompromising voices on the republican side was Mary MacSwiney, whose brother, Terence MacSwiney, had recently died on a hunger strike. MacSwiney conjured up quite a different Abraham Lincoln from Griffith's version in her argument against the voices of compromise. "We stand for the preservation of the existing Republic, which exists in consequence of the Declaration of Independence [of 1916], no matter how much the Deputies who have foresworn it may choose to sneer at it," she declared in the Dáil in May 1922, "and any action that we have taken we have taken on that basis and that basis alone." The republican movement had not been bluffing in 1916, and it was "not bluffing now, no matter what the consequences may be." Did her opponents really think the Treaty was "worth civil war?" They could only answer her by asking "Is the Republic, is the independence of Ireland, worth civil war?" To this question, MacSwiney answered "Yes, a thousand times yes, it is worth civil war." "The unity and independence of Ireland are as much worth civil war to Ireland," she concluded, "as the unity of the United States was worth civil war to Abraham Lincoln." Ironically, MacSwiney's Lincoln—the intransigent wartime leader—was closer to Lloyd George's than to Arthur Griffith's.[17]

MacSwiney's sleight-of-hand in coupling the word "independence" with "unity" cast Lincoln in the unlikely role of nationalist liberator, an image that persisted in Irish republican circles for several decades. Although Lincoln had some sympathy with Irish and Hungarian nationalism early in his career, he was never a national freedom fighter of the type Irish republicans had in mind. The pro-Treaty side was closer to Lincoln's spirit in emphasizing the underlying principle that made unity worth fighting for in the first place—majority rule as the essence of democracy. Responding in the Dáil in May 1922 to MacSwiney's endorsement of war, Kevin O'Higgins suggested that the Treaty was indeed worth fighting for. He was prepared to wage a civil war not just for the Treaty and the Free State, but for the same principle Arthur Griffith had articulated—"for a vital fundamental, democratic principle—for the right of the people of Ireland to decide any issue, great or small, that arises in the politics of this country." Yet, from the republican perspective, this plea for majority rule was fatally flawed. Anti-Treaty politicians, such as de Valera and MacSwiney, saw Ireland as a unified entity and cited Lincoln in insisting that the minority in North-East Ulster had no right to dictate terms to the majority in the rest of the island, let alone to sever their connection with Ireland. Unable to reach agreement on questions of sovereignty, partition, and the nature of political democracy, the pro-Treaty and anti-Treaty forces duly went to war in June 1922.[18]

IV

When it became clear in 1925 that the Boundary Commission intended to transfer parts of the Irish Free State into Northern Ireland, rather than the other way round, Éamon de Valera, still in the political wilderness after the defeat of the republican side in the Civil War, seized the opportunity to condemn the Treaty, the Free State, and partition. "In the long list of England's outrages against our people," he declared on December 6, 1925, "there is none greater than this outrage of partition." All "sections and classes" in Ireland, "whatever their political or other opinions," he conceded, were "entitled to equal rights as citizens and fair play," but "no section, north or south, east or west" was "entitled to secede from this nation." "The southern states of the American Union had a far better case for secession than our Northern Unionists," de Valera insisted, "and President Lincoln faced four years of terrible civil war rather than permit it, and the opinion of the world has justified him—and the results have justified him." When Dáil Éireann approved an intergovernmental agreement dissolving the Boundary Commission (thereby preventing its recommendations from going into effect and recognizing the existing borders of Northern Ireland), de Valera responded in words that Lincoln would surely have recognized: "We deny that any section of our people can give away the sovereignty or alienate any part of this nation's territory."[19]

De Valera's return to power in the 1930s, when he formed three governments with his Fianna Fáil party, provided a national and international platform from which to publicize the problem of partition—especially to Irish Americans and to the people of the United States more generally. "It is a great privilege to be able to address American friends on this, Lincoln's birthday," he declared in a radio broadcast to the American people in 1933. "The veneration in which Abraham Lincoln is held by the American people is shared in no small measure by the people of Ireland. Having ourselves so long striven for freedom, we honour him as the liberator of a race." Like Mary MacSwiney, de Valera moved seamlessly from emancipation of the slaves to national freedom and unity, declaring that the Irish knew "only too well what America suffered in those years" when Lincoln had saved the United States. "We too have endured the bitterness of civil strife," he continued, "but we, unhappily, were unable to prevent the partition of our country." Partition "was a purely arbitrary act," de Valera insisted, "inspired solely by considerations of British imperial policy and contrary to the every interest of the Irish people." It was "the worst of all the many crimes committed by British statesmen against the Irish people during the last 750 years."[20]

Although de Valera frequently turned to Lincoln for inspiration, the two leaders had starkly different understandings of nationality. For de Valera, as his eight-century chronology suggests, Irish nationality stood outside historical time or constitutional form. The declaration of a sovereign republic in Easter 1916 had reasserted an existing nation rather than creating a new one. "Ireland is more than a political union of states," de Valera told the American people in 1933. "It has been a nation from the dawn of history, united in traditions, in political institutions, in territory." For Lincoln, by contrast, the American nation originated in the specific, concrete, and secular events of the American Revolution and rested on a shared commitment to abide by the principles of the Constitution. But the salient point is that both conceptions of nationality, the romantic and the constitutional, rendered secession (or partition) impossible.[21]

De Valera consistently invoked Lincoln in asserting the inviolability of the Irish nation. When, on January 26, 1942, shortly after the Japanese attacked Pearl Harbor, American troops disembarked in Northern Ireland without the Irish government having been consulted, de Valera responded in his dual capacity as head of government and minister for external affairs. The Irish people, he explained, had taken at face value Woodrow Wilson's principles of democracy and national self-determination at the end of World War I, voting for national independence and the establishment of a republic. In response, the British government had simply "cut the nation in two." Unlike Ireland as a whole, de Valera continued, the six counties of the North "formed no natural, historic or geographical entity. The area was chosen solely with a view to securing a majority within it for the anti-national minority." To partition "an ancient nation," he concluded, "is one of the cruellest wrongs that can be committed against a people." It could only result in the same "evils" that "Abraham Lincoln foresaw from the projected partition of the United States, when he determined to prevent it even at the cost of fighting one of the bitterest civil wars in history."[22]

As the twenty-six counties of southern Ireland evolved through three constitutional forms—the Irish Free State (1922–37), Éire (1937–49), and the Republic of Ireland (since 1949)—successive Irish leaders confronted the problem of partition. They were especially outspoken on the matter when they toured the United States. During the sesquicentennial year of 1959, for example, the president of the Irish republic, Seán T. O'Kelly, made a three-day ceremonial visit to Illinois, where he visited Lincoln's tomb and addressed the state legislature in Springfield. At the graveside, O'Kelly expressed his hope "that the ancient nation of Ireland will be reunited peacefully in accordance with the Democratic principles which that noble statesman fought for and died to uphold." In his speech to the legislature, O'Kelly expressed his wish to rededicate himself and the Irish people to the ideals Lincoln "served so well and to the death— freedom and unity." Like MacSwiney and de Valera, he readily juxtaposed these two terms, though freedom had a quite different connotation in the

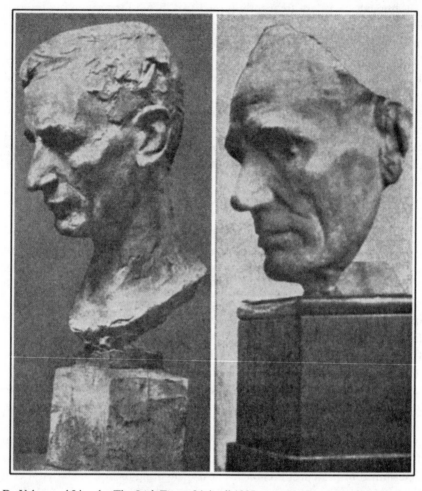

De Valera and Lincoln. The *Irish Times*, 24 April 1937, page 11 (Courtesy of the National Library of Ireland). "A Remarkable Resemblance will be noted between these two pieces of statuary," the *Irish Times* observed. "On the left: Mr. Jerome Connor's head of President de Valera on view at this year's Royal Hibernian Academy exhibition. Right: a mask of Abraham Lincoln taken a year before his death by Abraham Volk." The resemblance is not readily apparent, though the Irish nationalist and playwright Lady Gregory remarked, on meeting de Valera for the first time in 1921, that "I liked his face, good, honest, with something in it of Lincoln." *Lady Gregory's Journals,* ed. Daniel J. Murphy, 2 vols. (New York: Oxford University Press, 1978), I:300.

American case (abolition of slavery) than in the Irish (national independence). For O'Kelly, as for his republican predecessors, freedom and unity amounted to the same thing: a single nationalist government for the island of Ireland.[23]

O'Kelly's main subject in his address to the Illinois legislature was partition and, once again, he pressed Lincoln into the unlikely role of nationalist liberator. On this occasion he quoted from a speech Lincoln had made at Indianapolis on February 18, 1861, while en route to Washington to assume the presidency as the Southern states were seceding. "On what rightful principle may a state, being more [*sic*] than one-fiftieth part of the nation in soil and population," Lincoln asked, "break up the nation and then coerce a proportionally larger subdivision of itself in the most arbitrary way?" Yet in Ireland, O'Kelly pointed out, "six northern counties" remained "split away from the now independent republic." Lincoln therefore had "a special significance," for the Irish people, the Irish president declared, and "we are proud to think that Lincoln understood and sympathized with the efforts of our people to achieve independence."[24]

Within ten years of O'Kelly's visit to the United States, the "evils" that Éamon de Valera associated with secession led to a civil war, not between the two Irelands but within the province of Northern Ireland. Although this thirty-year period of violence, known to contemporaries as "the Troubles," raised perennial questions about Union, it featured surprisingly few references to Abraham Lincoln. As the conflict moved toward resolution in the 1990s, however, images of Lincoln once again became more frequent in Irish political conversation, with the most-quoted words coming, predictably, from the second inaugural address. Dick Spring, the Irish deputy prime minister (*tánaiste*) and minister for foreign affairs, cited the second inaugural in the Dáil on December 15, 1993 to celebrate a breakthrough in the peace process known as the Downing Street Declaration, whereby the British and Irish governments recognized the right of the people of Northern Ireland to choose between Union with Great Britain and a united Ireland. The president of Sinn Féin, Gerry Adams, meeting the Ulster Unionist leader, David Trimble, in public for the first time in September 1998, promised "malice toward none" as they strove to bind "up the nation's wounds" and moved toward "a just and lasting peace." Adams did not say which "nation" he had in mind—the Republic of Ireland, Northern Ireland, or a united Ireland—and Trimble offered no public response to his counterpart's magnanimity.[25]

By 2009, the bicentennial year of Lincoln's birth, the prospects of lasting peace in Northern Ireland looked considerably better than a decade earlier, but there had been some ironic twists in Lincoln's path through Irish politics along the way. When the leader of the Democratic Unionist Party, Peter Robinson, invoked Lincoln's image at the Smithsonian Folk Life Festival in Washington, D.C., in June 2007 to celebrate the new Northern Ireland, he did so in a quite distinctive way. "As I stand here and look towards the Lincoln Memorial I am reminded of the suffering that the United States experienced and the strong nation that emerged following its Civil War," Robinson declared. "Lincoln said— 'A house divided against itself cannot stand.' That's an important lesson for us all." Unlike his nationalist predecessors, however, Robinson was referring not to the united island of Ireland but, instead, to a self-governing Northern

Ireland that would remain permanently part of the United Kingdom. Yet both parts of Ireland, like the remainder of the United Kingdom, were by now well established parts of yet another Union. Future debates on Irish sovereignty will concern the balance of power within Europe. Whether the figure of Abraham Lincoln will feature in these debates, and in which of his various forms— republican, democrat, emancipator, wartime leader, unionist—will depend on the issues at stake.[26]

Notes

I would like to thank Enda Delaney, Diarmaid Ferriter, Roy Foster, Alvin Jackson, and my colleagues and graduate students at Boston College for reading drafts of this paper.

1. *Irish Times*, July 29, 1920.

2. *Dublin Daily Express*, April 29, 1865, quoted in U.S. Department of State, *Appendix to Diplomatic Correspondence of 1865. Abraham Lincoln, Late President of the United States of America, and the Attempted Assassination of William H. Seward, Secretary of State, and Frederick W. Steward, Assistant Secretary, On the evening of the 14th of April, 1865. Expressions of Condolence and Sympathy Inspired by These Events* (Washington, DC: Government Printing Office, 1866), 370. For resolutions passed by Irish municipal councils, religious groups, and others, see 173, 180, 190, 204–8, 221–22, 252. John Mitchel, the American-based Irish nationalist exile, was a rare exception to the pattern of grief and sympathy. See "The Continuation of the Jail Journal," in Mitchel's *Irish Citizen* (New York), July 16, 1870, National Library of Ireland; James Quinn, *John Mitchel* (Dublin: University College Dublin Press, 2008), 74.

3. *Ulster Observer*, April 27, 1865; *Dublin Daily Express*, April 29, 1865; "Resolutions passed at a meeting of the democratic classes of Dublin," in *Appendix to Diplomatic Correspondence of 1865*, 206, 370–72, 419.

4. For a critique of the Union as "a mockery" in light of the Irish famine, written by an otherwise moderate Irish nationalist, see Isaac Butt, "The Famine in the Land," *Dublin University Magazine* 29 (April 1847), excerpted in Peter Gray, *The Irish Famine* (New York: Harry N. Abrams), 155–57.

5. W. E. Gladstone, *The Irish Question* (New York: Charles Scribner's, 1886); Joseph M. Hernon, Jr., "The Use of the American Civil War in the Debate over Irish Home Rule," *American Historical Review*, 69 (July 1964), 1022–23; HC, vol. 304, cols 1205–1206, April 9, 1886; speech of Joseph Chamberlain at Liverpool, October 25, 1881, quoted in J. L. Garvin and Julian Amery, *The Life of Joseph Chamberlain*, 6 vols. (London: Macmillan, 1932–51), *Volume One, 1836–1885*, 345; Goldwin Smith to G. W. Curtis, February 11, 1886, quoted in Elisabeth Wallace, *Goldwin Smith: Victorian Liberal* (Toronto: University of Toronto Press, 1957), 92. Gladstone made a pro-Confederate speech in Newcastle on October 7, 1862, which he later regretted.

6. *Irish Times*, February 12, 1909; *The Times* (London), February 12, 1909.

7. *Irish Times*, December 26, 1910, quoting the *Spectator*, December 24, 1910. The original passage, with slight variation in content, can be found in Henry J. Raymond, *The Life and Public Services of Abraham Lincoln* (New York: Darby and Miller, 1865), 134.

8. *Irish Times,* November 29, 1913.

9. Ronald John McNeill, *Ulster's Stand For Union* (London: John Murray, 1922) at http://infomotions.com/etexts/gutenberg/dirs/1/4/3/2/14326/14326.htm, accessed August 23, 2007, Project Gutenberg eBook #14326. McNeill conveniently ignored the fact that Southern secessionists, although they were prepared to rupture the Union, wanted to preserve the American status quo in one critical respect, by protecting slavery.

10. *Irish Times*, July 29, 1920; Martin Quigley, *A U.S. Spy in Ireland* (Dublin: Marino Books, 1999), 118.

11. Eamon de Valera, *Speeches and Statements by Eamon de Valera, 1917–73* (Dublin: Gill and Macmillan, 1980), 51–52, 68.

12. De Valera, *Speeches and Statements*, 65, 66, 68; *Freeman's Journal* (Dublin), August 30, 1921. For a similar argument by another moderate nationalist newspaper, see the *Irish Independent*, June 12, 1919. The *Freeman's Journal* and *Independent* merged in 1924.

13. David Lloyd George to Eamon de Valera in *Irish Times,* August 27, 1921; Lincoln's First Inaugural, March 4, 1861, in Roy P. Basler et al., eds., *The Collected Works of Abraham Lincoln [CW]*, 9 vols. (New Brunswick, NJ: Rutgers University Press, 1953–55), 4:269.

14. De Valera, *Speeches and Statements*, 59–61, 81–86, 92–94.

15. Dáil Éireann debates, http://historical-debates.oireachtas.ie/, Volume 3, January 7, 1922, 340 (accessed March 16, 2008); Abraham Lincoln, "Letter to the editor of the *Sangamo Journal*," June 13, 1836, *CW*, 1:48. The *Sangamo Journal* was a Whig newspaper published in Springfield, Sangamon County, Illinois.

16. Lincoln to John Hay, May 7, 1861, quoted in Tyler Dennett, ed., *Lincoln and the Civil War in the Diaries and Letters of John Hay* (New York: Dodd, Mead & Company, 1939), 19–20; Dáil Éireann debates, Volume 3, January 7, and May 19, 1922, 341, 460–61.

17. Dáil Éireann debates, Volume 2, May 17, 1922, 424–25.

18. "Call for a Kossuth Meeting, January 5, 1852," *CW*, 2:115; Dáil Éireann debates, Volume 2, May 19, 1922, 464.

19. De Valera, *Speeches and Statements*, 121–23, 126.

20. Ibid., 234, 235.

21. Ibid., 235.

22. Ibid., 464–65; *New York Times*, January 28, 1942; *Irish Times,* January 28, 1942.

23. *New York Times*, March 18, 24, 1959; *Chicago Daily Tribune*, March 26, 1959; *Irish Times,* March 26, 1959.

24. *Chicago Daily Tribune*, March 26, 1959.

25. Second Inaugural Address, *CW*, 8:333; Dáil Éireann debates, Volume 437, December 15, 1993; *Guardian Unlimited*, September 11, 1998, http://century.guardian.co.uk/1990–1999/Story/0112755,00.html (accessed March 20, 2008).

26. Abraham Lincoln, "A House Divided," speech at Springfield, Illinois, June 16, 1858, *CW*, 2:61; Peter Robinson, speech to the Smithsonian Folk Life Festival, June 27, 2007, *northern ireland: see feel discover*, http://www.rediscoverni.com/index1/folklifefestival/opening-ceremony/peter_robinson_s_speech.htm (accessed January 3, 2008).

10

Defining a Legacy

LINCOLN IN THE NATIONAL IMAGINARY OF INDIA

Vinay Lal

There is no question that, insofar as American political figures resonate at all in South Asia, Abraham Lincoln remains, more than two hundred years after his birth, the supreme embodiment of the meaning and possibilities of "America" for most South Asians. This essay seeks to explore the extent and limits of his presence in South Asian, especially Indian, political and intellectual culture. Several years before his assassination would install him (as it was said) among the immortals, Lincoln's name was apparently already known to some in India. The ferocious Indian rebellion of 1857, where no brutality had been spared on either side, was suppressed to great effect, and Queen Victoria would eventually attempt to assuage the feelings of her wounded subjects across the ocean with a proclamation promising peace, prosperity, and greater attentiveness to the needs of India. Nevertheless, the feeling may also have persisted that India had entered into a new period of servitude, and it is reasonable to surmise that the American debates over slavery, in which Lincoln had played a prominent part, may have aroused the sentiments of some Indians looking for signs of hope from other quarters. In the late 1850s, an Indian merchant by the name of Dossabhoy Framjee Cama arrived in Washington, D.C. This enterprising Parsi was apparently so drawn toward Lincoln that some years later, during his presidency, Cama appeared outside the gates of the White House and resisted all attempts to dislodge him until he had obtained a likeness of the "Great Emancipator." Having gained the permission of an astonished president to sit for the artist Daniel Huntingdon, Cama reportedly carried back the painting "back in triumph to Calcutta."[1]

The greater the person, it may be argued, the more apocryphal the stories that circulate about him or her. There is, as far as I am aware, no official record of Lincoln ever having been visited by Dossabhoy Cama, who came from a family that had made something of a name in merchant shipping.[2] Such imagined links with Lincoln in India continue today in many private schools around the country, where framed prints of a poem entitled "Letter to His Son's Teacher" set before children the example of a public life guided by moral principles:

> He will have to learn, I know,
> that all men are not just,
> all men are not true.
> But teach him also that
> for every scoundrel there is a hero;
> that for every selfish Politician,
> there is a dedicated leader . . .

The "Letter to His Son's Teacher" is mistakenly if invariably attributed to Lincoln, but I very much doubt that anyone in India is willing to be persuaded otherwise. If Lincoln did not pen any such letter, it is equally true that the sentiments it expresses can be construed as those to which Lincoln would have given his firm assent. Indeed, the "Letter to His Son's Teacher" acquired such popularity in India in recent years that it even had the endorsement of the National Council for Educational Research and Training (NCERT), the country's premier body for primary and secondary education. The NCERT may, in its wisdom, have embraced the view that the precise authorship of the letter is less important than the nobility of the sentiments it espouses. This is one measure, characteristically Indian in many respects, of Lincoln's assimilation into the canon of the greats: much like the nameless authors of the Vedas and the Upanishads, his writings have become repositories of timeless truths, exemplary as exhortations to moral conduct and prudent thought. Historians are, I suspect, more apt to judge the reach of Lincoln's name and reputation by considering the weight of his "influence" on leading figures or major socio-political phenomena, but it may well be that in India, and elsewhere perhaps, the more enduring signs of his universal appeal reside in the fact that he is now part of the folklore of many distinct local cultures.

The idea of "influence" is notoriously elastic, and it does not easily lend itself to analytical insights. "On the table in his office," a notable biographer has written of Jawaharlal Nehru, "two things were always present: a gold statuette of Gandhi and a bronze hand of Lincoln."[3] The "influence" of Gandhi on Nehru is indisputable: indeed, "influence" here appears to be a rather effete if not anemic word, wholly inadequate for conveying the larger than life presence that Gandhi came to occupy in the life of Nehru and the nation at large. It is Nehru who captured the vast dimensions of Gandhi's life in the pithy phrase, "Gandhi is India." Yet, of course, the matter can scarcely end there, since there is a compelling case to be made for the argument that, in most matters critical to the conduct of domestic planning and foreign policy, Nehru effected a radical departure from the teachings of his master. Gandhi's "influence" on Nehru consequently appears considerably diminished once, having put aside the magic spell that Gandhi had cast on him, we turn our attention to the prescription that Nehru followed in seeking India's advancement. Lincoln, on the other hand, hardly appears in Nehru's writings. In Lincoln, Nehru may have found a statesman who matched his own literary aspirations. And, yet, beyond the obvious similarities between two statesmen who presided at the helm of political affairs when looming crises of division and secession wrought a pall over the future, one wonders what it might have been that drew Nehru to Lincoln.

There are many other registers through which one might read the idea of influence. Is it, for instance, a greater measure of a person's "influence" to suggest that his name appears in the country's school textbooks as a figure worthy of emulation than if the same person was a fount of inspiration to an oppressed people but otherwise appeared to have left no lasting impression on them? In a study of schools in the state of Gujarat, one linguist found that students being educated in the English medium were assigned readings on Lincoln in grade six, but those being educated in the vernacular, or Gujarati, were not given such readings.[4] One might thus reasonably reach the conclusion that awareness of Lincoln among the English-educated is greater than it is among those educated in Indian languages. However, what appears to be the logical inference, namely that Lincoln is influential among the educated strata, and more precisely among those who have had perhaps a greater exposure to Westernization and modernization, is not warranted by the facts of Indian society. Dalit thinkers and activists, who occupy the bottom rung of Indian society, and are cognizant of the resemblance that the historical conditions of their oppression bear to slavery in the American South, have looked to Lincoln as the Great Emancipator. Similarly, as a study of popular Tamil biographies of Lincoln suggests,[5] the vernacular literature in India may be more receptive to Lincoln than the publishing houses that cater to the graduates of English-medium public schools. The vernacular literature has remained truer to its twin moorings in Indian devotional literature as well as the nineteenth-century tradition of biographies of moral leaders, and the Tamil biographies of Lincoln bear all the marks of works intended to instill in the young noble thoughts, perseverance in a good cause, celebration of hard work, and a firm belief that adversity is intended to bring out the best in human beings. Tamil biographers of Lincoln dwell at length on his humble origins, disciplined work habits, humanitarianism, and empathy for the poor and the wretched. As one scholar of these biographies notes, "Lincoln's story—a poor man who made his way to the White House through personal integrity and sheer hard work—captures the imagination of the Tamils."[6]

The quest for Lincoln's legacy, the experience of India thus suggests, cannot be undertaken only as a study in intellectual history. The frequency with which he is quoted has less to do with the recognition that he was an extraordinarily effective and eloquent wielder of words and far more to do with representations of him as pragmatic, incorruptible, a leader of men, steadfast in his resolve—and a martyr, much like Gandhi, to the causes of liberty and human dignity. Some, expecting to see the name of Lincoln writ large in contemporary Indian intellectual history, might perhaps find it less than gratifying that his name is routinely brought into service to inspire and instruct the young but does not appear in contemporary debates about politics or the nature of the "good society." In the back page of the "Young World" supplement to a recent issue of the national daily, the *Hindu*, Lincoln's words are prominently displayed: "People are just about as happy as they make up their minds to be."[7] The narrative of "American exceptionalism," one suspects, is turned on its head: where Americans might view the ascendancy of a person from a log cabin to the White House as a quintessentially American experience, possible only in the New World, the tendency in India has been to assimilate Lincoln into a well-established tradition of life stories which dwell upon the triumph of the human spirit over adversity. Lincoln, we might say, is the apposite subject of those juvenile biographers who are intent upon establishing the extraordinariness of ordinary lives.[8]

There is a sizable body of literature on Lincoln in Indian languages, and lives of him are available in most if not all of the principal Indian languages.[9] S. Gurdial Singh, a Punjabi novelist who was conferred in 1999 the country's most prestigious literary award for lifetime achievement, confessed in a recent interview, "I have always been spurred on to a greater awareness of my limitations. It is only when you read biographies of men like Lincoln that you discover how little you are able to do or actually succeed in doing."[10] Would Gurdial Singh have encountered a life of Lincoln in English, Punjabi, Hindi, or indeed some other language? And is his estimation of Lincoln representative of the Indian encounter with the American president, an encounter that was seldom loud or transparent but was nonetheless informed by a sense that Lincoln, having presided over the fortunes of his country at a critical moment in its history and grappled with the most difficult questions of slavery and secession, had shown, through his prudence, sagacity, and moral uprightness of purpose, the way forward for other nations similarly placed? What kind of engagement with Lincoln does one find in the writings of Indian nationalists, and is it possible to aver that intellectuals and activists have been more profoundly moved by his teachings than other groups?

There has been, as I have suggested, some speculation about the place of Lincoln in the nationalist imagination, and the names of Gandhi and Nehru have on occasion been linked to him. It comes as no surprise that Indian elites under colonial rule were more conversant with British rather than American literature and politics, and there is little to suggest that American writers were even known in India. Similarly, one is hard pressed to find more than a handful of persons in the early phase of the nationalist movement, until the early part of the twentieth century, who were educated in the United States. The first Indian students only arrived in the United States around 1901.[11] A hugely disproportionate number of the members of the Indian National Congress, the principal organization of nationalist opinion, were trained in the law in Britain, and a perusal of the writings of the first generation of Indian nationalists, pursuant to the founding of the Congress in 1885, suggests their familiarity with the writings of British philosophers and thinkers such as Edmund Burke, David Hume, John Stuart Mill, and Jeremy Bentham, and even an intimacy with the contours of British intellectual life. Mohandas Gandhi, who had arrived at the Inner Temple in the 1880s to earn legal credentials, was perhaps the first figure from his generation to move away from the celebratory anglophilia that characterized the Indian, especially Bengali, intellectual elite.

Gandhi's first acquaintance with American writers extended primarily to Emerson and Thoreau.[12] How exactly Gandhi came to acquire knowledge of Lincoln is not known, but the circumstances under which he came to endorse him as "the greatest and noblest man of the last century" are clear enough.[13] Gandhi had arrived in South Africa in 1893, unaware that what he had intended to be a brief sojourn, while he searched for a purpose in life and a means of livelihood less exacting than a stint in British India's law courts, would stretch to a two-decade long stay during which he would pioneer mass nonviolent resistance to political oppression. Barrister Gandhi found that his education, credentials, and sartorial tastes did not prevent him from being lumped with other Indians as a "coolie," and in time he came to forge a struggle designed to end the vicious discrimination to which Indians in South Africa were then subjected. In 1903, mindful of the need for a publication that might forcefully present the grievances and sentiments of South Africa's Indian community, Gandhi founded a newspaper called *Indian Opinion*.

As the struggle against racial discrimination intensified, Gandhi endeavored to strengthen the resolve of those who had enlisted by giving them the examples of men and women whose lives he thought were worth emulating. At this stage of his life, Gandhi saw biography as an exemplary aid to young people not only in their quest for greatness, but also for the more immediate and pressing task of deriving suitable models for moral action. Over successive weeks in the pages of *Indian Opinion* in 1905, he penned short biographies of Socrates, Mazzini, Gorky, Tolstoy, George Washington, Thoreau, and Lincoln. Tolstoy's admiration for Lincoln, famously described by him as a "humanitarian as broad as the world," is well known, and it would be an arresting chapter in the history of ideas if it could be demonstrated that Gandhi came to an awareness of Lincoln from reading Tolstoy. While Gandhi evidently had a familiarity with Tolstoy's writings well before their exchange of letters in 1909,[14] it is nevertheless difficult to date precisely the moment when he might have become acquainted with Tolstoy's near veneration of Lincoln as a "Christ in miniature."[15]

Gandhi's biographical sketch of Lincoln, which appeared in the pages of *Indian Opinion* on August 26, 1905, must be reckoned as among the first pieces written on Lincoln in Gujarati. "It is believed," he wrote, "that the greatest and the noblest man of the last century was Abraham Lincoln," but Gandhi does not say "believed" by whom.[16] The passive construction invites attention: though the rest of the article implies Gandhi's assent to this generally held view, his reticence in a bold affirmation of his belief may have stemmed from an inadequate knowledge of Lincoln and, even more likely, from his unwillingness to commit himself to a proposition when the nineteenth century had produced so many other great luminaries, among them Tolstoy himself. Gandhi's sketch of Lincoln's life dwells on Lincoln as a self-made man, the horrors of slavery— and, correspondingly, Lincoln's courage in acting to free all slaves from their bondage—and the humility of the president even after he had attained much "eminence." Lincoln "received very little education until he was fifteen years old," wrote Gandhi, and he adds that Lincoln "could hardly read or write and earned his meagre living, wandering from place to place." Gandhi then describes Lincoln meandering about America on a country raft, and how it was only when Lincoln was around twenty years old that he thought of improving his prospects in life by self-study and eventually apprenticeship to a lawyer.

There is, in Gandhi's description of Lincoln, far more than the ordinary approbation of a life of Emersonian self-reliance. A close reading in 1904 of Ruskin's *Unto This Last*, which Gandhi characterized as having cast a "magic spell" on him, had convinced Gandhi of the profound utility of manual labor in the development of character, and similarly he had by then arrived at the conclusion that most formal schooling was, if anything, a hindrance to the development of true moral character. There is nothing in Gandhi's assessment of Lincoln to suggest that he viewed him as a supreme example of what might be achieved in a caste-less or modern society. To the contrary, it is the extent to which Lincoln did not partake of the fetishes of modern civilization, characterized by the elevation of mind over the heart, ratiocinative work over bodily labor, unadulterated greed over the spirit of cooperation, that he became an embodiment of humaneness, generosity, and humility. Having described the brutal practices of slavery, and Lincoln's fearless and singular determination "to wage war against those hundreds of thousands of men who depended for their living on the system and to set free the slaves from bondage," Gandhi closed with an enunciation of the twin themes of Lincoln's martyrdom and the fact that Lincoln, however much he remained an American, "regarded the whole world as his native land." Gandhi, who conceptualized *satyagraha* as a mode of nonviolent resistance that called upon its practitioners to even sacrifice their lives in a noble cause, believed that "Lincoln sacrificed his life in order to put an end to the sufferings of others."

Lincoln resurfaced in Gandhi's writings on a few rare occasions in subsequent years, but over the last two decades of his life there is barely any mention of him. In 1919, shortly after Gandhi had initiated the first mass movement of nonviolent resistance to colonial rule, an open letter addressed to him from a "Pennsylvanian" published in the *Times of India* advised Gandhi that a genuine revolution in India could only be achieved with the substantive reform of education and the transformation of his countrymen's moral habits.[17] Taking recourse to the example of Lincoln, Gandhi's correspondent reminded him that Lincoln, upon admission to the bar, "openly declared that he would not take a case until he had first satisfied himself that it was a true case." Lincoln, in pronouncing that "I am not bound to win, but I am bound to be true," had set the bar very high and it was for Indians to follow his example. His position would have deeply resonated with Gandhi, who trained as a barrister but found, much to his dismay, that the end of litigation was generally not the pursuit or establishment of truth but the declaration of victory. As was his established practice, Gandhi issued an open letter in reply—which, significantly, adverts to two of the Pennsylvanian's "illustrious countrymen," Lincoln and Thoreau. "I have endeavoured to the best of my ability," wrote Gandhi in high praise of Lincoln, "to translate into my life one of his sayings, namely, 'Let us have faith that right makes might, and in that faith, let us, to the end, dare to do our duty as we understand it.'"[18]

It is no accident that Gandhi picked this particular quotation, which occurs at the end of Lincoln's address at Cooper Union in New York City in February 1860.[19] Here, as on other previous occasions, Lincoln was at pains to express his conviction that slavery could not be defended, and it could not be permitted to overrun America in its "Free States": "If slavery is right, all words, acts, laws, and constitutions against it, are themselves wrong, and should be silenced, and swept away"; and if slavery is wrong, its "enlargement" and "extension" could not be countenanced. Lincoln's address was also notable for its unequivocal critique of John Brown's spectacular incitement of slave rebellion at the federal armory at Harpers Ferry. Though Lincoln had applauded Brown at a speech in Kansas for his opposition to slavery, indeed for his "great courage" and "rare unselfishness," he was also certain that the course of action taken by Brown had to be repudiated. Whatever political considerations might have motivated him to declare his opposition to "violence, bloodshed and treason," Lincoln at the same time condemned Brown's raid as a "violation of law" that was also, "as all such attacks must be, futile as far as any effect it might have on the extinction of a great evil."[20]

Is it possible to gesture at much more precise significations of a shared moral, political, and discursive universe between Lincoln and Gandhi, beyond the bland assertion that both may be viewed as "enduring touchstones of humanistic vision for freedom and democracy,"[21] or that the vision they followed "was great in terms of its humaneness"?[22] If, in the broadest terms, Lincoln and Gandhi are to be viewed as exemplars and visionaries who enshrined the ideas of "freedom" and "democracy" as the noblest endeavors of the human race, what are we to make of the fact that even as Gandhi could speak of the "satanic nature of the civilization" represented by Europe and launch a withering critique of modern industrial civilization,[23] Lincoln could declare with

MARTYRS OF HUMANITY
FEBRUARY 12, 1948

This image was published on Lincoln's birthday on February 12, 1948, less than two weeks after Gandhi's assassination on January 30. The cartoonist, D. R. Fitzpatrick, had a long association with the *St. Louis Post-Dispatch*. Image from D. R. Fitzpatrick, *As I Saw It: A Review of Our Times with 311 Cartoons and Notes* (New York: Simon & Schuster, 1953), 151.

supreme confidence that "Just now, in civilization, and the arts, the people of Asia are entirely behind those of Europe; those of the East of Europe behind those of West of it; while we, here in America, *think* we discover, and invent, and improve, faster than any of them."[24] There are, it appears, other conundrums as well: the young Lincoln had voiced strong opposition to the war with Mexico, but the young Gandhi, even while critical of the use of violence to resolve conflicts, nevertheless embraced the view that Indians in South Africa were duty-bound, as subjects of the British Empire, to assist the British in a brutal war against the Boers. In later years, Lincoln would lead the country in a protracted and bloody struggle against the secessionist South, while Gandhi, whose abhorrence for war had become unqualified, committed the Congress party to a position of neutrality in the war between the Allied and Axis powers. Having spent his entire life under the aegis of colonial rule, and harboring no illusions about the alleged gentlemanliness of the British rulers of India, Gandhi retained a healthy suspicion of wars that, however apparently just the cause, were rooted in what he viewed as an addiction to violence.

We can turn our attention once again to Lincoln's Cooper Union address and Gandhi's evident approbation of his remarks in an attempt to identify more precise points of congruence. Gandhi, who is recognized principally as an advocate of the rights of suppressed people, sought however to resuscitate for the twentieth century the language of "duties,"[25] so much so that he would eventually embrace the view that "in swaraj [freedom] based on ahimsa [non-violence], people need not know their rights, but it is necessary for them to know their duties."[26] Gandhi recognized Lincoln, alongside Mazzini, as one of the last great articulators of the conception of duty—and of the need, as Lincoln had said, to "stand by our duty, fearlessly and effectively."[27] Second, in Lincoln's critique of John Brown, Gandhi discerned a reverence for the law that was clearly shared between the two men. Gandhi's campaigns of civil disobedience have sometimes been critiqued, even by those otherwise sympathetic to his moral vision, as conducive to a spirit of lawlessness, but such a reading is insensitive to the consideration that, even while Gandhi opposed particular laws that he deemed to be unjust, he unfailingly upheld the majesty of the law in general. Third, in Lincoln's assessment of the futility of violent revolutionary schemes, Gandhi saw a vindication of his own oft-critiqued ambivalence towards anti-colonial rebels whose patriotism he admired even as he deplored their advocacy of violent resistance. "John Brown's effort was peculiar," Lincoln told his audience, and in "its philosophy, corresponds with the many attempts, related in history, at the assassination of kings and emperors. An enthusiast broods over the oppression of a people till he fancies himself commissioned by Heaven to liberate them. He ventures the attempt, which ends in little else than his own execution."[28] Much later, Gandhi would be roundly condemned for having failed, as his critics alleged, to save the life of Bhagat Singh, charged and convicted of the crime of political assassination by the colonial state.[29] Indeed, as Gandhi explained in a 1921 preface to his seminal text of 1909, *Hind Swaraj*, he had written the little book "in answer to the Indian school of violence and its prototype in South Africa. I came in contact with every known Indian anarchist in London. Their bravery impressed me, but I felt that their zeal was misguided. I felt that violence was no remedy for India's ills, and that her civilization required the use of a different and higher weapon for self-protection."[30]

Much more could be said of Gandhi and Lincoln—perhaps idealists in their view of the possibilities of human endeavor, but equally pragmatists in politics whose lives were shaped by a profound religiosity and reverence for "the rule of law"—in this vein, but what of Gandhi's contemporaries? It would not be inaccurate to suggest that Indian nationalist thinkers generally had little to say about Lincoln, and he is seldom invoked in their writings. As I have previously suggested, the lives of the first generation of Indian nationalists following the Indian rebellion of 1857–58 and the founding of the Indian National Congress in 1885, are characterized by a pervasive anglophilia. The patriarch of the Nehru clan, Motilal Nehru, had his clothes stitched in England, though like many others he would eventually be swayed by Gandhi and become an ardent advocate of *swadeshi* (self-reliance). That Motilal was, for an educated Indian gentleman and lawyer of his time, widely read cannot be doubted, and Lincoln's speeches and writings would have come to his attention. Speaking on the fifth anniversary of the Jallianwala Bagh massacre of 1919, as Motilal and others pressed forth with Gandhi's plan of noncooperation amidst opposition from those styled as "moderates," Motilal quoted Lincoln's words from his second inaugural address as an expression of the sentiments held by him and other "extremists": "With malice towards none, with charity for all, with firmness in the right as God gives us to see the right, we strive on to finish the work we are in."[31] Motilal had some evident attachment to these precise words: while conveying the greetings of the Legislative Assembly to Britain's Labour Party the same year, he again concluded his speech with an exhortation to emulate Lincoln in his "broad-minded wisdom."[32]

Collections of Motilal's speeches and writings do not, however, point to any sustained engagement with the corpus of Lincoln's work. It has been argued that Motilal's rather more famous son, Jawaharlal, "made frequent references to Lincoln in his writings and speeches," but a perusal of the some forty volumes of Nehru's collected writings does not warrant this conclusion.[33] Nehru never disguised his attraction to socialist thinkers, even if many Marxist intellectuals, especially in the aftermath of independence and the gradual evisceration of the dream of equality that the dawn of freedom had wrought, persisted in viewing him as a representative of the bourgeoisie. The sheer proximity to Gandhi, which repeatedly brought Nehru to an awareness of the Mahatma's uncanny ability to resonate with the masses, allowed him to overlook the intense religiosity in which Gandhi's life was bathed; but it may be questioned, at the very least, whether Nehru took Lincoln's appeals to the "higher law" in a similar spirit.[34] To be sure, Nehru was scarcely oblivious of Lincoln, and there is every reason to think that his humanitarianism was supremely endearing to Nehru. Thus, on a state visit to the United States in 1949, when he visited the Lincoln Memorial and other official monuments, Nehru described himself as wanting to visit those sites "not for the sake of mere formality, but because they have long been enshrined in my heart and their example has inspired me as it has inspired innumerable countrymen of mine." The men commemorated at such memorials, Nehru told the House of Representatives in his formal address, were the "torch-bearers of freedom, not only for this country but for the world."[35] Nehru's private correspondence displays a similar sensitivity to Lincoln's teachings and writings. So, in a letter written to his daughter Indira in 1943, Nehru approvingly brings to her attention Pericles' funeral oration with the observation that it is "strongly reminiscent of Lincoln's speech on a like occasion at Gettysburg."[36]

The one constituency that was unquestionably drawn to Lincoln were the Dalits, and it is perhaps no coincidence that their leader, B. R. Ambedkar, seeking to signal his departure from the practice prevailing among Indian students who opted for an overseas course of study, chose to study in the United States, at Columbia University, rather than in Britain. Like Gandhi, Nehru, Patel, and many others before him who aspired to enter public life, Ambedkar trained as a lawyer; after returning to India upon the termination of his studies, Ambedkar would assume the leadership of the Dalits. His public life drew him into numerous controversies, particularly over his relentless critiques of upper-caste Hindu society. His ideas on the elimination of brutal and systemic forms of discrimination against the Dalits, or Untouchables as they were then called, attracted much resistance. Nevertheless, upon the attainment of Indian independence, Ambedkar was called upon to preside as chairman of the constitution drafting committee. His closing speech, as the Constitution was about to be adopted in late 1949, drew attention to the wide disparities in India and to the aspirations of the Dalits to forge a new life for themselves under a new constitution. "This urge for self-realization in the down-trodden classes must not be allowed to develop into a class struggle or class war," Ambedkar cautioned, for "it would lead to a division of the House. That would indeed be a day of disaster. For, as has been well said by Abraham Lincoln, a house divided against itself cannot stand very long."[37]

We do not know how deeply read Ambedkar was in Lincoln's writings. He acknowledged one supreme master, the Buddha, and in the closing years of his life he led tens of thousands of Dalits in conversion to Buddhism. His other main instrument for the advancement of the Dalits, the lowest of the low in the deeply stratified society of India, was the creation of a political party. "So impressed was Ambedkar with Lincoln," one commentator has recently opined, "that when he launched a political party for Dalits, he called it the Republican Party of India."[38] What is indisputably true is that, by the 1930s, Ambedkar had acquired a global reputation as the man who endeavored to emancipate the Dalits from the shackles of caste slavery. Characterizing Ambedkar as "one of the few men who have risen from the malodorous sink which is below the lowest caste of India," *Time* magazine in March 1936 devoted an editorial to him entitled "Untouchable Lincoln."[39] Yet, a deeper analysis of the intellectual and moral impression of Lincoln's writings on Ambedkar must surely necessitate a closer look at Ambedkar's large compendium of works, rather than rest on the presumption that both men decried the division of men into haves and have-nots, slave owners and slaves. Just what kind of Lincoln was being invoked by Ambedkar and the Dalits? Were Dalits aware of the immense discrepancies and paradoxes in the image of Lincoln who, as the Great Emancipator, still found it difficult to concede complete equality between blacks and whites?[40]

In assessing Lincoln's legacy in India, we are moved to ask, "To what extent can Lincoln be viewed as a world historical figure?" If decolonization and the emancipation of hundreds of millions of people from colonial yoke was one of the principal achievements of the second half of the twentieth century, a movement that was indisputably given its most forcible expression in the advent of Indian independence, can it be said that the most enduring images of Lincoln— as the emancipator of slaves and the architect of the Union who famously prophesied that "a house divided against itself cannot stand"[41]—contributed to this momentous development? Lincoln surely strikes a chord in nearly everyone who has struggled against racism, but did he figure prominently in the discussions about human rights that ensued in the 1930s and 1940s and culminated in the creation of the Universal Declaration of Human Rights?[42] In India, much more so than in most, if not nearly all, countries that achieved liberation from colonial rule, there has been a vigorous debate on human rights since independence and the suppression of various communities has been the subject of sustained if not always effectual critique. I am not, however, aware that Lincoln has ever been invoked in such debates, and contemporary discussions, such as those which took place in Durban in 2001 on the occasion of a large international convention on the elimination of racism and "all other forms of discrimination," have largely bypassed Lincoln. It may well be that the diminished role of the United States in recent years in such forums has led to the marginalization of some American thinkers and writers.

My narrative of Lincoln's legacy in India inescapably leads to a second and widely diverging conclusion. As is true of so much of the political culture of South Asia, the juxtaposition of India and Pakistan, now arch enemies and yet more than mere neighbors, can be instructive for our purposes.[43] When in late 2007 General Pervez Musharraf announced the suspension of constitutional rights and the proclamation of an emergency, he summoned the authority of Lincoln in defense of his efforts to safeguard Pakistan from destruction. "Abraham Lincoln usurped rights to preserve the union," Musharraf intoned on national television, and he perforce was now being compelled to do the same: "Pakistan comes first. Whatever I do is for Pakistan, and whatever anyone else thinks is secondary." As Lincoln had written in 1864, "By general law life and limb must be protected; yet often a limb must be amputated to save a life; but a life is never wisely given to save a limb. I felt that measures, otherwise unconstitutional, might become lawful, by becoming indispensable to the preservation of the constitution, through the preservation of the nation."[44] Musharraf had drawn not upon *Bartlett's Quotations*, or some other reference book, but rather on Richard Nixon's book *Leaders* where one encounters the following passage: "Lincoln's consuming passion during the time of crisis (the American Civil War 1861–65) was to preserve the Union. Towards that end he trampled individual liberties. His justification was necessity."[45]

That Musharraf, who assumed power through a coup d'état and ruled Pakistan with an iron fist for a decade, should so effortlessly have invoked Lincoln as his supreme authority may be unnerving to Lincoln's admirers even if they may find it flattering that Lincoln lives on in the most unexpected ways. But we are better positioned to appreciate the irony if we call to mind the two figures who entered into a deeper moral and political engagement with the life and thought of Lincoln than anyone else in India. Gandhi was the principal architect of the Indian independence movement, just as Ambedkar would earn a unique place for himself in the life of the nation as the moving force behind the Constitution of India and, in popular imagination, as the fearless champion of the unfettered right of Dalits to lead lives of dignity and equality. In Ambedkar, Gandhi found his most principled and determined foe. Gandhi idealized the Indian village, Ambedkar abhorred it; and if Gandhi was resolutely opposed to modern industrial civilization, Ambedkar was an energetic advocate of modernization and Westernization. These are simplifications, but they do not disguise the justifiably widespread impression that Ambedkar and Gandhi stand for largely different conceptions of the good life, moral progress, and the nature of human endeavor.[46] The future of India, it is sometimes argued, will be determined in good measure by the reception accorded to Gandhi and Ambedkar in different constituencies. It is, in any case, a striking testimony to the profound moral vision, ecumenism, and the purposefulness of his life that Lincoln could have drawn to himself the two most compelling and opposed figures in the recent history of India. It may well be that, in India's quest to accommodate both Gandhi and Ambedkar, there are cues to how Lincoln himself will fare in the tumultuous times that appear to lie ahead.

Notes

1. M. V. Kamath, *The United States and India 1776–1976* (Washington, DC: Embassy of India, 1976), 185.

2. The only mention I have found of Dossabhoy Cama is in W. H. Coates, *The Old "Country Trade" of the East Indies* (London: Cornmarket Press, 1969), 89. If, indeed, Cama did visit Lincoln and carry back to India his portrait, it may well be the one listed in the collections of the Prince of Wales Museum, Mumbai.

3. M. J. Akbar, *Nehru: The Making of India* (Delhi: Penguin Books, 1989), 565. Earlier biographies of Nehru do not mention the "bronze hand of Lincoln," and I could find no reference to it in what is perhaps the best known of the biographies of Nehru, the 3-volume work by S. Gopal. One Indian scholar of Lincoln has written that "Mahatma Gandhi wrote favorably of him and Jawaharlal Nehru hung a painting of him next to his desk in his study." See M. Rajendra Pandian, "Lincoln's Reputation Among the Tamils in South India: A Professional and Personal Influence" in William D. Pederson and Frank J. Williams,

eds., *Creative Breakthroughs in Leadership: James Madison, Abraham Lincoln and Mahatma Gandhi* (New Delhi: Pencraft International, 2007), 286.

The story of "Lincoln's hand" might seem apocryphal, in keeping with many of the other stories that have been generated about Lincoln, but for the fact that the source is a little-known speech by Nehru himself. In December 1956, in an address that Nehru gave in Washington, DC, he described a gift he had received from an American professor in 1951 and which he had ever since "treasured greatly." That was, Nehru said, "a mould in brass of Abraham Lincoln's right hand. It is a beautiful hand, strong and firm, and yet gentle. It has been kept ever since on my study table, and I look at it every day and it gives me strength. This may perhaps give you some idea of our thinking and our urges in India. For, above all, we believe in liberty, equality, the dignity of the individual and the freedom of the human spirit. Because of this, we are firmly wedded to the democratic way of life, and in our loyalty to this cause we will not falter." See *Jawaharlal Nehru's Speeches*, Volume 3: March 1953–August 1957 (New Delhi: Publications Division, Ministry of Information & Broadcasting, Government of India, 1958), 46.

It is possible that the bronze cast of Lincoln's right hand was gifted to Nehru by Arthur E. Morgan, chairman of the Tennessee Valley Authority from 1933 to 1938. Morgan came to have a long relationship with India, inspired in great measure by his attraction to the ideas of Gandhi. See Aaron D. Purcell, "Collaboration and the Small Community: Arthur Morgan and the Mitraniketan Project in Kerala," *The Historian* 65 (2003), 643–64.

4. Vaidehi Ramanathan, "Written Textual Production and Consumption (WTPC) in Vernacular and English-medium Settings in Gujarat, India," *Journal of Second Language Writing* 12 (2003), 139–40. Indian school textbooks in English suggest that stories about Lincoln are often part of the curriculum, largely to impress on young minds that "the chance of any little backwoods boy to become president of the United States" should never be minimized. The quotation appears in T. C. Collocott, ed., *New Radiant Reader*, Book 9 (New Delhi: Allied, 1976; 24th impression), lesson 16, a text used in class 9 in Bombay schools in 1978. See Narendra Nath Kalia, "Images of Men and Women in Indian Textbooks," *Comparative Education Review* 24, no. 2, part 2: Women and Education in the Third World (June, 1980), S217.

5. Pandian, "Lincoln's Reputation Among the Tamils in South India," 279–92. This study is confined to the state of Tamil Nadu, but it is doubtful, for example, that the Tamils of Sri Lanka, a considerable number of whom were long engaged in a bitter and exceedingly violent secessionist conflict with the Sinhalese-dominated Sri Lankan state, would have been similarly inspired by Lincoln.

6. Ibid., 279.

7. *The Hindu* (January 25, 2008), "Young World," 8.

8. As an illustration, see the biography, one in a long series, titled *Abraham Lincoln*, by Jyotsna Bharti (New Delhi: Spider Books, 2007).

9. The World Catalog lists books on Lincoln in the four principal languages of South India—Tamil, Telugu, Kannada, and Malayalam—as well as Hindi, Urdu, Gujarati, and Punjabi. A biography of Lincoln appeared in Telugu as early as 1907. See the appendix in this book by George Scratcherd. Even today, many Indian books, particularly those appearing in Indian languages and from small publishing houses, have no ISBN; consequently, the likelihood that there are books on Lincoln that do not appear in the World Catalog is very great.

10. Rana Nayar, "S. Gurdial Singh, a Punajbi Novelist, Jnanpith Award Winner," online at http://www.sikhphilosophy.net/history-of-sikhism/189-s-gurdial-singh-punjabi-novelist-jnanpith.html (accessed April 20, 2009).

11. Vinay Lal, *The Other Indians: A Political and Cultural History of South Asians in America* (New Delhi: HarperCollins, 2008), 23–27.

12. For further details, see Vinay Lal, "Gandhi's West, the West's Gandhi," *New Literary History* 40 (2009), 281–313.

13. M. K. Gandhi, "Abraham Lincoln," in *The Collected Works of Mahatma Gandhi*, 100 vols. (New Delhi: Publications Division, Ministry of Information and Broadcasting, Government of India, 1969–), 4:393. Hereafter cited as *CWMG*. The entire edition is available online, in PDF: www.gandhiserve.org/cwmg/cwmg.html.

14. See Kalidas Nag, *Tolstoy and Gandhi* (Patna: Pustak Bhandar, 1950).

15. See Norman W. Provizer, "On Hedgehogs, Foxes and Leadership: Uncovering the Other Tolstoy," *The Leadership Quarterly* 19, no. 4 (August 2008), 453–54.

16. Gandhi, "Abraham Lincoln," *CWMG,* 4:393–95.

17. The letter from the "Pennsylvanian," *Times of India* (August 13, 1919), is reproduced as Appendix VI in *CWMG*, 18:463–68.

18. Gandhi, "Letter to 'The Times of India'" (August 20, 1919), *CWMG*, 18:303–5.

19. Address at Cooper Union, New York City (February 28, 1860): see Abraham Lincoln, *Selected Speeches and Writings*, ed. Don E. Fehrenbacher (New York: Vintage Books/The Library of America, 1992), 251.

20. Cited by Richard Carwardine, *Lincoln: A Life of Purpose and Power* (New York: Alfred A. Knopf, 2006), 96.

21. Chanchala K. Naik, "Democracy and Emancipation: Reading Lincoln Through Gandhi," in Pederson and Williams, eds., *Creative Breakthroughs in Leadership*, 268–69.

22. Balaji Ranganathan, "Abraham Lincoln's Speeches and Mahatma Gandhi's *Hind Swaraj*: A Vision to a Possible Future," in Pederson and Williams, eds., *Creative Breakthroughs in Leadership*, 266.

23. The word "satanic" appears in *CWMG*, 21:241, though that is not its only occurrence; for Gandhi's critique of modern civilization, see M. K. Gandhi, "A Word of Explanation" [1921], in *Hind Swaraj or Indian Home Rule* (Ahmedabad: Navajivan Publishing House, 1939 [1909]).

24. Lincoln, "Lecture on Discoveries and Inventions, Jacksonville, Illinois" (February 11, 1859), *Lincoln: Speeches and Writings*, 207.

25. Vinay Lal, *Gandhi, citizenship, and the idea of a good civil society*, Mohan Singh Mehta Memorial Lecture, April 2008 (Udaipur: Seva Mandir, 2008).

26. *CWMG*, 75:178.

27. Address at Cooper Union, *Lincoln: Speeches and Writings*, 247.

28. Ibid., 246.

29. The most even-handed discussion of this vexed matter is to be found in A. J. Noorani, *The Trial of Bhagat Singh* (Delhi: Oxford University Press, 2001 [1996]), 233–53.

30. M. K. Gandhi, "A Word of Explanation" [1921], in *Hind Swaraj or Indian Home Rule* (Ahmedabad: Navajivan Publishing House, 1939 [1909]), 15.

31. *Selected Works of Motilal Nehru*, Ravinder Kumar and Hari Dev Sharma, eds., (New Delhi: Vikas Publishing House, 1986), IV:209 [speech of April 13, 1924].

32. Ibid., 339 [speech of February 14, 1924].

33. Uwe Luekben, "A Humanitarian as Broad as the World: Abraham Lincoln's Legacy in International Context," *German Historical Institute Bulletin* 42 (Spring 2008), 136.

34. I am mindful that it was William H. Seward, Secretary of State in Lincoln's cabinet, who appealed to the "higher law." However, whatever Lincoln's own fidelity to the Constitution, he also allowed the "voice of conscience" a supreme place in human affairs. This is what is designated by my usage of "higher law."

35. "A Voyage of Discovery," October 13, 1949, in *Selected Works of Jawaharlal Nehru: Second Series* (New Delhi: Jawaharlal Nehru Memorial Fund, 1992), 13:301–2.

36. Letter of June 5, 1943, in *Selected Works of Jawaharlal Nehru: First Series*, S. Gopal, ed. (New Delhi: Orient Longman, 1980), 13:159.

37. B. R. Ambedkar, Speech on the Draft Constitution, November 26, 1949, in *Dr. Babasaheb Ambedkar: Writings and Speeches*, Vasant Moon, ed. (Government of Maharashtra, Education Department, 1994), 13:1218.

38. Shobhan Saxena, "The audacity of hope," *Times of India* (November 9, 2008). A similar assertion is made by Eleanor Zelliot, "Understanding Dr. B. R. Ambedkar," *Religion Compass* 2 no. 5 (2008), 808.

39. See anon., "Religion: Untouchable Lincoln", *Time* (March 16, 1936), at http://www.time.com/time/magazine/article/0,9171,755912,00.html (accessed April 20, 2010).

40. Nishikant Waghmare, "India's Lower Castes" (June 3, 2007), writes with obvious disdain of Gandhi's "shameless" defense of caste and offers as a contrasting outlook the views of Lincoln: "As I would not be a slave, so I would not be a master. This expresses my idea of democracy." This article, published on countercurrents.org, is available online at http://www.countercurrents.org/waghmare030607.htm (accessed May 1, 2009). But I do not see in Waghmare's article a nuanced understanding either of Gandhi or of Lincoln. Gandhi's critical distinction between *varna* and caste aside, his conservative pronouncements were often at odds with his practices where he took unusual liberties and risks; on the other hand, Waghmare is clearly oblivious to Lincoln's profound ambivalence on the question of social and intellectual equality between blacks and whites.

41. "House Divided" speech (June 18, 1858), in Lincoln, *Selected Speeches and Writings*, 131.

42. Paul Gordon Lauren, *The Evolution of International Human Rights* (Philadelphia: University of Pennsylvania Press, 1998), makes no mention of Lincoln; and I think that is largely the case in the scholarly literature, though it is conceivable that a perusal of the draft documents and transcripts of committee meetings may suggest a more enhanced place of Lincoln in the discussions. Professor Jörg Nagler has quite rightly suggested that Franklin D. Roosevelt was a keen admirer of Lincoln, and the considerable impression of FDR's ideas on the debates surrounding the question of human rights perhaps points to the necessity of assessing Lincoln's influence in more subtle ways. I am grateful to Professor Nagler for his insightful comments on my paper.

43. See Vinay Lal, "The Strange and Beguiling Relationship of Pakistan and India," *Amerasia Journal* 34, no. 1 (2008), 99–111.

44. Letter to A. G. Hodges, April 4, 1864, as reproduced in Ronald C. White, Jr., *The Eloquent President: A Portrait of Lincoln Through His Words* (New York: Random House, 2005), 394.

45. Richard Milhous Nixon, *Leaders* (New York: Touchstone Books, 1990). Ikram Sehgal, editor of Pakistan's *Defence Journal*, has described how, in an interview with him,

Musharraf pulled out Nixon's book and began reading extracts about Lincoln. See Sehgal, "90 minutes in an hour of crisis," *Media Monitors Network* (January 22, 2002), online: http://mediamonitors.net/ikramsehgal60.html (accessed September 1, 2009).

46. For a nuanced view, see D. R. Nagaraj, *The Flaming Feet: A Study of the Dalit Movement* (Bangalore: South Forum Press, 1993).

11

A Man for All Seasons

LINCOLN IN SPAIN

Carolyn P. Boyd

Many Spaniards have found inspiration in Lincoln's life and career over the past 150 years, seeing in him the embodiment of their own political and social ideals.[1] What is striking is the president's perceived utility as a symbol to Spaniards whose political and cultural values have otherwise diverged remarkably. As might be expected, admiration for Lincoln has mirrored Spanish attitudes toward the United States more generally. Relations between the two nations have often been strained, owing to hemispheric rivalries, religious prejudice, and divergent political traditions. At the same time, cleavages within Spanish society along lines of class, religion, region, and ideology have produced disparate responses to the United States as an emblem of modernity, democracy, and progress. To the extent that Lincoln has been understood to embody democratic values, his fluctuating fortunes as a political symbol have reflected these cleavages. Moreover, Spaniards who have viewed Lincoln as a heroic or virtuous figure have tended to project on to him qualities they have found lacking in their own society. The multiple identities they have variously ascribed to Lincoln tell us more about their concerns, values, and hopes for their nation than they do about Lincoln himself.

In the nineteenth century, admiration for Lincoln was a feature of an oppositional political culture that sought to democratize and modernize the Spanish constitutional monarchy. Among the first reformers to venerate Lincoln were the Spanish abolitionists, who perceived the intimate connection between the restriction of civil and political rights under Spain's liberal constitution of 1845 and the enslavement of laborers of African descent in Spain's Caribbean empire. By the 1860s Spain was the only European power still to permit slavery in its colonial possessions, a humiliating distinction that reinforced the conviction among progressives that abolition was only one element in a larger project of national regeneration that must include moral, political, economic, and social reform.[2] As one republican leader put it, "It is necessary that Spain awaken;

that its citizens intercede on behalf of the slaves; that the clergy demand the fulfillment of the laws of Christ;. . . . if not, slavery will kill our country. Nations
pay for the crime of slavery with long centuries of misfortunes."[3]

The abolitionists interpreted Lincoln's election in 1860 and the outbreak of
war early the next year as signs that the American Republic would at last be
true to its founding principles. Many were journalists, intellectuals, and politicians aligned with the Progresista or Democratic parties, who were troubled by
the contradiction between democratic ideology and practice in the new nation.[4]
The U.S. example had long allowed anti-abolition forces to contend that slavery and democracy were not incompatible. Moreover, as long as the American
Republic suffered from the "illness" of slavery, it was difficult to argue that
republicanism was a morally superior alternative to monarchy. Counting on
Lincoln's well-known opposition to slavery to rectify this dilemma, Spanish
progressives felt justified in claiming that American republicanism provided a
"model for all the peoples of the world . . ."[5]

Most members of the Spanish political class rejected this claim, however,
believing the conservative liberal monarchy to be the best safeguard of their
interests. Among the most vehement critics of republicanism were the Carlists,
a counterrevolutionary movement that had fought an unsuccessful war against
the liberal monarchy in the 1830s and remained unreconciled to liberalism, let
alone republicanism. In 1862, the Carlist newspaper, *El Pensamiento Español*,
argued that the war in the United States was the inevitable consequence of its
godless political institutions:

> The history of this model republic can be summed up in a few words.
> It came into being by rebellion. It was founded on atheism. It was
> populated by the dregs of all the nations in the world. It has lived with-
> out law of God or man. Within a hundred years, greed has ruined it.
> Now it is fighting like a cannibal, and it will die in a flood of blood
> and mire. Such is the real history of the one and only state in the world
> which has succeeded in constituting itself according to the flaming the-
> ories of democracy. The example is too horrible to stir any desire for
> imitation in Europe.[6]

Believing that the future of democratic republicanism depended upon the
immediate end of slavery in the United States, Spanish abolitionists were disappointed by the conciliatory tone of Lincoln's first inaugural address. They worried that his appeal to reason and compromise was insufficient to rally people
to his cause and would lead to the triumph of the more impassioned partisans
of the Confederacy. Early judgments of the new president were harsh:

> Lincoln is far from being a political talent of the first rank, much less
> the one needed in the current circumstances. He possesses firmness and
> serenity but lacks imagination and spirit. The cold inflexibility of the men

of the North is only appropriate in normal situations, and in this extraordinary case, one misses the activity and creative genius that animates the men of the South.[7]

Moreover, Lincoln's insistence on the indissolubility of the Union puzzled Spanish republicans, most of who subscribed to the "pactist" or contractual theory of federalism.[8] Believing that bonds among self-governing states should be voluntary and contingent upon mutual consent, they were skeptical of Lincoln's argument that the Confederacy lacked the right to secede. Indeed, their enthusiasm for the American federal republic sprang in good measure from their opposition to the rigid centralization of the Spanish state and to its architects in the conservative liberal party, known as the Moderados. Carl Schurz, the U.S. minister to Madrid, informed the president that European opinion would only swing to the North if the cause were a noble one, like abolition rather than a dispute over the right of secession.[9]

After the Emancipation Proclamation, however, the democratic-left no longer questioned Lincoln's capacity for leadership. While Spanish conservatives labeled the Proclamation a "first-rate political blunder," "inopportune," and "vindictive,"[10] progressives hailed it as a long-overdue, if still incomplete, solution to the fundamental cause of the war.[11] Lincoln had at last redeemed the promise of the American Republic, according to the republican journalist and orator, Emilio Castelar: "The puritans founded the colony; the great men of the past century, the Republic; but Lincoln has sanctified it."[12]

The Spanish Abolitionist Society was founded shortly after the Emancipation Proclamation, growing quickly to 700 members.[13] Among its leaders was the influential Romantic poet Carolina Coronado, the wife of the American chargé d'affaires, Horatio Perry. At her salon in Madrid, intellectuals, politicians, and literary figures of all political persuasions met for discussion, although her dedication to abolitionism and other liberal causes eventually distanced her from the court and aristocratic circles in which she had previously travelled.[14]

Lincoln's early reputation in Spain owed a great deal to Coronado's influence. In an "Ode to Lincoln" published after the election of 1860, she hailed the new president as the "faithful son of the glorious, just, kind-hearted Washington," whose mission was to restore the honor of both her native land and her adopted one:

> Grand example of Christian courage
> today you raise your human voice
> against the injustice of slavery
> so that the proud genius
> of the original people
> may recover its book of sacred laws.[15]

In an open letter widely reprinted during the Civil War, Coronado praised Lincoln, "the patriarch, the prudent one, the friend of peace," for understanding that even pacifists must sometimes take up arms for a just cause.[16] Shortly after Lincoln's assassination, she published yet another poem in his honor, "The Redeeming Eagle," in which she called on Lincoln to aid Spain in its quest for redemption from the sin of slavery:

> Tell me how it was; inspire my mind.
> Tell me, how, to the admiration of the world
> did you wipe away the black stain
> that vilely tarnished your brilliant crest?
> How did you put out that awful pyre,
> A second Inquisition, that across the Atlantic,
> Bartolomé, with an unwise light
> ignited there, to later regret?[17]

As this and other poems published in the wake of Lincoln's death suggest, Lincoln's assassination sealed his reputation as a martyr to the principle of freedom. Lincoln was mourned not only as "the second Christ of the blacks," but also as the redeemer of the American Republic and by extension, all of humanity.[18] Poems in the popular press compared the assassin John Wilkes Booth to such notorious villains as Nero and Tiberius.[19] As the news of Lincoln's death spread, the American embassy received expressions of sorrow from all over the country, while other private and public entities wrote directly to the U.S. government to offer their condolences.[20]

Abolitionists were disappointed when the end of slavery in the United States did not immediately produce a similar result in Cuba and Puerto Rico, but their hopes rose again in September 1868, when a military coup led by the liberal General Juan Prim ended the Bourbon monarchy, sent Queen Isabel II into exile, and brought a coalition of Progresistas, Radicals, and Democrats to power. In a poem dedicated "To the Abolition of Slavery in Cuba," written shortly after the September Revolution, Carolina Coronado once again invoked Lincoln, the "immortal eagle," while pointing out the unsustainable contradiction between Caribbean slavery and the democratic goals of the new revolutionary regime in the peninsula:

> If the immortal eagle already set free
> the Africans from their shame,
> why do the brothers who are their neighbors
> in the Antilles remain enslaved?
> By what right, noble Castile
> do you keep their hands in chains,
> when, guided by the call of liberty,
> you break sovereign scepters?[21]

During the next six years—known in Spanish history as the Revolutionary Sexennium—the Abolitionist Society stepped up its campaign, in which the United States and its sixteenth president were more than ever a point of reference. They quoted Lincoln's "house divided" speech to support their contention that the separatist insurgency that had broken out in Cuba could only be defeated if liberty were guaranteed for all citizens of the empire.[22] Allusions to the sacrifice of the "immortal Lincoln" on behalf of a suffering humanity, sometimes in explicitly messianic terms, were a staple of abolitionist rhetoric and poetry.[23] Both those favoring immediate emancipation and those defending a gradualist approach could find support for their position in Lincoln's published views, and his name was frequently invoked to lend a veneer of authority and morality to competing arguments. But although emancipation was finally legislated in 1873 for Puerto Rico, where the number of slaves was relatively small, in Cuba fear of racial conflict and the profitability of the sugar industry delayed full abolition until 1886. The memory of Lincoln as the Great Emancipator thus remained an important weapon in the abolitionist arsenal for two decades after his death.

The myth of Lincoln, the hero of the democratic revolution, was similarly nurtured in the hectic incubator of the Revolutionary Sexennium of 1868–74, a period of political and social instability that included the adoption of a new democratic constitution, the coronation of King Amadeo I of the House of Savoy, his abdication and the declaration of the Spanish Republic in 1873, Carlist, Cuban separatist, cantonalist and Internationalist insurrections, and two military coups that culminated in the restoration of the Bourbon monarchy in 1874.[24] Throughout these upheavals and beyond, Spanish progressives retained their admiration for Lincoln, whose life and death symbolized the triumph of liberty in the broadest possible sense. According to Coronado, slavery was only one of the tyrannies that Lincoln, "The Redeeming Eagle," had vanquished:

> In you was born the new dynasty
> that will reign in the ageless world,
> that majesty of majesties
> that the heavens only confer upon virtue.
> The sceptre, without human tyranny,
> the crown without mad vanities,
> watered with your pure blood
> and consecrated in the New World.
> Humble woodcutter, monarchs go
> to place flowers on your tomb,
> and rich ships and humble barques
> lower their flags of many colors;
> for you in provinces of the world entire
> eminent orators raise their voices

and the Christian church with its various rites
lifts your glory to infinitude.[25]

As these stanzas suggest, for Spanish progressives like Coronado the international outpouring of sorrow provoked by Lincoln's assassination represented a revolution in hierarchies, the birth of a new age in which kings paid their respects at the tomb of a humble rail-splitter. The Progresista daily, *La Iberia*, compared the homage paid to Lincoln to the universal mourning that had accompanied the death of Richard Cobden, the British Radical politician, free-trader, and pacifist, just a few days before Lincoln's assassination: "Lincoln and Cobden! That is, two obscure workers, born to nothing, *plebeians*, as they would have said less than a century ago, attend Parliaments, write letters to Kings and rise above all the traditions and dominate all the aristocracies. Progress is visible, great, consoling!"[26]

In the ideology of the middle-class left, Lincoln personified the moral, self-actualizing citizen who enabled democracies to prosper. At the same time, the ambiguities in Lincoln's character and career permitted a broad spectrum of groups who otherwise disagreed on substantive matters to claim the president as their own. In general, the qualities that progressives professed to find in Lincoln offered a reverse image of the defects they perceived in their own society. An iconic figure whose stature was unrelated to birth or rank, Lincoln was a ruler whose homely virtues contrasted dramatically with the pomp, profligacy, and irresponsibility of the Spanish monarchy. In republican discourse Lincoln's life exemplified the rewards of democracy, republicanism, freedom of conscience and expression, and political and social equality—in sum the political values that the revolutionaries of 1868 had found lacking in the Isabelline monarchy and that animated their vision of the new Spain they hoped to create.

In many ways Lincoln represented an idealized vision of the United States of America, "that great Republic that is the despair of reactionaries and the shame of pessimists."[27] Despite reservations about the "mercantile" and expansionist tendencies in American culture, Spanish reformers believed the United States embodied the progressive spirit of the century, and its constitution served as the model for the democratic Spanish constitution of 1869.[28] Convinced of the "moralizing virtues" of individual liberty, they interpreted Lincoln's character and career as the natural outcome of the American political system.[29] His evident humanity, modesty, and respect for public opinion served to assuage apprehensions aroused by the unexpected display of American military and industrial power during the Civil War.

The image of Lincoln that took shape in Spain during the 1870s and 1880s owed much to two influential public figures, Emilio Castelar and Rafael María de Labra. Collaborators in the progressive press, the Abolitionist Society, the Madrid Athenaeum, the republican movement, and the Cortes, they were politicians whose moral vision and rhetorical skills earned them the respect of their contemporaries in Spain and abroad. Castelar, born into a liberal middle-class family in 1832, enjoyed an international reputation as a master of the florid oratorical style so popular in the nineteenth century. He first made his mark in the 1850s and '60s in the Athenaeum, the University of Madrid, and the pages of *La Discusión* and *La Democracia*, two leading republican dailies, where he fiercely attacked colonial slavery, the monarchy, and the conservative generals, clerics, and politicians who ruled Spain with an iron fist. Deprived of his university post in 1865 and forced to flee Spain the following year, he returned after the September Revolution and was elected as a member of the newly formed Federal Republican Party to the Constituent Cortes that drafted the constitution of 1869. When the abrupt abdication of King Amadeo I in 1873 led to the proclamation of the Spanish Republic, Castelar served as minister of state and then as its fourth—and last—president. Although he initially opposed the Bourbon restoration, Castelar eventually founded the Possibilist Party to work for democratization within the framework of the constitutional monarchy, a pragmatic compromise that alienated him from his more doctrinaire republican co-religionaries.[30]

Labra, son of a liberal Spanish general, was born in Havana in 1840. During his long career he distinguished himself as a tireless proponent of abolition, colonial autonomy, and educational reform. As a republican deputy to the Cortes and later as senator, he represented both Cuba and Puerto Rico before their independence in 1898. President of the Abolitionist Society and editor of its newspaper, Labra played a decisive role in the abolition of slavery, but he failed in his efforts to secure greater autonomy for the overseas possessions. In 1876 he joined a group of progressive university professors in founding the Institución Libre de Enseñanza, an influential private academy whose ideas about educational reform shaped the next generation of teachers, policy makers, and public intellectuals in Spain. Alongside these activities, Labra was an advocate for such progressive causes as prison reform, women's education, and international law.[31]

Like many democratic reformers of their generation, both Castelar and Labra were disciples of the idealist German philosopher Karl Friedrich Krause, a student of Hegel.[32] The Spanish Krausists defined man as a rational and moral being whose spirit evolved through acts of exploration and self-creation. Knowledge of the natural laws of morality and justice depended upon individual discovery and rational reflection, not dogma or divine revelation. An ideology of both protest and renewal, Krausism was a prescriptive for modernization in a society that had largely escaped the intellectual and cultural repercussions of the Reformation and the Enlightenment. At the same time, its evolutionary idealism appealed to middle-class reformers with little appetite for revolution, particularly after the upheavals of the Revolutionary Sexennium. Led by the Institución Libre de Enseñanza after 1875, the Krausists poured their energies into educational reform, believing that the preparation of active, aware citizens was a necessary precondition for democratic change. The task of education, according to the founder of the Institución, Francisco Giner de los Ríos, was to "make men"—"sincere, natural, sober, magnanimous, creative, manly, modest men, healthy in body and soul, invincible friends of the good and implacable enemies of evil."[33] Until its demise during the Spanish civil war, the Institución campaigned tirelessly to transform Spanish education by replacing authoritarian educational practices premised on rote memorization with active methods based on discovery and lived experience.

For Castelar and Labra, telling the story of Lincoln, the self-made man, was a form of civic education. Like books of saints and martyrs for Catholic believers or Plutarch's *Lives* for gentlemen, biographies of self-made men would provide ordinary Spaniards with models to venerate and more important, to emulate. As Labra noted:

> [O]ne can never applaud enough the English and North American custom of disseminating, by means of pamphlets and books, the personal history of great figures who, by virtue of their real merits or the preoccupations and wishes of the public, represent the great enterprises and the periods of modern history. . . . It would be difficult to find a more appropriate way of putting the history of the country within reach of the generality of people, especially today when Kings have become simple mortals and human life unfolds in many different spheres.[34]

As tools of political mobilization and civic instruction, such biographies possessed an enormous appeal for democratic reformers. Labra included lives of Toussaint Louverture, William Gladstone, and the enlightened Portuguese reformer, the Marqués de Pombal, in a collection of political biographies he published in 1887; Castelar wrote a number of short biographical sketches of figures like Garibaldi, Gambetta, Juárez, and Carolina Coronado, as well as his portrait of Lincoln.[35] For both men, Lincoln represented an iconic figure who embodied the individual moral qualities they believed to be essential to democratic republicanism.

Biographies of self-made men like Lincoln were clearly intended to counter the socialist and anarchist ideologies that had begun to receive support among the working classes during the Revolutionary Sexennium and that expanded their appeal significantly after the legalization of workers' associations in 1881. One Spanish educator writing at the turn of the century noted approvingly that in England and the United States biographies served as a "lightning rod on the social edifice, deflecting the electrical charge of revolutionary passions."[36] But it would be a mistake to dismiss such books as counterrevolutionary, for they were in fact written with a revolutionary intent: to democratize the existing order by broadening popular political participation and demolishing social hierarchies. In a conservative Catholic society where workers were taught to accept earthly submission in anticipation of a heavenly reward, attributing

Lincoln's fame and achievements to individual effort in the context of democratic opportunity held revolutionary implications. Nevertheless, socialist
and anarcho-syndicalist movements evinced little interest in Lincoln as a role
model. For them, the key to the revolutionary transformation of society lay in
collective action rather than individual self-improvement.

Over the course of his career Castelar described Lincoln's life and character many times in lectures, essays, and books. The first instance may have
been an essay Castelar published in 1864 that compared Lincoln and Benito
Juárez, two American patriots then fighting for republicanism, liberty, and
independence from European intervention.[37] The best known of his portraits, in which Lincoln appeared as a "new Moses" who had died "in the
very moment of his victory, like Christ, like Socrates, like all redeemers"
became, in translation, a staple of declamatory literature in the United States
at the turn of the century.[38] Embedded in a parliamentary speech delivered
during the Revolutionary Sexennium, Castelar's portrayal of Lincoln conveyed both an appreciation of American institutions and a critique of Spanish ones. According to Castelar, Lincoln's character was decisively shaped by
the environment in which he was born and grew to manhood. His intrinsic
human qualities—humility, dedication to principle, and patriotism—reached
their fullest potential in the "primeval forests" of America, where men were
free to achieve their dreams through hard work and determination. A "child
of Nature," lacking formal instruction, he was an inspiring autodidact who
had learned to read from the Bible. (Castelar frequently attributed Lincoln's
liberal values to his presumed Christian faith, an implicit rebuke to the Spanish church, which equated liberalism with atheism.)[39] His political values
were shaped in the state and local institutions that encouraged political participation and civic engagement on a broad scale. In contrast to the stifling
administrative centralization in Spain, the autonomous municipality lays at
the heart of the decentralized and federated United States, offering ordinary
folk like Lincoln, "a school of liberty."[40]

One of the qualities Castelar most admired in Lincoln was what he often
called "serenity" or "prudence." However critical of the established order,
Castelar was neither a Jacobin nor a socialist, preferring to rely on the laws of
history and nature and the beneficent effects of republican institutions to secure
the liberty, prosperity, and social harmony that he believed were the ultimate
destiny of humankind. For Castelar, Lincoln represented the ideal statesman—
beholden neither to the past nor to privilege, firm of purpose, decisive in action
but respectful of the rule of law, temperate, and pragmatic. In America, a new
land without history, such moderation in pursuit of revolutionary change came
naturally. In old Europe, however, the "double despotism" of an intolerant
church and an absolute monarchy had induced reformers to become "violent
and revolutionary and consequently not very democratic, not very liberal and
not very republican."[41]

Despite his admiration for Lincoln's prudence and devotion to peace, Castelar also praised his unflinching determination to go to war to preserve liberty and national unity. No democratic society could wish for peace at any price. In a characteristically grandiloquent phrase, he reminded his readers that "A republican state always prefers the storms of a tempestuous revolution to the sepulchral silence of despotism."[42] As president of the Republic in 1873, Castelar staked his own political career on the principle of national unity, which he believed to be "a principle of obvious indisputability, of inarguable force."[43] Compelled by circumstance to confront Internationalist and cantonalist revolts in southern and eastern Spain, Carlist insurrection in Catalonia and the Basque Provinces, and an ongoing rebellion in Cuba, Castelar did not hesitate to suspend both the constitution and his democratic convictions and to call upon the army, justifying his actions with reference to Lincoln's assumption of extraordinary powers during the Civil War.

But Lincoln the savior of the Union was less attractive than Lincoln the Great Emancipator to many Spaniards, for whom the memory of Lincoln's "tyranny" overshadowed his image as a secular saint.[44] Castelar's many enemies on the right opportunistically criticized the republican habit of "deifying" Lincoln, who "without the least scruple, without the most minimal vacillation, started a civil war of extermination and without quarter" against a territory whose only crime was to make use of its sovereign powers to rebel against the Union.[45] But federal republicans were equally troubled by Lincoln's willingness to prioritize national unity over civil liberties and Southern self-determination. Castelar, unrepentant, staunchly defended his hero to the end. In his opinion, in public memory Lincoln had "risen to the heavens, fluttering his wings of light among the heroes and martyrs and redeemers of humankind."[46]

Like Castelar, Rafael María de Labra was initially drawn to Lincoln because of the Emancipation Proclamation. During his twenty-year anti-slavery campaign, he frequently quoted from Lincoln's speeches and claimed him as an ally. The biography that he published in 1883 attributed Lincoln's greatness to the interplay of character, environment, and history. Labra saw Lincoln and his precursor Toussaint Louverture as leaders chosen by providence to rectify three hundred years of human malice and greed. But whereas Louverture's fate was to voice a protest, Lincoln's destiny was greater—to redress the martyrdom of the Haitian revolutionary and to rescue democracy from the stain of slavery. Labra shared Castelar's admiration for Lincoln's simplicity and authenticity: his rough appearance, speech, and manners, his work ethic, his honesty, and his ability to speak to the concerns of ordinary citizens. Other American leaders might have possessed greater intelligence, education, and refinement, but none surpassed him in dedication to the "eternal cause" of human freedom. Labra also emphasized Lincoln's perseverence, a quality he found lacking among Spain's popular classes, which alternated between fits of revolutionary insurrectionism and profound apathy. Lincoln's distinction, in Labra's view, lay in his *character*, the same quality that had raised George Washington above his gifted contemporaries. The superiority of democratic systems was that they were more likely to produce the patient and prudent leaders willing to sacrifice self-interest to the greater good.[47]

Castelar and Labra were the most eminent of Lincoln's biographers, but less prominent reformers also appreciated Lincoln's value as a model of modesty, temperance, and self-improvement at a time of rising working-class unrest. A biography of Lincoln was chosen to inaugurate a new series of books about "Illustrious Workers" in 1868, whose purpose was "to inform the working class about its triumphs; to make it understand practically that it can rise above the place in which it finds itself to the highest positions in society; to inspire it, at the same time, with feelings of dignity, within its sphere and its class, and with the value of intelligent cooperation in the work of society."[48] Another volume, titled *Martyrs of the Republic*, which appeared after the proclamation of the Republic in 1873, featured biographies of such renowned apostles of liberty as Lincoln, Mazzini, Garibaldi, and Kossuth, as well as Spanish martyrs to the republican cause. The essays in this two-volume work portrayed lives of "heroic beauty, noble deeds and examples of courage and patriotism, which only liberty can inspire," but they also stressed that heroism rested upon everyday virtues within reach of all. Lincoln embodied the moral superiority of democratic republicanism: "Lincoln should be called the martyr of liberty, the martyr of the great republican idea, of that idea that is the synthesis of disinterest, abnegation and justice."[49]

The goal of these and other contemporary biographies by middle-class reformers was to inculcate popular faith in the power of individual endeavor to overcome poverty and social disadvantage.[50] Self-made men like Lincoln exemplified the idea that anyone could achieve success by dint of hard work, courage, and perseverance. The challenge for this literature of uplift was to strike a balance between Lincoln's identity as the quintessential American, the child of nature born on the frontier; his extraordinary character, which enabled him to rise to lead the nation at its moment of greatest peril; and the universal human qualities that gave his life pedagogic value. Most authors solved the dilemma, as did Castelar and Labra, by defining Lincoln's greatness as the felicitous outcome of the providential laws of history, propitious circumstances, and personal effort. Emphasizing only his unique gifts would have diminished his utility for those seeking to encourage working-class rectitude and ambition. As one biographer put it:

All men, by the mere fact of being men, possess the germ of the virtues that adorned Lincoln. Their ultimate development depends upon the use that we make of the circumstances that surround us . . . We are the makers of our own developing existence . . . Nothing will seem impossible to the spirit decidedly resolved on achieving the end of existence, which is nothing other than perfection.[51]

The spate of biographies that appeared in the twenty years or so after Lincoln's death dwindled thereafter. The centenary of his birth produced one major biography, but no monuments or other public tributes to the president.[52] Mounting tension with the United States, which culminated in the loss of Cuba and Puerto Rico in the Spanish-American War of 1898, had disillusioned many former admirers of the American Republic. Both Labra and Castelar publicly condemned American imperialism, which they saw as a betrayal of the values of Lincoln and the founders. As Castelar proclaimed: "Franklin, Washington, Lincoln, those benefactors of Humanity, cannot turn into Xerxes, Pharaoh, Attila, those scourges of God."[53] Also contributing to the decline of Lincoln hagiography after the turn of the century was the dramatic expansion of the socialist and anarcho-syndicalist movements, whose leaders rejected the meliorist individualism so popular with middle-class republicans.

Lincoln's popularity in Spain after 1898 also fell victim to the impassioned debate over Spanish national identity and history that pitted modernizers against Catholic traditionalists. Conservatives who defined the nation in terms of its traditional Catholic identity had never admired American politics and culture. While the figure of Lincoln remained attractive to democratic reformers, they became less inclined to borrow heroes and symbols from abroad, in order to forestall criticism from Spanish conservatives who were only too willing to condemn their opponents as traitors and heretics enamored of all things foreign, while positioning themselves as the defenders of "true Spain" and its traditional Catholic values. To deny these critics the opportunity to disparage their patriotism and to substantiate their claim that Spain had its own democratic tradition, progressives turned to indigenous heroes rather than to foreign models. Even after the proclamation of the Second Republic in 1931 brought to power a new generation of progressive reformers, Lincoln and the international democratic heroes of the nineteenth century were conspicuously absent from their discourse.[54] To be sure, the American battalions who fought on behalf of the Second Spanish Republic during the Spanish civil war of 1936–39 became collectively known as the Abraham Lincoln Brigade, but the name was selected for its symbolic significance for American volunteers and supporters, not for Spaniards.

A few biographies featuring Lincoln were published by Spaniards in exile after the end of the civil war,[55] but in Spain itself biographies of Lincoln only began to reappear in appreciable numbers in the 1950s and 1960s. In contrast to the previous century, when the democratic opposition used Lincoln to critique the conservative status quo, Lincoln's promoters were now to be found on the right. Seeking to normalize relations with Europe and the United States and to launch a project of capitalist economic modernization, the Franco regime approved publication of numerous biographies of Lincoln, the self-made man and Civil War leader, including several written for children.[56] The regime seems to have calculated that Lincoln's moral virtues—simplicity, religious faith, loyalty to family and country, love of learning—would reinforce its campaign to transform the Spanish people into a nation of hardworking, politically quiescent producers and consumers. Equally attractive were Lincoln's "house divided" speech and his commitment to national unity, which provided implicit parallels with the regional and constitutional conflicts that divided Spain in the 1930s. In contrast, after Franco's death in 1975 and the subsequent transition to democracy, schoolbook biographies and popular translations reflected the renewed interest in Lincoln as the exemplar of democratic virtue.[57]

Three works for adult audiences published by Spanish authors in the thirty years after the transition to democracy demonstrate the malleability of the Lincoln myth and the diversity of the causes in which it can be enlisted.[58] In all three, Lincoln's life and times are narrated and interpreted so as to shed light on contemporary political concerns in Spain. The first was published in 1989 by Victor Alba, the pen name of a radical Catalan journalist who spent thirty-five years in exile before returning to Spain after the death of Franco. Alba's biography, written from a leftist perspective, highlights the democratic, working-class Lincoln and his devotion to government of, by, and for the people. In contrast, a scholarly biography by Julián Ruiz Rivera, a professor of American History at the University of Seville, portrays Lincoln as the embodiment of a democratic political system governed by pragmatism and compromise. Published in 1991, it reflects the fear of ideological extremism and social conflict that permeated Spanish political life in the years immediately after the democratic transition.

More polemical is the life-and-times biography of Lincoln, the savior of the Union, published in 2002 by the prolific right-wing journalist César Vidal. In this lengthy narrative, the preservation of the Union is Lincoln's paramount concern, and federalist ideology and what Vidal labels "Southern nationalism" are assigned ultimate responsibility for the outbreak of the Civil War. The implied comparisons to Catalan and Basque nationalists become explicit in the revised version of the biography that Vidal published in 2009 with the subtitle, "Unity against Self-Determination," in which he intermittently interrupts the narrative to reflect upon Catalan and Basque demands for political devolution and the threat these pose to the integrity of the Spanish nation.[59] Elsewhere in the biography, Vidal emphasizes the important role that religion played in Lincoln's life, a reproach, presumably, to the secularizing policies of the governing Socialist Party.

The Spanish right has also turned to Lincoln to fend off mounting demands from the left for a true accounting for the crimes and injustices of the Franquist regime. In his biography of Lincoln, Vidal praises the American president's desire to put national reconciliation ahead of the need for vengeance, an implicit rebuke to those seeking retrospective justice for the victims of Franquist repression. For a 2009 article in *The New Yorker* about efforts to exhume the body of the assassinated poet Federico Garcia Lorca, an American reporter interviewed don Fernando Serrano Súñer y Polo, the son of Franco's brother-in-law, Ramón Serrano Súñer, who was a Nazi sympathizer, head of the Spanish Falange (Spain's fascist party), and minister of the Interior and Foreign Affairs during World War II. D. Fernando, who contends that the Falange has been "misinterpreted," reminded his American interlocutor that not all those who died in the war were victims of Franco. Then, after expressing admiration for Lincoln's commitment to reconciliation, he recited the Gettysburg Address by heart.[60]

As these examples suggest, in Spain Lincoln has remained a man for all seasons. Just as in the nineteenth century, however, the appropriation of the Lincoln myth by groups across the political spectrum sheds greater light on contemporary political conflicts than it does on Lincoln and his age.

Notes

1. I would like to thank Professor Gregorio de la Fuente of the Universidad Complutense of Madrid, who provided bibliographical guidance at the beginning of this project, and Victoria Blacik, a Ph.D. candidate at the University of California, Irvine, who provided essential research assistance.

2. Christopher Schmidt-Nowara, *Empire and Antislavery: Spain, Cuba, and Puerto Rico, 1833–1874* (Pittsburgh: University of Pittsburgh Press, 1999).

3. Emilio Castelar, *Perfiles de personajes, y bocetos de ideas* (Madrid: Librerías de A. de San Martín, 1875), 270–71.

4. *La Iberia*, December 22, 1860; Castelar, *Perfiles de personajes*, 264.

5. María Victoria López-Cordón, *La revolución de 1868 y la I República* (Madrid: Siglo Veintiuno Editores, 1976), 368.

6. Donaldson Jordan and Edwin J. Pratt, *Europe and the American Civil War* (New York: Octagon Books, 1969), 251–52.

7. *La Iberia*, March 27 and December 21, 1861.

8. Ibid., June 6, 1861.

9. James W. Cortada, *Spain and the American Civil War: Relations at Mid-Century, 1855–1868* (Philadelphia: American Philosophical Society, 1980), 57–58.

10. Jordan and Pratt, *Europe and the American Civil War*, 252; *El Lloyd Español*, October 23, 1862.

11. *La Iberia,* December 24, 1862 and January 21, 1863.

12. Emilio Castelar, *Cuestiones políticas y sociales* (Madrid: A. de San Martin/A. Jubera, 1870), 57.

13. Paloma Arroyo Jiménez, "La Sociedad Abolicionista Española, 1864–1886," *Cuadernos de historia moderna y contemporánea*, no. 3 (1982); Jorge Maluquer de Motes Bernet, "El problema de la esclavitud y la Revolución de 1868," *Hispania* 31, no. 117 (1971); Schmidt-Nowara, *Empire and Antislavery: Spain, Cuba, and Puerto Rico, 1833–1874*.

14. Ramón Gómez de la Serna, *Mi tía Carolina Coronado* (Buenos Aires: Emecé Editores s. a., 1942); Alberto Castilla, *Carolina Coronado de Perry: biografía, poesía e historia en la España del siglo XIX* (Madrid: Ediciones Beramar, 1987); Isabel María Pérez

González, *Carolina Coronado: etopeya de una mujer* (Badajoz: Departamento de Publicaciones, Diputación Provincial de Badajoz, 1986); Adolfo de Sandoval, *Carolina Coronado y su época* (Zaragoza: Librería General, 1929); Lisa L. Surwillo, "Poetic Diplomacy: Carolina Coronado and the American Civil War," *Comparative American Studies* 5, no. 4 (2007).

15. Carolina Coronado and Gregorio Torres Nebrera, *Obra poética* (Mérida: Editora Regional de Extremadura, 1993), 731–33.

16. Carolina Coronado and Gregorio Torres Nebrera, *Obra en prosa* (Mérida: Editora Regional de Extremadura, 1999), 352.

17. Surwillo, "Poetic Diplomacy: Carolina Coronado and the American Civil War," 418.

18. *El Abolicionista Español*, July 15, 1865.

19. Ibid., August 15, 1865.

20. Isaac Carilo y O'Farrill, "La muerte de Lincoln," *Escenas contemporáneas*, April 1865, 150; M. del Palacio, "Revista de la semana," *El Periódico Ilustrado*, no. 9 (1865): 66; United States Dept. of State, *The assassination of Abraham Lincoln, late President of the United States and the attempted assassination of William H. Seward, Secretary of State, and Frederick W. Seward, Assistant Secretary, on the evening of the 14th of April, 1865: expressions of condolence and sympathy inspired by these events* (Washington: Government Printing Office, 1867); "Crónica política," *Gil Blas* 5, 50 (1868).

21. Castilla, *Carolina Coronado de Perry: biografía, poesía e historia en la España del siglo XIX*, 175.

22. Rafael M. de Labra, *La cuestión social en las Antillas Españolas: Discurso pronunciado en la conferencia del 26 de febrero de 1872*. Conferencias anti-esclavistas 6 (Madrid: Secretaría de la Sociedad Abolicionista Española, 1872), 13.

23. *El cancionero del esclavo. Colección de poesías laureadas y recomendadas por el jurado en el certámen convocado por la Sociedad Abolicionista Española*, (Madrid: Publicaciones Populares de la Sociedad Abolicionista Española, 1866).

24. Rafael Serrano García, ed., *El sexenio democrático*, Ayer 44 (Madrid: Asociación de Historia Contemporánea: Marcial Pons Ediciones de Historia, 2001).

25. Coronado and Torres Nebrera, *Obra poética*, 2, 836.

26. *La Iberia*, May 1, 1865.

27. Rafael M. de Labra, *De la representación é influencia de los Estados-Unidos de América en el derecho internacional. Conferencia dada en la Institución Libre de Enseñanza de Madrid, el día 1º de abril de 1877* (Madrid: A. J. Alaria, 1877), 38.

28. Joaquín A. Oltra, *La influencia norteamericana en la constitución española de 1869*, Estudios de historia de la Administración (Madrid: Inst. de Estudios Administrativos, 1972).

29. Emilio Castelar, *Las guerras de América y Egipto: historia contemporánea* (Madrid: Oficinas de la Ilustración Española y Americana, 1883), 25.

30. David Hannay, *Don Emilio Castelar* (London: Bliss Sands and Foster, 1896); José Antonio Hernández Guerrero, Fátima Coca Ramírez, and Isabel Morales Sánchez, *Emilio Castelar y su época: Actas del I Seminario Emilio Castelar y su época: ideología, retórica y poética, Cádiz, diciembre de 2000* (Cádiz: Universidad de Cádiz Servicio de Publicaciones: Fundación Municipal de Cultura, 2001); Carmen Llorca, *Emilio Castelar, precursor de la democracia cristiana* (Madrid: Biblioteca Nueva, 1966); María Cruz Seoane Couceiro, *Oratoria y periodismo en la España del siglo XIX* (Madrid: Fundación Juan March, 1977); Jorge Vilches García, *Emilio Castelar, la patria y la república* (Madrid: Biblioteca Nueva, 2001).

31. Fernando Bayrón Toro, *Labra: biografía, bibliografía e ideas sobre abolición de la esclavitud, autonomismo, el Tratado de París de 1898* (Mayagüez, P.R.: Editorial Isla, 2005); María Dolores Domingo Acebrón, *Rafael María de Labra: Cuba, Puerto Rico, Las Filipinas, Europa y Marruecos, en la España del sexenio democrático y la restauración (1871–1918)* (Madrid: Consejo Superior de Investigaciones Científicas, 2006); Guillermo Domíniquez Roldán and Real Sociedad Económica de Amigos del País (Cuba), *Rafael Maria de Labra: estudio leído en la Sociedad Económica de Amigos del País el día 10 de enero de 1919* (Habana: Imprenta "El Siglo XX," 1920).

32. Manuel García Castellón, "Influencia krausista en el abolicionismo español del siglo XIX: la Sociedad Abolicionista Española (1865–1887)," in *Actas de la 11th Annual Afro-Hispanic Literature and Culture Conference* (Diáspora: Southern Arkansas University, 2001), 158–65. At http://www.ensayistas.org/critica/spain/garcia.htm. For Spanish Krausism, see Gonzalo Capellán de Miguel, "El primer krausismo en España: ¿moderado o progresista?" in *Las máscaras de la libertad: el liberalismo español, 1808–1950*, ed. Manuel Suárez Cortina (Madrid: Marcial Pons Historia, 2003), 169–201; Juan López-Morillas, *The Krausist Movement and Ideological Change in Spain, 1854–1874*, 2nd ed. (New York: Cambridge University Press, 1981); Manuel Suárez Cortina, "Krausoinstitucionismo, democracia y republicanismo de cátedra," in *El gorro frigio. Liberalismo, democracia y republicanismo en la Restauración*, ed. Manuel Suárez Cortina (Madrid/Santander: Biblioteca Nueva/Sociedad Menéndez Pelayo, 2000), 91–125.

33. Manuel Tuñón de Lara, *Medio siglo de cultura española (1885–1936)*, 3rd ed. (Madrid: Editorial Tecnos, 1973), 46.

34. Rafael M. de Labra, *Estudios biográfico-políticos* (Madrid: Impr. de La Guirnalda, 1887), 118–19.

35. Ibid.; Emilio Castelar, *Garibaldi* (Firenze: Coi tipi dei Successori Le Monnier, 1882); Emilio Castelar, *Leon Gambetta*, 2nd ed. (Madrid: El Día, 1883); Emilio Castelar, *Retratos históricos* (Madrid: Oficinas de la Ilustración Española y Americana, 1884); Emilio Castelar y Ripoll, "Doña Carolina Coronado," in *Discursos y ensayos*, ed. José García Mercadal (Madrid: Aguilar, 1964), 231–44.

36. Luis A. Santullano, "Ideales de la pedagogía anglo-americana," *La Escuela Moderna* 25, 1 (1903), 46.

37. Castelar, *Cuestiones políticas y sociales*, 49–58.

38. Emilio Castelar y Ripoll, *Discursos parlamentarios de don Emilio Castelar en la Asamblea Constituyente*, vol. 3 (Madrid: A. de San Martín/A. Jubera, 1871), 362–64; Harry Cassell Davis and John Cloyse Bridgman, *Three Minute Declamations for College Men*, 2d ed. (New York: A. Hinds and Company, 1890), 220–21; George Riddle, *A Modern Reader and Speaker* (New York: Duffield, 1908), 125–26; Edwin Du Bois Shurter, *Public Speaking: A Treatise on Delivery: With Selections for Declaiming* (Boston: Allyn and Bacon, 1903), 215–17.

39. *La Iberia*, May 10, 1876.

40. Ibid., May 12, 1870; Castelar y Ripoll, *Discursos parlamentarios de don Emilio Castelar en la Asamblea Constituyente*, 277; Castelar, *Cuestiones políticas y sociales*, 50.

41. Castelar, *Retratos históricos*, 285.

42. Castelar, *Las guerras de América y Egipto: historia contemporánea*, 9.

43. Emilio Castelar, *Discursos parlamentarios y políticos de Emilio Castelar en la restauración*, vol. 3 (Madrid: A. de San Martín, 1885), 24, 29.

44. *La Iberia*, August 31, 1873; *La Dinastía*, January 16–17, 1889, May 10, 1891, May 21 and 24, 1893.

45. *La Iberia*, August 31, 1873.

46. Ibid., September 6 and 9, 1873.

47. Labra, *Estudios biográfico-políticos*, 103–75.

48. Manuel Corchado y Juarbe and José Feliu, *Abraham Lincoln*, Obreros ilustres (Barcelona: Impr. de los hijos de Domenech, 1868), 7.

49. *Los mártires de la República: cuadros históricos de los sufrimientos, de las penalidades, de los martirios de todos los grandes apóstoles de la idea republicana . . ./por una sociedad de escritores republicanos*, 2 vols. (Barcelona: Biblioteca Escogida, 1873), 2:112.

50. J. Meca, *Abraham Lincoln íntimo: apuntes histórico-anecdóticos de su vida y de su época* (Barcelona: Montaner y Simón, 1909); Enrique Leopoldo de Verneuill, *Historia biográfica de los presidentes de los Estados Unidos* (Barcelona: Montaner y Simon, 1885); Emilia Serrano de Wilson, *Americanos célebres: glorias del Nuevo Mundo* (Barcelona: Sucs. de N. Ramírez, 1888); Enrique Piñeyro, *Hombres y glorias de América* (Paris: Garnier Hermanos, 1903).

51. Corchado y Juarbe and Feliu, *Abraham Lincoln*, 15–16, 23.

52. J. Meca, *Abraham Lincoln, íntimo. Apuntes histórico-anecdóticos de su vida y de su época* (Barcelona: Montaner y Simón, 1909).

53. Emilio Castelar, *Crónica internacional* (Madrid: Editora Nacional, 1982), 349–53, (quotation 351); Rafael M. de Labra, *Estudios de derecho público: aspecto internacional de la cuestión de Cuba* (Madrid: A. Alonso, 1900), 3–4.

54. Carolyn P. Boyd, *Historia Patria: Politics, History, and National Identity in Spain, 1875–1975* (Princeton, NJ: Princeton University Press, 1997).

55. Benjamín Jarnés, *Escuela de libertad. Siete maestros: Bolívar, Hidalgo, Lincoln, Martí, San Martín, Sucre, Wáshington* (México, D.F.: Editora Continental 1942); Celso Romero Peláez, *Lincoln, el leñador. Drama en tres actos* (Santiago de Chile: Ed. Tegualda, 1948); Bernardo Villarrazo, *Abraham Lincoln: su lección y mensaje* (Madrid: Langa y Cía., 1954).

56. Juan Alarcón Benito, *Mares del sur: seguido de Sendas de libertad y De la empresa de las indias* (Madrid: Escelicer, 1966); Juan Aragón, *Figuras estelares* (Barcelona: Editorial Bruguera, 1974); José de Murguia, *Abraham Lincoln*, vol. 19, Colección "Hombres, leyendas, historia" (Madrid: G. del Toro, 1971); Enrique de Obregón, *Lincoln* (Barcelona: Ediciones AFHA Internacional, 1971); María Luisa Celaa, *Abraham Lincoln* (Bilbao: Editorial Cantábrica, 1968).

57. *Abraham Lincoln: El libertador de los esclavos*, 8th ed. (Barcelona: Ediciones Toray, 1992); Francisco-Luis Cardona Castro, *Lincoln*, especial. ed., Grandes biografías (Madrid: Edimat Libros, 2002).

58. Víctor Alba, *Lincoln* (Barcelona: Planeta, 1989); Julián Bautista Ruiz Rivera, *Abraham Lincoln: el sueño americano* (Sevilla: Universidad de Sevilla, 1991); César Vidal Manzanares, *Lincoln*, 2d ed. (Madrid: Acento Editorial, 2002).

59. César Vidal Manzanares, *Lincoln: la unidad frente a la autodeterminación* (Barcelona: Planeta, 2009).

60. Jon Lee Anderson, "Letter from Andalusia: Lorca's Bones," *The New Yorker*, June 22, 2009, 47.

12

"That Great and Gentle Soul"

IMAGES OF LINCOLN IN LATIN AMERICA

Nicola Miller

It has been claimed that Lincoln's name has resonated more powerfully in Latin America than in any other part of the world. His assassination, which was interpreted by Latin Americans as martyrdom, prompted public expressions of mourning, especially in Cuba, Argentina, and Chile.[1] He became an iconic figure in Latin America during the late nineteenth century and remains so today: the centennials, including the recent bicentennial, have been officially marked throughout the region. There is a *Calle Lincoln* (Lincoln Street) in most Latin American cities, and in Argentina and Cuba there are towns that bear his name. From the pioneering (yet plagiarized) biography in Spanish by leading Argentine statesman Domingo Sarmiento, published in mid-1865, to Fidel Castro's claim in 1981 that "Lincoln belongs to us," a multitude of references to him can be found in the writings and speeches of Latin American intellectuals and politicians of varying views.[2] Sarmiento (1811–88) saw himself as the Argentine Lincoln, Benito Juárez (1806–72) was referred to as the Mexican Lincoln, and Cubans have drawn parallels between Lincoln and their own founding father, José Martí (1853–95).[3]

Amid the diversity of representations of Lincoln across Latin America, there are three images that can be identified as salient, and three historical periods when they became so. This essay will first consider Lincoln as nation-builder, in the Civil War decade; then Lincoln as natural man, in the late nineteenth century; and, finally, Lincoln as *americanista* (meaning an advocate of shared modern republican values throughout the Americas), in the era of the Good Neighbor Policy (the 1930s and 1940s). Latin American interest in Lincoln was at its height during these periods, although it has consistently been present, with only Washington—and perhaps FDR—rivaling him as a lastingly significant reference point. As elsewhere, Latin American fascination with Lincoln once again increased in 2009, the bicentennial year, not least because of the place that Barack Obama gave Lincoln in the story of his own political career.

Lincoln as Nation-Builder: Reason over Force

After Washington came the invincible spirit of Lincoln, who finished the liberating work that the aristocratic gentleman of the South had not dared to attempt.

—Domingo Sarmiento

Sarmiento's rapidly produced biography, *Vida de Abran Lincoln* (1865), which he compiled while in Washington during May and June 1865, was for several decades the main source on Lincoln for Latin American readers.[4] It went to a second edition in less than a year, and there was even a third printing, primarily to satisfy demand in colonial and slave-owning Cuba, where the U.S. Civil War resonated particularly powerfully. Sarmiento expressed frustration that only a few hundred copies had been sold in Argentina and Chile at the time, but records of the private libraries of Latin American intellectuals testify to its widespread presence among the educated.[5] During the 1860s, Latin America's information about the United States was heavily reliant on the writings of individual travelers such as Sarmiento. Some copies of U.S. or European newspapers got through to Latin America's capitals, but they were often delayed and interrupted, hence the disproportionate effects of Sarmiento's work of compilation in shaping Latin American perceptions of Lincoln.[6] There were other texts, of course, but the widespread and lasting influence of Sarmiento's vision is attested to by citation or borrowing in later accounts well into the twentieth century.[7]

As he stated at the outset, Sarmiento wrote only the introduction, parts of the concluding chapters and a few passages of explanation for the Latin American reader; the rest of the book was translated—from two unacknowledged contemporary U.S. biographies—by his secretary, "Bartolito" Mitre, son of President Bartolomé Mitre (1862–68).[8] Both of the U.S. biographies contained a variety of extracts from Lincoln's speeches and writings, and much of the value of Sarmiento's work lay in introducing Latin American readers to Lincoln's own words. Sarmiento's volume included full texts of Lincoln's speech to Congress opposing the Mexican War (January 1848) and of the Emancipation Proclamations (September 1862 and January 1863). However, his transcription of the Gettysburg Address—which is far shorter—was doctored to suit his own purposes.

Sarmiento's treatment of this latter, already canonical, speech reveals a great deal about the principles determining his selection of material on Lincoln. He cited all but the final sentence of the first paragraph, but then went on to gloss over the second paragraph. Lincoln's well-known words,

we here highly resolve that these dead shall not have died in vain—that this nation, under God, shall have a new birth of freedom—and that

government of the people, by the people, for the people, shall not perish
from the earth,

were conveyed by Sarmiento, in authorial—and authoritative—voice as follows:

> [Lincoln] went on to explain the solemnity and importance of this cere-
> mony, and concluded by saying that with this act *the nation was proclaim-
> ing at the top of its voice* that the fallen of that battle had not sacrificed
> their lives in vain, because, with God's guidance, the liberty bathed in
> their blood would be reborn, and that the government of the people, by
> the people and for the people is not destined to perish from the face of
> the earth.[9]

In other words, "the nation" has acquired, for Sarmiento, a capability for historical agency that Lincoln did not accord it. Moreover, the defining feature of
Lincoln, for Sarmiento, was that he had demonstrated the viability of actually
building a nation on the founding ideals of the United States (which were also
those of Argentina). By thwarting the widespread European expectation that
the United States would disintegrate under the pressure of war, Lincoln had
triumphantly shown how unfounded was the view that "the sovereign people
[of the United States], those happy inventors of railways, telegraphs and steam-
ships, who were so competent at accumulating wealth through patient industry
or the audacious *go-ahead* spirit, would flinch . . . in the face of death."[10] Both
in peace and now in war, the United States had proved to be the epitome of
what a modern republic should be.[11]

Sarmiento interpreted the U.S. Civil War in terms of a comparison between
modern and ancient understandings of republicanism. The true cause of the
hostilities, he argued, was not slavery, but a clash of cultures arising from the fact
that the South was "the intermediary between Europe and America." Southern
slave owners were "gentlemanly in the extreme, brave and tenacious in their
ideas"; they ran their government as they ran their mansions, with a strong sense
of racially determined social hierarchy. "This," declared Sarmiento, was "the
Roman type." "How," he demanded, "could they not despise the commercial,
industrial, plebeian, *parvenu* inhabitant of the North?" And yet, "the North,
with all the forces of a nineteenth-century Republic, goes marching onwards,
with its schools, its machines, its immigration, its factories, its companies, its
equality."[12] In his view, slavery was only "the immediate cause of the war, and
its extinction the most obvious consequence"; beyond that, "in the entrails of
the Republic, as an institution," far deeper problems were at work, notably how
to secure popular consent.[13] Lincoln's genius, for Sarmiento, lay in his ability to
harness the abolition movement, which the Argentine writer described in highly
gendered terms as a "great cry of redemption" emanating "from the entrails" of
"Mrs. Beecher Stowe," to the cause of nation-building.[14] Sarmiento's influential
conclusion about Lincoln was that he had "completed the United States as a

[form of] government, by bringing it forth unscathed from internecine conflict; as a society, by erasing the stain that tainted its liberties by abolishing slavery; as a people, by coming to power through the influence of his word, his conviction alone, and carrying with him to the Presidency the working people whose hands were roughened if honorable, but whose minds were cultivated."[15]

Sarmiento's fascination with Lincoln is readily understandable in the context of Argentine history. The great fault-line there for much of the nineteenth century was between Unitarians and Federalists, a divide that was less about alternative conceptions of the state than about the conflict of interest between Buenos Aires, the wealthy port where import and export revenues were collected, and the rest of the provinces of the Federation of the River Plate. Unitarians sought to unite the country under the rule of Buenos Aires, concentrating wealth there and allowing only limited autonomy to the other states; Federalists sought to reduce the power of Buenos Aires and to strengthen state's rights in order to transfer wealth to the interior. Liberal Unitarians ultimately defeated Federalists in the civil war of 1851–52. The Constitution that emerged in 1853 was, however, a compromise between the two movements and the dispute continued to dominate Argentine politics until 1880, when a more lasting settlement was engineered. When Sarmiento was writing about the U.S. Civil War, Argentina had already had its own experience of secession when Buenos Aires Province opted out of the Federation in 1854, leading to one civil war in 1859, when Buenos Aires was defeated, and another two years later, when Buenos Aires successfully reasserted its control over the nation. Tensions persisted, however, between the representatives of the centralizing state and the forces of local power. Sarmiento himself, as governor of San Juan province from 1862–4, had found his own attempts to introduce modern education, public works, infrastructure, and economic development thwarted by the activities of a local *caudillo* (a leader whose power is informal—often charismatic—and authoritarian).

It is well known among historians of Sarmiento that he both saw and sought to make others see parallels between himself and Lincoln. In a letter to his friend and advocate Mary Mann, he was open about his reasons for appropriating Lincoln:

> [I]n all the issues which interested me—the need to suspend the right of *habeas corpus* in case of insurrection and invasion . . . the war councils to try revolutionary ringleaders, and a thousand more, the opinion that I held (always the least popular one, of course), was that of the government of the United States, with Lincoln and Johnson as my supporters. My *Life of Lincoln* has invoked them in my defense.[16]

Thus, in choosing extracts from the two U.S. works, Sarmiento edited out the domestic political opposition to Lincoln in order to emphasize the image of a resolute leader whose willingness to suspend particular liberal principles, such as habeas corpus, in the cause of defending the whole liberal republican project, had enabled him to maintain civilian control and ultimately compel his country to unity. This image was shared by Juan Bautista Alberdi, who was far less enthralled with the United States than Sarmiento but who also identified the main lesson of the U.S. Civil War as the importance of unity and centralization—under firm civilian leadership—in creating a powerful nation.[17] Both Sarmiento and Alberdi came from a generation of Argentine statesmen who had despaired at the insistence of their predecessors in adhering to lofty liberal principles in the face of insurrection, which had resulted only in the defeat of liberalism by opponents who had little regard for such niceties of political conduct.

In different ways, these debates were played out in most Latin American countries during the nineteenth century. What was at stake was the defense of republicanism against monarchism (which was resurgent in Mexico during the 1860s and persisted in Brazil until 1889): in other words, the defense of the values of the New World against the Old. There were different interpretations of how and why Lincoln had been able to preserve the Republic: in divided Argentina, the emphasis was on the importance of central, unifying power; in over-centralized Colombia, in contrast, the U.S. Civil War was interpreted as illustrating the strength of a system that gave the states an effective mobilizing capability.[18] For liberal nation-builders across the region, however, what made Lincoln so compelling was his capability to sustain civilian power to defend the republican ideal, even in the midst of war.[19]

Lincoln as Natural Man

that other natural man, that great and gentle soul, Lincoln
—José Martí, 1887

In comparing Lincoln to Walt Whitman, the Cuban poet, journalist, and independence leader José Martí sharply reoriented the image of Lincoln away from Sarmiento's stern statesman toward Lincoln as natural man.[20] What Martí seemed to want to convey was the impression of Lincoln as an uncorrupted man of the people, who had lived close to nature, and who preserved the simplicity of his rural background even in the executive mansion. Martí wrote no single sustained work on Lincoln,[21] but referred to him often in his extensive writings about the United States, which were crucial in shaping perceptions across Latin America because Martí was one of the earliest Latin American writers to benefit from the syndication of newspaper articles. As the leader of the second war of Cuban independence, launched in 1895, he admired, as Sarmiento had done, Lincoln's willingness to fight for what he believed in. But Martí's main interest lay in Lincoln's authenticity. This preoccupation arose from the influence of Romanticism on his own political thought, which gave him a sense of the radical possibilities of democracy that went far beyond the positivist-influenced liberalism that by then was increasingly dominant in Latin American states, where elites tended to give priority to order over progress.

Martí referred repeatedly to Lincoln's unaffected closeness to the humble people, his ability to express their sorrows, and his compassion for them, to the extent that "the spirit of Christ" was in him.[22] As president, "Lincoln, that sublime son of those 'from below'" wept,[23] Martí noted approvingly, "because his generals were going to shoot, as deserters, a few poor peasant lads who had not learnt to love war."[24] In Martí's eyes, Lincoln's poor, rural upbringing lent him an unrivaled legitimacy as a leader of his people who fulfilled the ideals of U.S. independence: "out of the truth of poverty, with the innocence of the forest and the sagacity and power of the creatures that inhabited it, emerged, in the hour of the national readjustment, that good, sad guide, the woodcutter Lincoln."[25] Lincoln's background enabled him to do what Martí, in his famous manifesto for the cultural independence of Latin America, "Nuestra América" ("Our America," 1891), urged all governments in Latin America to do, namely to govern not according to precepts borrowed from places with a wholly different history, but, rather, with knowledge and understanding of "the elements that constitute [their own] country."[26] One example he gave was Lincoln's treatment of Secretary of War Simon Cameron, who was removed from office because of public outrage at corruption scandals early in 1862. Lincoln, according to Martí's account, "understood that someone who had become a possible presidential candidate through trickery and intrigue would not lose all of his power because he had been caught out in yet another intrigue [and that] in a time of war and [nation-building] it was important to subdue with kindness those dangerous friends who could not be defeated." Lincoln sent Cameron to Russia rather than to jail, which was, in Martí's eyes, evidence of the "sagacity and leniency" of "a true statesman" who had a profound understanding of the conditions in which he was operating.[27]

In the context of the Cuban politics of that era, it is unsurprising that Martí was not only interested in Lincoln, but also had an interest in making his own mark upon Lincoln's image. Cuba's own struggles over sovereignty became entangled with the politics of slavery to an extent that made the U.S. Civil War seem especially relevant. Cubans were encouraged in such comparisons by their familiarity with the views of Spanish Liberal supporters of the Unionist cause, such as Emilio Castelar and Francisco de Frías, who drew explicit parallels between the U.S. Civil War and the situation in Cuba. The U.S. Civil War was interpreted, according to leading Cuban historian Emeterio Santovenia, as "the triumph of liberty over slavery."[28] The strong Cuban sense that Lincoln was a part of their own history is illustrated by Santovenia's rather speculative claim that "the roots of the Gettysburg address grew in Cuba" (through a rather vague connection between Cuban intellectual

José de la Luz y Caballero and U.S. Unitarian minister and scholar Theodore Parker).[29] What is certain is that the adventures of two Cubans who fought for the Union and were present at Gettysburg were followed avidly in Cuba through the pro-Lincoln newspaper *El Siglo*.[30] A refrain often heard in the Cuban fields during the 1860s was:

> Avanza, Lincoln, avanza (Advance, Lincoln, advance)
> Tu eres nuestra esperanza (You are our deliverance [lit. "hope"]).[31]

The official ten-volume *Historia de Cuba* (1952) described how, as the cause of emancipation became bound up with the cause of Cuban independence, "the image of Lincoln, both in modest dwellings and in mansions that housed progressive young altruists, came to be an expression of the deepest Cuban aspirations."[32]

Martí, who denounced the European-oriented universities of Latin America for blinding young Latin Americans to the beauty of their own history and culture, found it especially important that Lincoln was an autodidact whose wisdom derived from experience rather than formal education. He reported the story of Lincoln's redrafting of Seward's version of his inaugural address in order to draw a distinction between true poetry of the human soul and pompous, vacuous verbiage. Lincoln's intervention showed, he wrote "how the talent . . . for putting each word in its place is learnt not in the study of rhetoric but in a feel for words," because Seward, with all his education, had "proposed a very florid paragraph . . . full of vain pomp that obscured and weakened a beautiful image," whereas Lincoln, the autodidact, by making a few deft changes "converted the poor phrase into one of extraordinarily powerful beauty."[33] Interest in Lincoln's autodidacticism continued to be widespread in Latin America well into the twentieth century.[34]

This image of Lincoln as natural man was picked up by the highly influential Uruguayan cultural commentator José Enrique Rodó, whose celebrated essay *Ariel* (1900) established the parameters of debate about the differences between Latin America and the United States for at least three decades. Rodó presented Lincoln as natural man in order to make a particular argument of his own, namely that the best way to prevent democracy from lapsing into mediocrity was to promote meritocracy. "The essential character of a democratic society," he wrote, "will always be the immanent justice that permits everyone to stand out by their strengths and merits, and makes each person the architect of his or her own destiny. . . . [It was this spirit of justice that] one day raised Lincoln, the woodcutter of Illinois, to the Capitol in Washington."[35] For Rodó, as for Martí, Lincoln was someone whose wisdom came from experience, who was instinctively able to decipher the great book of life: just as Columbus found therein "a premonition of his unexpected discovery" and Luther "the virile impulse towards liberty and reason," so "in [this book of life] Lincoln learnt to love the slaves."[36] The intellectual context of this characterization of Lincoln as innately committed to social justice was Rodó's rejection of the crude versions of utilitarianism that had come to prevail among Latin American elites in the late nineteenth century. The young Uruguayan idealist was primarily concerned to ensure that negative materialist values (greed, conspicuous consumption, selfishness) did not come to dominate in Latin American societies as he argued they had come to do in the United States. Rodó, therefore, projected the image of Lincoln rising naturally and deservedly through the irresistible force of his "redemptive idea."[37]

The Latin American reaction against positivism and materialism led by Rodó was compounded by the rise of U.S. interventionism in the region after the Spanish-American War of 1898. Theodore Roosevelt's aggressive claim to act as the "policeman of the Americas," the colonial status of Puerto Rico, and the compromised independence of Cuba, all contributed to a growing sense of disillusionment with the United States. In response to the U.S. intervention to bring about the Republic of Panama in 1903, the Colombian intellectual Carlos Alberto Torre lamented: "The government of the United States has returned the world to barbarism. . . . We have lost our isthmus, but the United States has lost its honor. Oh, Lincoln! Today is the day you were truly assassinated!"[38] It was at this time that a related idea began to find expression, namely that Lincoln was representative not of any specifically U.S. values but of broader modern human ideals, which were, Latin Americans began to argue, better preserved in Latin America than in the now-degenerate United States. Tolstoy's famous claim that Lincoln was "a humanitarian as broad as the world" was often echoed in Latin America, where there was a good deal of sympathetic interest in Tolstoy's thought.[39] By the 1920s, when virtually all Latin American leaders had come to see the Monroe Doctrine (the 1823 statement that European colonial expansion in the Americas would be regarded by the United States as a threat to its own interests) as an instrument of U.S. imperialism, Lincoln was widely represented as the last upholder of the ideals of the Founding Fathers, who were thought to have been dishonored and demeaned by all his successors.[40]

The main emphasis in early twentieth-century Latin American accounts of Lincoln, then, was precisely on his ability to let himself be guided by a natural humanity innate to everyone rather than by any acquired characteristics. He was seen as unique in *not* fashioning himself, an idea captured in a speech made by the Mexican diplomat José Manuel Puig Casauranc, at Springfield, Illinois, on February 11, 1932. Locating Lincoln in the pantheon of liberators of the Americas—Bolívar, Washington, Hidalgo—Puig Casauranc argued that what distinguished Lincoln was "the *simple humanity*" in which his genius was cloaked. Remaining always "humble and humane," Lincoln's ability to make contact with people enabled him to intuit "*what actually existed,*" in contrast to the tendency of political leaders to see themselves as exceptionally gifted, when "in reality, [their genius was] no more than a sublimation of characteristics common to everyone."[41] The image of Lincoln as the incarnation of popular wisdom was reinforced by stories about his natural ability to get on with people from all walks of life. For example, Osvaldo Orico, writing in the early 1940s, when the question of racial integration was prominent in Brazilian politics, told an anecdote about Lincoln walking through Washington and meeting a black man, "dirty and in rags," who "greeted him without ceremony." Lincoln "responded with great cordiality" and, when his secretary asked him if he knew what kind of man had addressed him, replied, "I cannot allow anyone to outdo me in courtesy."[42] Some members of the Latin American Left picked up on the same quality, citing Marx's description of Lincoln as a "sincere son of the working class."[43] This image of Lincoln as an authentic natural man, close to his people, unblinkered by abstract theories, is also evident in Castro's favorite (and probably apocryphal) Lincoln quotation: "As Lincoln said, you can fool all of the people some of the time, but you cannot fool all of the people all of the time."[44]

Lincoln as *americanista*

Lincoln, the precursor of the Good Neighbor.
—Emeterio Santovenia, 1951

Lincoln's image as *the* great *americanista* dates back to Sarmiento, who acclaimed him as the incarnation of "those affinities that exist between the two Americas,"[45] but it came to prominence with Franklin Roosevelt's Good Neighbor Policy in the 1930s. The influential mid-twentieth century Cuban historian Emeterio Santovenia marshaled a lot of evidence, mostly from 1861–62, in support of his claims for Lincoln's spirit of inter-American cooperation.[46] He cited Lincoln's warning to Spain that their landing of troops in Santo Domingo was considered an unfriendly act toward the United States; his persuading of Congress to recognize Haiti as an independent republic; and his diplomatic campaign to secure good relations in Latin America, particularly with Mexico. In Santovenia's widely read account, the promotion of good relations with Latin America came to be linked in Lincoln's mind with the need to abolish slavery to preserve the Union: "A community of republics ruled morally by mutual respect among them all, without respect to geographical size or racial composition, was in perfect harmony with a nation that was about to stop being half slave and half free."[47] During the mid-twentieth century, "Lincoln" became emblematic of the possibility of mutually respectful, collaborative relations between the United States and Latin America. In order to understand why, it is necessary to explore both how Lincoln's attitude toward Latin America was received at the time as well as how it was reinterpreted in the light of FDR's policy.

Although the "rise of the U.S. empire" is conventionally dated to the late nineteenth century, in Latin America, particularly in Mexico and Central America, serious alarm about the expansionist tendencies of U.S. leaders date back at least to the Mexican War (1846–48), when Mexico lost over one-third of its territory, including California. The filibustering expeditions of William Walker during the 1850s were seen in Latin America not as the personal whim of a wayward individual, but as a calculated insult by the U.S. government, encouraged and supported by popular opinion, particularly after President Pierce formally recognized Walker's government.[48] In general, the 1850s saw a significant increase in expansionist rhetoric, which unsurprisingly fueled Latin American fears, and from their perspective the aggressive attitude resumed and intensified after the Civil War, with Andrew Johnson, James Blaine,[49] McKinley and—above all—Theodore Roosevelt. For Latin Americans, Lincoln was *an exception* among U.S. presidents in that he spoke about Latin American countries with respect and sought to cultivate good relations with them, sending reputable U.S. public figures with an interest in the region to act as diplomatic representatives.[50]

Before the Civil War, then, there was a high level of wariness about the United States throughout Latin America. Although Latin Americans continued to differ as to whether the United States should be included in initiatives toward hemispheric unity, increasingly the view that the United States was a threat came to prevail, as was the case at meetings in Lima (1847–48) and in Santiago (1856), when Chile, Ecuador, and Peru signed a treaty to promote stronger ties across Spanish America, an agreement motivated in no small part by hostility toward the United States. There was certainly a case to be made that many Latin American countries had an interest in seeing the United States divided. Lincoln therefore had grounds for concern that the Confederacy would succeed in securing recognition in Latin America, or—more realistically—that the Latin American countries would adopt a neutral stance in the conflict.

In the event, Lincoln's government was remarkably successful in representing the South as the source of filibustering and expansionism and the Union as the bulwark of democratic self-government, emancipation, and security against European interventionism. The only Latin American country to declare neutrality was the Empire of Brazil (which also, unsurprisingly, followed the European powers in recognizing the Hapsburg monarch Maximilian, who was installed as emperor of Mexico by French troops in 1864). The Spanish American republics refused to grant belligerent status to the Confederacy, although they were not prepared to follow Seward's injunction to treat Southern ships as "pirates."[51] Sarmiento portrayed the defeat of the South, the defeat of slavery, and the defeat of U.S. expansionism as one and the same thing.[52] Benito Juárez, fighting against Maximilian, continued to see the triumph of the Union as a prerequisite for the ousting of French troops from Mexico and rebuffed the approaches of the only Confederate agent to be sent to Latin America.[53] In

Chile, the Chamber of Deputies passed a motion stating that "the fact alone of the termination of the [U.S. civil] war, and the reconstruction of the North American Union, gives such reassurance of a safe present and a peaceful future to South American republics."[54]

In the "brief period of unparalleled friendship" during the U.S. Civil War,[55] a combination of good envoys, U.S. offers to mediate, and a generally respectful tone in relations did a great deal to create a sense of shared interests between the Unionists and Latin American liberals. Lincoln's own credibility in Latin America was greatly enhanced by his record of opposition to the Mexican War. Secretary of State William Seward also helped to ease relations with Latin American countries by adopting a more moderate approach to the vexing question of U.S. compensation claims arising from losses during the wars of independence.[56] Moreover, U.S. overtures to Latin American governments were further helped by the liberal victories in a series of struggles for power with conservatives across the continent: it is unlikely, for example, that Rosas or Urquiza would have been willing to mark the 4th of July with serenades as did Mitre in 1863 in Argentina, or that relations would have been officially declared to be "more than cordial, [indeed] fraternal" before the start of the Liberal Republic in Chile (1861–91).[57]

The main reason, however, that Latin American governments were sympathetic to the Unionist cause was the threat of European intervention. This was felt most acutely in Mexico, which was confronted, a leading diplomat lamented, with "the harsh alternative of having to sacrifice either our territory and our nationality to [the United States] or our liberty and independence to the thrones of the European despots."[58] France was not only occupying Mexico but also actively interfering in Ecuador, encouraged by a pro-monarchy Conservative Party. Spain sent troops into Santo Domingo in 1861 and seized the Chincha Islands, with their valuable guano deposits, from Peru in 1864. In light of these events, the position of those who argued that the United States should be enlisted in support against European incursions into the hemisphere became far more plausible after 1861 than it had been before. Once again, the notoriously ambivalent Monroe Doctrine assumed the guise of a promise rather than a threat, and in 1862 discussions resumed about the formation of a hemispheric alliance against European intervention.

In practice, Lincoln did not actually do a great deal to help Latin America. Indeed, with hindsight it could well be argued that he helped to put in place the structures that underpinned the consolidation of unequal relationships later in the century. That was not widely recognized at the time, but there were voices of disillusionment, notably the Mexican diplomat Matías Romero, who remembered Lincoln telling him before his inauguration that he would "do anything within his power in favor of the interests of Mexico" and who had maneuvered long and hard to make Lincoln fulfill that very promise by giving Juárez military support to oust the French.[59] Lincoln's refusal to intervene openly in favor of Mexican liberals, despite the fact that he turned a blind eye to a lot of arms smuggling across the border,[60] led Romero to conclude that Lincoln had never really been interested in Mexico, that he had expressed concern only because of public opinion, and that he was therefore a weak leader, too much inclined to compromise.[61] But this was a minority view and, in any case, Lincoln's discreet aid came to be seen in a far rosier light after his successors flatly refused to help Chile and Peru defend themselves against Spain in 1866 or—and this was seen as the greatest betrayal—to help Cuba win its independence. By mid-1869, Cuban independence fighters, who by then had launched the first war of independence (1868–78), were of the view that if they could only secure U.S. recognition of them as belligerents, then they would soon win.[62] The refusal of the Grant administration to lend support, which was compounded by attempts to act as a mediator with Spain, caused profound disillusionment, and provoked some exaggerated claims about what Lincoln might have done had he still been president. Thus Lincoln acquired a lasting image as the friend of Latin America who would help out when asked but otherwise not interfere.

The slave-holding colony of Cuba excepted, Lincoln's role as emancipator of the slaves has not at any stage been the main focus of interest in Latin America. The Emancipation Proclamation itself was cited relatively rarely, less often than his speech against the Mexican War, his inaugural address, or the Gettysburg Address.[63] Even the slave-holding Empire of Brazil is only partly an exception. Joaquim Nabuco, abolitionist leader in Brazil during the 1880s, later ambassador to Washington, and the only Latin American invited to speak at the commemoration held there in 1909, declared with hindsight that: "Through what Lincoln did, . . . we could win our cause without a drop of blood being shed."[64] However, during the 1860s in Brazil, when the debates about slavery were limited to the ruling elite, the U.S. experience of emancipation was more often held up as a negative model (fueling slave owners' fears about a radicalized black army) than a positive one.[65] In the 1880s, when abolition became a matter of wider social concern, the U.S. example came to be seen as symbolic of the modernization that was increasingly perceived as desirable in Brazil. Even so, according to Nabuco's own account,[66] the campaigning organizations that were formed drew more inspiration from British experiences than from U.S. ones. It was notable that when President Kennedy went to Brazil in 1961, it was a copy of the Gettysburg Address that he signed,[67] not the Emancipation Proclamation—symbolizing the fact that it was republican government that was identified as the shared experience of the two countries, not emancipation.

Indeed, there has been comparatively little discussion in Latin America of some of the stock-in-trade features of Lincolnism in the United States, such as the debate about whether he emancipated the slaves out of moral principle or exploited abolition to serve his own political ends. The fact that the Emancipation Proclamation arose out of a strategic war aim, as well as out of moral repudiation of slavery, did not cause concern among Latin Americans (as it did in France). In countries where mid-nineteenth-century liberals were widely of the view that the previous generation had caused havoc by trying to implement abstract principles with no regard for what was politically possible, it was precisely the timely convergence of strategy and principle that they admired. In general, there has been little debate about Lincoln in Latin America, since references to him are overwhelmingly favorable, but usually fleeting: invocations of his name have served a talismanic function as touchstones of transcendental virtues—moral strength, compassion, respectfulness—that the writer/speaker wishes to claim by association. Flashes of his humor have occasionally emerged, but in general, Latin Americans have preferred their Lincoln in a serious mood (Sarmiento endorsed the criticism that one French biographer of Lincoln had inappropriately adopted too "witty" a tone).[68] Latin Americans have shown little interest in the image of Lincoln as the embodiment of "common sense" and self-reliance, which have been constructed in Latin America as Anglo-Saxon values inferior to the Latin American concern with solidarity, empathy, and imaginativeness. In Latin America, Lincoln has usually been seen less as a symbol of specifically U.S. values and more as one of the great men of the Americas, representing the whole hemisphere's generic commitment to modern republicanism.[69] For Latin Americans, he is associated with the United States only in the sense that he represented the last gasp of its founding idealism.

Notes

1. Ramiro Guerra y Sánchez, ed., *Historia de la nación cubana* (Havana: Editorial Historia de la nación cubana, 1952), IV:32; Nancy Brandt, "Don Yo in America: Domingo Faustino Sarmiento's Second Visit to the United States, 1865," *The Americas* 19:1 (July 1962), 21–49, 25; and Benjamín Vicuña Mackenna, "A Lecture Before the 'Traveler's Club' of New York on the Present Condition and Prospects of Chili," December 2, 1865, in Daniel J. Hunter, *A Sketch of Chili* (New York: S. Hallet, 1866), 13–29, 17.

2. Fidel Castro, speech denouncing Radio Martí, October 25, 1981, Castro Speech database, http://lanic.utexas.edu/la/cb/cuba/castro.html, accessed April 7, 2009. All translations from Spanish are mine unless otherwise stated.

3. Emeterio Santovenia and Raul Shelton, *Martí y su obra* (Miami: Educational Publishing Corp., 1970), IV:166, where Lincoln was described as "the archetype of Martí."

4. Domingo Faustino Sarmiento, *Vida de Abran Lincoln* [sic], *décimo sesto presidente de los Estados Unidos* (New York: D. Appleton & Ca, 1866), xliv.

5. Emeterio Santovenia, *Sarmiento y su americanismo* (Buenos Aires: Editorial Americalee, 1949), 109–10; Benjamín Vicuña Mackenna, *Estudios i catálogo completo i razonado de la Biblioteca Americana coleccionada por el Sr Gregorio Beéche* (Valparaíso: Imprenta del Mercurio, 1879), 57–78.

6. From Colombia, Salvador Camacho Roldán noted in 1861 that "only some editions of the New York *Herald* had arrived from May, and two from . . . June," because of Civil

War in Colombia. See his "Guerra civil en los Estados Unidos de Norte" [1861], in *Escritos varios* (Bogotá: Librería Colombiana, 1892), 249–59, 255.

7. Apart from Salvador Camacho Roldán's articles on the Civil War, in his *Escritos varios*—see note 6, the Chilean Benjamín Vicuña Mackenna, who also visited the United States in 1865, wrote a series of commentaries, which are collected in Hunter, *A Sketch of Chili* (Hunter was his secretary). Osvaldo Orico, *Homens da America Libertadores de povos do continente* (Rio de Janeiro: Editorial Getulio Costa, 1944), carries the same discussion of the inscription at the Capitol (112–13) as Sarmiento's text (*Vida de Abran Lincoln*, xxii–iii).

8. The sources have been identified as Frank Crosby, *Life of Abraham Lincoln, Sixteenth President of the United States* (Philadelphia: John E. Potter, 1865), and the anonymously published work of David B. Williamson, *Illustrated Life, Services, Martyrdom, and Funeral of Abraham Lincoln* (Philadelphia: T. B. Peterson & Bros., 1865). See Enrique Carilla, "Sarmiento y su *Vida de Lincoln,*" *Revista de humanidades* (Buenos Aires), I:1 (1961), 167–77. Comparing the U.S. texts with Sarmiento's, it quickly becomes clear that he did simply interweave passages from the two of them, inserting quotations from Lincoln.

9. Sarmiento, *Vida*, 214. My emphasis.

10. Ibid., xvii.

11. Ibid., xlvii–xlviii.

12. Ibid., xxvi.

13. Ibid., xix and xxiii.

14. Ibid., xxviii.

15. Ibid., xliii-iv.

16. Sarmiento, letter of May 12, 1866 to Mary Mann, in Barry Velleman, *"My Dear Sir": Mary Mann's Letters to Sarmiento* (Buenos Aires: Instituto Cultural Argentino Norteamericano, 2001), 16.

17. Juan Bautista Alberdi, *El imperio del Brasil y sus planes de reconstrucción territorial y dinástica en detrimento de la América Republicana* (Paris: Imprenta Rochette, 1869), 23–24.

18. Salvador Camacho Roldán, "Guerra civil en los Estados Unidos del Norte (Año de 1863)" [1864], in his *Escritos varios*, 260–83, esp. 260–63.

19. In Colombia, Camacho Roldán, who had evidently read Sarmiento's biography, also saw Lincoln as a bulwark against militarism. See his *Notas de viaje* (Bogotá: Publiciones del Banco de la República, 1973), II:337; and his *Escritos varios*, 268.

20. José Martí, "El poeta Walt Whitman" [1887], in his *Obras completas* (Havana: Editorial de Ciencias Sociales, 1975), 13:131–43, 133 [hereafter *OC*].

21. A narrative account of Lincoln's policies during the Civil War can be found in Martí's article "El General Grant" [1885], in *OC*, 13:3, 83–115.

22. José Martí, Letter to the editor of *La Nación* [Buenos Aires], August 15, 1889, New York, in *OC*, 12:287–95, 294.

23. "Roscoe Conkling" [1888], in *OC*, 12:175–83, 181.

24. Martí, "El General Logan" [1887], in *OC*, 12:305–7, 306.

25. José Martí, "Congreso Internacional de Washington" [1889], *Nuestra América* (Barcelona: Lingkua, 2006), 79.

26. José Martí, "Nuestra América" [1891], in Julio Ramos, *Divergent Modernities: Culture and Politics in Nineteenth-Century Latin America*, trans. John D. Blanco (Durham, NC: Duke University Press, 2001), 295–303 (quotation 296).

27. José Martí, letter to the editor of *La Opinión Pública* [Montevideo], July 8, 1889, New York, in *OC*, 12:271–76 (quotation 273).

28. Santovenia, "Lincoln, el precursor . . .," 488.

29. Ibid., 490.

30. Ibid., 488.

31. Hermino Portell Vilá, *Historia de Cuba en sus relaciones con los Estados Unidos y España* (Miami: Mnemosyne Publishing, 1969), II:171.

32. Guerra y Sánchez, *Historia*, 31.

33. Martí, "Recuerdos: Franklin, Washington, Lincoln y Webster," no date, in *OC*: 13:407–9.

34. For example, the Argentine Cupertino del Campo's one-page summary of Lincoln's life featured the fact that he had only three months' schooling, but "he taught himself by himself, reading and re-reading the Bible and the few books that with difficulty he could get hold of." Cupertino del Campo, *Prohombres de América* (Buenos Aires: Asociación de Difusión Interamericana, 1943), no page numbers. Chile's main newspaper, *El Mercurio*, noted in 1959 that in many respects Lincoln was a product of his times, but "the unusual thing about him was his determination to teach himself." "La memoria de Lincoln y la opinión universal," *El Mercurio* (Santiago), February 13, 1959, 3.

35. José Enrique Rodó, "El trabajo en el Uruguay" [1908], in Emir Rodríguez Monegal ed., *Obras completas* (Madrid: Editorial Aguilar, 1957), 653 [hereafter Rodó, *OC*].

36. Rodó, *OC*, 361.

37. Ibid., 968.

38. Carlos Alberto Torres, *Idola fori*, ed. Rubén Sierra Mejía (Bogotá: Instituto Caro y Cuervo, 2001), 602–3.

39. Arnold Gates, "La memoria de Lincoln y la opinión universal," *El Mercurio*, February 13, 1959, 3.

40. M. Castro Morales, "Estados Unidos en la historia del derecho," *Amauta* (Lima), Año II, no. 9 (May 1927), 29–32. See also "Mensaje de Alfredo Palacios, El Presidente de la Unión Latino-Americana a la juventud universitaria y obrera de los Estados Unidos," *Amauta* (Lima), Año II, no. 8 (April 1927), 34–36 (quotation 36), in which he associated Lincoln with the motto of "America for all humankind," in contrast to the Monroe Doctrine's "America for the Americans."

41. J. M. Puig Casauranc, "Abraham Lincoln, flor de humanidad," in *Mirando la vida* (Mexico: no publisher stated, 1933), 43–49, quotations from 47–49.

42. Orico, *Homens da América*, 112.

43. "Carta de Marx," *La Vanguardia* (Buenos Aires), April 15, 1965, 3.

44. See, for example, "Statement by Cuban Premier Fidel Castro in reply to statements made by Chilean President Eduardo Frei," March 20, 1966; "Castro comment on sugar, Chilean land reform," April 15, 1966; "Castro reiterates debt nonpayment," July 8, 1985, all from Castro speech database.

45. Sarmiento, *Vida*, xiv.

46. Emeterio S. Santovenia, "Abraham Lincoln" [1948] and "Lincoln, el precursor de la Buena vecindad" [1951], in his *Estudios, biografías y ensayos* (Havana: no publisher stated, 1957), 435–99. Rafael Helidoro Valle, "Lincoln y su pasión americana," *La Prensa*, February 12, 1959, 6, which was written from Mexico, was a summary of Santovenia's interpretation. The influence of Santovenia's ideas is explicit, too, in the speech by Cuban

Congressman Segundo Curti Messina, *Lincoln. Oración pronunciada el Día de las Américas* (Havana: Impresora Modelo, 1949), 49.

47. Santovenia, "Abraham Lincoln," 463.

48. See, for example, Chilean Francisco Bilbao's bald assertion: "Walker is invasion, Walker is conquest, Walker is the United States," in his article "El Congreso Normal Americano" [1856], *Obras completas*, ed. Manuel Bilbao (Buenos Aires: Imprenta de Buenos Aires, 1866), I:287–304, esp. 297.

49. For the view that "Gin" Blaine represented the turning point, see Benjamín Vicuña Mackenna, *Blaine* (Santiago: Imprenta Victoria, 1884).

50. For details on Lincoln's representatives in Latin America, see Nathan L. Ferris, "The Relations of the United States with South America during the American Civil War," *Hispanic American Historical Review* 21 (1941), 51–78, esp. 52. Thomas Nelson was especially popular in Chile and the appointment to Mexico of Thomas Corwin, a public figure of high renown, who was particularly famous for his opposition in the Senate to the Mexican War, was intended and received as a sign that Lincoln's administration took Mexico seriously.

51. Ferris, "Relations," 54.

52. Sarmiento, *Vida*, xxxii.

53. Brian Hamnett, *Juárez* (London: Longman, 1994), 157; Robert Ryal Miller, "Arms Across the Border: U.S. Aid to Juárez during the French Intervention in Mexico," *Transactions of the American Philosophical Society* (December 1973), 10.

54. Benjamín Vicuña Mackenna, "Motion offered in the Chamber of Deputies of Chili," June 3, 1865, in Hunter, *A Sketch of Chili*, 113–16, esp. 115.

55. Ferris, "Relations," 78.

56. Ibid., 74.

57. Ibid., 76.

58. Matías Romero, "Letter to the Minister of Foreign Relations of Mexico," Washington, April 4, 1862, in Burr and Hussey, *Documents*, 147–48 (quotation 148).

59. Translated citation from Romero's diary, in Miller, *Arms Across the Border*, 9.

60. Miller, *Arms Across the Border*.

61. Harry Bernstein, *Matías Romero 1837–1898* (Mexico: Fondo de Cultura Económica, 1973), 114. Peruvian José Gregorio Paz Soldán was also critical of Lincoln, arguing that he had made it impossible for Peru to buy the weapons needed to fight Spain in the Pacific. See Santovenia, *Sarmiento y su americanismo*, 81.

62. Francisco J. Ponte Domínguez, *Historia de la Guerra de los Diez Años* (La Habana: Academia de la Historia de Cuba, 1958), 36.

63. For examples of citations of the Gettysburg Address see: Luis Alberto Sánchez, *Un sudamericano en Norteamérica: ellos y nosotros* (Lima: Universidad Nacional Mayor de San Marcos, 1968), 321; Osvaldo Orico, *Homens da America*, 121–22; *La Nación* (Buenos Aires), April 14, 1965, 6; and Carlos Denegri, "Abraham Lincoln," *Excélsior* (Mexico City), April 14, 1965, 3A.

64. Joaquim Nabuco, "Lincoln and the Character of American Civilization," in *Abraham Lincoln. The Tribute of a Century 1809–1909*, ed. Nathan William MacChesney (Chicago: A. C. McChung & Co., 1910), 436–38 (quotation 437).

65. Natalia Bas, "The Model of the United States in Brazilian Debates on the Abolition of Slavery, 1861–1888" (draft chapter of Ph.D. thesis, University College London, 2009).

66. Joaquim Nabuco, *Abolitionism: The Brazilian Antislavery Struggle*, trans. and ed. Robert Conrad (Chicago: University of Illinois Press, 1977).

67. John F. Kennedy, "Recorded Greetings to the President and People of Brazil," April 3, 1961, http://www.presidency.ucsb.edu/ws/index.php?pid=8040, accessed May 11, 2009.

68. Sarmiento, *Vida*, xiii.

69. Articles about him have often appeared under the rubric "Hombres de América" ("Men of the Americas"), for example, Djed Bórquez, "Hombres de América. La vida luminosa de Abraham Lincoln," *Excélsior* (Mexico City), February 12, 1959, 6 and 9. See also the international conference organized by the Cuban Alternative Martiana para las Américas, held in Mexico in May 2009, "Martí, Juárez, and Lincoln in the Soul of Our America," Latin American Studies Association Web site: http://www.cubasection.org/php/noticia.php?id=135, accessed May 11, 2009.

13

"A Standard of Our Thought and Action"

LINCOLN'S RECEPTION IN EAST ASIA

De-min Tao

Abraham Lincoln's image in East Asia ranges widely, from an exemplar of honesty and self-reliance to a larger-than-life champion of human equality and popular rights. This essay moves beyond the realm of legend and myth to examine some of his concrete influences in China and Japan by tracing his contacts with the region during his presidency. It then assesses the construction and adaptation of Lincoln's image in East Asia, which has been used for a range of purposes, including as a role model for promoting an industrious spirit and democratic values, as a political tool of opposition party leaders, and as a means of criticizing American politics and foreign policy.[1]

I. Lincoln's Attitude toward China and Japan

During the mid-nineteenth century, Western imperialism and capitalist expansion brought the world together to an unprecedented extent. Karl Marx noted this globalizing tendency in a letter of 1858 addressed to his colleague, Friedrich Engels: "The proper task of bourgeois society is the creation of the world market, at least in outline, and of the production based on that market. Since the world is round, the colonisation of California and Australia and the opening up of China and Japan would seem to have completed this process."[2] From the date of the letter, October 8, it is clear that Marx took the Treaties of Tientsin between China and four Western powers, and the Ansei Treaties between Japan and five Western powers signed respectively in June and July that year, as the symbol of the full opening of East Asia. The former was concluded as the result of China's defeat in the Arrow War with Britain and France, which led to the opening of the capital city of Peking and the nearby port city of Tientsin to foreign diplomats, traders, and missionaries. This paved the way for further Western penetration into northern China, given that the five treaty ports, including Canton and Shanghai, had already been opened along China's southeast coast in the wake of the Opium War and the Treaty of Nanking in the early 1840s. The latter was initiated by Townsend Harris, the first American consul general to Japan, by taking advantage of the Arrow War's impact on the Shogun government, and thereby gaining what Commodore Perry failed to achieve during his ice-breaking visits of 1853 and 1854—opening of trading ports and extraterritoriality for American citizens in Japan.[3]

It was under these circumstances that Lincoln had to deal with some difficult issues arising from the newly developed foreign relations with China and Japan early in his presidency. In late 1860, just three days before Lincoln's victory in the presidential election, Samuel Wells Williams, secretary of the American legation in Beijing, submitted a letter to Secretary of State Lewis Cass, stating that a total of $400,000 had been paid by the Chinese government for claims on account of losses sustained by American citizens during the Arrow War. After paying the claims, "there will remain the sum of a little more than $200,000 in the hands of the United States' authorities in China, and subject to their direction." Williams proposed that the surplus funds be used to establish "a school of a high rank in China, where the natives of that empire can be taught the languages and science of western countries, under the tuition of competent men, with the object of making them serviceable to their own countrymen and government."[4] It appears that Lincoln favored this proposal to establish a Western-style academy for Chinese students. Although such an academy did not materialize until fifty years later, the occasion demonstrated Lincoln's foresight in embracing an alternative that would have served as the basis for an amicable relationship between China and the United States.[5]

Lincoln's diplomatic contact with Japan was similarly cordial. In the spring of 1860, the first Japanese diplomats arrived in Washington, D.C., to exchange the Ansei Treaty.[6] Based on its terms, Japan had already opened the three treaty ports of Yokohama, Nagasaki, and Hakodate in 1859 and was obliged to open the two major cities of Edo and Osaka and the two treaty ports of Kobe and Niigata. However, the inflation and political conflicts caused by the opening of Yokohama prompted the Shogun to seek a five-year postponement in the opening of these cities and ports. Lincoln replied on August 1, 1861 with characteristic tact, ensuring that his representative Townsend Harris, now the first minister to Japan, would be fully instructed to "proceed not less from a just regard for the interest and prosperity of your empire than from considerations affecting our own welfare and honor."[7] Treating the Japanese ruler as a kind of equal, Lincoln ended the letter: "wishing abundant prosperity and length of years to the great state over which you preside, I pray God to have your Majesty always in His safe and holy keeping." As a result, the United States, along with the allied powers, agreed to grant a five-year extension to the Shogun.[8] Lincoln's direct interactions with East Asia during his presidency, limited though they were, nevertheless displayed a sense of graciousness and compassion toward the region, thereby contributing, in no small manner, to his rising popularity in the decades to come.

II. The Spread of the Lincoln Story from Tokyo

As a matter of fact, on March 12, 1862, some seven months after sending that letter to the Shogun, Lincoln had a chance to chat in the White House with Joseph Heco, a young Japanese American who had served as an interpreter for the American legation in Edo (or Tokyo, as it became known after the Meiji Restoration in 1868), and who was seeking a position in the U.S. Navy with the help of Secretary of State William Seward. A native of Bansh province, Heco's ship was cast adrift in the Pacific in early December 1850 on his way home from a sightseeing trip to Edo. Fortunately, the thirteen-year-old boy and his fellow shipmates were picked up by the American freighter *Auckland*, which brought the survivors to San Francisco. Once in America, Heco attended a Catholic school in Baltimore, got baptized at the age of seventeen, and was naturalized as a U.S. citizen at the age of twenty-one.[9]

Heco recalled the brief but pleasant meeting: "The President was tall, lean, with large hands, darkish hair streaked with grey, slight side-whiskers and clean shaved about the mouth . . . He shook hands with me very cordially, and then he made a great many inquiries about the position of affairs in our country." Thus, he confirmed through personal experience the president's reputation as "a most sincere and kind person, greatly beloved by all those who came in contact with him, and more especially by his party and his friends."[10] In 1863, Heco resigned his job at the American legation and returned to Japan, where he became a prominent journalist, government official, and businessman. He published Japan's first newspaper, *Kaigai Shimbun* (*The Overseas News*) in 1864, which earned him the reputation as "the father of Japanese journalism." Indeed, it was through Heco's paper that many Japanese learned of Lincoln's assassination in July 1865.

Many English books were translated and edited for popular consumption after the 1868 Meiji Restoration as part of the national push toward learning from and catching up with the West.[11] For example, Japanese versions of Samuel Smiles's *Self-Help* and John Stuart Mill's *On Liberty*, published in 1870 and 1871 respectively, quickly became bestsellers. In December 1890 the first biography of Abraham Lincoln by Kaiseki Matsumura (1859–1939) appeared in Tokyo. Matsumura had an eclectic and wide-ranging education in many different private academies, where he learned Confucianism in Kyoto, English in Osaka, and Christianity in Yokohama. His Lincoln biography, which raced through thirteen editions, was the product of an education that emphasized moral development.[12] Its pages stressed, at times superlatively, Lincoln's guileless honesty and determination in the face of adversity, describing him as a

"good teacher for the impoverished," as well as a "model for our nation's politicians."[13] Matsumura compared Lincoln's death to that of Wang Yangming's,
the famous neo-Confucian philosopher and politician of early modern China,
in its dignity and to Jesus Christ's in its heroic martyrdom.[14]

Matsumura's pioneering biography undoubtedly inspired many of his contemporaries and later generations, including subsequent authors of Lincoln's
Japanese biographies. For example, Sakusaburō Uchigasaki (1877–1947),
made the following statement in the preface to his own 1929 enlarged biography of Lincoln.

> It was in 1890 when I was studying at an elementary school in Sendai
> that I first got to know Lincoln's name. Reading Kaiseki Matsumura's
> *Biography of Lincoln*, I began to admire the great man who was entirely
> different from heroes of the traditional mold. Every time I encountered a
> crisis and had to overcome temptation during my youth, it was this biog-
> raphy that gave me directions and courage. When I was twelve years old,
> I repeatedly read the *Taikōki* (Biography of Hideyoshi Toyotomi), but
> when I became a fifteen-year-old boy, I began to worship Lincoln, and
> read his biography whenever I got depressed.[15]

Uchigasaki had studied at Tokyo Imperial University's English department
before going to Oxford for training in theology. Later, he became a popular
publicist and a professor at Waseda University and was six times elected a
member of the House of Representatives beginning in 1924.

Lincoln's story became even more widespread in Japan upon its inclusion
in 1903 in the national textbook for moral education for upper-level pupils
in elementary schools. This booklet, containing twenty-eight lessons, preached
values such as patience, courage, loyalty to the family, and patriotism, through
the use of anecdotal stories to highlight the moral of the lesson. Lincoln, the
only foreign person included in the textbook, featured in five lessons including
those on studying, honesty, sympathy, and personal freedoms. These themes
were exemplified through episodes in Lincoln's life that were more personal
than political in character. Though emancipation appeared in the text, the Lincoln introduced to Japanese schoolchildren was the young Abe who worked
for three days to make up for damaging a neighbor's book, the young man
who walked a mile to return a few pennies to a store customer, and the fron-
tiersmen who rescued a distressed pig stuck in mud.[16] The space allotted to
Lincoln is noteworthy, especially considering that the contemporary Meiji
emperor's achievements and teachings were introduced in three lessons, and
a famous Tokugawa Shogun's merits and insights were appraised in just two
lessons. Given the very high rate of compulsory elementary school attendance
during this time in Japan (95 percent in 1905)[17], a whole generation of Japanese
effectively grew up with Lincoln as a foreign, yet familiar, role model, alongside

more traditional figures from Japanese and Chinese histories. For instance, Yaichi Akiyama, another Japanese Lincoln biographer, recalled in *The Great Man Lincoln*: "When I was a fourth grade pupil, I studied Lincoln's story for the first time through the textbook for moral education, which left a dramatic impression on my mind."[18]

The great Japanese biographers of Lincoln in the early twentieth century—Sakusaburō Uchigasaki, Yaichi Akiyama, and Ōson Sakurai—were indebted to Inazō Nitobe (1862–1933). A famous scholar and diplomat whose likeness can still be found today on the 5,000 yen banknote, Nitobe assisted scholars through encouragement and help in obtaining Lincoln-related materials. Nitobe attended the Sapporo Agricultural College (now Hokkaidō University), where he received an American-style education rooted in Christian principles. He pursued further studies at Johns Hopkins University in the United States and at Halle University in Germany. His multifaceted career included stints as a technocrat responsible for agricultural policies in Taiwan and Manchuria, a professor at his alma mater and the Kyoto Imperial University, and an under-secretary general of the League of Nations where he was the founding director of the International Committee on Intellectual Cooperation (predecessor to UNESCO). Nitobe was best known for his book *Bushido: The Soul of Japan* (1900), which was written in English and introduced samurai ethics and Japanese culture to Western readers. *Bushido* reflected his lifelong goal to become a "bridge across the Pacific," serving as a cultural broker between his countrymen and the international community.[19] As such, in addition to introducing Japan to the world, he also wrote and helped others to write books to introduce the outside world to Japanese audiences.

Tales of Lincoln (1912) by Ōson Sakurai is one such work. In its afterword, Nitobe revealed that he had written several chapters jointly with Sakurai. Nitobe began the project in 1909 as part of the commemoration of the centennial of Lincoln's birth, but was too busy to finish the work himself, so he passed it on to Sakurai to complete. In the afterword, he enthusiastically called Lincoln "the kindest man among the great men, and the greatest man among the kind men,"[20] which surely left the reader with a strong impression of Lincoln's character. At the end of his life, Nitobe also wrote a foreword for Yaichi Akiyama's *The Great Man Lincoln* (1933). The following passage reveals Lincoln's appeal to the Japanese in the late nineteenth and early twentieth centuries.

It is an old story around 1879 or 1880 that I first got to learn about Lincoln. One day at a library in Sapporo, I came up with the foolish ambition to read all the books that I could get my hands on to, and thus a book entitled *From Log-cabin to the White House* caught my attention. Without even knowing it was a biography, once I started reading it, I was fascinated by almost every page, and could not help but read through it without rest. When I finished reading, I got a deep feeling that this was truly a great man, and a biography of a great man was truly interesting. From that day on, I became a passionate worshipper of Lincoln; my study was full with books about Lincoln, and he became an idol in my *kamidana* [a home altar].

Lincoln lived in a different time and space, and therefore we cannot physically follow his steps. However, we can take him as a standard of our thought and action. Even Lincoln himself, had he not read George Washington's biography, would not have thought about becoming a man like Washington, and might have ended up as an ordinary person, and died in obscurity among the commoners. If Lincoln is likened to a golden temple, we at least can become a golden needle. Marble could be a grand monument to be looked up at by all people, but it also could be used as a stone weight for making pickles. In other words, although there are differences in position and achievement between Lincoln and us, we can draw no distinction in terms of personal quality.

There are a few books on Lincoln by our countrymen. But to study a great man as Lincoln, is equivalent to studying Mount Tai [the great mountain near Confucius' hometown in Shandong Province, China]; that is to say, it can be approached from anywhere and observed from all sides. And the truth about Lincoln cannot be exhausted by just a few books. For example, it is not an easy task to gain a full understanding of Lincoln, even if we limit our interests to only his religious faith. . . . Biographies on extraordinary men like Lincoln are not only a stimulus to young people with lofty ambitions, but should be read by all persons— regardless of his or her occupation, age, or class.[21]

After Nitobe's death, Toyohiko Kagawa, the Christian social reformer and international preacher in early twentieth-century Japan, made a pilgrimage to the historic sites connected with Lincoln. He was invited to give the Rauschenbusch Lectures at Colgate-Rochester Divinity School in April 1936, in memory of the American social gospel leader. During his travels, Kagawa made thoughtful and impressive comments at every Lincoln site he visited. When he observed the log cabin at Rockport Municipal Museum in Indiana, he reflected on the modest origins of a man he judged the world's greatest giant. When he traveled across the state of Illinois, and saw the vast prairie and the Mississippi River, he concluded that the eloquence of Lincoln's Gettysburg Address made him the plains' greatest poet. He attributed Lincoln's greatness to his love of learning. After visiting the site where Lincoln had worked as a ferryman on the Ohio River, Kagawa reflected:

[O]ne cannot say the reason that the young worker became a giant of the world was just a product of the environment. . . . [W]e have to think about Lincoln's spiritual strength. Today [because of the Great Depression], millions of laborers are in the same situation. However, Lincoln did not stop reading books even when he was doing a ferryman's job. He kept reading even when he was hired by someone else, and this was the reason that he could rise in life to become a giant.[22]

After visiting the Lincoln Memorial in Washington, D.C., Kagawa commented that Lincoln was the father of America's restoration and the teacher of mankind forever, stating, "as long as Americans remember Lincoln over George Washington, the American spirit will be everlasting, and flourish forever."[23] When Kagawa greeted the largest crowd ever gathered in the Knights of Columbus auditorium in Springfield in February 1936, he told them:

> It is quite an honor and privilege for me to visit this city of President Lincoln. Today I was given a chance to visit New Salem, and it was an inspiration to me. An Emperor of Japan once said that the greatest personality in the world's history is Abraham Lincoln. Even the great Emperor of Japan considered himself inferior to Abraham Lincoln. . . . Abraham Lincoln does not belong to this country alone. He belongs to the world. He belongs to Japan also. Millions and millions of souls in Japan are inspired by his life. Millions and millions of people of the colored race are inspired because he emancipated the colored people. And we, too especially respect him.[24]

The image of Lincoln promoted in prewar Japan was predominately that of a "success story" to inspire diligence and industriousness in individuals. What was lacking was a discussion of Lincoln's political principles and commitment to democracy. Even in Nitobe's praise for the Gettysburg Address, he did not mention the famous phrase, "government of the people, by the people, for the people."[25] This is because by the time of the publication of Matsumura's Lincoln biography in 1890, the Satsuma-Chōsh faction, which preferred the German-style authoritarian state, had monopolized the major positions in the government and responded to the increasing calls for popular rights with a conservative turn in its policies.[26] The promulgation of the Meiji Constitution and the *Imperial Rescript on Education*, in February 1889 and October 1890 respectively, elevated the emperor to a living god and emphasized loyalty and devotion to the throne. Therefore, the word "democracy" (expressed in Japanese as *Minken,* people's rights, or *Minshu,* rule by the people), which had motivated a generation during the early Meiji period, gradually became a kind of taboo in society. Even Sakuzō Yoshino, the leading political scientist at Tokyo Imperial University, had to resort to borrowing an old Confucian term of *Minpon* (people are the basis and source of the governance) to articulate his ideas for a real constitutional government and party politics.

Only after World War II, when the allied occupation authorities initiated a series of "democratization" policies in Japan, did such aspects of Lincoln's legacy begin to receive their due attention in Japanese publications. The most symbolic and influential events in the process of democratization were the emperor's renouncement of his divinity on January 1, 1946 and the adoption of a new constitution drafted mainly by the American officials on November 3 the same year. The significance of the former was best described by the following poem written then by a French-trained sculptor Kōtarō Takamura:

> The Occupation army saved us from starvation
> And we narrowly escaped destruction.
> At that moment the Emperor came forward
> And proclaimed "I am not a living god."
> As day followed day, the weight was lifted from my eyes,
> The burden of sixty years disappeared at once.[27]

Now that the taboo was removed, the democratic principles of Lincoln that had been downplayed for decades assumed center stage in the new Lincoln biographies. For example, the prominent biographer Ken Sawada placed the "government of the people . . ." phrase on the title page of his life of Lincoln, and the leading geographer Usao Tsujita pointed out in his *Lincoln* that

> today, when our country is going to restart as a democratic nation, in spite of our different personal preferences, we have to take a new look at and make new research on Lincoln. Intellectuals should be free from a preconceived notion and unreasonable prejudice that Lincoln was merely a famous self-made man who could serve as a role model for boys for encouraging their learning and cultivating their honesty. . . . Lincoln as a figure needs to be accepted once more by our Japanese society for getting to know America and what a democracy means. We may get a sense of where Japan is heading by just parroting the phrase of "government of the people." . . . Unless our country is able to turn out many persons like Lincoln, it can never be a civilized nation."[28]

In addition, Takeo Ono used *Lincoln: The Embodiment of Democracy* as his book title and Toshihiko Satō's was *The Father of Democracy: Lincoln.*[29] This version of Lincoln became the subject of postwar school textbooks.[30] Lincoln as champion of democracy, however, did not preclude his commercial deployment, most notably in comic book form, by Japan's answer to Walt Disney— Osamu Tezuka.[31]

III. China's Opposition Party Leaders' Embrace
of the Gettysburg Address

Lincoln did not reach the same level of popular recognition in late nineteenth- and early twentieth-century China as he did in Japan. When he featured in Chinese journal articles, it was often the translation of originals written in

Japanese. His appearance in Chinese school textbooks appears to have been limited to English language readers, which would have been beyond the capabilities of most Chinese.[32] Nonetheless, Chinese intellectuals were undoubtedly attracted to Lincoln's story, both for its example of the self-made man and for the democratic principles the American politician embraced. This was particularly the case with Sun Yat-sen, the founding father of the Republic of China (ROC), and Mao Tse-tung, the major leader of the People's Republic of China (PRC), both of whom were longtime opposition party leaders.

When a larger Chinese fleet was defeated by a smaller, yet tactically superior and better disciplined, Japanese navy in the Sino-Japanese War of 1894–95, some observers concluded that the battle highlighted China's inability to keep pace with Japan's Western-style modernization. However, inspired by Japan and the United States' experiences in nation-building, China launched its own series of reform programs, which eventually led to the 1911 Revolution under Sun's influence that changed Asia's largest monarchy into a republic, and the Northern Expedition of 1926–28 which defeated the powerful warlords and established the Nanking government under Generalissimo Chiang Kai-shek, the new leader of the Nationalist Party or Kuomintang (KMT) founded by Sun. These political miracles in which opposition leaders of common background rose to power were closely watched and admired by the Japanese. As the Lincoln biographer and politician Sakusaburō Uchigasaki stated:

> When I investigated our country's history of party politics, I found unexpectedly that it drew indirectly on Lincoln . . . When the news [of emancipation] arrived, people realized that this was the spirit of the age and the direction of world opinion, and the movement for a constitutional government [in Japan] thus began to rise. Sun Yat-sen's "Three Principles of the People" finally took shape and the nationalist government was established in Nanking. The new thinkers in the south who had been under the oppression of the northern military dictatorship, now grasped the government. This had a great impact on Japan's movement for a constitutional government. Sun's Three Principles . . . derived from the hint he got from Lincoln when he was learning in the United States. If this was true, the Lincoln that had passed away has now been revived in the Republic of China.[33]

Uchigasaki's view was not an isolated one. Fellow provincial and prominent political scientist Sakuzō Yoshino thought similarly,[34] as did Tsuyoshi Inukai, a famous opposition leader and a great admirer of Sun.[35]

Sun Yat-sen (1866–1925) was a transnational figure heavily influenced by Western ideas, just like Inazō Nitobe. The son of a Cantonese peasant, Sun's childhood hero was Hong Xiuquan, the leader of the Taiping Rebellion of 1851–64 against the Qing dynasty (1644–1911). When he was a teenager, Sun joined his older brother for three years in Honolulu, where he enrolled in a Church of England boarding school and learned the ideas of Lincoln and Alexander Hamilton.[36] Beginning in 1895, he was forced to live in exile in Europe, America, Canada, and Japan for sixteen years because of his radical politics. His kidnapping by the Chinese Legation in London in 1896 earned him international fame as China's leading revolutionary.[37] After the 1911 Revolution, Sun became the provisional president of the ROC and a founder of the KMT.

Sun's Three Principles of the People—which refers to People's National Consciousness (*minzu*), or nationalism; People's Rights (*minzhu*), or democracy; and People's Livelihood (*minsheng*), or socioeconomic well-being—was often compared to Lincoln's famous expression in the Gettysburg Address, a "government of the people, by the people, and for the people."[38] In a 1919 lecture on the history of Western politics, he used the expression to praise the United States for establishing a truly democratic republic, and maintained that in the political system championed by Lincoln, the people became the rulers and the leaders became public servants.[39] Sun invoked Lincoln's phrase as a sort of democratic ideal toward which China—whose people were growing increasingly disillusioned with the rule of its Manchurian dynasty—should aspire. To be sure, Sun's Three Principles were actually an eclectic combination of ideas which drew from his transnational background, and its specific essence differed from that of Lincoln's in significant ways.[40] Nevertheless, insofar as Lincoln's message was appropriated by Sun to unify the will of a nation at a historical watershed, it could be said that Lincoln's spirit was, indeed, revived in China.

Compared with Sun Yat-sen, Mao Tse-tung (1893–1976) was born into a richer peasant-merchant family. He was exposed to ideological debates on liberalism, democratic reformism, anarchism, and utopian socialism during World War I and its aftermath, before eventually becoming a founding member of the Chinese Communist Party (CCP) in 1921. When the CCP formed the first United Front (1923–27) with the KMT for preparation of the Northern Expedition, Mao was responsible for political propaganda. Unlike many other politicians, he was concerned more about the peasants, who constituted the great majority of China's total population of four hundred million. After the Long March, Mao finally became the undisputed leader of the CCP and its Red Army based in Yan'an, located in northwest China. After the Marco Polo Bridge Incident on July 7, 1937, he formed the second United Front (1937–45) with the ruling party KMT to withstand the Japanese invasion, and his bases and troops were reorganized as part of the national administrative and military systems under Chiang Kai-shek. He told the American reporter Edgar Snow that sometime before or after the 1911 Revolution "I learned about the United States for the first time from an article on the American Revolution, and still remember a sentence from it: 'after eight years of hard fighting, Washington won out and established his nation.' From *Biographies of Great Heroes*, I further got to know Napoleon, Catherine II, Peter the Great, Wellington, Gladstone, Rousseau, Montesquieu, and Lincoln."[41]

The defeat of the Japanese invasion resulted in a new conflict in China, this time waged between Communists and Nationalists. This struggle spawned a competition between the two sides to enlist foreign support and sympathy. It is a sign of Lincoln's reach and elasticity in East Asia that both sides deployed him as an instrument of public diplomacy. When a Reuters correspondent asked Mao in late September 1945 what his conception was of a free and democratic China, the Communist leader invoked Lincoln. "A free and democratic China," Mao asserted,

> will have the following characteristics. Its government officials at all levels, including even the central government, will all be chosen in universal elections with secret ballots, and will be responsible to their electors. It will carry out Mr. Sun Yat-sen's Three People's Principles, Lincoln's principle of 'of the people, by the people, and for the people,' as well as Roosevelt's Atlantic Charter. It will guarantee the independence, solidarity, and unity of the country, and its cooperation with other democratic powers.[42]

The ensuing Civil War of 1946–49 invited further comparisons with Lincoln. Mao drew power from peasants by launching a series of land-reform programs, a tactic not unlike Lincoln's mobilization of African Americans during the American Civil War. Indeed, the power Mao drew from the peasantry turned the tide of the conflict in the favor of the CCP, leading to the retreat of the KMT government to Taiwan.

Despite their many differences, both Sun Yat-sen and Mao Tse-tung echoed the Gettysburg Address when they were in the position of an opposition party leader. While Sun did not live to see the KMT hold power, he had anticipated that a true democracy must be gradually and patiently cultivated—indeed his vision would be realized in Taiwan in the 1990s. By contrast, although Mao ruled the PRC for twenty-seven years after 1949, he never put his democratic promises into practice. Even today, democratic reforms remain elusive on the mainland, though campaigners, such as recent Nobel Prize-winner Dr. Liu Xiaobo, continue to work toward these ends.

IV. The Uses of Lincoln in Diplomatic Interchanges between the United States and East Asia

As elsewhere, a notable feature of Lincoln's image in East Asia has been its malleability. This in part reflects the elasticity of his words and deeds, which has allowed him to be invoked in diplomatic exchanges for purposes ranging from the strengthening of alliances to self-justification in disputes over issues of human rights and national sovereignty.

The former case was manifested by a special stamp issued in the United States in 1942 and by its equivalent issued in Taiwan in 1959. As part of efforts to express American support for the "overrun countries" and their "heroic resistance" against the Axis Powers in World War II,[43] a five-cent "China Commemorative Stamp" was issued on July 7, 1942 in Denver by the U.S. Post Office Department. While the stamps for other overrun countries were simply an image of their respective national flags, this featured Lincoln and Sun, side by side, along with their famous democratic doctrines written in English and Chinese characters, respectively. Between the two likenesses, there is a map of China with the image of a sun from the national flag of the ROC, with the inscriptions "July 7, 1937," "July 7, 1942," and the Chinese government's wartime guidelines of "Fight the War and Build the Country" (in Chinese). The particulars of the stamp were chosen with great care (perhaps reflecting not only President Roosevelt's interests in stamps, but also the importance he assigned to the China front during the Second World War):[44] July 7, 1942 was exactly five years after the Marco Polo Bridge Incident, which marked the outbreak of the second Sino-Japanese War; Denver was the very city in which Sun resided when the 1911 Revolution occurred; and the value of the stamp, five cents, was the normal rate for sending a letter from the United States to China. In addition, at a ceremony on July 7, 1942, at the White House, Frank Walker, then U.S. Postmaster General, presented a set of stamps to the Chinese ambassador in Washington, D.C., and a first-day cover to Chiang Kai-shek, after which a total of twenty-one million stamps, including 170,000 first-day covers, were sold.[45] If the stamp reflected in part the imperatives of wartime propaganda, it also embodied the transnational movement of ideas that had created a global democratic consciousness.[46]

Since both China's Nationalists and Communists were allies of the United States at the time, they competed to claim the mantles of Sun Yat-sen, Lincoln, and other heroes. When the relationship soured between Chiang Kai-shek and

This 1942 U.S. postal stamp illustrates the connection between Sun Yat-sen and Lincoln. Taiwan issued a similar stamp in 1959, which can be found on this book's cover.

U.S. Chief of the General Staff Joseph Stilwell, Mao's secretary Hu Qiaomu seized the opportunity to present the Communists as the legatees of American traditions. In a special editorial in *Jiefang Daily* (*Liberation Daily*) that appeared on the Fourth of July, Hu declared that "The work we Communists are carrying out right now is exactly the work that Washington, Jefferson, Lincoln, and others have already achieved in the United States; there is no doubt it will earn the sympathy of a democratic America . . . The United States is currently providing generous aid to China's war of resistance and democratic movements, for which we are very grateful. Long live the Fourth of July! Long live democratic America!"[47]

During the Cold War, it was Chiang Kai-shek and the KMT government, now based in Taiwan, who appropriated Lincoln in their effort to secure American support. Perhaps the most visible example occurred during the 1959 sesquicentennial of Lincoln's birth when the government issued a commemorative stamp, which placed Sun and Lincoln shoulder to shoulder in front of the backdrop of the colorful national flags of the ROC and the United States. As a news report described, the decision was made at a time "when Chinese and American nations are joining hands to resist Communist invasion," as well as "for the cause of carrying on the traditional Sino-American friendship, commemorating the two great democratic prophets, and protecting human rights and upholding justice."[48]

The political uses of Lincoln as a means for promoting Sino-American relations were not restricted to the periods of World War II and the Cold War. In fact, it was continued and renewed in the 1990s, when both Beijing and Washington attempted to construct a strategic partnership. President Jiang Zemin's familiarity with Lincoln served as a conversational ice-breaker during his 1997 meeting with President Bill Clinton. Upon being shown an original manuscript of Lincoln's Gettysburg Address, Jiang pleasantly surprised his American hosts by reciting aloud the document which he memorized as a high school student in the 1940s. This episode, as one commentator observed, had the effect of facilitating "the most probing and candid discussion of the human rights issue in their five meetings."[49] The uses of Lincoln, however, were not limited to polite socializing. Prior to his 1997 trip, Jiang cited Lincoln's opposition to slavery in an interview with the *Washington Post*, attempting to deflect criticisms over Tibet by accusing the United States of applying a double standard in its treatment of the issue. "Lincoln was a remarkable leader, particularly in liberating the slaves in America. . . . When it comes to slavery in China, most of China got rid of slavery long ago, except in Tibet, where it was not until the Dalai Lama left that we eliminated serfdom. . . . The impression I get is that you [Americans] are undoubtedly opposed to slavery, yet you support the Dalai Lama."[50] Taiwanese separatism also offered Chinese Communists the opportunity to deploy the image of Lincoln the national consolidator on behalf of their objectives. "The purpose of your civil war was to unite America together,"

Jiang asserted on another occasion, "yet on the issue of Taiwan your people support separating Taiwan and China and cannot understand how strongly 1.2 billion people feel about reunification of the motherland. This makes people think the standards you apply to others are not the same as those you apply to yourselves."[51] Jiang has not been the only recent Chinese statesmen to interpret Lincoln and the American Civil War through the lens of the Taiwan issue. A similar use of Lincoln was made by Zheng Bijian, a high-ranking advisor to China's leadership who popularized the term, "China's peaceful rise." In an article for the journal *Chinese Youth,* Zheng likened the Taiwan issue to the problem faced by Lincoln during the Civil War: "Look at President Lincoln, and how adamantly he opposed secession. . . . How come Lincoln's battle to preserve the Union was completely justified, whereas our steadfast efforts to maintain a unified motherland is not?"[52]

As in China, Lincoln's name was also used by some influential leaders in Japan to criticize America's unfair treatment of its citizens, especially concerning the two major issues of Japanese immigration and its postwar constitution. The Asian Exclusion Act (known more commonly in Japan as the Japanese Exclusion Act) of 1924 came as a deep blow to many Japanese, some of whom had previously been strong believers in the openness of American society. The Act imposed a ban on Japanese immigration to the United States on the grounds that such immigrants were crowding the job market and causing social unrest, a problem first raised by the California legislature after the Russo-Japanese War. Notable Japanese such as Viscount Eiichi Shibusawa "could not believe that this restrictionist legislation came from the country that gave birth to Washington and Lincoln, and has advocated justice and equality as its national creed ever since its inception."[53] Shibusawa, a pioneering banker and industrialist who was involved in the founding of hundreds of companies and schools during his lifetime, was one of the few Japanese who recognized the rising influence of the American business model and political leadership on the world stage early in the twentieth century. He thus sought to avoid the kind of conflicts that would lead to a fatal clash with the United States. In 1909, he led a business delegation on a three-month tour of the United States to build ties with American business, religious, and academic circles. He encouraged Japanese participation in the 1915 Panama-Pacific International Exposition in San Francisco, and persuaded the Japanese delegation to accept the Washington Naval Treaty while attending the Washington Conference of 1921–22 as an observer.[54] Thus, it was not at all unaccountable that he was so disillusioned with the Act.

Toyohiko Kagawa, who happened to be in the United States during the passage of the Asian Exclusion Act, used a sermon to tell a fifteen-thousand-strong audience in Southern California: "I have stopped singing America's national anthem. . . . The white people may enjoy freedom, but the yellow race does not. In the name of Abraham Lincoln, I am ashamed of the United States!"[55] And Inazō Nitobe, the foremost advocate of Lincoln in Japan, who lectured widely in America to counter anti-Japanese sentiments there, was especially shocked at the news of the passage of the Act. "It is absolutely outrageous," he declared, "I am deeply sorry for the United States. Until this law is revoked, I swear I will never step foot on American soil."[56] It is apparent that many Japanese people perceived the Act as Japan's national humiliation, an idea that played no small role in the escalation of U.S.-Japanese tensions in the interwar years.

As mentioned earlier, Japan adopted the American-drafted Constitution of Japan in 1946 under Allied Occupation. This, too, was considered an act of national humiliation by some Japanese leaders. On July 30, 1953, Yasuhiro Nakasone, a young politician who was attending a summer seminar at Harvard University chaired by Professor Henry Kissinger, indicated his discontent in a speech at an international forum there. Nakasone argued that "If Lincoln's words 'Government . . . by the people' have any truth, a constitution for the Japanese should be made by the Japanese . . . I have no doubt that when such a constitution is made, Americans will be satisfied and pleased with the result—the birth of a real democracy in Japan."[57] Two years later, he joined the non-partisan "League of the Diet Members for an Autonomous Constitution," and publicized a song called "Revising the Constitution." In 2007, the league was renamed as "League of the Diet Members for Making a New Constitution," and Nakasone became its president. Nakasone has devoted much of his long political career, which has included three stints as prime minister in the 1980s in which he aligned with Ronald Reagan (the so-called "Ron-Yas" relationship), to the issue of constitutional reform.

In conclusion, when both China and Japan were in the process of a historical transition from a traditional to a modern state in the late nineteenth and twentieth centuries, they turned increasingly outward in search of potential models to follow. The values that Lincoln represented had strong appeal to these nations, whose dramatic rise on the global stage mirrored that of Lincoln's nineteenth century America. Lincoln's personal values also found traction in East Asian cultures, not least for the prescription they offered for individual and national development—perseverance, hard work, liberty, and democracy. While certain aspects of his legacy were selectively applied in the process of adoption, and still others are increasingly employed as a foil for diplomatic interchanges between the region and the United States, such versatility of use also speaks to the fundamental reach of Lincoln's ideas, which have transcended various boundaries to function as a common point of reference between all nations.

Notes

1. I am grateful to Mr. Hitoshi Honda of Meisei University Library, who kindly allowed me free use of the rich collection of the Tokyo Lincoln Center. I also wish to thank Mr. Davis Mengel, chief of the Special Access and FOIA staff at the National Archives

and Records Administration (NARA) in Washington, DC; Mr. Pan Kuang-che, director of Hu Shih Memorial Hall, Institute of Modern History at Academia Sinica; and Ms. Shen Weiwei, doctoral student at Kansai University, for their assistance in discovering relevant materials in the United States, Taiwan, and China.

In this essay, Japanese names are presented in the Western convention of personal names preceding family names, whereas Chinese names follow the Chinese convention of family names preceding personal names, for the sake of notational consistency with the existing literature. Unless otherwise noted, all translations are my own.

2. "Marx to Engels in Manchester," Marx & Engels Internet Archive, accessed October 10, 2010, http://www.marxists.org/archive/marx/works/1858/letters/58_10_08.htm.

3. See John K. Fairbank, Edwin O. Reischauer, and Albert M. Craig, *East Asia: Tradition and Transformation*, rev. ed. (Boston: Houghton Mifflin, 1989), chap. 16–17.

4. U.S. State Department, "Dispatches from U.S. Ministers to China 1843–1906" (M92-Roll 20: February 13, 1860–July 26, 1861), at NARA in Washington, DC.

5. Tyler Dennett, *Americans in Eastern Asia: A Critical Study of United States' Policy in the Far East in the Nineteenth Century* (New York: Macmillan, 1922), 330.

6. See Masao Miyoshi, *As We Saw Them: The First Japanese Embassy to the United States (1860)* (Berkeley: University of California Press, 1979).

7. Abraham Lincoln, "Reply to the Tycoon of Japan on Opening of Treaty Ports," in *The Works of Abraham Lincoln: State Papers 1861–1865,* ed. John H. Clifford and Marion M. Miller, (New York: The University Society, Inc., 1908), 2:246. The Shogun was referred to as "Tycoon" in formal diplomatic communications at the time.

8. However, due to the war between Satsuma domain and Britain in 1863, and between Chōshū domain and the combined fleet of four powers including the United States in 1864, Japan had to open the named cities and ports (except Kobe) in 1865.

9. See Haruyoshi Chikamori, *Joseph Heco* [in Japanese] (Tokyo: Yoshikawa Kobunkan, 1963); Haruyoshi Chikamori, *Joseph Heco: Documenting the Unexpected Life of a Japanese Who Had Met Lincoln* [in Japanese] (Tokyo: Japan Britannica, 1980). Heco's native name was Hikozō Hamada.

10. Joseph Heco, *The Narrative of A Japanese: What He Has Seen and the People He Has Met in the Course of the Last Forty Years*, ed. James Mursoch (San Francisco: American-Japanese Publishing Association, n.d.), 1:299–302.

11. During the Meiji Restoration, the Tokugawa shogunate was defeated, and power and land ownership were returned from the samurai class to the emperor. The uprising was orchestrated by a group of young, reform-minded men from the domains of Satsuma and Chōshū, who later formed the core of the new leadership—also known as the Meiji oligarchy—that set out on major political and social reforms based on Western models.

12. Kaiseki Matsumura, *Biography of Lincoln* [in Japanese] (Tokyo: Maruzen Shōsha Shoten, 1890).

13. Ibid., introduction.

14. Ibid., 179.

15. Sakusaburō Uchigasaki, preface to *Lincoln* [in Japanese] (Tokyo: Jitsugyō no Nippon, 1929).

16. Ministry of Education, *An Advanced Elementary School Textbook of Morals (for second grade instruction)* [in Japanese] (1903; repr., Tokyo: Ministry of Education, 1910), table of contents, 17–24.

17. Fairbank, Reischauer, and Craig, *East Asia*, 532.

18. Yaichi Akiyama, *The Great Man Lincoln* [in Japanese] 3rd. ed. (1933; Tokyo: Kyo-bun-kan, 1940), 1.

19. Shigeru Fujii, *Morioka's Great Predecessors* [in Japanese] 3rd. ed. (2000; Morioka: Morioka City Middle School Principals' Council, 2008), 51–117. It is said that Theodore Roosevelt was so impressed by *Bushido* that upon finishing the book he immediately ordered an additional thirty copies, five of which he passed along to his children so that they might learn from the "noble character and resolute integrity" of the Japanese.

20. Ōson Sakurai, *Tales of Lincoln* [in Japanese] 3rd. ed. (1912; Tokyo: Teibi Press, 1913), preface and 424–26.

21. Yaichi Akiyama, *Great Man*, ii–iii. It is said that Lincoln shared the spot on Nitobe's home altar with Jesus Christ and Socrates. Nitobe's memory of his first contact with the Lincoln story may have been flawed, for he graduated from the Sapporo Agricultural College in 1881, and *From Pioneer Home to the White House: Life of Abraham Lincoln: Boyhood, Youth, Manhood, Assassination, Death* by William M. Thayer was first published in 1882 (Boston: James H. Earle). The same author's *From Log-cabin to White House* (Norwich, CT: Henry Bill Pub. Company) published in 1881 concerned the life of President James A. Garfield.

22. Toyohiko Kagawa, "Making the World as My Home," in *The Complete Works of Kagawa Toyohiko* [in Japanese] (Tokyo: Kirisuto Shinbunsha, 1963), 23:417.

23. Ibid., 417–22.

24. Emerson O. Bradshaw, Charles E. Shike, and Helen F. Topping, eds., *Kagawa in Lincoln's Land* (New York: National Kagawa Coordinating Committee, 1936), 18–19. As a pacifist, Kagawa was critical of the martial decoration at Lincoln's tomb: "It is regrettable that the monument was decorated with tanks and cannons, but no images of the emancipator. I felt deeply that the republicans of the United States did not understand the spirit of emancipation." Toyohiko Kagawa, *Complete Works*, 23:421.

25. Sakurai, *Tales*, 418–20.

26. See Fairbank, Reischauer, and Craig, *East Asia*, chap. 18.

27. Irokawa Daikichi, *The Culture of the Meiji Period*, trans. and ed. Marius B. Jansen (Princeton, NJ: Princeton University Press, 1985), 9–12. See also Carol Gluck, *Japan's Modern Myths: Ideology in the Late Meiji Period* (Princeton, NJ: Princeton University Press, 1985).

28. Ken Sawada, *A Biography of Lincoln* [in Japanese] (Tokyo: Chōbunkaku, 1946); Usao Tsujita, *Lincoln* [in Japanese] (Tokyo: Daigadō, 1947).

29. Takeo Ono, *Lincoln: The Embodiment of Democracy* [in Japanese] (Tokyo: Hōei-sha, 1959); Toshihiko Satō, *The Father of Democracy: Lincoln* [in Japanese] (Tokyo: Iwasaki shoten, 1960).

30. See Kunio Yanagita and Masakatsu Naruse, *New Language Reader (for 1st year Junior High School)* [in Japanese] (Tokyo: Tokyo Shoseki, 1962), 104–11.

31. Osamu Tezuka, ed., *The Day of Emancipation* [in Japanese], World History, vol. 11 (Tokyo: Chūōkōron-sha, 1984).

32. See, for example, "The Assassination of American President Lincoln" [in Chinese] *Zhongwai Dashi Bao*, 2, August 25, 1899; "Lincoln's Childhood House," illustration, *Xinmin Congbao*, 19, October 31, 1902; "Calligraphy by Lincoln," [in Chinese] *Zhonghua xueshengjie*, 1: no. 9, September 25, 1915. The 1915 article includes a printed image of a handwritten letter of condolence from Lincoln, dated November 21, 1864, addressed from the White House to a Boston mother whose five sons had supposedly died in the Civil War.

33. Sakusaburō Uchigasaki, *Lincoln* [in Japanese] (Tokyo: Jitsugyō no Nippon, 1929), ix.

34. De-min Tao, "The Japanese Responses to the May Fourth Literary Revolution: The Cases of Yoshino Sakuzō and Aoki Masaru" [in Japanese], in *China as Cultural Phenomenon* (Osaka: Kansai University Press, 2002).

35. De-min Tao, "Naito Konan and the Eastern Cultural League: Pan-Asianism in the Early Showa Period" [in Japanese], Supplementary Issue No. 3 to *Journal of East Asian Cultural Interaction Studies* (Osaka: Kansai University, December 2008); Neil Martin, "Sun Yat Sen: In Defense of Nationalism, the Republic, and the American System of Political Economy," The Schiller Institute, accessed March 4, 2008.

36. Martin, "Sun Yat Sen"; Fairbank, Reischauer, and Craig, *East Asia*, 743.

37. Wang Ke-wen, ed., *Modern China: An Encyclopedia of History, Culture, and Nationalism* (New York & London: Garland Publishing, 1998), 339–41.

38. Ibid., 352.

39. Wang Er-min, "The Concept of Public Servant and the Idea of People as Sovereignty in Modern China" [in Chinese], in Wang's *Second Series of Essays on Modern Chinese Intellectual History* (Beijing: Social Sciences Academic Press, 2005), 427.

40. For example, Sun's Principle of National Consciousness (*minzu*) was originally conceived as a rallying call for the Han Chinese—organized along narrow ethnic lines—to wrest back control of their land from the Manchurian rulers and imperialist foreigners—as opposed to the Lincolnian notion of preserving the Union from potential dissolution. Concerning the differences in Chinese and American understanding of democracy, see Elizabeth J. Perry, "Chinese Conceptions of 'Rights': From Mencius to Mao—and Now," *Perspectives on Politics* 6, no. 1 (2008), 37–50.

41. Edgar Snow, *Autobiography of Mao Tse-tung* [in Chinese], trans. Wang Heng (Taipei: Taiwan shufang, 2002), 22.

42. "Answers to Questions Raised by Reuters News Agency Correspondent Gamble, September 27, 1945," quoted in Arthur Waldron's editorial, "What Should Bush Say at Tsinghua University," *Taipei Times,* February 2, 2002; Minoru Takeuchi, ed., *Collected Works of Mao Tse-tung* (Tokyo: Sososha, 1971), 9:335.

43. Maud and Miska Petersham, *America's Stamps: The Story of One Hundred Years of U.S. Postage Stamps* (New York: Macmillan, 1947), 116–19.

44. FDR noted to his son during the Cairo Conference: "You should consider that if China were not around, or if it to be were defeated, how many divisions of Japanese troops would be transferred to other fronts to fight. They could immediately occupy Europe, occupy India. They could do so without effort, and advance into the Middle East . . . and join Germany to make pincer attacks and get together in the Near East, shutting out Russia, smashing Egypt, and severing all the transportation lines that pass through the Mediterranean." Yang Tianshi, "Refuse German Suggestion for a Joint Attack on India and Prevent the Joining of Forces by Germany and Japan: An Interpretation of Chiang Kai-shek's Diary" [in Chinese], *Minpao Monthly*, 45, no. 9, (September 2010), 70–74.

45. "FDR and the First Stamp of Sun Yat-sen in the United States" [in Chinese], American ed., *Wenhuipao*, November 13, 2007, accessed October 10, 2010, http://www.chinesetoday.com/news/show/id/26652.

46. One of the reasons for this judgment was that World War II has been propagated as a war between the "democratic powers" and the "fascist powers," although countries like Soviet Russia and the ROC—whose status as a permanent member of the United Nations'

Security Council was replaced by the PRC in 1971—were not democratic countries by Western standards. And to some extent, the propaganda-derived perception of World War II still matters in today's post-Cold War world.

47. Yang Yusheng, *The Chinese Views of America* [in Chinese] (Shanghai: Fudan University Press, 1996), 183.

48. "A Stamp in Which the Two Great Democratic Prophets of China and the United States are Put Together" [in Chinese], *United Daily News* (*Lianhe pao*, a major newspaper in Taiwan), December 16, 1959.

49. Robert L. Kuhn, *The Man Who Changed China: The Life and Legacy of Jiang Zemin* (New York: Crown Publishers, 2004), 321.

50. Ibid., 316.

51. Ibid., 316–17.

52. Zheng Bijian and Ye Xiaoshen, "Zheng Bijian: Peaceful Rise and Peaceful Development are One and the Same" [in Chinese], *China Economic Net* (originally published in *Chinese Youth*), September 21, 2007, accessed August 4, 2009, http://www.ce.cn/xwzx/gnsz/szyw/200709/21/t20070921_12994705_1.shtml.

53. Shibusawa Seien Kinen Zaidan Ryūmonsha, ed., *Biographical Material on Shibusawa Eiichi* [in Japanese], 46 vols. (Tokyo: Shibusawa Seien Kinen Zaidan Ryūmonsha, 1958–1963), 34:182.

54. Masato Kimura, *Shibusawa Eiichi: The Pioneer of Popular Economic Diplomacy* [in Japanese] (Tokyo: Chūōkōron-sha, 1991), 61–152.

55. Kagawa, *Complete Works*, 23:423.

56. Sadao Asada, *U.S.-Japanese Relations between the Two World Wars: The Navy and the Policy-making Process* [in Japanese] (Tokyo: Tokyo University Press, 1995), 310.

57. William Theodore de Bary et al., *Sources of Japanese Tradition: Volume 2, 1600 to 2000* (New York: Columbia University Press, 2001), 1088–89.

14

National Unity and Liberty

LINCOLN'S IMAGE AND RECEPTION IN GERMANY, 1871–1989

Jörg Nagler

The attempt to trace Lincoln's image and reception in Germany for the time span of more than one hundred years presents a considerable challenge since different political systems need to be considered. After the creation of the German Reich in 1870–71, Germany became a thriving industrial nation and power. Following the First World War, it became the Weimar Republic, then the Third Reich, next a divided Germany in the Cold War, and finally a reunified country after 1989–90.[1]

This analysis of the transnational images, memory, legacy, reception, and perception of Lincoln will concentrate less on the historical figure himself and more on the individuals and collective entities that responded to Lincoln and generated these evocations and images. Such images, whether of other nations or their key historical figures, are always cultural productions involving cognitive processes that inherently use familiar contents out of the cultural reservoir of the recipients.[2] These processes—which are never static—are deeply rooted in the history and culture of each respective community or nation; they help us understand the specific historical circumstances under which Lincoln became a figure recognized as a "humanitarian as broad as the world" (Tolstoy).

Who were the major producers and carriers of these images, and what were their intentions? How did they receive their information about Lincoln? Did changing American views and interpretations of Lincoln have an impact on the German side?[3] The reception and legacy of Lincoln in Germany needs to be embedded in overall German-American relations, including the mass emigration of some two million Germans to the United States in the nineteenth century, which led to close ties between the two nations.[4]

Given the lack of evidence on how ordinary Germans perceived Abraham Lincoln, this chapter will focus on politicians, intellectuals, labor leaders, and artists. It will examine under what historical contexts, with what intentions, and in what ways they referred to Lincoln. It will consider why and how certain social and political groups in Germany utilized the image and iconography of Lincoln to support their own objectives. In addition it will also consider which Lincoln images dominated: the unifier, the emancipator, the modernizer, the democrat who used the power of a democratic state, the egalitarian self-made man from humble origins, or the defender of workingmen's rights.

On Abraham Lincoln's birthday in 1913, the German ambassador to the United States, Count von Bernstorff, at the invitation of the Abraham Lincoln Association, delivered a commemorative speech entitled "Lincoln as Germany Regarded Him" before the joint assembly of the Illinois legislature and other invited guests at the State Armory in Springfield. Besides filio-pietist remarks praising the contributions of German-Americans during the American Civil War and their supposedly decisive vote for Lincoln in 1860, the ambassador emphasized the strong and unrelenting support of Prussia and other German states for the cause of the Union. He portrayed Lincoln as the strong unifier, a national leader with a will to fight for unity and freedom—not unlike Bismarck who pursued his national goals with blood and iron[5]—but then also stressed his personal characteristics. Bernstorff further depicted Lincoln as a hero to whom German-Americans felt a strong attraction. But what Germans on both sides of the Atlantic most admired in Lincoln as "the greatest leader in the greatest crisis of your national life," he continued, was that in him (in contrast to Hamlet) "the native hue of resolution was not sicklied o'er with the pale cast of thought." In repeatedly linking war and nation-building and justifying war as a *sine qua non* for the creation of a nation, he stressed a supposedly common development between the United States and Germany for which Lincoln in German eyes had become a symbol: "The craving of the soul of the German nation for unity is the last but not least reason I should mention which influenced our people in their sympathy with Abraham Lincoln and his policy."

The ambassador's depiction of Lincoln outlines one core element in German perceptions of the sixteenth American president. The interest in Lincoln's image in Germany cannot be dissociated from the American Civil War, as well as the Germans' simultaneous struggle for national unity. Close to 200,000 German-born soldiers fought in the Union armies, and their approximately 500,000 letters sent back to Germany contributed to the shaping of a positive Lincoln image in their homeland.[6] Besides the transatlantic migration of people, the migration of ideas and ideologies influenced each other. The stream of mass immigration included an important and significant group the ambassador had mentioned: the exiled so-called Forty-Eighters who had participated in the abortive German revolution of 1848–49. Along with these 4,000 to 5,000 activists, there arrived highly politicized immigrants who eagerly participated in the political process of their new home country, especially in the new Republican party, as journalists, and as active members in the trade unions. Some of the Forty-Eighters, such as Carl Schurz, Francis Lieber, and Gustave Koerner, knew Lincoln very well and directly transmitted information about him back to Germany.[7]

Although Bernstorff mentioned the term several times in his speech, for him freedom did not play a major role in Lincoln's legacy, although it did for social and political groups yearning for a freer and more democratic society, who perceived Lincoln as the defender of freedom and democracy. Ever since the revolution of 1848–49, an admiration for the liberal-republican American democracy was especially evident among German socialists and social democrats, who perceived the American Civil War as a social revolution and class struggle. For them Lincoln became a prime symbol, especially as he had called the free laborer the "bulwark of democracy." Wilhelm Liebknecht, one of the founding fathers of the German Social Democracy and a close friend of Karl Marx, was the first to publish Marx's letter signed on behalf of the International Working Men's Association, which congratulated Lincoln on his re-election in November 1864.[8] Liebknecht belonged to the group of German socialists who perceived the United States as a positive example for Germany, conveyed in his famous 1873 dictum "In Germany there is our America."[9] Liebknecht's well-publicized speaking tour in 1886 through the United States with Edward Aveling and Eleanor Marx-Aveling, the daughter of Karl Marx, only strengthened his belief in American republicanism.[10] In his enthusiastic travel account *Ein Blick in die Neue Welt* (*A Glance at the New World*), published a year after his trip, he reiterated his admiration for Lincoln and the results achieved by the Civil War: "Where is the heroic European people that could offer something similar? And men like Old John Brown who went joyfully into death in order to annihilate slavery—and Lincoln who surmounts the greatest of the great with his plainness and who strolled the path of duty ahead of his people into death. Aren't these ideal aims, ideal struggles, ideal men? Where do we have one's peers?"[11] Though the book was received critically by some socialist factions, Liebknecht represented an important wing of the Social Democratic Party, which maintained a positive perception of the United States and continued to admire Lincoln for decades to come.

In addition to convergence between social democratic reform thought in Germany and progressive thought in America, the German intellectual elite took an increasing interest in developments in the turn-of-the-century United States.[12] During Theodore Roosevelt's presidency, scientific, and academic exchanges were strengthened and prestigious German intellectuals such as Max Weber and Georg Jellinek studied diverse aspects of American history and society. Communication channels were intensified—also by increasing numbers of German travelers[13]—and the accessibility of information on the United States improved. However, a critical skepticism predominated in the discourse on America, especially within the educated middle class who believed in German cultural superiority and developed an anti-American sentiment.[14] In this late phase of Imperial Germany, when the United States and Germany

increasingly became competitors in economic, political, and educational matters, pro- and anti-American elements competed against each other. This fight
over the meaning of the United States reflected the broader concern of how
Germany should handle the forces of modernity. Lincoln was quoted and
sometimes admired by German anti-Americans, as well as by pro-Americans.
The former group saw in him the pure example and representation of a "good
America" that ever since his assassination had followed the wrong path. They
used Lincoln's image as a humanitarian and enlightened internationalist to val-
idate their criticism of American culture and policy.[15]

During the Lincoln centennial in 1909, several commemorative meetings
were held in Germany. Two major events took place in Berlin, one at the residence of the American ambassador, the other at the University of Berlin, which
included academics as well as representatives from the Foreign Office, including
the former German ambassador in Washington Theodor von Holleben and
the cultural minister.[16] Such activities were accompanied by numerous publications on the "Great Emancipator," such as Carl Schurz's Lincoln biography
published in 1908, one of nine Lincoln biographies written by German authors
during these decades.[17] In the political arena of the Wilhelminian era, however,
Lincoln was almost never mentioned. Between 1871 and 1918 the German parliament did not once refer to Lincoln.[18] Only Social Democrats outside of parliament referred to Lincoln and commemorated the fiftieth anniversary of his
assassination in April 1915 in their central publication, the *Vorwärts*. Lincoln
was portrayed as a symbol of hope amidst war. Although Woodrow Wilson
was highly popular among Social Democrats, he never surpassed Lincoln.[19]

The Weimar Republic, as the first functioning German democracy, with its
ubiquitous discourses on Americanization, modernization, and Westernization, offers an interesting case of Lincoln's reception in Germany. Although
German intellectuals were bitterly divided in their opinions of America, the
general population seemed to have more positive leanings toward the modern,
Western country that had created jazz and the Model T Ford. The national
right, however, called the Weimar Republic a superficial "American import."[20]
In this climate Social Democrats sustained their fascination with Lincoln and
Americanism.[21] On November 9, 1918 when Social Democrat Philipp Scheide-
mann (born in the year of Lincoln's assassination) proclaimed the German
Republic, he explicitly used Lincoln's dictum from the Gettysburg Address in
the slightly changed version "all for the people and by the people." Scheide-
mann became the second chancellor of the Weimar Republic under president
Friedrich Ebert and later visited Lincoln's tomb in Springfield during a lecture
tour in the United States in 1925.[22] After his death in 1925, Social Democrat
Ebert—first president of the Weimar Republic—was dubbed "the Abraham
Lincoln of German history" by Theodor Heuss for his role in preserving the
German union in the first months after the First World War. Heuss, a liberal
Reichstag member during the Weimar Republic who subsequently served as

the first president of the Federal German Republic,[23] first compared the two—albeit utterly different—figures as self-made men who climbed up the social ladder with self-discipline and then mastered the national crisis they faced: "Lincoln appeared out of the dark of a young people; Ebert came out of the shadow of the rear houses of an old people's history. They stood in the twilight and the passion of rumpled years, they themselves tamers of their own passions and men of their own formation . . . Lincoln was killed by bullets, Ebert had been killed by defaming words."[24] In subsequent years, this comparison and its symbolism was often used to elevate Ebert's national significance.[25] Democratic Weimar Germany, experiencing a cultural and economic rapprochement to the United States, made the 1920s a heyday in the reception of Lincoln.[26] Thomas Dixon's 1920 play, *A Man of the People: A Drama of Abraham Lincoln*, was translated into German the same year;[27] and another Lincoln drama, written by German author Hermann Luedke, *Abraham Lincoln. Ein Schauspiel*, appeared in 1928 and was first performed at the prestigious Meiningen theatre house in Thuringia. A *New York Times* journalist offered the opinion that "Luedke's drama represents [the] president as firm only on slavery." Indeed the play portrayed Lincoln as a rustic lawyer and good-natured president who too easily yielded to the pressures of his political surroundings and only showed perseverance in one achievement: the abolition of slavery.[28]

Of all the Lincoln biographies written during the Weimar Republic, most notable was Emil Ludwig's 600-page opus, simultaneously published in Germany and the United States in 1930. Ludwig, an international celebrity author, drew the scorn of historians who charged writers like him for their "unscientific" approach to writing biographies.[29] Internationally, Ludwig was seen as a "representative of the new Germany" due to his strong criticism of right-wing groups and militarism.[30] Two years earlier, President Calvin Coolidge had received Ludwig at the White House, accompanied by German ambassador Friedrich Wilhelm von Prittwitz. Ludwig told the president that he had acquired fresh views on American life and amassed much first-hand information about Lincoln. He subsequently told the *New York Times* that he was quite impressed by Coolidge's knowledge and views on Lincoln.[31] A few days before Lincoln's birthday in 1930, the *New York Times* printed a three-page essay by Ludwig entitled "A New Lincoln: A World Figure," which shed light on the German image of Lincoln. Ludwig offered a bracing comparison between Lincoln and chancellor Otto von Bismarck, who had become an almost mythic figure for the Germans:

> Considered from the purely national point of view, both Bismarck and Lincoln may be called leaders and saviors without whom their peoples would have been disunited—without Bismarck Germany would have remained divided, without Lincoln America would have been rent into two. Considered from the point of view of genius, Bismarck seems the

superior, his undertaking more original, more active and bolder, its result more astonishing, his impress upon the world greater. But when one compares the characters of the two, Lincoln comes out ahead, and this is the real reason for the later beginning and the greater duration of his influence . . . But he [Lincoln] did not lie in the knowledge which he acquired slowly and which placed him upon the Olympus of history. It was precisely these peculiarly American qualities, products of the soil and essentially simple, which made him so different from all the statesmen Europe produced in the nineteenth century.[32]

Ludwig's Lincoln biography attempted to inspire his German readership to believe in the "potentialities of democracy" at a time when his country was already slipping away from republican into authoritarian structures. The book did not become a bestseller in Germany, unlike his biography on Bismarck. After Hitler came to power Ludwig's books—including his life of Lincoln—were burned in public.[33] But in 1930 there was still optimism about Germany's cultural and political relationship with the United States. The *New York Times* published an assessment from a Berlin correspondent headlined "Links between Germany and America," which contended that it was no accident that Ludwig's Lincoln biography was published simultaneously in both countries. The correspondent saw it as a sign of ties between men of letters and of strengthening of common "intellectual impulses which travel back and forth across the ocean."[34] The Rockefeller Foundation aimed to foster the still fragile democracy by financing the German Abraham Lincoln Stiftung (ALS).[35] This short-lived foundation (1927–1934) promoted the democratization of German society and especially supported educational reforms as a basis for a more open society. The names of the advisors to the Abraham Lincoln Stiftung and its fellows read like the German *Who Is Who* of the intellectual elite, the majority of whom were progressives, such as Walter Gropius, Herman Hesse, Paul Tillich, Kurt Hahn, and Eugen Rosenstock-Huessy. Some of them later joined the resistance to the Nazi regime, were persecuted, and emigrated to the United States.[36] Neither the American founders of the Stiftung nor the scholarship recipients explicitly discuss why the name of the sixteenth president was chosen for their organization.

In 1938 a radio play entitled *Abraham Lincoln* written by playwright Walter Gilbricht was broadcast in Germany, and a year later, at the outbreak of the Second World War, Gilbricht finished his play *Abraham Lincoln. A Drama in Five Acts*.[37] The play was not performed until the 1950s. Not surprisingly, under the Nazi regime Lincoln does not appear to have had a profile in German society.

In March 1949, four years after the war ended, the German weekly magazine *Der Spiegel* published a poll of whom the Germans considered history's greatest statesman. *Time* magazine saw the results as an "an enlightening glimpse into that enigma, the collective German mind. Though they may have been chastened, the Germans had lost none of their admiration for strong men." It was no surprise that 3,937 out of 8,500 votes were cast for Otto von Bismarck. *Time* worried that the re-education process in Germany had thus far been a failure and more work remained to be done. But in fact the list of fifty states- men included seven Americans, including Franklin D. Roosevelt at number nine, followed by Lincoln at number seventeen, and George Washington just one rank behind him.[38]

Germany's postwar political borders hardened as U.S. and Soviet satellites developed into West and East Germany. References to Lincoln by West Ger- man politicians and the general public were rare at the time immediately after the war. As the Cold War set in, freedom became a central term of this engage- ment, and when Americans looked back to their heroic figures, Lincoln seemed the ideal figurehead to represent that principle to the world. The strategy of containment not only encompassed the military and economic mobilization of the nation, but also a mental mobilization leading to a positive moral prepared- ness against Soviet expansionism. In this historical phase, Lincoln became "a major political export." Never before had the significance of one particular American figure been so emphasized by officials interested in the molding of a positive image of the United States abroad. The acceptance of Lincoln as the representative of a genuine Americanism and its value system became the measuring stick of how successfully a foreign nation was able to counterbal- ance communists' expansionism. Whoever was for Lincoln was by this logic against communism, an issue of great importance for Germany, the nation on the frontline of the Soviet bloc. Success stories in this regard were then attrib- uted to Lincoln's legacy.[39]

The United States Information Agency (USIA) and Voice of America radio concentrated its efforts on lecture series, films, book gifts, and official ceremonies to spread the word of the Great Emancipator in the fight against communism.[40] The so-called America Houses established by USIA in all major German cities served as centers for re-educating Germans through cultural programs. Several great American presidents appeared on the front covers of the America Houses' programs, but foremost was Lincoln.[41] Altogether 37 books related to Lincoln were published in West Germany between 1947 and 1958, including eight biographies and one book on Lincoln's religion.[42] Some Lincoln biographies published in the Weimar Republic were reprinted, in one case with the added subtitle, "The creative power of democracy."[43] Through these and other ways Lincoln's life was used for the democratic re-education of Germans.[44]

The postwar American emphasis on Lincoln as the Great Emancipator reflected deep societal changes in the United States, which in turn affected the presentation of his image in foreign countries.[45] As a divided nation somewhat akin to the North and the South before the outbreak of the Civil War, Lincoln became the key American historical figure for Germans. American politicians in occupied West Germany repeatedly reinforced these comparisons. U.S. High Commissioner John J. McCloy compared the task of first Federal chancellor Konrad Adenauer with that of Lincoln and later stated that Adenauer's attitudes reminded him of Lincoln's hopes for reconstruction after the Civil War. According to McCloy, Adenauer did not want "to divide the German people irrevocably" into "sheep and goats."[46] When the Americans asked for more death sentences for Nazi perpetrators, Germans pleaded for greater leniency, referencing Lincoln and his charity toward the defeated Confederacy.[47]

The rich symbolism of the divided city of Berlin did not escape the attention of American politicians, propagandists, and citizens. This city and its inhabitants were situated at the front of the Cold War that could turn hot anytime. Besides the military support, Berliners needed ideological American backup. In October 1950 a "Freedom Bell," analogous to the American Liberty Bell, was dedicated in a ceremony at the Schöneberger Rathaus in the presence of 400,000 to 500,000 Berliners. The civil-religious character of the event became evident during the reading of the inscription on the rim of the bell, which adapted one of the core sentences of the Gettysburg Address to the global context of the Cold War: "That This World under God shall have a new Birth of Freedom." German politicians in Berlin realized the symbolic attractiveness of the Freedom Bell with the Lincoln quote and did not miss opportunities to connect Berlin's fate with the bell, soon to be dubbed the "World Freedom Bell," and with the words of the Gettysburg Address.[48]

The central promoter of Lincoln's reception in post–World War II West Germany was Willy Brandt. Formerly persecuted by the Nazis and exiled in Norway and Sweden, he served as mayor of the divided city of Berlin from 1957 to 1966, and chancellor of West Germany from 1969 to 1974. It came as no surprise that Lincoln's famous dictum "A house divided against itself cannot stand" became the central *leitmotif* in his policy concerning a disunited Germany. According to his second wife, Brandt preferred this (biblical) Lincoln quotation over all others.[49] In his autobiography he emphasized how strongly Lincoln had shaped his view on history ever since his youth.[50]

In the midst of the Cold War, Brandt became an important person for American foreign policy and propaganda—a fact of which he was aware. He was already a celebrated figure when he toured the United States in the 1950s.[51] While in the country, Brandt received a Lincoln bronze bust from the Research Institute of America.[52] In 1959 Brandt was invited to give the key commemoration speech at a banquet of the Abraham Lincoln Association in Springfield— one of the major sesquicentennial celebrations in America. Brandt spoke before representatives of twenty-one nations, among them British ambassador Sir Harold Cassia and his French colleague Hervé Alphand, and some other 1,500 dignitaries, who assembled at the State Armory. Forty-six years before, ambassador von Bernstorff had delivered his Lincoln speech at the same venue. After two world wars, however, the circumstances were quite different. Behind

Willy Brandt delivering his keynote address at the sesquicentennial banquet of the
Abraham Lincoln Association in Springfield, Illinois on February 12, 1959. (Image
courtesy Getty Images)

Brandt a large banner stating "A house divided against itself cannot stand"
was displayed.

Brandt concentrated on major concepts and turning points in Lincoln's
legacy for himself and Germany. In the first part of his speech, he emphasized
Lincoln as the national unifier so important to the divided German nation,
also stressing the global aspect: "We here today, all the American people and
millions of freedom-loving men and women throughout the world are hon-
oring that great man, Abraham Lincoln, who in martyrdom has gone down
in history as the unifier of his people. But this man does not belong to you
alone, my friends." As Bernsdorff had once pointed out, Brandt emphasized
what German-Americans had contributed to Lincoln's election in 1860, men-
tioning key historical figures Carl Schurz, Gustav Koerner, and Francis Lieber.
He then referred to the enduring perception of Lincoln from the German social
democratic perspective: Lincoln as the friend and supporter of workingmen's
interests. Brandt told the audience that he too came from humble origins: "As
a man who has emerged from the labor movement, I wish to point out . . . that
it was Abraham Lincoln who called the free laborer a bulwark of democracy,
and that he considered those particularly worthy to be trusted who toil up from
poverty. This spirit of impartiality and of faith in equal opportunity was also
understood on the other side of the ocean."

The third aspect of Lincoln's legacy (and to Brandt, most important)
reflected the new American interpretation of Lincoln after the Second World

War: Lincoln as a moral leader and apostle of international struggle for freedom, a forerunner for human rights. Brandt's familiarity with Lincoln's speeches became evident when he indirectly referred to the "chords of memory" from Lincoln's first inaugural address. Brandt adroitly connected Lincoln's legacy with the future development of Germany by transcending the national question to a global Cold War context. When he mentioned the Soviets' attempt to make Berlin a "free" demilitarized city, he again referred to Lincoln and his reflections on the multiple meanings of freedom. His speech culminated by connecting Lincoln's Gettysburg Address to the situation of divided Germany, and especially Berlin, concluding: "The Freedom Bell also reminds us of the immortal work of Abraham Lincoln. . . . Engraved on our Freedom Bell are these noble words from the Gettysburg Address: 'That this world,' Lincoln said 'nation,' but today he, too, would include the whole world, 'under God shall have a new birth of freedom.'"[53] Brandt's words reflected a deep knowledge of American history and especially the diverse facets of the Lincoln legacy. A week later *Time* magazine reported on the Springfield event with the headline: "Berlin's Lincoln Expert" and quoted the program chairman as saying: "Brandt is a fighter for freedom, just as Lincoln was."[54]

Brandt's Lincoln speech in Springfield had an enduring importance for the Social Democratic Party. In October 1960, shortly before he was nominated as their candidate for chancellor, widely distributed party flyers showed a cover photograph of Brandt standing before the "house divided" banner in Springfield[55] It should be pointed out that in Germany this biblical proverb from Matthew 12:25 was not commonly used.[56]

Meanwhile, within Germany, the USIA focused on introducing Lincoln sesquicentennial activities as one of their greatest propaganda efforts in the Cold War. A dispatch from USIA West Germany received at the close of the sesquicentennial stated that "The Lincoln Sesquicentennial fell upon fertile ground in West Germany where Abraham Lincoln undoubtedly is the most widely known and respected American statesman. The Germany of today is apt to find much immediate significance . . . in the ideals and problems of freedom and national unity with which Lincoln was so intimately and prominently associated."[57]According to the USIA, Germans participated extensively in the observance in all major West German cities. American soldiers stationed in Frankfurt built a replica of Lincoln's log cabin birthplace in front of the American Cultural Center with timber donated by a Taunus mountain village. A full-size replica of it was presented to Willy Brandt for permanent display in West Berlin. The opening ceremony, attended by many government officials and representatives from different institutions, received nation-wide publicity and the cabin exhibit was visited by more than 45,000 people during the year, many of whom also came from the Russian sector. A film of Brandt's visit to Springfield was screened in various public showings; in Berlin some 10,000 viewers came to see it in one showing at the Sports Palace. USIA branches in West Germany, in cooperation with the German Society for American Studies, sponsored a Lincoln essay contest in German high schools, supported by cultural and educational authorities at the local and state levels who acted as screening panels for the 5,000 entries. Winners were flown to Berlin for a presentation ceremony, where an address by Brandt was a feature of the program. USIA claimed that "more than two million people throughout West Germany [were] being constantly [made] aware of the many programs, exhibits, contests, and ceremonies conducted in commemoration of this anniversary observance."[58]

When Chancellor Brandt visited Lyndon B. Johnson in the White House in the 1960s, he had done some background reading about the president before meeting him. Brandt, however, got Johnson's childhood mixed up with Lincoln's and asked if it was true that he had been born in a log cabin, to which Johnson replied, "No, I was born in a manger."[59] In the 1970s Brandt's international reputation was boosted by his *Ostpolitik*, and he became associated with visionary and charismatic qualities similar to those of his own idol. In the eyes of some observers, Brandt possessed strong leadership qualities and had not only succeeded in reconciling the left-wing elements and the Atlanticists of his party, but had also pushed his country to an accelerated European integration.[60]

From his keynote address in Springfield through the reunification process in 1989, Brandt continuously referred to Lincoln. The press noted that as foreign minister and as chancellor he displayed a Lincoln bust in his office. Brandt and later Chancellor Helmut Schmidt repeatedly quoted Lincoln in parliament, in interviews, and during their speaking tours through both Germanies.[61]

Brandt's common reference to Lincoln was part of a conscious strategy to bolster his political image in Germany and enhance his popularity, especially among educated Germans. That does not mean, however, that he only used Lincoln's legacy for political purposes. His memoirs and reports from close friends portray Brandt as a genuine believer in and admirer of the moral integrity of Lincoln. Brandt was convinced that Lincoln should serve as a political role model for Germans. Lincoln's legacy and aura were used by American propagandists, but at the same time Germans actively manipulated it to pursue their own political goals.[62]

In the months preceding the German reunification, the former chancellor repeatedly visited the German Democratic Republic and again often quoted Lincoln's line "A house divided against itself cannot stand" in public appearances. Brandt now associated Lincoln more with national unity than with the rights of workingmen, as Social Democrats had. "In all the years I have read and thought about Lincoln," he said in 1989, "I always was fascinated by him, because he was a visionary and pragmatist at the same time." Those qualities, according to Brandt, were needed to solve the German question. Brandt applied the "house divided" metaphor to various historically specific German circumstances: "For many years I have asked for understanding abroad that we [Germans] cannot live forever as an internally divided people because of the Nazi era. I have often referred to a sentence by Lincoln, which does not stem from him but which he in turn got from the Bible—a fact that is nothing to be ashamed of—that a house divided against itself cannot stand."[63] During the Cold War, he had applied it to the situation of a divided Germany and subsequently during the reunification process of 1989–90. Once Germany had been united, however, Brandt realized that a "mental split" not unlike the old Berlin wall still ran through the nation, and that Lincoln's dictum could still be applied to this new and unaccustomed situation. In 1998 Egon Bahr, former federal minister for special affairs and close associate of Brandt, delivered a lecture on him in Berlin, quoting Brandt from 1966: "One people cannot live permanently—without losing its inner balance—when it cannot say yes to its fatherland." As Bahr added, this was the "Brandt version" of his so oft-repeated "house divided" quotation. Bahr gave it a contemporary new meaning when he pointed out that nine years after reunification the mentality and social reality of both Germanies still remained different and divided.[64]

Late in achieving national unity, Germany always had a keen interest in the American Civil War. Wars paved the way for the formation of the German Empire—Prussia's defeat of Austria and France. This process of unification and nation-building in a transatlantic context deepened the German admiration for Lincoln. From the creation of the German Reich in 1870–71 to the reunification of Germany in 1989–90, Lincoln's image as the national unifier played an important social and political role. Simultaneously, however, his image as the egalitarian self-made man who defended the rights of workingmen, and the archetypal democrat, had a strong appeal especially to labor leaders, socialists, and social democrats.

This strong German interest has yielded one of the highest numbers of Lincoln biographies published in any country outside the United States. German historians, journalists, and politicians have produced no less than thirty-eight full-fledged lives of the president. In addition, there are German translations of some standard American biographies, including Carl Sandburg's multivolume life. The numerical peaks in these publications occurred during the Weimar Republic and the postwar period in the Federal Republic, but the surge of further interest during the period of Lincoln's bicentennial, which saw the publication of three new biographies, revealed the continuing power of the sixteenth president to fascinate and engage a German readership.[65]

Notes

1. Though the number of historiographical works on the German image of the United States has increased of late, there still is a need for a systematic analysis of German perceptions of American national figures such as Lincoln. An exception is the older work by Ernst Fraenkel, "Das deutsche Wilsonbild," *Jahrbuch für Amerikastudien*

5 (1960), 66–120. On the recent most relevant historiography, see David E. Barclay and Elisabeth Glaser-Schmidt, eds., *Transatlantic Images and Perceptions: Germany and America since 1776* (New York: Cambridge University Press, 1997); Volker Depkat, *Amerikabilder in politischen Diskursen: Deutsche Zeitschriften von 1789 bis 1830* (Stuttgart: Klett-Cotta, 1998); Werner Kremp, *In Deutschland liegt unser Amerika: Das sozialdemokratische Amerikabild von den Anfängen der SPD bis zur Weimarer Republik* (Münster: LIT-Verlag, 1993); Alexander Schmidt, *Reisen in die Moderne: Der Amerika-Diskurs des deutschen Bürgertums vor dem Ersten Weltkrieg im europäischen Vergleich* (Berlin: M. Niemeyer, 1997); Viktor Otto, *Deutsche Amerika-Bilder: Zu den Intellektuellen-Diskursen um die Moderne 1900–1950* (München: Fink Wilhelm, 2006); Baltmannsweiler, ed., *Amerikanisches Deutschlandbild und deutsches Amerikabild in Medien und Erziehung* (Baltmannsweiler: Pädagogischer Verlag Burgbücherei Schneider, 1990).

2. Jörg Nagler, "From Culture to Kultur: American Perceptions of Imperial Germany, 1871–1914," 131–35, and, Wolfgang Helbich, "Different, But Not Out of This World: German Images of the United States between Two Wars, 1871–1914," 109–29, both in Barclay and Glaser-Schmidt, eds., *Transatlantic Images and Perceptions*.

3. On the changing American interpretations of Lincoln's legacy, see Merrill D. Peterson, *Lincoln in American Memory* (New York: Oxford University Press, 1994).

4. Hans W. Gatzke, *Germany and the United States: A "Special Relationship?"* (Cambridge, MA: Harvard University Press, 1980), 38.

5. The *New York Times* headline read: "Diplomat praises Lincoln: Von Bernstorff Tells How Germans Aided the Emancipator," *New York Times*, February 13, 1913, 5; *Addresses delivered at the Celebration of the Hundred and Fourth Anniversary of the Birth of Abraham Lincoln* (Springfield, IL: Abraham Lincoln Association, 1913), 13–24; Barry Schwartz, *Abraham Lincoln and the Forge of National Memory* (Chicago: University of Chicago Press, 2000), 261. The tradition of a banquet commemorating Lincoln on his birthday organized by the Abraham Lincoln Association started during the Lincoln Centennial. Two German speakers have since been invited: Bernstorff in 1913 and Willy Brandt in 1959. See http://www.abrahamlincolnassociation.org/pastbanquetspeakers.asp. For a comparison of Lincoln and Bismarck, see Carl Degler, "The American Civil War and the German Wars of Unification: The Problem of Comparison," in Stig Förster and Jörg Nagler, eds., *On the Road to Total War: The American Civil War and the German Wars of Unification, 1861–1871* (New York: Cambridge University Press, 1997), 53–72. The introductory note to the Bernsdorff lecture reads: "In popular education, in music, in agricultural and industrial science, indeed in every field of original research, the world looks to Germany. Our own debt can never be told in words. We cannot forget with what devotion our Germans sustained Mr. Lincoln in his struggle to preserve the Union. To our crucible of civilization, the German immigrant has furnished a sturdiness and integrity of character, and a spirit of patriotism, which gives to him and to those who may follow him, a special welcome to our shores." *Addresses delivered at the Celebration*, 12.

6. Just one example may suffice. A German immigrant wrote home after Lincoln's election in 1860: "A. Lincoln, the man of freedom, the enemy of slavery, the man of equal rights, has been elected our president. . . . I have sent you some magazines . . . and also a portrait of Abe Lincoln." Translated from the German and cited in Wolfgang Helbich and Walter D. Kamphoefner, eds., *Germans in the Civil War: The Letters They Wrote Home* (Chapel Hill: University of North Carolina Press, 2006), 302. It has been estimated that

between 1820 and 1914 alone almost 280 million letters were sent home by these immigrants. See Wolfgang Helbich et al., eds., *Briefe aus Amerika: Deutsche Auswanderer schreiben aus der Neuen Welt 1830–1930* (München: Beck, 1988), 31.

7. Jörg Nagler, *Frémont contra Lincoln: Die deutschamerikanische Opposition in der Republikanischen Partei während des Amerikanischen Bürgerkrieges* (Frankfurt/New York: Peter Lang, 1984).

8. Georg Eckert, "Wilhelm Liebknecht über Abraham Lincoln," in Imanuel Geiss and Jürgen Wendt, eds., *Deutschland in der Weltpolitik des 19.und 20.Jahrhunderts* (Duesseldorf: Bertelsmann Universitätsverlag, 1973), 121–32. For Lincoln's standing in the German labor movement, see the unpublished paper, Bettina Hofmann "The Lincoln Image and the German Labor Movement, 1861–1914," delivered at the conference " 'A Humanitarian as Broad as the World': Abraham Lincoln's Legacy in International Context" at the German Historical Institute, October 4, 2007.

9. Hartmut Keil, "German Socialist Immigrants and Political Institutions," in Marianne Debouzy, ed., *In the Shadow of the Statue of Liberty: Immigrants, Workers, and Citizens in the American Republic 1880–1920* (Chicago: University of Illinois Press, 1992), 263.

10. *New York Times*, September 20, 1886, 3; and November 26, 1886, 8; Jost Hermand, "Ein Blick in die Neue Welt" (1887). Wilhelm Liebknechts Bericht über seine USA-Reise im Jahre 1886, in Wolfgang Beutin et al., eds., *Eine Gesellschaft der Freiheit, der Gleichheit, der Brüderlichkeit* (Frankfurt: Peter Lang, 2001), 29–44; William Frederic Kamman, *Socialism in German American Literature* (Philadelphia: Americana Germanica Press, 1917), 32.

11. Wilhelm Liebknecht, *Ein Blick in die Neue Welt* (Stuttgart: J. H. W. Dietz, 1887), 272.

12. James T. Kloppenburg, *Uncertain Victory: Social Democracy and Progressivism in European and American Thought, 1870–1920* (New York: Oxford University Press, 1986); Kremp, *In Deutschland liegt unser Amerika,* 9.

13. Alexander Schmidt, *Reisen in die Moderne: Der Amerika-Diskurs des deutschen Bürgertums vor dem Ersten Weltkrieg im europaischen Vergleich* (Berlin: Akademie Verlag, 1997).

14. Jürgen Heideking, "Amerikanische Einflüsse auf die Weimarer Reichsverfasung und das Grundgesetz für die Bundesrepublik Deutschland," in Jürgen Elvert and Michael Salewski, eds., *Deutschland und der Westen im 19. und 20. Jahrhundert* (Stuttgart: Franz Steiner, 1993), 248.

15. Andrei S. Markovits, "European Anti-Americanism (and Anti-Semitism): Ever Present Though Always Denied," *Center for European Studies Working Paper Series* 108 (2004), 9–10.

16. Nathan William MacChesney, ed., *Abraham Lincoln; The Tribute of a Century, 1809–1909. Commemorative of the Lincoln Centenary and Containing the Principal Speeches made in Connection therewith* (Chicago: A.C. McClurg & Co., 1910), 510.

17. According to Worldcat, there were 32 Lincoln-related books published from 1871 to 1914, including nine Lincoln biographies written by German authors.

18. See the protocols (Verhandlungen des Deutschen Reichstags) for the Reichstag online: http://www.reichstagsprotokolle.de/index.html.

19. *Vorwärts*, April 14, 1915 (Number 102).

20. Brendon O'Connor, ed., *Anti-Americanism: Comparative Aspects* (Oxford: Greenwood World Publishing, 2007), 166.

21. Kremp, *In Deutschland liegt unser Amerika*, 217–18.

22. Philipp Scheidemann, *The Making of New Germany: Memoirs of a Social Democrat*, 2 vols. (London: Hodder & Stoughton), 2:113; Christian Gellinek, *Philipp Scheidemann: Eine biographische Skizze*, (Köln: Böhlau, 1994), 31; Christian Gellinek, *Northwest Germany in Northeast America: Immigration Waves from Central Europe and Their Reverberations Until Today* (Münster: LIT Verlag, 1997), 67.

23. Theodor Heuss, "Der Abraham Lincoln der deutschen Geschichte," in Max Peters, *Friedrich Ebert: Erster Präsident der Deutschen Republik* (Berlin: Arani, 1950), 169–78 (Heuss delivered the speech in the German Bundestag on February 28, 1950); Walter Mühlhausen, "Friedrich Ebert in German Political Memory," in Astrid M. Eckert, ed., *Institutions of Public Memory: The Legacies of German and American Politicians* (Washington, DC: German Historical Institute, 2007), 120–21. The British *Observer* had already compared Ebert with Lincoln in 1923, *The Observer*, November 11, 1923.

24. Theodor Heuss, *Die großen Reden: Der Staatsmann* (Tübingen: Wunderlich, 1965), 118; Mühlhausen, "Friedrich Ebert in German Political Memory," 120–21.

25. Walter Mühlhausen, "Ebert," 121. See also, "A German Lincoln or the Stalin of the SPD," *Zeit*, February 28, 1975.

26. A look at the publications in this respect is again revealing. According to Worldcat fourteen corresponding books, including six Lincoln biographies by German authors, were published during the Weimar Republic. Compared to the annual frequency of Lincoln publications in Imperial Germany, this indeed was a much higher rate.

27. Translated as *Präsident Lincoln: Schauspiel in 4 Akten* (Leipzig: K. Scholtze, 1920).

28. *New York Times*, November 13, 1928, 26.

29. Hans-Jürgen Perrey, "Der Fall Emil Ludwig-Ein Bericht über eine historiographische Kontroverse der ausgehenden Weimarer Republik," *Geschichte in Wissenschaft und Unterricht*, 43 (1992), 169–81. The *New York Times* also criticized Ludwig's approach. The review headline read: "A Grotesque View of Lincoln in Emil Ludwig's Biography." The reviewer then continued: "His use of a 'new historical method' results in a blending of the standardized portrait with some unfortunate distortions." *New York Times*, February 9, 1930, BR 3. For Ludwig see, Franklin C. West, "Success Without Influence: Emil Ludwig during the Weimar Years," *Leo Baeck Institute Yearbook*, 30 (1985), 169–89; Jürgen Kuczynski, "Emil Ludwigs Lincoln," *Die Weltbühne*, 26 (April 8, 1930), 537–39.

30. West, "Success without Influence," 170.

31. *New York Times*, March 4, 1928, 34. Ludwig also visited both John D. Rockefeller and Thomas Edison, who were wintering in Florida. West, "Success Without Influence," 169.

32. *New York Times*, February 9, 1930, SM2.

33. West, "Success Without Influence," 187, 189.

34. *New York Times*, May 11, 1930, 66.

35. Malcolm Richardson et al., eds., *Weimars transatlantischer Mäzen: die Lincoln-Stiftung 1927 bis 1934. Ein Versuch demokratischer Elitenföderung in der Weimarer Republik* (Essen: Klartext Verlag, 2008).

36. Malcolm Richardson, "A Search for Genius in Weimar Germany: The Abraham Lincoln Stiftung and American Philanthropy," *Bulletin of German Historical Institute* 26 (2000), http://www.ghi-dc.org/publications/ghipubs/bu/026/b26richardsonframe.html. Malcolm Richardson: http://www.ghi-dc.org/publications/ghipubs/bu/026/b26richardsonappx.html#ap1.

37. Axel J. Vieregg, ed., *Gesammelte Werke in zwei Bänden by Peter Huchel*, 2 vols. (Frankfurt: Suhrkamp, 1984), II:457; Walter Gilbricht, *Abraham Lincoln. Drama in fünf*

Akten (Berlin, 1939). The play was later performed in Leipzig on December 23, 1955. Josef Tobias and Jochen Weber, *Die neuere Entwicklung des Theaters in der Sowjetischen Besatzungszone* (Bonn: Deutscher Bundes-Verlag 1957), 18.

38. *Der Spiegel*, March 5, 1949, 32; *Time*, March 14, 1949.

39. Barry Schwartz, *Abraham Lincoln in the Post-Heroic Era: History and Memory in Late Twentieth-Century America* (Chicago: University of Chicago Press 2008), 97.

40. *New York Times*, July 23, 1946, 33; Schwartz, *Abraham Lincoln in the Post-Heroic Era*, 96.

41. *Abraham Lincoln: Das Leben eines Unsterblichen* (Hamburg: P. Zsolnay, 1958).

42. See the data provided by Worldcat.

43. Albrecht Montgelas, *Abrabham Lincoln: Die schöpferische Macht der Demokratie* (Hamburg: Drei Türme Verlag, 1949).

44. In the decade after 1945 over 1,400 works of American prose fiction were published in Germany. See Ralph Willett, *The Americanization of Germany, 1945–1949* (New York: Routledge, 1989), 55.

45. Barry Schwartz, "Iconography and Collective Memory: Lincoln's Image in the American Mind," *The Sociological Quarterly* 32 (1991), 301–19.

46. Thomas Alan Schwartz, *America's Germany: John J. McCloy and the Federal Republic of Germany* (Cambridge, MA: Harvard University Press, 1991), 82.

47. Joshua Rubenstein, *The Unknown Black Book: The Holocaust in the German-occupied Soviet Territories* (Bloomington: Indiana University Press, 2007), 39.

48. Andreas Daum, "America's Berlin 1945–2000: Between Myths and Visions," in Frank Trommler, ed., *Berlin: The New Capital in the East. A Transatlantic Appraisal* (Washington, DC: AICGS, 2000), 58–59.

49. Brigitte Seebacher-Brandt, *Willy Brandt* (München: Piper Verlag, 2004), 361; see also Judith Michel, *Willy Brandts Amerikabild und-politik 1933–1992* (Gottingen: Vandenhoeck & Ruprecht, 2010), 34–35.

50. Willy Brandt, *Begegnungen und Einsichten* (Hamburg: Hoffmann und Campe, 1976), 80.

51. Daum, "America's Berlin," 58.

52. *New York Times*, February 12, 1959, 15. The bronze bust was a work of Leo Cherne, executive director of the institute.

53. *New York Times*, February 13, 1959, 21; *The Times*, February 13, 1959, 8; Thomas F. Schwartz, "Lincoln and the Cold War," *A Newsletter of the Abraham Lincoln Association*, 6 (2004), 2, 4–5; *Lincoln Sesquicentennial Commission, Abraham Lincoln Sesquicentennial, 1959–1960: Final Report* (Washington, 1960), 70–71; Willy Brandt, *Erinnerungen* (Zürich: Propylänen, 1989), 64; Jörg Nagler, *Abraham Lincoln: Amerikas großer Präsident* (München: Beck, 2009), 9.

54. *Time*, February 16, 1959.

55. Gaines Post, *Memoirs of a Cold War Son* (Iowa City: University of Iowa Press, 2000), 136.

56. Wolfgang Mieder, " 'A House Divided': From Biblical Proverb to Lincoln and Beyond," in Warren S. Brown, ed., *Understanding Wisdom: Sources, Science, and Society* (Philadelphia: Templeton Foundation Press, 2000), 84–85; Wolfgang Mieder, *"A House Divided": From Biblical Proverb to Lincoln and Beyond* (Burlington, VT: Proverbium, 1998).

57. *Lincoln Sesquicentennial Commission Final Report*, 123.

58. Ibid., 123, 125.

59. Quoted in Dinopoulo Elias et al., eds., *Trade, Globalization and Poverty* (New York: Routledge, 2008), 232.

60. Werner Lippert, "Richard Nixon's Detente and Willy Brandt's *Ostpolitik*: The Politics and Economic Diplomacy of Engaging the East" (Unpublished dissertation, Vanderbilt University, 2005), 2; William E. Griffith, *The Ostpolitik of the Federal Republic of Germany* (Cambridge, MA: MIT Press, 1978), 176–85.

61. *Der Spiegel*, August 29, 1980, 25; Willy Brandt, *Bundestagsreden* (Bonn: AZ Studio 1972), ii. For further references to Lincoln made in the speeches of Willy Brandt, see Jürgen Leinemann, "Ein grübelnder patriot" ("A pensive patriot"), *Der Spiegel*, October 10, 1992, 21; and "Erst das Land, dann die Partei" ("First the land, then the party"), Ibid., February 24, 1992, 25.

62. Tina Leich, "Die Inszenierung der Kanzlerkandidaten im Wahlkampf 1969 oder 'auf die Wirkung kommt es an,'" in Stefan Schwarzkopf, ed., *Die Anatomie des Machtwechsels: Die sozialdemokratischen Regierungsübernahmen von 1969 und 1998* (Leipzig: Leipziger Universitätsverlag, 2007), 47.

63. Willy Brandt in an interview on August 28, 1978, *Spiegel*, No. 35 (1978), 34.

64. Egon Bahr, *Willy Brandts europäische Außenpolitik* (Berlin: Bundeskanzler-Willy-Brandt-Stiftung, 1998), 3.

65. Ronald Gerste, *Abraham Lincoln: Begründer des modernen Amerika* (Regensburg: Pustet, 2008); George Schild, *Abraham Lincoln: Eine politische Biographie* (Paderborn: Schöningh, 2009); Nagler, *Abraham Lincoln*.

15

From Colonization to Anti-colonialism

LINCOLN IN AFRICA

Kevin Gaines

It is a great irony that Africans' embrace of Lincoln, which peaked during their mid-twentieth century independence struggles against European colonialism, grew out of the "Great Emancipator's" advocacy of colonization, or the resettlement of former slaves back to Africa. Lincoln was hardly unique in supporting colonization, sharing the widespread belief of the time that whites would never accept blacks as equals in the United States. Throughout the antebellum era, colonization to Africa remained a far more popular, and ambiguous, form of opposition to slavery than the more radical position of abolitionism. Colonizationists encompassed pro-slavery politicians as well as anti-slavery Republicans, including Harriet Beecher Stowe. Like Stowe, many viewed the resettlement of African Americans to their ancestral homeland in largely religious terms. Colonization, in their view, promised redemption from the horrors of slavery, as former slaves enacted divine providence through the evangelization of Africa. With this objective in mind, Presbyterians established a university in Pennsylvania, which eventually took on the name Lincoln University in honor of the fallen emancipator, for the purpose of training Africans and African Americans to spread the Gospel in Africa. In 1957, Lincoln University's most illustrious African graduate, Kwame Nkrumah, presided over the independence of the West African nation of Ghana as its first prime minister. Nkrumah pursued an ambitious agenda of African continental union and liberation that brought him worldwide fame and notoriety, while engaging quite substantively with the meaning of Lincoln's legacy, and its implications for his nation and Africa. So it was that the colonization movement, which sought to rid the United States of its former slaves, had the unintended result of merging the destinies of Africans and Americans, a fortuitous outcome from the standpoint of Nkrumah and other U.S.-schooled Africans. As perhaps the crowning irony in this story of historical affinities between Africa and America,

Nkrumah and Lincoln were again linked in 2009, the bicentennial of Lincoln's birth and the centennial of Nkrumah's.

Given the global circulation of the image, legend, and legacy of Abraham Lincoln as a consummate symbol of American democracy and freedom, it should come as no surprise that African anti-colonial nationalists in the mid-twentieth century found in Lincoln an inspiration for their struggles for self-determination. While the record of commentary about Lincoln among educated, English-speaking Africans is far from voluminous, there is enough of it to raise several intriguing questions. How did Africans obtain information about Lincoln? What did Lincoln's image mean to them? And finally, why was this fascination with Lincoln among an admittedly select group of African leaders so fleeting?

To fully understand Africans' fascination with Lincoln, it is helpful to note the complexity of African Americans' views of Lincoln. In his oration at the Freedmen's dedication of the monument to Abraham Lincoln in Washington, D.C. in 1876, Frederick Douglass made the classic statement of African Americans' ambivalence toward Lincoln. Compelled by the occasion to speak unvarnished truth, Douglass noted that Lincoln had been "the white man's President, entirely devoted to the welfare of white men," ready, at least in the early years of his administration, to sacrifice the human rights of blacks in order to uphold the welfare of whites. "[Y]ou and yours were the objects of his deepest affection and his most earnest solicitude. You are the children of Abraham Lincoln. We are at best only his step-children; children by adoption, children by forces of circumstances and necessity." Still, Douglass allowed that although "the Union was more to him than our freedom or our future, under his wise and beneficent rule we saw ourselves gradually lifted from the depths of slavery to the heights of liberty and manhood." Lincoln had been no abolitionist, but his moderation helped assure the demise of slavery. "Viewed from the genuine abolition ground, Mr. Lincoln seemed tardy, cold, dull, and indifferent; but measuring him by the sentiment of his country, a sentiment he was bound as a statesman to consult, he was swift, zealous, radical, and determined."[1]

Little wonder that Lincoln provided the contested terrain upon which blacks would continue to debate the meaning of their existence in the United States. Fond memories of Lincoln as emancipator clashed with the unsentimental view of Lincoln the pragmatist, susceptible to the prejudices of his era. The subject of Lincoln could elicit sharp tensions between integrationists and nationalists, radicals and conservatives, at times in explosive fashion. In 1933, Arthur Schomburg, the Afro-Puerto Rican scholar and collector of all manner of books, manuscripts, prints, and paintings by or related to people of African descent, bolted angrily from a Brooklyn meeting at which he was guest speaker. The chair of the meeting, the black journalist Ted Poston, had disputed Schomburg's claim that Lincoln was a man without prejudice. Poston countered that if left up to Lincoln, African Americans would still be slaves, a statement that infuriated Schomburg.[2]

However disputed his legacy, African Americans enlisted Lincoln's image to mobilize ideological support for their own freedom struggles. Historian Scott Sandage identified the 1939 concert by Marian Anderson at the Lincoln Memorial as setting the tone for the civil rights movement's strategies of non-violent protest. Black activists, Sandage argues, "refined a politics of memory at the Lincoln Memorial," promulgating a civic religion of national unity and consensus to help amplify the voices of blacks and legitimate the cause of civil rights in national politics. Noting the "ambivalent relationship between African Americans and the icon called Abraham Lincoln," Sandage notes that black civil rights leaders "strategically appropriated Lincoln's memory and monument as political weapons, in the process layering and changing the public meanings of the hero and his shrine."[3]

Though Africans may not have engaged Abraham Lincoln's image and memory as extensively and with as conflicted feelings as did African Americans, nevertheless, a similar process of appropriation has been at work. Africans enlisted Lincoln as a resource in their opposition to European colonialism from the mid-1880s to the 1960s, finding in him a symbol of freedom. It was of great importance that Lincoln had presided over the demise of slavery, his image all but displacing that of the Founding Fathers of the revolutionary era in the minds of generations of Africans. In Africa, as throughout the rest of the world, Lincoln has proven to be a most malleable icon.

How did English-speaking Africans learn about Lincoln? Most likely, Africans received knowledge of Lincoln in two ways. First, through the cultural influence of American, African American, and British missionary educators in west, central, and southern Africa from the late nineteenth century well into the twentieth. During the late nineteenth century, the travels of African American seamen to Cape Town, one of the busiest port cities in Africa, provided another source of knowledge about Lincoln. In addition, African American jubilee vocal quartets toured internationally, and during the late nineteenth century, such groups performed in every major city in South Africa. According to historian James Campbell, these pathways of communication provided a wide range of Africans, whether educated or not, with a basic familiarity with African American history and its central narrative of slavery and emancipation. Such knowledge would have provided a sturdy foundation for the turn of the century collaboration between black South African ministers and African American missionaries of the African Methodist Episcopal Church.[4]

From the mid-nineteenth century onward, another source of knowledge about Lincoln came from African American colleges such as Lincoln University, which also enrolled students from the African continent with the purpose of training them for missionary efforts back home. These American-educated Africans would have been important additional sources of information about the reform movement of emancipation and freedman's education, within which Lincoln's image would have loomed large, particularly as part of emancipation day celebrations among blacks for generations after his death. Indeed, during the early twentieth century there is evidence that American and African American missionaries invoked the memory of Lincoln to generate ideological and material support for African missionary work. It should be noted here that American missionaries, black or white, were invariably trespassers in a field that European missionaries and colonial authorities viewed as their proprietary domain. By the late nineteenth century, when the white South's campaign to reverse the civil and political rights gained by African Americans under Reconstruction was in full swing, many African American missionaries in Africa were at pains to defend their fitness for citizenship and equality by asserting their unique contribution to the uplift and redemption of Africa. Invoking Lincoln in their promotional literature also may have been an attempt to resuscitate the flagging spirit of abolitionism and evangelical reform. Lincoln was introduced into the promotional discourse by missionaries of the African Methodist Episcopal (AME) Church, the African American National Baptist Convention (NBC), and the predominantly white American Baptist Home Mission Society, raising the possibility that stories about Lincoln would have entered the curriculum of these missionary schools.[5]

Another likely source of information for English-speaking Africans of the independence era was a series of religious tracts published during the 1940s by London's Sheldon Press on behalf of the International Committee on Christian Literature for Africa. The series, the African Home Library, featured brief biographies of such figures as "Harriet Tubman: Who Led the Slaves to Freedom," British anti-slavery leaders William Wilberforce and Lord Shaftesbury, and Abraham Lincoln. Selections in the African Home Library were not confined to the theme of slavery and abolition, however; these biographies were listed alongside books adapted from Old and New Testament stories, assorted Bible stories and the like. Mrs. George Schwab, an American writer who wrote the life of Lincoln, hewed closely to the familiar myths about her subject, including his aptitude for physical labor, his youthful hunger for education, his honesty and kindness, and above all, his opposition to slavery, which, along with the matter of Lincoln's piety, was substantially overstated. The Gettysburg Address was reprinted in Schwab's book. The lesson Schwab drew from Lincoln's assassination was the peaceful succession of power, indicating the strength of a "government of the people and for the people." More research is needed to discern whether books from the African Home Library were circulated in Africa and if so, to what locations. Interestingly, with the permission of the International Committee on Christian Literature for Africa and the Sheldon Press, a Mende language version of the Schwab text was published in the West African British colony of Sierra Leone in 1955.[6]

If the purveyors of such tracts in English, Mende, or any other African languages intended to secure the allegiance of Africans to the colonial status quo, theirs was a risky approach. Indeed, great men and women in the British and American histories of abolition and emancipation would likely be irresistible objects of study for young English-speaking colonial subjects striving for self-respect and political independence. The historian Derek Peterson has shown how Kenyans imprisoned by the British invoked the history of abolitionism as a means of exposing and condemning the abuses of colonial authorities. By associating their plight with slavery, detainees also asserted themselves as the true exemplars and guardians of what they considered to be British standards of justice and civilization.[7]

Though fragmentary, this historical background invites the expectation of finding Africans ready to acknowledge Lincoln or quote from his speeches and writings. Just as Lincoln's familiar image and legacy would have been serviceable to missionary educators of Africans, so, it seems that Lincoln resonated with young Africans as a symbol of their own aspirations for freedom and liberation.

For young Africans of the nationalist generation, coming of age in the mid-twentieth century amid the humiliations of colonialism, Lincoln's image, alongside knowledge of histories of African resistance to Western conquest and African American freedom struggles, were resources in their formative struggles for intellectual independence, cultural identity, and moral authority. Nelson Mandela, a boyhood convert to Methodism and a product of British colonial schooling, recounts how during the early 1940s, as a student at the University of Fort Hare, a bastion of the liberation movement, he played the role of John Wilkes Booth in a play on the life of Lincoln. The play had been adapted by Mandela's classmate, Lincoln Mkentane, who, not surprisingly, claimed for himself the title role. This particular identification with Abraham Lincoln raises several questions. Was young Mkentane given his English first name by a teacher, as Mandela, named after Admiral Horatio Lord Nelson, had been? Or did Mkentane's parents seek an alternative to British imperial history in choosing the name Lincoln? Mandela notes that Lincoln Mkentane had come from a distinguished Transkein family, and that Mkentane's recitation of the Gettysburg Address received a standing ovation. The play's moral, as Mandela recalled, "was that men who take great risks often suffer great consequences."[8] Precisely what was Abraham Lincoln's appeal to these Fort Hare students and their audience? Was it Lincoln's penchant for a religious language of suffering, sacrifice, and redemption? Or was it Lincoln's determination in choosing the perilous course of war to save the Union? Did their meditation on the "great risks" taken by Lincoln help reconcile themselves to the necessity of fighting injustice?

To return to colonial Kenya, around the same time, roughly the 1940s, Gikuyu university students were required by their instructors to recite the Emancipation Proclamation, as part of a curriculum that resisted British colonial instruction. Through this assignment every student had the opportunity to perform the role of the Great Emancipator, and wartime commander in chief.

Much more than a mere pedagogical exercise, the act of uttering the words, "I Abraham Lincoln," and declaring "all persons held as slaves within any State or designated part of a State, the people whereof shall then be in rebellion against the United States, shall be then, thenceforward, and forever free" could hardly be experienced as anything other than a transgression of the colonial order. At such moments, the Kenyan students and their instructors recast Lincoln's proclamation as a moment of resistance, voicing a thinly veiled version of their own anti-colonial aspirations. "I do order and declare that all persons held as slaves within said designated States, and parts of States, are, and henceforward shall be free": these words conjured an imagined future marked by an end to colonial oppression and a new dispensation of freedom, independence, and power.[9]

These two examples attest to much more than the fact that knowledge of Lincoln was available to young Africans of the nationalist era. Lincoln's pivotal role in the African American narrative of slavery and freedom made him an icon of anti-colonial resistance. During the 1930s, through the efforts of Lincoln University, the name of the Great Emancipator would be associated with the training of West Africans intent on their own liberation, several of whom would hold leadership positions in post-independence African governments. Nnamdi Azikiwe, president of Nigeria, and Kwame Nkrumah, the prime minister of Ghana, were among the most prominent of Lincoln's African alumni. At Lincoln, Nkrumah and Azikiwe interacted with its largely African American student body, became acquainted with the school's abolitionist public culture, and undoubtedly learned of African Americans' mixed feelings about Abraham Lincoln.[10]

While it is difficult to know the extent of the circulation of Mrs. Schwab's primer on Lincoln throughout Africa, some of those destined for leadership made political use of their knowledge of Lincoln. Julius Nyerere, prime minister of Tanganyika, found in Lincoln inspiration for his campaign for a liberal and nonracial basis for Tanganyikan citizenship that would include indigenous Africans, South Asians, and Arabs. Nyerere found precedent and encouragement in Lincoln's defense of the principle "all men are created equal" against the Know Nothing party's racism and nativism back in 1850s America. "When the know-nothings get control," Nyerere quoted Lincoln, "it will read, all men are created equal except the negroes and foreigners and [C]atholics. When it comes to that . . . I shall prefer emigrating to some country where they make no pretense of loving liberty, where despotism can be taken pure, without the base alloy of hypocrisy." Carrying the day with his argument, Nyerere noted the slippery slope that would result from breaking the principle of nonracial citizenship, predicting the day "when we will say people were created equal except the Masai, except the Wagogo, . . . etc. We will continue breaking these principles."[11]

Kwesi Armah, Ghana's high commissioner in London, drew even more extensively on Lincoln's words to defend Ghana's neutrality in the Cold War conflict between the United States and the Soviet Union. Lincoln was instrumental to Armah's plea that the superpowers avoid nuclear catastrophe. Referencing two fallen presidents in the same breath, Armah wrote, "I kept harking back to the words spoken by my boyhood hero, Abraham Lincoln, a century, almost to the day, before we took a sad farewell of John Kennedy." Quoting from the Gettysburg Address, Armah alluded to Lincoln and Kennedy as "those honoured dead" resolving "that these dead shall not have died in vain; that this nation, under God, shall have a new birth of freedom; and that government of the people, by the people, and for the people, shall not perish from the earth. . . ." For Armah, the survival of life on earth, rather than the experiment of American democracy was at stake. In reiterating his position of nonalignment with respect to the Cold War, Armah "humbly" rephrased Lincoln's words: "A world divided against itself cannot stand. I believe this world cannot endure permanently, half slave and half free."[12]

Through Lincoln's image, Armah linked the destinies of Africa and America, joining the history of the United States, once a fledgling union fighting for its survival in a Civil War, with the challenges facing Ghana and other new African states. Writing during the tumultuous days of the U.S. civil rights movement, Armah's gloss on Lincoln's "new birth of freedom" urged support for racial equality. For Armah, such a "new birth" also encompassed the ongoing liberation struggles against white minority rule in southern Africa. Armah's rephrasing "without apology" of the quotation from Lincoln's house divided speech not only asserted the unsustainability of superpower conflict, but also suggested that the Cold War was in fact a diversion from addressing the fundamental inequality of the global order, "half slave and half free."[13]

In quoting Lincoln, Armah followed the example of his boss, Kwame Nkrumah, whose engagement with Lincoln's image and memory was arguably as sustained as that of any other African leader of his day. In coming to the United States for his education, Nkrumah, like Azikiwe, diverged from the usual pursuit by anglophone Africans of advanced degrees in England. Nkrumah took to heart Azikiwe's advice that a British education might dampen his anti-colonial fervor and resided in the United States for over a decade, beginning in 1935, going on to earn a masters degree from the University of Pennsylvania.

Years later, upon his return to the United States, as prime minister of the new nation of Ghana, Nkrumah was greeted by euphoric African American crowds. A forceful critic of colonialism, Nkrumah had insisted that Ghana's independence was meaningless without the total liberation of the African continent. But Nkrumah walked a fine line between his support for African nationalist movements still struggling for independence, and his ardent pursuit of U.S. assistance for the construction of a hydroelectric dam at Ghana's Volta River, the centerpiece of his plans for Ghana's industrial development and modernization.[14]

Having dealt with hostile elements in the British press, Nkrumah was eager to sway public and Congressional opinion to his favor in the United States. During his whirlwind visit to the United States in 1958, Nkrumah visited the Lincoln Memorial, the scene of pro-civil rights demonstrations with Marian Anderson's Easter Sunday concert in 1939, and the Prayer Pilgrimage for Freedom the year before, at which Martin Luther King Jr. delivered his "Give Us the Ballot" speech. At the memorial, Nkrumah laid a wreath, mingled with tourists, and posed for several photographs in front of the massive statue of Lincoln. It is worth noting that Nkrumah also paid a visit to Mount Vernon, the residence of George Washington, a curious backdrop for communicating a pro-civil rights message. The Lincoln Memorial's recent use by supporters of civil rights was not lost on Nkrumah and his State Department handlers. Both would have embraced the visual association with Lincoln as a symbol of emancipation and an American civic religion of freedom and democracy.

Posed in front of the statue, impeccably attired and aloof of expression, sharing the frame with white tourists in the background, Nkrumah's image as head of state seemed far removed from the stock visual representation of the hierarchical relationship of Lincoln standing over the kneeling freed slave, described by the historian David Brion Davis as "the emancipation moment."[15] At the request of the U.S. government, the occasion of Nkrumah's visit to the Lincoln Memorial was commemorated on a postage stamp issued by Ghana marking the Lincoln sesquicentennial in 1959. On that stamp, Nkrumah is posed in front of the statue, his forward-looking gaze echoing that of Lincoln's marble visage. In 1965, Ghana issued four commemorative stamps of Lincoln to mark the centennial of his assassination.

To celebrate the Lincoln sesquicentennial, the United States Information Agency (USIA) planned a global outreach campaign, including programs and exhibits in several African countries. On the whole, the USIA and embassy officials seemed unaware of an indigenous knowledge of Lincoln, or of African American history, that might have enriched the quality and reception of Lincoln among African audiences. U.S. officials seemed intent on diverting Africans' discussions of Lincoln away from the burning issue of civil rights in the United States, an objective that Nkrumah resisted in his remarks delivered for the Voice of America broadcast, *In Search of Lincoln*. Nkrumah claimed that Lincoln's significance for Africans was his role in "the eventual emancipation of peoples of African descent in the United States," and ending the "evil" of slavery. Noting the continuing need for vigilance in the name of justice and equal treatment, Nkrumah lamented that Lincoln's egalitarianism "tends to be forgotten even in these enlightened times."[16]

For Nkrumah, the United States of America provided the model for his vision of African unity, a United States of Africa. In 1963, Nkrumah published his book *Africa Must Unite*, its appearance timed to coincide with the inaugural meeting of the Organization of African Unity in Ethiopia. This

Kwame Nkrumah visiting the Lincoln Memorial in Washington in 1958. (Image courtesy of Getty Images)

book was the ideological centerpiece, throughout Africa and the West, for Nkrumah's pursuit of an African continental union government. Nkrumah cited several precedents in making his case for a political union of African states. He lauded Simon Bolívar's vision, sadly thwarted, of a Union of South American States. In Nkrumah's view, perhaps influenced by his disappointing negotiations with the U.S. government and the Kaiser Corporation over the building of the Volta dam, political unity was a vital precondition for Africa's economic development. In unity, Africa stood a greater chance of resisting balkanization and conditions of economic neocolonialism imposed by the West. Where Bolívar failed, Lincoln had succeeded. "The United States of America, but for the firm resolve of Abraham Lincoln to maintain the union of the states, might well have fallen into a disintegration which would have barred the way to the tremendous acceleration of development that an enormous agglomeration of land, resources and people made possible." For Nkrumah, the choice was clear. The fragmentation of "national exclusivism" was to be rejected for the road of union.[17]

For Nkrumah, Lincoln was the true founder of the modern United States of America, in effect, the architect of its vast industrial might. It was Lincoln's victory in the Civil War that imposed the Union on the vanquished South. Noting Lincoln's reluctance to interfere with the institution of slavery, Nkrumah argued that the survival of the Union required the abolition of slavery. Writing at a moment in which much of southern Africa remained under the control of white minority rule, Nkrumah argued that Lincoln's eventual embrace of emancipation justified "our Pan-African stand that complete freedom is imperative for African Unity." Again, Nkrumah stressed the direct relationship between the continuance of the Union and the nation's industrial expansion.[18]

What was behind Nkrumah's strategic references to Lincoln in his arguments in support of an African union government? Insofar as Nkrumah was addressing Westerners, particularly Americans, his historical allusions to Lincoln as the savior and architect of the modern United States were perhaps intended to counter Western perceptions of fundamental differences between Africa and Europe (or the West more generally).[19] Fellow African heads of state were another crucial audience for Nkrumah's discussion of Lincoln. Yet one suspects that Nkrumah's emphasis on Lincoln's act of preserving the Union by force of arms as commander in chief would strike rival African heads of state as a worrisome argument for African union government.

In any case, Nkrumah failed to persuade enough fellow heads of state of the virtues and necessity of African unity. Nkrumah, who took an increasingly confrontational stance toward the United States and the West, was overthrown by a military coup in 1966 while away from Ghana. From exile, he remained a leading spokesman for African liberation. But talk of Lincoln was nowhere to be found in his later political writings. Nor would other African leaders find in Lincoln a compelling exemplar for their political agendas. By the late 1960s and beyond, as African liberation movements in southern Africa met with violent repression and embraced armed struggle, Africans could look closer to home for examples of martyrdom. Patrice Lumumba, the democratically elected prime minister of the Congo, ousted by a secession movement, and slain by Belgian troops in 1961, was such an example. The Martinique-born writer and activist Frantz Fanon was an early advocate of armed struggle for the African revolution, and was widely viewed as a martyr, though leukemia was the cause of his untimely death. There were other African martyrs, victims of political assassination, including Amilcar Cabral, Tom Mboya, Eduardo Mondlane, and Chris Hani. Nelson Mandela, released from prison in 1992 after twenty-seven years, became a universal symbol of sacrifice and reconciliation worthy of a Lincoln.

The moment of Lincoln's appeal among African leaders was fleeting. It reflected a brief span of some thirty years, from the 1930s to the 1960s, when many African nationalists viewed the United States as an anti-colonial ally, in large part due to their identification with African Americans' freedom struggles. Just as significant was the fact that for many young Africans, the United States, unlike European colonial empires, seemed largely untainted by colonialism, and Lincoln, as emancipator, common man, and martyr, epitomized the nation's democratic promise. By the mid-1960s, supporters of African liberation realized that colonialism in Africa would not yield without armed struggle and bloodshed. To those fighting for social justice in the United States it was apparent that civil rights legislation had failed to solve persistent problems of poverty, as well as inadequate housing and schools. For African Americans and Africans demanding self-determination, Lincoln's image was diminished, from the majestic icon of freedom on the Mall to the two-dimensional racial paternalism of "the emancipation moment," the image of Lincoln towering over a submissive slave, which had crystallized African Americans' ambivalence toward Lincoln.

Another likely explanation for the paucity of references to Lincoln by the late 1960s was the growing perception among Africans of the United States as an enemy to African aspirations. Just as the meaning of Lincoln's image was transformed over time in the minds of African Americans, so did the image of the United States suffer at home and abroad due to the Vietnam War, the assassinations and urban rebellions of the late 1960s, and continuing racial strife. This critical stance toward the United States as global hegemon opposed to African liberation was a profound departure from the perception of many earlier African nationalists who held favorable views because of their education in the country and their identification with African American struggles for equality.

All told, there are many Lincolns, or many sides of Lincoln, with which Africans might identify, or ignore, as the case may be. There is Lincoln the emancipator. But for Africans who gained their freedom from colonialism through armed struggle, the idea of emancipation by edict might seem unrealistic. There is the Lincoln of the Civil War, the defender of the Union. Here it is true that the press often compared Lincoln with Nigeria's General Gowon, who kept that nation together in the face of the Biafran Civil War of 1967. Then there is Lincoln as agent of national reconciliation. For playing a similar role in post-apartheid South Africa, Archbishop Desmond Tutu received the Lincoln Leadership Prize of the Lincoln Presidential Library and Museum in Springfield, Illinois, in 2008. In a similar vein, Ellen Johnson Sirleaf, the president of Liberia, praised Lincoln as a "defender of liberty" and an inspiration for her country's transition to democracy after nearly three decades of civil war.[20] And finally, there is Lincoln, the deeply flawed white racist and colonizationist who, nevertheless, was capable of extraordinary growth under extreme duress, an image of him handed down to us by Frederick Douglass, but curiously, one that does not appear to have caught on among those Africans who invoke his memory.

With the worldwide interest in Barack Obama, whose admiration for Lincoln is well known, there is the possibility of a revival of interest in Lincoln among Africans. But if the engagement with Lincoln's political thought and role in U.S. history is to flourish, it will necessarily have to bring Lincoln's legacy to bear on contemporary African problems of political conflict, autocratic governance, and the need for greater protection of the rights of minorities and women in African states. No doubt young Africans continue to have access to information on the life and career of Lincoln through their schooling and perhaps the Internet. In retrospect, perhaps Africans' engagement with Lincoln was too superficial—even opportunistic—to displace other pre- and post-colonial historical figures from their political imagination, and thus to have lasting significance. Today, years after Lincoln's name captured the hope and idealism of young Africans' struggles for national independence, there seems to be a symmetry of misrecognition between Africans and Americans.[21] With few exceptions, Africans, by and large, no longer view Lincoln as relevant to their present-day problems and challenges. And a significant number of Americans seem dimly aware, if not resistant, to a reckoning of the place of Africa in the history of the United States, its origins and founding as a slave society, the crisis of the Civil War, and emancipation.

Notes

1. Frederick Douglass, "Oration in Memory of Abraham Lincoln," April 14, 1876, Lincoln Park, Washington, DC. http://teachingamericanhistory.org/library/index.asp?document=39.

2. Winston James, *Holding Aloft the Banner of Ethiopia* (London: Verso, 1998), 202–3.

3. Scott A. Sandage, "A Marble House Divided: The Lincoln Memorial, the Civil Rights Movement, and the Politics of Memory, 1939–1963," *Journal of American History* 80 (June 1993), 136.

4. James Campbell, *Songs of Zion: The African Methodist Episcopal Church in the United States and South Africa* (Chapel Hill: University of North Carolina Press, 1998), 125–27.

5. David W. Blight, *Race and Reunion: The Civil War in American Memory* (Cambridge, MA: Harvard University Press, 2001), 306; T. J. Morgan, "What Spelman Stands For." *Spelman Messenger*, December 1901: 1–7; and Lewis G. Jordan, "Where Is the Money?" *Mission Herald*, August 1912: 2. For a recent study of the activities of African American missionaries in Africa, see Brandi Hughes, "Middle Passages: The Redemption of African America in the African Mission Field, 1862–1905" (Ph.D. diss., Yale University, 2008).

6. Mrs. George Schwab, *Abraham Lincoln* (London: The Sheldon Press, 1945); George Schwab, Ebraham Linco_n/nyiemo_i mame_i (Bo: Sierra Leone: Protectorate Literature Bureau, 1955).

7. Derek R. Peterson, "The Intellectual Lives of Mau Mau Detainees," *Journal of Modern African History* 49 (2008), 73–91.

8. Nelson Mandela, *Long Walk to Freedom: The Autobiography of Nelson Mandela* (Boston: Little Brown and Company, 1994), 40.

9. Derek Peterson, *Creative Writing: Translation, Bookkeeping, and the Work of Imagination in Colonial Kenya* (Portsmouth, NH: Heinemann, 2004), 154–55.

10. Nnamdi Azikiwe, *Liberia in World Politics* (London: Arthur H. Stockwell, Ltd., 1934), 40–41. Indeed, Azikiwe scornfully quoted Lincoln's negative view of African Americans, as articulated during the Lincoln-Douglas debates: ". . . I am not, nor ever have been, in favor of bringing in any way the social and political equality of the white and the black races. . . ." Quoted in Evelyn Rowand, "The Effect of Lincoln University on the Leaders of British West Africa" (Master's Thesis, Department of History, University of Alberta, 1964), 27–28.

11. Julius K. Nyerere, *Freedom and Unity: Uhuru na Umoja: A Selection from Writings and Speeches, 1952–1965* (London: Oxford University Press, 1967), 126–29.

12. Kwesi Armah, *Africa's Golden Road* (London: Heinemann, 1965), 142.

13. Ibid.

14. Kevin Gaines, *American Africans in Ghana: Black Expatriates in the Civil Rights Era* (Chapel Hill: University of North Carolina Press, 2006).

15. Sandage, "A Marble House Divided," 148.

16. For the original sound recording, see, Abraham Lincoln Sesquicentennial Commission, *In Search of Lincoln*, RG 148, Motion Picture, Sound, and Video Records Section, Special Media Archives Services Division (NWCS-M), NARA II.

17. Kwame Nkrumah, *Africa Must Unite* (London: Heinemann, 1963), 189.

18. Ibid., 210–11.

19. V. Y. Mudimbe, *The Invention of Africa: Gnosis, Philosophy, and the Order of Knowledge* (Bloomington: Indiana University Press, 1988), 107.

20. Ellen Johnson Sirleaf, "Founding Father," *The New York Times* (February 15, 2009); http://www.nytimes.com/2009/02/16/opinion/16sirleaf.html?_r=2&ref=abraham_lincoln.

21. I am indebted to David W. Cohen for this insight.

16

Hating and Loving the "Real" Abe Lincolns

LINCOLN AND THE AMERICAN SOUTH

David W. Blight

For a very long time, Americans of all backgrounds, as well as foreigners who visit the United States, have viewed the South as the country's most distinctive section—by history, culture, and by all manner of stereotypes. Culturally justified or not, the Civil War and the North's leader, Abraham Lincoln, provide the most pivotal markers in the development of perceptions of the South as a place, a world of attitudes and experiences, indeed a burdensome past set apart from the whole of the nation's history. The premise of this paper begs the question, who or what is a Southerner? When trying to harness the story of how "Southerners" in the United States have used, appropriated, hated, loved, and remembered Abraham Lincoln, we must first recognize the truism—there were and are many Souths. The near absurdity, or at least plurality, in this question of Lincoln and the South might be represented by the useless fact that Lincoln shared one great thing in common with William Faulkner: they both worked in a post office when they were young, and both apparently with the same diffidence and spotty attendance.

In one sense, of course, Lincoln was a Southerner—by birth, family, and friendship connections to one part of the border South. He was born near Hodgenville, Kentucky; his father, Thomas, and his mother, Nancy Hanks, were originally from Virginia. Lincoln married a born and bred Kentuckian, Mary Todd, who had grown up in a slaveholding family. His three law partners, John Stewart, Stephen Logan, and William Herndon were all native Kentuckians. And many of his best friends—Joshua Speed, Orville Browning, Ward Lamon—were from below the Ohio River. And yes, there was the flatboat journey down the Mississippi River to New Orleans as a young man, which was undoubtedly a formative experience and memory. Some have also concluded that Lincoln likely spoke with a kind of Kentucky accent. But what does all of this actually tell us about Lincoln's worldview, his ideas, and his character?

An historian of the Ohio-Kentucky region, Christopher Phillips, has cautioned that we not make too much of Lincoln's personal ties to Kentucky or even of the influence of his "Southernness," suggesting that the Illinois of his adulthood was far different from the Kentucky of his youth. And Southern historian and Jefferson Davis biographer, William Cooper, has argued that a deep flaw in Lincoln's silence, indecision, and over-estimation of Southern "unionism" in the secession crisis was that the president-elect knew virtually no deep South politicians and had no personal relationships with the leaders (nor even some critics) of secession from the Carolinas to Texas.[1] Much is made of Lincoln's relationship with Alexander H. Stephens from when they were in Congress together in the late 1840s, but they exchanged virtually no correspondence between then and early 1861. None of this record or evidence would ever get in the way of one strand of Southern writers and spokesmen who would *make* Lincoln a Southerner and adopt him as one of their own, especially for white supremacist and segregationist purposes.

But there are many strands of Southern adoption of Lincoln. In his *Lincoln and the South* (1946), James G. Randall made much of Lincoln's Southernness, and that book still rewards a reading, if for no other purpose than to see Randall's noted "Needless War" school approach played out through Lincoln. Randall claims Lincoln was "immersed in southern influences" his entire life. He considered young Abe Lincoln's fascination with *rivers* a southern thing, like Samuel Clemens apparently. He stressed his marriage and time spent in and around Lexington observing the world of slavery in Mary Todd's family. He further claims it was Lincoln's "southern type of friendliness" that made him kind to black people. And Randall made a special case for the significance of the "border" in making Lincoln's life and consciousness, fashioning Kentucky as the geographical seat of compromise and "adjustment." He says Lincoln really understood Kentucky but Kentuckians did not understand Lincoln. In Randall's view, it was the "Kentuckiness" in Lincoln that made him so devoted to preserving the Union. By exalting the Crittendens, Clays, and even the Breckinridges of Kentucky, Randall implicitly at least denigrated the Republicans (especially the radicals), while associating Lincoln with the then honored tradition of American compromise. Randall, like most of us, found the Lincoln he wanted, a "moderate . . . border mind," a man whose "opposites were the extremists on both sides."[2] But there were moderates of a similar outlook from Maine and Michigan as well.

If Carl Sandburg could love Lincoln nearly to death precisely because he was a man of paradox, the same has been true of Southerners who have grudgingly respected or virulently loathed, and then over time genuinely loved (in some cases), the man whose government and armies conquered them and destroyed one version of a historical South. It could be said that there was no "Old South" until Lincoln and the Union troops killed it. The Southerners' Lincoln has been as paradoxical as anyone else's, even as this region has been the geographical and ideological home of Lincoln-hating over time. Southerners have taken the "Lincoln myth" and peeled it away down to some useful reinventions of their own. The peeled myth, like the pruned rose bush, often sprouts even more enduring leaves and blossoms, or thorns and poisons. There is a Southern scholars' Lincoln and a popular culture Lincoln; novelists and poets have had their sway over Lincoln's image, as have all manner of politicians from small-town mayors to presidents. But great distances often prevail between the many kinds of Southern images of Lincoln, just as they have in the American North or West or the world over. And the reactions, beginning with the war itself, can be as raw as they are sometimes transcendent.

In her remarkable wartime journal, "Brokenburn," Kate Stone, a Louisiana planter, slaveholder, and sister of Confederate soldiers, left these depressed and gleeful reactions to Lincoln's assassination in 1865. After declaring that she cannot "believe" the news of Robert E. Lee's surrender, Stone records on April 28 (from Tyler, Texas, where she fled with some of her family and a few of her slaves): "We hear that Lincoln is dead . . . 'Sic semper tyrannis,' as his brave destroyer shouted as he sprang on his horse. All honor to J. Wilkes Booth, who has rid the world of a tyrant and made himself famous for generations." By May 15, Stone opened a diary entry with: "Conquered, Submission, Subjugation are the words that burn into my heart, and yet I feel we are doomed to know them in all their bitterness." All was "gloom . . . like the shadow of death." Then she wrote at length of her hatred of Lincoln. "Poor Booth, to think that he fell at last. Many a true heart at the South weeps for his death . . . Caesar had his Brutus . . . and Lincoln his Booth. Lincoln's fate overtook him on the pinnacle of his fame, or rather infamy. We are glad he is not alive to rejoice in our humiliation and insult us with his jokes. The circumstance of his death forms a most complete tragedy."[3]

Most in the wartime generation of Confederates would never find a way to get comfortable with Lincoln's image or memory. Some, especially among Confederate leadership, saw quickly in Lincoln's murder a harder fate for the postwar South, lamenting Booth's act, and they were likely right. But many newspaper reports of the assassination came from a raw sense of defeat and rage. The editor of the *Texas Republican* declared "it certainly a matter of congratulation that Lincoln is dead, because the world is happily rid of a monster that disgraced the form of humanity." And the *Houston Telegraph* announced: "From now until God's judgment day the minds of men will not cease to thrill at the killing of Abraham Lincoln." And even E. A. Pollard, in his famous 700-page-plus *The Lost Cause* (1867), referred to Lincoln's death as "tragical . . . at the hands of one of the most indefensible but courageous assassins that history . . . ever produced."[4] Pollard launched in print this idea that Lincoln's murder was "tragic," maybe even a real blow to the South's ultimate fate, but at the same time denouncing and hating the cause for which he lived and died. Alive, Lincoln would be ripe for virulent hatred; dead, he would be too, but that hatred had to be managed, manipulated, transformed.

Lincoln-hating has a long history, not only in the South, and it has taken many forms. But few ex-Confederates held to a diehard line on despising Lincoln more openly and eccentrically than former Confederate soldier Pink Parker of Troy, Alabama. When Parker returned to his home at the end of the war, he found his house burned, his slaves freed, and his livestock gone. He remained utterly unreconstructed and on every anniversary of Lincoln's death he donned his Sunday finest and marched about town wearing a homemade badge declaring his joy in the "death of Old Abe Lincoln." In 1906, Parker offered the town a large granite monument with the inscription: "Erected by Pink Parker in honor of John Wilkes Booth for killing old Abe Lincoln." Town officials apparently declined the monument, so Parker placed it in his front yard where it remained for fifteen years, attracting tourists, until his death.[5]

At the other extreme, Southern African Americans who were former slaves loved Lincoln and appropriated him to their ends of freedom, safety, and political and civil rights in an increasingly hostile South. Lincoln has also occupied an important place in a black sacred American nationalism (a black civil religion) born of the epic of emancipation. For at least two generations after the war, Lincoln's place in black public memory was all but sacrosanct. Whatever the truth about just how much Lincoln had or had not been black folks' advocate, by and large, Southern blacks recruited the *martyred* Lincoln to their cause. By the turn of the twentieth century, and certainly by the time of the centennial of Lincoln's birth in 1909, black commemorative activity emerged everywhere, in tiny villages and large cities. Lincoln had always been a central part of African American emancipation day celebrations; in the desperate circumstances of the Jim Crow South, he became even more important as a symbol.

The idea that "Lincoln freed the slaves" has attained the status of a cliché in our time, usually telling us more about the user of the phrase than anything historical. Today the phrase is often under a certain scholarly and public skepticism among some, while it still flourishes in Lincoln adoration among some establishment scholars (and certainly in the public's imagination). But at many black gatherings commemorating freedom, Lincoln's image was front and center. To blacks at the beginning of the twentieth century, Lincoln as icon had come to represent much more than a personal and presidential act of emancipation. The Proclamation itself, almost always read at these occasions, had become for blacks their own kind of national treasure, their own founding document. It was "the issuance of their Magna Carta" that they should celebrate on January 1 every year, declared the National Afro-American Council in 1906, an organization created by the journalist T. Thomas Fortune.[6] Whether blacks saw the Proclamation as the foundation of their citizenship, or whether they viewed Lincoln as their literal liberator, most had adopted their own civic logic: in segregated, racist America, where their rights were temporarily crushed, if

Lincoln had not freed the slaves, then the nation had not done so either; and if the nation had not freed them, then they had no future as citizens at all. For so many Southern blacks, Lincoln's place in the emancipation drama stood as an official declaration of their belonging in the land of their birth, secured by blood in war, and sanctioned by the highest authority of the nation. In the United States, where a Southern black man or woman could not claim that "Lincoln freed the slaves" (meaning the United States freed the slaves and laid down the Thirteenth, Fourteenth, and Fifteenth amendments), then fear and hopelessness were the only options. Loving Lincoln meant believing that 1865 really was a new beginning, a new birth to *their* American history.

Lincoln's portrait in front of a Southern black church at an emancipation commemoration or on any common day was a collective statement of citizenship and identity. Blacks, of course, also recollected how as refugees, soldiers, camp hands, and laborers they had freed themselves. But theories of self-emancipation had little historical grounding in the early twentieth century, and were of marginal value in wresting the right to vote back from white suprema-cists. Strategically, and with genuine sentiment, therefore, blacks honored Lincoln in season and out. And they did so within a religious worldview that saw emancipation in Biblical time, a historical process of centuries and more. In their view, God had come to earth, appointed a time and place, and, indeed, appointed a leader as liberator. In the Christian cosmology through which many freedmen and their children came to understand their emancipation, God had entered history, chosen his people and his moment, and, of course, as in the Bible, chosen a Moses.

On emancipation day, January 1, 1909 in Augusta, Georgia, a black Baptist minister, Silas X. Floyd, delivered a speech, "Abraham Lincoln: Sent of God," at a large gathering sponsored by churches, fraternal orders, and the local Lincoln League. Lest there was any doubt about this millennial link between emancipation, God's designs, and Lincoln, the audience only needed to hear the title and follow the metaphors. Floyd was young and charismatic; he represented the post-freedom generation preaching to the freedom generation. He admonished those blacks who wished to forget that "our race was once enslaved in this country." "Did you ever see . . . a Confederate veteran who desired to forget that he wore the gray," asked Floyd, "or was unwilling to teach his children that he once proudly marched in battle behind Lee and Gordon, Jackson and Johnston? Did you ever see a Union soldier who was ashamed of the part he took in the Great War, or who felt humiliated to tell his children about it?" Floyd reminded his audience that they too had a great story to tell:

And don't you remember that when the children of Israel under the leadership of Moses were on the march from Egypt . . . to Canaan . . . don't you remember that, after they had safely crossed the Red Sea, the Lord commanded them to set up memorial stones by which the event should be remembered? And yet some old Negroes wish to forget all about slavery—all about the past—and stoutly maintain that we have no right to be celebrating this day that brought freedom to race . . . May God forget my people when they forget this day.[7]

This speech sizzles with generational conflict and is told in the common coin of Old Testament understandings. But at the heart of Floyd's message is not only that Southern blacks could not afford to forget the past, but that as long as ex-Confederates displayed their memory and dominated popular discussion of the meaning of the war, former slaves and their descendents had to try to keep pace in their own way. If Lee was God's Christian soldier sent to represent a holy cause in glorious defeat, then Lincoln was God's appointed agent of black and American liberation. When the children of Israel assembled their memorial stones, they too were obedient and reluctant in the face of God's commands, inspired and frightened by their faith, their heroism, and their history. And their Moses, before he became Moses, had been reluctant and troubled before he did his weighty duty. And neither quite made it to the promised land.

Behind all the public commemorations of emancipation, a deep folk spirit of Lincoln remembrance can be discerned among ordinary black folk. In 1910, Mary White Ovington, a white social worker and a founder of the NAACP, recorded the recollections of numerous ex-slaves in southern Alabama. Ovington found an interesting range of old folks who told of personal pain, hardship, family breakups, labor conditions, and progress toward property ownership. A woman identified only as "Granny" recited the most compelling story. Very old, with African features, Granny told of being sold away from her four children in North Carolina, sent in the slave trade westward to Alabama, and forced to give birth to a fifth child fathered by her new, cruel master. She remembered crying when her master's son died in the Confederate army because he was a "kind chile." She related tales of being whipped, of her desperate fears of running away, and of surviving on her faith in "Master Jesus."[8]

As Ovington was about to leave, she asked Granny about the photograph of Lincoln on the mantle in her cabin. "I love dat face Miss," Granny answered. "I love it so dat der lady down here, she done gib me der picture. Dose eyes, dey follow me, dey's so kind. I don't know how to tell you how much I lub dat man dat made us free—an' all der oders, too, dat helped." Granny and Ovington are both reminded of a lyric from a plantation song as "they looked out on the fields where men guided the mules in the plowing."[9] This interview is likely a collaborative work of nostalgia, a dose of neo-abolitionist pathos, and a genuine window into freed people's memory all at once. It also shows us the power of black folk memory of Lincoln; the picture above Granny's mantle stood for hundreds of thousands of others just like it. Was this naïve monarchism (as Russians serfs put faith in the czar rather than their noblemen masters), or some kind of primitive fetishism? Or was it a collective civic logic announcing hope in the face of hardship and sometimes horror?—a visual talisman for Granny's generation declaring that slavery had once been defeated and could be again.

Between Pink Parker and Granny, or between E. A. Pollard and Silas Floyd there were unbridgeable gulfs. Not only their memories, but their worlds, never met. What animated all of them, of course, in this sea of myth was one fundamental truth—Lincoln . . . or something or someone had freed the slaves. That fundamental fact of the postwar South had everything to do with how "Southern" images of Lincoln would evolve. Over time, Southern Lincoln-haters as well as grudging admirers, would have to decide whether emancipation was essentially a good or an evil for the South. Lincoln's Southern reputation in its many forms over time rose and fell, and rose again on this question. It was Pollard after all who set a tone on this question in the immediate aftermath of the war. In language still used by Lincoln-haters today, he called emancipation a "deliberately planned robbery of the Southern people," and the Proclamation a "bold iniquity . . . an act of malice toward the master rather than one of mercy to the slave . . . a crime . . . in the name of humanity . . . a cruel and shameful device . . . of a wicked and reckless war."[10]

This tradition of Lincoln-hating has waxed and waned in Southern history, and it has certainly eroded measurably in recent decades. But several forms can be discerned over time. Southerners have never been alone in despising or opposing Lincoln. Wartime Democrats especially spewed more venom on Lincoln than we would want to conjure up. And some abolitionists bitterly attacked the president, especially early in the war. Over time, in the twentieth century, the Old Left and some black critics have either lambasted Lincoln for his conservatism or dismissed and condemned him for his racism. But Southerners have dominated Lincoln-hating and still do.

The Confederate indictment of Lincoln bored deep into Southern consciousness from the very beginning of the war. In his essay on the "Anti-Lincoln Tradition" in 1982, historian Don Fehrenbacher left this startling observation: "Lincoln's role in southern eyes was that of a military conqueror—a ruthless Attila bent upon the destruction of a superior civilization. In fact the Confederate image of Abraham Lincoln in the 1860s bears a striking resemblance to the American image of Adolf Hitler in the 1940s." During the war Lincoln was labeled everything from "tyrant" to "fiend" to "monster." In all sorts of popular media he was represented as a "buffoon," a drunkard, a libertine, a coward, a murderer, and a "pornographic storyteller."[11]

A growing and important array of white Southerners over the late nineteenth and early twentieth centuries would accept, even appreciate, Lincoln for his apparent leniency toward the South and Reconstruction. They would lament his death, including famously Jefferson Davis, who exercised a certain personal grace regarding Lincoln's memory, while nonetheless vehemently asserting a state's rights defense of the Confederacy to his dying day. "New

South" advocates like Henry Grady of Atlanta and his circle admired Lincoln and tried to appropriate him to their aims of economic and social progress.

But many diehard champions of the Lost Cause (professional Southerners and ex-or neo-Confederates) would very much keep Lincoln front and center as *archenemy* in their fantasy-melodrama of the Civil War as they wished it remembered. In popular memory no one worked harder at Lincoln vilification (or with more sheer nastiness) than the powerful, notorious, eccentric Mildred Rutherford, historian general of the United Daughters of the Confederacy (UDC) for more than a decade in the early twentieth century. From her base in Athens, Georgia, her crusade took many forms, but especially essays and textbooks for Southern schoolchildren who, she believed, must be given the "truth" about Lincoln. Rutherford threw "truths" around as though they were pieces of candy to be popped like pills of medicine down the throats of young people. A short list of the haymakers ("truths") that Rutherford purveyed includes that Lincoln was a slaveholder; that as a quartermaster in the Mexican War he tried to starve American soldiers; that he contributed money to John Brown's raid on Harpers Ferry; that the Gettysburg Address had really been written by William H. Seward; and that in 1867 Ulysses Grant had imposed a forty-five-year censorship on any newspaper that criticized Lincoln. Rutherford was hardly alone in the UDC; she was merely a conspicuous and particularly visible representative of a large number of middle- and upper-class white Southern women who produced all manner of materials to indoctrinate white youth in the ways of Confederate righteousness and Yankee perfidy. Among Rutherford's comprehensive monthly lesson plans for schools was one in 1915 that required a comparison of Jefferson Davis and Abraham Lincoln on the question: "Which violated the Constitution?"[12] The prescribed answers were neither subtle nor cliffhangers.

An early and concerted attack on Lincoln in book form was published in 1901, *The Real Lincoln,* by Charles Landon Carter Minor, a Confederate veteran, Virginia aristocrat, and president of Virginia Polytechnic Institute. Minor wrote as though preparing a historical-legal brief against Lincoln. In an odd, perhaps disingenuous spirit of North-South reconciliation, Minor claimed he wanted to allay sectional bitterness—caused, he believed, by the false legends about Lincoln foisted on Southerners. Minor used Northern witnesses from the collections of oral history produced by William Herndon and Ward Lamon to produce a litany of hundreds of quotations, a compendium more than a book, in the service of character assassination. This popular work that went through many editions was little more than the Lost Cause at its most vicious and spurious, forged from the personal destruction of Lincoln's image. Minor's selections portrayed Lincoln as a reprobate, a drunk, an infidel, cruel to his parents, vulgar in his habits and jokes, and even as a misguided revolutionary.[13]

The "real" Lincoln in his many Southern manifestations would continue to appear all over the cultural landscape. One of the most intriguing uses of

Lincoln by a Southern writer was that of Thomas Dixon. Dixon stood in a growing tradition of Southern white supremacists who tried to fashion Lincoln as part of their own cause, even their own kith and kin. They found especially useful his Charleston, Illinois, speech in the Lincoln-Douglas debates where Lincoln gave his most thorough rejection of racial equality, and they applauded his advocacy of colonization for blacks. Joel Chandler Harris, for example, wrote a famous little story, "The Kidnapping of Abraham Lincoln." The lead character, Billy Sanders, a "Georgia cracker," combines with a ne'er-do-well young aristocrat; they go through Union lines to grab Lincoln, spirit him back into the Confederacy, and somehow win the war. But when Sanders meets Lincoln the two develop a "secret admiration" for each other. Harris gives his sentimental readers the careworn, burdened Lincoln who sits down with Sanders and swaps yarns. "Down our way," says Sanders, "they say you're a Yankee, but if that's so, the woods are full of Yankees in Georgia, all born and raised right there." Lincoln laughs loudly and answers: "You're paying me the highest compliment I've had in many a day." The two Confederates can't go through with the abduction and one says he feels like he'd be "kidnapping his grandfather."[14]

Dixon took all of this sentiment much further. Born in 1864 in North Carolina, Dixon grew up with Reconstruction, which he hated with deep passion. He became a Baptist minister after studying law and history and achieved fame for his sensationally racist sermons. Those sermons turned into novels and plays, *The Leopard's Spots* (1902) and *The Clansman* (1905), each of which sold more than a million copies; the latter became the basis for the epic film *The Birth of a Nation*, in 1915. In *The Clansman,* Lincoln is called the "Great Heart"; he is essentially a Southerner misplaced in the presidency during the war. In *The Southerner: A Romance of the Real Lincoln* (1913), Dixon wrote a turgid, 550-page reinvention of Lincoln into an American (but very Southern) folk hero whose destiny it had been (until Booth) "to heal the bitterness of the war and remove the Negro race from physical contact with the white race." To Dixon, Lincoln's greatness lay in his racism, in whiteness, and his willingness to use the crisis of the Civil War to find a solution to the American race problem—which meant removal of black people from the country. Dixon's Lincoln is one swathed in idyllic myth and unadulterated Civil War nostalgia; he is the hero as divine agent who had to be sacrificed for a cause to find ultimate triumph. At the time of Lincoln's assassination, writes Dixon, "his prophetic soul had pierced the future and seen with remorseless logic that two such races as the Negro and Caucasion could not live side by side in a free democracy." And Dixon employed the central villains of the Reconstruction legend as Lincoln's real betrayers: "The Radical theorists of Congress were demanding that these black men, emerging from four thousand years of slavery and savagery should receive the ballot and the right to claim the white man's daughter in marriage. They could only pass these measures over the dead body of Abraham Lincoln."[15]

Perhaps no Southerner ever carried on a more prolonged and bitter campaign of Lincoln-hating than Lyon Gardiner Tyler, the son of President John Tyler. As a scion of an old Virginia family, Tyler had many agendas, not least of which was an endless defense of his father's political career (he was the fourteenth of sixteen children of Tyler's, the fifth of seven by a second wife). But when filio-piety was not his purpose it was a devotion to Lost Cause ideology and a burning hatred of Lincoln that animated Tyler's work as a historian and educator. He started as a teacher, then became a member of the Virginia legislature in the late 1880s, and then took a faculty position at the College of William and Mary, where he eventually became president. "I accept the results of the war [Civil War]," he once remarked as late as 1929. "I am commercialized, industrialized and northernized."[16] At least the third of these was certainly not true.

At William and Mary, Tyler created his own journal, *Tyler's Quarterly Historical and Genealogical Magazine,* which he edited for nearly twenty years. Over and over again, Tyler wrote articles, or reprinted others' work, arguing standard Lost Cause tropes: the South had never fought for slavery, they had never been defeated on the battlefield, the Confederacy was the true heritage of the American Revolution, Reconstruction was an oppressive occupation of a sovereign people, and especially that the war's worst—indeed criminal—result of emancipation was the greatest downfall of American history. "The emancipation of the slaves," he maintained, "accomplished as it was in the most ruinous fashion by Lincoln and his cohorts, put back the South a hundred years at least, and it is still paying the penalty of the conquered." As the prime villain of the drama, of course, Tyler attacked Lincoln in season and out. The Emancipation Proclamation, Tyler declared, was "the true parent of Reconstruction, of legislative robbery, negro supremacy, cheating at the polls, rapes of white women, lynching, and the Ku Klux Klan."[17] The South bore no responsibility for any of these developments, Tyler argued. But Lincoln did.

Tyler devoted many pages and years to trying to demolish what he called the "Lincoln myth." His Lincoln was a vulgar, "coarse," demonic destroyer, not merely a dictator but a bloodthirsty killer, fashioned by national "propaganda" into a "social Christ." Tyler relished attacking historians such as Frederick Bancroft and the bestselling author James Ford Rhodes for their favorable portrayal of Lincoln. "The incompetent Lincoln," he growled, "despite his vacillating conduct and filthy conversation, is canonized as the 'First American!'" Booth's shot, said Tyler, had assured "to Lincoln an estimate in the eyes of the North far beyond his actual worth." He completely rejected the idea that had Lincoln lived, Reconstruction policies in the South would have been much more lenient. Lincoln, claimed Tyler, "positively reveled" in destroying the South and in "impure" and "callous" inhumanity. Tyler's Lincoln, as might be said in Southern slang, was a low-down no-count at best, and a cold-blooded mass killer at worst. Tyler did actually make one point in 1931 that even today's staunchest protectors of Lincoln as the perfect model might consider: "One of the principal factors in the perpetuation of the Lincoln tradition," wrote Tyler, "has been and still is to accept everything and anything Lincoln said as ipso facto truth. There is no parallel to the infallibility attributed to Lincoln outside the infallible authority to the Bible by ecclesiastical tradition."[18] Tyler's consuming hatred of Lincoln lasted until his death, coincidentally on February 12, 1935.

Lincoln-hating in recent times has taken yet further twists and turns. Tyler's old Lost Cause venom transformed into a Reagan-Bush era venom from the political and academic Right. Some of this community of historical writing on Lincoln and the Civil War emanates from white supremacist and neo-Confederate impulses of the late twentieth and early twenty-first centuries, and some of it is staunchly libertarian, anti-statist, even utopian, while Lincoln-hating stands in for the hated "big government." Two books emerge among a crowded subfield of neo-Confederate, pro-secession, largely ersatz scholarship: Charles Adams's *When in the Course of Human Events: Arguing the Case for Southern Secession* (2000), and Thomas J. DiLorenzo's *The Real Lincoln: A New Look at Abraham Lincoln, His Agenda, and an Unnecessary War* (2002).[19]

Why pay attention to these books? The simple answer is that they sell well, better than some canonical works on Lincoln and the Civil War of recent years that might be considered part of a liberal orthodoxy forged around the works of James McPherson, Eric Foner, and others. But more important, along with such recent books as *The Politically Incorrect Guide to American History*, by Thomas E. Woods, Jr., given huge publicity by Fox News, MSNBC, and other media outlets, and which had a stint on the *New York Times* bestseller list, these works provide a historical undergirding for a broadening, conservative, and libertarian attack on the actual legacies of the original Republican party, the Progressive movement, the New Deal regulatory state, the Great Society, and the Civil Rights movement.[20] Carefully researched, well-written academic history (even by those authors who reach broad audiences) is merely one more target of a conservative network of enthusiasts who love Whiggish, happy, redemptive American history. Their real targets are the "liberal elites" who allegedly control the academy, brainwash generations of students, and too often remain in their cocoons, scorned and irrelevant to the ways history is used in the civic arena.

In a recent essay in *Reviews in American History*, Daniel Feller took on the Adams and DiLorenzo books, as well as a third, by Jeffrey Hummel, *Emancipating Slaves, Enslaving Free Men: A History of the American Civil War*. Feller points out that the Library of Congress catalogues my book, *Race and Reunion: The Civil War in American Memory* (2001) right next to Tony Horwitz's *Confederates in the Attic* (2002), and Adams's defense of secession (with mine apparently in the middle). "Though Adams and Blight sit adjacent on the shelves," writes Feller, "the gulf between them, both in viewpoint and audience, is nearly bottomless. Contemplating that gulf provokes some disturbing thoughts."[21] In Lincoln scholarship and pedagogy, we should at least peer across this disturbing gulf.

Adams, an economist by training, is self-described as the "world's leading scholar on the history of taxation." DiLorenzo, a Southerner by roots and outlook, teaches economics at Loyola College in Maryland and has been active in the "League of the South." Both authors consider the slavery issue as a mere pretext for the larger reason Lincoln and Republicans went to war—to advance the centralized, leviathan state. Both authors despise Lincoln and argue that the war's greatest legacy is federal "tyranny" over the states and especially over individual liberty. Secession was not only understandable, but right and holy. And Lincoln's war was a series of "criminal" policies. It was a war waged, in Adams's and DiLorenzo's view, for increased taxation, for higher tariffs, and business profits. Adams compares Lincoln's ruthlessness in prosecuting a war to unconditional surrender to that of Stalin and Hitler in World War II. Adams considers Lincoln a virulent racist and calls the second inaugural address "psychopathic," a mere cover for his larger motive—the total destruction of Southern civilization. During Reconstruction, according to Adams, the Union Leagues were the terrorist wing of the Republican party and the Ku Klux Klan a harmless, necessary veterans' organization. Three of Adams's chapters had first been published in the white supremacist magazine, *Southern Partisan*.[22]

This is all standard Lost Cause dogma of a fairly extreme brand updated to fit current times, and it could have been written in 1890 or 1913 by any number of first or second generation ex-Confederates. But as Feller writes, it is not merely a "brainless rant." It has all the usual scholarly apparatus, footnotes, and bibliographical essay. Adams's work is a screed full of some wild roundhouses, but it also reads much like a Glenn Beck monologue on Fox News, a Newt Gingrich news conference in 1994, a Grover Norquist press release about the condition of the American polity in 2004, or the internal memos of the billionaire funders of the Tea Party in 2010. It is history serving a political persuasion: facts spun into a compelling narrative for the scorned and rebuked, white Christian conservatives of America who believe their faith in God, country, and righteousness, as well as their hatred of taxation of any kind, are somehow under attack. Adams's Lincoln, like the Tea Party movement, offers nourishment for the new federalists and state's rightists who believe government and taxation (as well as a black president who linked himself symbolically to Lincoln) to be America's great domestic enemies.[23]

DiLorenzo's book is even more extreme in its sheer hatred of Lincoln. *The Real Lincoln* may have taken cues from the 1901 book of the same name by Charles L. C. Minor. That book, at the high tide of Lost Cause writing, trashed Lincoln as unheroic, un-Christian, and a counter-example to the noble Christian soldier, Robert E. Lee. But primarily DiLorenzo twists Lincoln's presidency into a libertarian manifesto for an age of conservative complaint. DiLorenzo's Lincoln provoked the Civil War to bring into being the modern "welfare-warfare state." Rather than as the Great Emancipator, the sixteenth president should be remembered, says DiLorenzo, as the "great centralizer."[24]

What mainstream America celebrates in Lincoln's conception of the Civil War as the "rebirth" of freedom, DiLorenzo sees as the "death of federalism." His Lincoln is the dictatorial godfather of big government.[25] Leaders of secession were the Civil War's real heroes, according to DiLorenzo, because their cause had nothing to do with slavery—only with resisting federal tyranny. His real subject is the economic legislation passed by the Lincoln administration and the Civil War Congress—protective tariffs, the Morrill Act (subsidized land-grant colleges), federal subsidies to railroads, nationalized money, the income tax, the Homestead Act, and most egregious of all, emancipation by military force (the theft of individual property), and the huge extensions of federal power in the Fourteenth and Fifteenth amendments.

In 2006, DiLorenzo updated and trumpeted his assault on Lincoln even more forcefully in a new book, *Lincoln Unmasked: What You're Not Supposed to Know about Dishonest Abe.* In some nineteen breezy, vicious chapters, DiLorenzo seems to have made himself into the Lyon Gardiner Tyler of our era. He takes up Tyler's obsession with the alleged "Lincoln myths" and the "Lincoln cult," and again makes the Illinoisan into a dishonest abolitionist, a racist, and especially a defender of railroad corruption. Most of all, DiLorenzo harps repeatedly on his central theme: "All certified members of the Lincoln cult are champions of big government" and "the deification of Lincoln has always been part of a not so-hidden agenda to expand the size and scope of the American state far beyond what the founding fathers—especially Jeffersonians—envisioned." Lincoln "destroyed" the Constitution, as did the New Deal and the Great Society, and hence, in DiLorenzo's right-wing rallying cry, libertarians must save it.[26]

There is little likelihood that the DiLorenzos of the Right will make significant numbers of Americans hate Lincoln, but much of his argument looks like only a slightly angrier, heightened version of the campaign manual of movement conservatives during the George W. Bush administration. They can never appear to hate Lincoln—and do not need to—but they do tend to hate government, and they are very much interested in confirming judges and passing legislation that would roll back the activist-interventionist government, and the beginnings of the regulatory state, that the original Republicans created. The struggles over historical memory—which version of the past or of a great president's legacy shall win out in pubic debates—are very much about how Americans define the nature of our democracy in relation to the past. And Lincoln's image and reputation are once again at the heart of how Americans debate the course of policy in the wake of the economic collapse of 2008 and the election of Barack Obama.

There remains one major Southern body of thought and writing on Lincoln to assess. Lincoln became the focus of a Southern literary and scholarly tradition in the latter half of the twentieth century, especially among many Southern-born historians and novelists who came north for a graduate education and to teach. The list of those who came to largely admire Lincoln and devote portions, if not most, of their careers to studying the sixteenth president is long and formidable: Avery Craven, Bell Wiley, David Donald, David Potter, T. Harry Williams, C. Vann Woodward, and others. As a group, they would make an intriguing book-length study for an intrepid researcher. Some were expatriates of a kind who must have discarded a good deal of baggage from their youths about Lincoln to then spend years writing about him.

Donald, following the lead of his mentor, James Randall, might be said to have launched this school with his 1955 essay, "Abraham Lincoln and the American Pragmatic Tradition." Donald greatly admired the tendencies he saw in Lincoln: his anti-doctrinaire approach to political issues; his political realism above ideology; a willingness to grow and change even on some fundamental positions; and his refusal, as a good pragmatist, to make "irredeemable pledges against the future." Above all, he saw a Lincoln who always distrusted "absolutists," which Donald admiringly interpreted as Lincoln's "expression of his tragic realization of the limitations of human activity."[27]

It is this same pragmatist that the poet-novelist Robert Penn Warren came to embrace as well. In his life-long lover's quarrel with his native South, much of it written from Yale and Connecticut, Warren may have embodied best the twentieth-century Southern intellectual's need to get right with Lincoln. It was the moderate, border state, Whiggish lover of ambiguity that many Southern writers could make their own. One wonders just how much embracing Lincoln allowed the ironic and sometimes tragic worldviews and sentiments of many Southerners to therefore embrace America as well. In his *Legacy of the Civil War*, written for the centennial in 1961, Warren lovingly quotes Donald and T. Harry Williams on Lincoln's pragmatism. From his own dark view of human nature, his need to distribute guilt and blame for slavery and the war to all of humanity, and in his own neverending need to blister his own South with criticism, Warren seems to have found in his fellow-Kentuckian a way to plant his own American flag. After reading *Legacy of the Civil War* in manuscript, C. Vann Woodward wrote to this friend: "I wonder that you don't make something of Kentucky, Lincoln-Warren country between revelation-happy Yank and deduction-bitten Reb, Alsace-Lorraine of pragmatism between the crusaders."[28] For Woodward, Warren, and so many other Southerners to this day, Lincoln became an Alsace-Lorraine, a state of mind perhaps that allowed for a full intellectual fruition of their American experience.

Even this group of brilliant Southern writers and historians have sought and found the Lincoln they need and believe in. Theirs may be closer to that illusive thing, the "real" Lincoln, that we all seem to endlessly seek. Only someone of sufficient paradox and ambiguity, for Southerners or anyone else, could inspire so many divergent versions of the "real."

Notes

1. Papers presented by Christopher Phillips and William Cooper, ("Lincoln and the South" conference, The American Civil War Center at Tredegar, Richmond, VA, March 13, 2009).

2. J. G. Randall, *Lincoln and the South* (Baton Rouge: Louisiana State University Press, 1946), 1–116, esp. 45, 47, 57.

3. John Q. Anderson, ed., *Brokenburn: The Journal of Kate Stone, 1861–1868* (Baton Rouge: Louisiana State University Press, 1995), 333, 339–41.

4. The Houston papers quoted in Bell I. Wiley, *Abraham Lincoln: A Southerner's Estimate after 110 Years,* Mellon Lecture (New Orleans: Tulane University, 1975), 2–3; Edward A. Pollard, *The Lost Cause: A New Southern History of the War of the Confederates* (1867; rpr. New York: E. B. Treat & Co., n.d.), 750–52.

5. Parker in Wiley, *Abraham Lincoln: A Southerner's Estimate*, 3–4.

6. *New York Age*, December 27, 1906, Hampton University Clipping File, fiche, 272. On black memory of Lincoln in the early twentieth century, see David W. Blight, *Race and Reunion: The Civil War in American Memory* (Cambridge, MA: Harvard University Press, 2001), 369–70.

7. *Atlanta Constitution*, January 2, 1909; and see Blight, *Race and Reunion*, 336–37.

8. Mary White Ovington, "Slaves' Reminiscences of Slavery," *Independent* 68 (May 26, 1910), 1131–34.

9. Ibid., 1135–36.

10. Pollard, *Lost Cause*, 359–60.

11. Don Fehrenbacher, "The Anti-Lincoln Tradition," orig. pub. 1982, in Fehrenbacher, *Lincoln in Text and Context* (Stanford, CA: Stanford University Press, 1987), 198–99.

12. On Rutherford and UDC, Mildred Rutherford Scrapbooks, nos. 6, 9, 60, Museum of the Confederacy, Richmond, VA. Among Rutherford's speeches are such titles as "Wrongs of History Righted," and "Historical sins of Omission and Commission," in UDC Addresses, Museum of the Confederacy. See Blight, *Race and Reunion*, 279–81, 289–90; Karen L. Cox, *Dixie's Daughters: The United Daughters of the Confederacy and the Preservation of Confederate Culture* (Gainesville: University of Florida Press, 2003), 104–6, 137–38; and Fehrenbacher, "The Anti-Lincoln Tradition," 205.

13. Charles L. C. Minor, *The Real Lincoln, from the Testimony of His Contemporaries,* 4th ed. (Gastonia, NC: Atkins-Rankin, 1928), copy in Yale University Library. A useful discussion of Minor is in Michel Davis, *The Image of Lincoln in the South* (Knoxville: University of Tennessee Press, 1971), 123–25.

14. Joel Chandler Harris, *On the Wing of Occasions. Being the Authorized Version of Certain Curious Episodes of the Late Civil War, Including the Hitherto Suppressed Narrative of the Kidnapping of President Lincoln* (New York: Doubleday, 1900), 190, 193, Beinecke Library, Yale University.

15. Thomas Dixon, *The Clansman: An Historical Romance of the Ku Klux Klan (*New York: Appleton, 1905), 31–32; Thomas Dixon, *The Southerner: A Romance of the Real*

Lincoln (New York: Appleton, 1913), 543. It is remarkable that Dixon dedicated *The Southerner* to "Our first Southern-born President since Lincoln, my friend and collegemate, WOODROW WILSON."

16. Lyon Gardiner Tyler, *General Lee's Birthday* (n. p., n. d.), 19, in Davis, *Image of Lincoln in the South*, 133.

17. *Tyler's Quarterly* (October, 1930), 81; *Tyler's Quarterly* (January, 1921), 149–50, Sterling Library, Yale University. Lyon Gardiner Tyler, *John Tyler and Abraham Lincoln: Who Was the Dwarf? A Reply to a Challenge* (Richmond: 1929), 16, in Davis, *Image of Lincoln in the South*, 131.

18. *Tyler's Quarterly* (April, 1920), 223; *Tyler's Quarterly* (July, 1925), 7; *Tyler's Quarterly* (January, 1925), 151–53.

19. Charles Adams, *When in the Course of Human Events: Arguing the Case for Southern Secession* (Lanham, MD: Rowman & Littlefield, 2000); Thomas J. DiLorenzo, *The Real Lincoln: A New Look at Abraham Lincoln, His Agenda, and an Unnecessary War* (New York: Three Rivers Press, 2002).

20. See James M. McPherson, *Battle Cry of Freedom: The Civil War Era* (New York: Oxford University Press, 1988); Eric Foner, *Reconstruction: America's Unfinished Revolution, 1963–1877* (New York: Harper & Row, 1987); Thomas E. Woods, Jr., *The Politically Incorrect Guide to American History* (Washington, DC: Regnery, 2005). For a review that exposes Woods's falsehoods and right-wing political agenda, as well as simply sloppy, pseudo-scholarship, see David Greenberg, www.Slate.com, March 11, 2005. Greenberg points out that some conservative academics have denounced Woods's book, while right-wing television hosts, Sean Hannity and Pat Buchanan, offered it praise and considerable air time. The book demonstrates, Greenberg asserts, that the far right of the Republican party increasingly exhibits a "scorn for intellectual authority altogether." Woods is also an active advocate of use by states of the doctrine of "nullification" against such enactments as the recent health care reform bill, and other measures.

21. Daniel Feller, "Libertarians in the Attic, or a Tale of Two Narratives," *Reviews in American History* 32 (June, 2004), 184.

22. Adams, *When in the Course of Human Events*, 109–25, 151–55, 205.

23. Feller, "Libertarians in the Attic," 189. On Norquist, leader of the advocacy group, Americans for Tax Reform, see John Cassidy, "The Ringleader: How Grover Norquist Keeps the Conservative Movement Together," *New Yorker*, August 1, 2005, 42–53.

24. On Charles L. C. Minor's book, *The Real Lincoln*, see Merrill D. Peterson, *Lincoln in American Memory* (New York: Oxford University Press, 1995), 193. DiLorenzo, *The Real Lincoln*, 233.

25. DiLorenzo, *The Real Lincoln*, 264, 6.

26. Thomas J. DiLorenzo, *Lincoln Unmasked: What You're Not Supposed to Know about Dishonest Abe* (New York: Crown Forum, 2006), 181–82.

27. David Donald, "Abraham Lincoln and the American Pragmatic Tradition," in *Lincoln Reconsidered: Essays on the Civil War Era* (1955 rpr. New York: Vintage, 1961), 132–42.

28. Robert Penn Warren, *The Legacy of the Civil War* (1961 rpr. Cambridge, MA: Harvard University Press, 1983), 16–18; C. Vann Woodward to Robert Penn Warren, September 4, 1960, C. Vann Woodward Papers, series 1, box 59, Sterling Library, Yale University.

17

Projecting Lincoln, Projecting America

Jay Sexton

Barack Obama masterfully employed Lincoln's image during his historic presidential campaign of 2008. Obama went to great lengths to cast himself as Lincoln's heir, even launching his presidential bid on the steps of the Old State Capitol where Lincoln once warned his countrymen that "a house divided against itself cannot stand." At his inauguration Obama took the oath of office on the very Bible Lincoln used for the same purpose nearly 150 years earlier. When Obama named erstwhile nemesis Hillary Clinton his secretary of state, he cited as precedent Lincoln's "team of rivals" strategy, also the title of a recent best seller on the Lincoln administration by Doris Kearns Goodwin, as precedent for nominating an intra-party rival from New York to this top cabinet position.[1]

Yet it should be remembered that Obama is not the only recent president to lay claim to the mantle of Lincoln. How quickly we forget that his predecessor, George W. Bush, also drew power from the sixteenth president. Like Obama, Bush peppered his public addresses with references to Lincoln; he also found inspiration in a biography of Lincoln that he read while in the White House; he too recognized the electoral benefit in campaigning alongside the Great Emancipator when presenting himself as leader of "the party of Lincoln."[2]

Less known was how Bush deployed Lincoln's image in international affairs. Confronted with rampant anti-Americanism following the invasion of Iraq in 2003, the Bush administration turned to America's most iconic and revered figure for help. Shortly after being named under secretary for public diplomacy in 2005, long-time Bush advisor Karen Hughes announced the opening of "Lincoln Corners" in public libraries in Asia. This scheme extended funds to libraries to devote a corner of their space to American publications, as well as to host seminars and lectures on the United States. "I'm a big believer in those Lincoln Corners," Hughes asserted, "because it is a program that brings [to foreign peoples] a little piece of America."[3] While Hughes opened these

Lincoln Corners in Malaysia and Pakistan, the State Department completed a new Lincoln anthology for its Web site and prepared a traveling poster-board exhibit that chronicled Lincoln's life. And when Bush made the case for an interventionist foreign policy in his second inaugural address in 2005, he presented his statecraft as an extension of the thinking of his Republican predecessor. At the climax of the address, Bush quoted Lincoln as justification for an interventionist foreign policy: "The rulers of outlaw regimes can know that we still believe as Abraham Lincoln did, 'Those who deny freedom to others deserve it not for themselves; and, under the rule of a just God, cannot long retain it.'"[4]

The Bush administration's public diplomacy initiative met at best with mixed results. Lincoln Corners were one of the few institutional counters to anti-Americanism in South Asia. They also promoted laudable values like women's rights (the Web site of the Lincoln Corner in Kuala Lumpur trumpets its recent program entitled "Women in Entrepreneurship: Secrets to Success"[5]). But the Lincoln Corners became the targets for the very anti-Americanism that they sought to moderate. The Lincoln Corner in Karachi, Pakistan, ran into problems when it became difficult to find locals, who feared for their safety, to operate them. Anti-Americanism in Pakistan was too much for even the Great Emancipator to combat. "Abraham Lincoln's portrait was hanging up," the Karachi Lincoln Corner coordinator stated in 2007, "but due to threats, and the law-and-order situation, last month we took it down."[6]

Nor could the Bush administration control the lessons foreigners took from Lincoln. It perhaps was a sign of the reach of the administration's public diplomacy effort that President Pervez Musharraf invoked Lincoln during a national crisis in Pakistan in the autumn 2007. But Bush administration officials certainly did not want Musharraf to point to Lincoln as justification for his declaration of emergency powers and suspension of the constitution. Musharraf's Lincoln address placed the Bush team in the position it sought to avoid—wedged uncomfortably between its ideological objective of spreading democratic government and its strategic alliances with unsavory, strong-armed regimes.

The Bush administration was not the first to attempt to capitalize on Lincoln's stature abroad, nor was it the first to run into problems in so doing. A forgotten element of Lincoln's legacy is the role his image has played in American public diplomacy. "Abraham Lincoln," one State Department official asserted in the mid-twentieth century, "is the most saleable product this nation has to offer."[7] It is Lincoln who graces the cover of the United States Information Agency's official history of America.[8] Though not as well known as the staples of U.S. public diplomacy—the Declaration of Independence, the mythic "American dream," and, perhaps most successful of all, jazz—Lincoln nonetheless has been a recurrent symbol in American propaganda.

This essay examines U.S. projections of the sixteenth president. American propaganda is an important element of the "Global Lincoln," though not in the straightforward sense that it dictated the nature of the Lincoln imagined by those around the globe, even if this was the intention of U.S. propagandists. Rather, the importance of Lincoln propaganda lay in how it contributed to the politicization of his image by associating it with the projection of American power. That American officials promoted Lincoln abroad helped make him a contested symbol and language of international relations, a *lingua franca* of public diplomacy in the "American century."

The United States was slow to integrate public diplomacy into its foreign policy. In contrast to European governments, many of whom formalized cultural operations in the late nineteenth century, Washington lacked a permanent public diplomacy apparatus until the mid-twentieth century. This partly was a result of traditional aversions to foreign entanglement and big government. But it also stemmed from ideological certitude. With most nineteenth-century American statesmen convinced that the principles of the Declaration of Independence were destined to sweep around the globe, there was little need to bother with European-style cultural diplomacy, which many in the United States interpreted as evidence of the intrinsic unpopularity of the ideas being promoted.

The lack of institutionalized public diplomacy, of course, did not mean that Americans shied away from promoting their culture, values, and practices. Some U.S. diplomats in the nineteenth century projected images of Lincoln abroad to advance American political interests.[9] In such instances, however, individual diplomats acted on their own accord, seizing the opportunity to use Lincoln as a political instrument in a specific context, rather than as part of a larger strategy formulated in Washington. Other American promoters of Lincoln acted independently of government, yet often served its interests nonetheless: missionaries, exporters, travelers, and authors all functioned as unofficial propagandists in the nineteenth century. Perhaps the most significant way Americans spread word of Lincoln abroad in the decades immediately after his assassination was through biographies sold or reprinted abroad. Herndon's *Life of Lincoln* and *Abraham Lincoln* co-authored by John Hay and John Nicolay, in particular, commanded a wide readership outside of the United States. Lesser known biographies and pamphlets on Lincoln also contributed to his global celebrity. It appears that Lord Charnwood, the Englishman whose 1916 study of Lincoln became a canonical work on both sides of the Atlantic, first became interested in Lincoln when as a boy he stumbled upon a biography published in London by traveling American journalist Charles Godfrey Leland.[10] One should not overstate the significance of such an example, for Charnwood's *Lincoln* was shaped more by his liberalism and the Great War than it was by the biography he read as a boy. But it does show that Americans helped Lincoln travel, particularly in the English-speaking world.

The form that this traveling Lincoln took varied. With Americans themselves in great disagreement on Lincoln's legacy, there was no single national line projected abroad. A reader in the Bodleian Library in Oxford in the 1930s might well pick up the *Lincoln* of Hay and Nicolay and conclude that Americans thought favorably of their sixteenth president. Or a reader might with equal plausibility select Edgar Lee Masters' *Lincoln the Man* and conclude that Americans did not think very highly of the Great Emancipator.[11] Shaping foreign perceptions of Lincoln was of such importance to some Americans that they were moved to send unsolicited letters to foreign libraries. One American wrote to the Bodleian Librarian in 1931 to protest "against the insanely audacious scurrility of a book on Lincoln by a degenerate, second-growth, rebel by the name of Masters. I most sincerely trust that the great Bodleian Library has not, nor will not, put such a book within reach of the Oxford students." (Alas, Oxonians have been able to call up Masters' book from the Bodleian's vast subterranean stacks since its publication in 1931).[12] Private promotions of Lincoln also could come into conflict with the views and policies of the U.S. government. While Congress passed neutrality legislation aimed at keeping the United States out of the Spanish Civil War in the 1930s, an assortment of American communists and anti-fascists ignored these restrictions and took the fight directly to Franco's nationalists through a volunteer force called the Abraham Lincoln Brigade. "Today it is left to the Communist Party to revive the words of Lincoln," declared Earl Browder, the general secretary of the Communist Party-USA. This certainly was not the view of Lincoln that officials in the Roosevelt administration wanted to project abroad.[13]

The discord among Americans concerning Lincoln's legacy confounded the few formal attempts that were made to project the sixteenth president in the decades after his death. These mostly occurred in government-supported schools within American colonial possessions, namely in the Philippines and in schools for Native Americans. Educators in both places viewed American history as a means of achieving their objective of "social engineering," as it was called in the Philippines, or "Americanizing the American Indians," in the parlance of Indian reservations. They calculated that Lincoln's biography would inculcate the somewhat paradoxical values they sought to promote: deference to the United States and an individualist spirit to counter traditional tribal loyalties. "The Indian heroes of the camp-fire need not be disparaged," one leading American educator stated, "but gradually and unobtrusively the heroes of American homes and history may be substituted as models and ideals."[14]

The history texts most often used in these schools, Scudder's *History of the United States for the Use of Beginners* (in Indian schools) and Baldwin's *Barnes's Elementary History of the United States Told in Biographies* (in the Philippines), presented Lincoln as an exemplar of this sort of patriotic, yet independent and self-made man. These texts celebrated Lincoln's character and early years, devoting surprisingly little space to his political principles and career. Both Scudder and Baldwin sidestepped any topic that might prove controversial, even those which might broaden Lincoln's appeal to Native

American and Filipino students, such as his opposition to the war of conquest against Mexico. Instead, these texts constructed a simplistic and linear biographical narrative of the archetypal self-made man. The self-made man theme appeared explicitly in lesson plans. At the end of the chapter on Lincoln, *Barnes's Elementary History* asked students to "name some of the qualities of his character which made it possible for him to become a great man."[15]

Yet the self-made man was not the only Lincoln that spoke to Native Americans and Filipinos. Sioux students might have wondered if the magnanimous Lincoln portrayed in their textbook—the Lincoln who had no intention of dictating the terms of peace to the defeated Confederacy—would have agreed with taking them away from their families, cutting their hair, and "civilizing" them in far-away schools such as Philadelphia's Lincoln Institute.[16] Filipino students might have contrasted the textbook Lincoln they were instructed to emulate with the Lincoln invoked by the American Anti-Imperialist League. The League's 1899 manifesto cited Lincoln to buttress its case for withdrawing from the Philippines (ironically, the manifesto used the same Lincoln quotation that Bush employed in 2005 to justify an interventionist foreign policy: "Those who deny freedom to others deserve it not for themselves; and, under the rule of a just God, cannot long retain it"[17]). That Lincoln's story did not invariably lead to the ends envisioned by American educators is revealed by Luis Taruc, a Filipino communist-nationalist who opposed the foreign occupation of his homeland in the mid-twentieth century. Like many men of his generation, Taruc idolized Lincoln and could recite by memory the Gettysburg Address. "I cherish Jefferson and Abraham Lincoln, especially Lincoln," he declared. But Taruc's Lincoln inspired not obedience or gratitude toward the United States, but resistance to foreign colonialism.[18]

These early formal projections were more successful in disseminating Lincoln than in controlling his image. But even in terms of the spread of Lincoln's image, the significance of such propaganda campaigns should not be overstated. More important to Lincoln's rising global celebrity than governmental projections was the larger geo-political context. The American promotion of Lincoln in the late nineteenth and early twentieth centuries owed much to the structures and circuits of the British Empire. Not only did Lincoln's story circulate within the vast British Empire, but Americans also used its networks—its communications lines and telegraphs, its publishing houses and missionary networks, its commercial routes and political contacts—to spread word of their sixteenth president. Influential American biographies, for example, were reprinted by London publishers and then disseminated around the British world.[19] In the case of the promotion of Lincoln, as in so much else, the British Empire complemented and fostered the expansion of the United States. Lincoln's global celebrity, of course, was also the result of the emergence of the United States as a global power. The increase in American power manifested itself not only in rising military might and the outright colonial expansion of

1898, but more often in the projection of the informal power of American commerce, culture, and ideas.[20] It is perhaps no coincidence that Lincoln's heyday in foreign lands corresponded with the projection of American power: in Latin America in the late nineteenth century, in Britain and Europe in the early twentieth, and in Africa and Asia in the Cold War.[21]

One of the attractions of Lincoln's story—to Americans and non-Americans alike—was that it helped to explain the emergence of the United States as a global power, a phenomenon which impacted ever more peoples in the decades after his assassination. This did not mean, of course, that all embraced the particular forms that American power took. Indeed, the conception of a mythic and flawless Lincoln functioned as the standard to judge, or even redirect, the actions of subsequent American statesmen. The malleable Lincoln could serve the interests of those from across the political spectrum: whereas Taruc deployed Lincoln to oppose the American occupation of the Philippines, British liberals invoked him to prompt the United States to more fully engage in international affairs. Whatever the specific objective, more and more peoples around the globe came to see Lincoln's utility in the court of international opinion and public relations.

The greatest attempt by the United States government to project and control Lincoln's image abroad occurred during the 1959 sesquicentennial of his birth. By this time the United States had institutionalized and professionalized public diplomacy. The watershed for this development was the two world wars, particularly the second. Confronted with enemies armed with sophisticated propaganda operations, American officials developed their own means of waging the battle for hearts and minds. The Office of War Information during the Second World War established an overseas branch that, among other things, broadcast over the airways the radio programming of Voice of America. The onset of the Cold War necessitated the continuation of public diplomacy efforts, though the bureaucratic structure to oversee such operations remained a matter of debate even after the Eisenhower administration created the United States Information Agency (USIA) in 1953. A hostile Congress cut the USIA's budget in 1957 and many called for it to be restructured or placed under the control of the State Department. George Allen, the USIA director, feared that there existed a "suspicion—that is particularly acute in Congress—that there is something fundamentally evil and un-American about a propaganda agency."[22]

The Lincoln sesquicentennial provided the USIA with a golden opportunity to demonstrate its value to critics in Congress. Working alongside it was the Abraham Lincoln Sesquicentennial Commission (ALSC), a body established by Congress in 1957 to coordinate commemorations of the sixteenth president. Headed by Republican Senator John Sherman Cooper of Kentucky, the commission appointed noted African American political scientist and diplomat

Ralph Bunche to oversee its international programs. Both the USIA and the ALSC recognized the bureaucratic and political utility of the sesquicentennial. A successful operation would demonstrate the value of a propaganda agency and federally sponsored commemoration commissions to domestic opponents (like the USIA, the ALSC attracted criticism, particularly when reports surfaced in 1958 of irregular expenditure of public funds).[23] In the larger picture, both the USIA and the ALSC viewed the promotion of Lincoln abroad as inextricably linked to the mobilization of patriotism and nationalism at home. The overseas activities of the sesquicentennial aimed to reassure Americans that one of their greatest statesmen and symbols attracted adherents abroad, that their traditions and ideals had traction across the globe, and that they were not alone in the battle against the Soviet Union.[24]

The Lincoln sesquicentennial could not have come at a better time for the United States. The Soviet's successful launch of *Sputnik* in 1957 was a public relations disaster for the United States. The nation that promoted its scientific enterprise and technological superiority now trailed the Soviet Union in the space race. More problematic was domestic racial conflict and the persistence of racial segregation in the American South. The 1957 confrontation in Little Rock regarding school integration was widely reported around the globe, thanks in part to Soviet propaganda. Little Rock undermined America's moral authority abroad. Secretary of State John Foster Dulles feared that the episode "is ruining our foreign policy. The effect of this in Asia and Africa will be worse for us than Hungary was for the Russians." A crowd in Caracas pelted the visiting motorcade of Vice President Richard Nixon a year later with shouts of "Little Rock."[25]

The sesquicentennial presented an opportunity to counter these public diplomacy setbacks. A self-educated man, Lincoln personified American enterprise and his role in ending slavery could be deployed to help erase memories of Little Rock. What ensued was one of the most sophisticated and coordinated public diplomacy operations of its time. Barely three weeks of the sesquicentennial year had passed before an official report boasted "that the Lincoln Sesquicentennial is already the most successful commemorative program since [the USIA] has been in business."[26] The scale and array of activities dwarfed previous commemorations of Benjamin Franklin and Theodore Roosevelt. The USIA distributed around the globe information packets on Lincoln, filled with photographs, brochures, and essays written by leading American scholars such as Carl Sandburg, David Potter, and David Donald. Ground agents of the United States Information Service (USIS), the name used by USIA branches in foreign countries, issued press releases, rented cinemas to show Lincoln films, and displayed Lincolniana in High Street windows. Voice of America broadcasts trumpeted Lincoln's achievements. American historians went on all-expense paid lecture tours and USIS agents worked with local educators to hold school events and Lincoln essay contests. Existing Lincoln statues hosted wreath-laying ceremonies, while new ones were unveiled.

The USIA left no stone unturned. American servicemen presented Berlin Mayor Willy Brandt with a real-size replica of Lincoln's boyhood log cabin. In Trinidad and Tobago, the USIA sponsored a "Lincoln Anniversary Walking Race" of nine miles, the distance a young Lincoln allegedly walked to visit a sick friend. Back at home, the USIA encouraged Americans to participate in the projection of Lincoln abroad. Under the "People to People" program, private citizens composed letters to foreign correspondents that unsubtly drew attention to the great Illinoisan. Prominent foreign visitors to Washington received Lincolniana in view of the cameras. An Apostolic envoy returned to the Vatican with a Latin translation of the Gettysburg Address; other foreign leaders packed into their bags miniatures of the bust of Lincoln by sculptor Leonard Volk. Senator Cooper presented representatives of eighty-two countries with complete microfilm editions of the Lincoln Papers. Those nations lacking microfilm facilities received copies of Basler's *Collected Works of Abraham Lincoln*.[27]

Any reader of the records of the USIA cannot but be impressed by its flexible and adaptive structure. Officials in Washington gave much leeway to their field agents to pursue their own initiatives. So long as an event or display promoted Lincoln in a positive light, the USIA supported the endeavor. The most successful enterprises were those that collaborated with host nations and tailored Lincoln to comport with local tastes. "Gandhi and Lincoln, men of common ideals," headlined one USIA press release in Madras ahead of a symposium organized by Indian scholars comparing the two leaders.[28] The sesquicentennial campaign went to great lengths to cast Lincoln in a cosmopolitan light. USIA activities and the lecture series of academics emphasized, for example, the connections Lincoln had with Juarez (in Mexico), Garibaldi (Italy), and trade-unionism (Great Britain).

This approach aimed to do more than simply to connect Lincoln to other leaders. It sought to use Lincoln as a means of Americanizing the heroes and traditions of other nations. In a memo to the USIA under the subject heading "Foreign Lincolns," ALSC Executive Director William Baringer offered his thoughts on how to present other national heroes in the light of Lincoln (fortunately, the USIA would correct the errors):

India's Lincoln—Mohandas Karachand Ghandhi [*sic*]; Brazil's Lincoln would have to be Simon Bolívar; England's Lincoln is not so simple—it would have to include, chronologically, William Pitt, the younger, who kept Napoleon out of England and thus performed a Lincolnian service to his native land. Secondly, there was Sir Robert Peel, who in the Reform bill of 1832 began the democratizing of the House of Commons franchise. Thirdly, after the Civil War, William Ewart Gladstone carried the enfranchising to the logical conclusion. So England's Lincoln would be Mr. Gladstone Peel Pitt, Jr. Japan's Lincoln is a tougher proposition.

That would have to be the nobles who overthrew the Shogunate and established constitutional monarchy in Nippon. What were their names? I have no idea, but they can be looked up, if important. To compensate for the failure to give names in the case of Japan—Switzerland's: Arnold Winkelried; Republic of Philippines: Manuel Queson [*sic*]; United States of Indonesia: Sukarno; Ghana: Kwame Nkruma [*sic*].[29]

This approach amounted to the Americanization of other nation's heroes, for Baringer made clear that such figures were Lincolns, not vice versa. American propaganda did not present Lincoln as the "American Gandhi" or the "American Nkrumah," even though this might have enhanced Lincoln's reputation in certain places. The greatest task before American officials in the sesquicentennial was not just to introduce Lincoln to foreign audiences, but to promote a version of Lincoln that advanced the political and diplomatic objectives of Cold War America. The "foreign Lincoln" strategy sought to achieve this by subsuming other icons into an American tradition that led inexorably away from communism and the Soviet Union. Most important, this tactic sought to moderate potentially subversive national heroes—particularly Third World anti-colonial nationalists—by presenting them as apostles of Lincoln's measured liberalism.

The Americanization of "foreign Lincolns" was the hallmark of the signature event of the USIA's sesquicentennial campaign, an hour-long Voice of America program entitled *In Search of Lincoln*. The program included statements from eight heads of state, as well as several ordinary people from around the globe, all of whom cited Lincoln as a great inspiration. The Lincoln these leaders and ordinary folks invoked varied: Ghanian Prime Minister Kwame Nkrumah emphasized anti-colonialism, while a housewife from his country spoke of Lincoln as the archetypal family man; West German Chancellor Konrad Adenauer called attention to Lincoln the democrat; South Vietnamese President Ngo Dihn Diem highlighted Lincoln's role as a national unifier. The brilliance of the Voice of America program was in how it glossed over the different and potentially subversive Lincolns these national leaders invoked by subsuming them into the narrative devise of a mystic, quasi-religious search for Lincoln in the world of 1959. *In Search of Lincoln* reduced the man to a set of simple catechisms that comported with the values, principles, and practices the USIA sought to promote abroad: "Lincoln, the convinced democrat"; "Lincoln the woodsman, rail-splitter, surveyor"; "the humanitarian"; "the consecrated unifier and pacifier of the greatest democracy of his time"; "the family man." Wherever the Voice of America looked for Lincoln, it found him "in living form . . . in people's minds . . . and in people's hearts." The world, in other words, was full of Abraham Lincolns; it was full of Americans.[30]

The USIA presented a Lincoln stripped of complexity in order to broaden his appeal and sidestep controversy. The Lincoln that appeared in U.S.

propaganda in 1959 was disproportionately the young Lincoln. As in the earlier textbooks used in schools for Native Americans and Filipinos, the Lincoln projected most often was the man who personified the ideal of democratic self-improvement, the ambitious rail-splitter by day who studied law by firelight at night. The USIA campaign included surprisingly little about Lincoln the statesman and president. Topics such as civil liberties, wartime politics, and race were avoided whenever possible. Though credited with freeing the slaves, the Great Emancipator trope appeared much less than one might assume. This was likely a result of its entanglement with racial issues and how it might invite examination of Lincoln's ambiguous position on civil rights for African Americans.

The USIA could not dictate or control all aspects of the sesquicentennial campaign. Foreign collaborators, academic lecturers, and even some USIS field agents strayed from the top-down directives from Washington, presenting fuller versions of Lincoln that spoke to local concerns. The many partnerships the USIA forged with private enterprise, both within and outside the United States, helped to broaden the sesquicentennial campaign, though it necessarily diversified the Lincoln that was being projected.[31] If many of these accounts of Lincoln were more nuanced and complex than the official propaganda, they still tended to present Lincoln in a favorable light. The same cannot be said of foreign audiences at USIA events. The records of the sesquicentennial are peppered with reports of audiences challenging the view of Lincoln sanctioned by American propagandists. An Indian intellectual questioned the phraseology and meaning of some of Lincoln's signature speeches; an attendee at an event in South Korea contended that slavery continued to exist in the United States after Lincoln's death; a Moroccan schoolboy reminded the USIA that "the recent disturbances of Little Rock show that the slave problem isn't settled yet."[32] Such comments were more than just interpretations of Lincoln the historical figure. Contesting the USIA's depiction of Lincoln became proxy for a political debate concerning the nature and projection of American power in the twentieth century. The more the USIA promoted Lincoln, the more he became a contested symbol, a metaphoric language in which to debate contemporary events.

It is a credit to the USIA that it at times invited, rather than suppressed, alternative interpretations of Lincoln. This was the case not only in its flexible structure and partnerships that gave surprising autonomy to those on the ground, but also in specific programs, most notably a series of Lincoln essay competitions for school children. This scheme brought Lincoln into schools around the globe, most of which did not normally include American history on the syllabus. USIS operatives lured schools into participating by offering books and teaching materials; it attracted students with the allure of $25 awards and the grand prize of an all expense paid trip to the United States. Many students nonetheless resented an American propaganda agency assigning them extra homework. "I was determined not to like the man I had to write about," the grand prize winner from St. Kitts, Christopher Vanier, later recalled in his memoir, "He was a dead, white, political leader, long gone: nothing to do with me."[33]

Such sentiments shaped Vanier's essay, which was an unlikely winner considering its repudiation of Lincoln hagiography. This precocious seventeen year old with no background in American history anticipated the revisionist account of Lincoln that scholars would develop in the coming decades. Vanier argued that "Lincoln in his glory is indebted to the Negro race, the poor and the downtrodden, because the major part of his eminence arises from his defence of them, and only through them did he fulfil his aspirations." Though Vanier acknowledged Lincoln's anti-slavery beliefs, he reminded his readers that, far from blazing the trail of emancipation, the American president "followed in the wake of British freedom lovers" who had abolished slavery in the British West Indies back in the 1830s. Yet for as much as Vanier wanted to knock Lincoln down from his pedestal, he found himself drawn to him, arguing that in the Civil War more than the "American nation [was] at stake—the whole cause of humanity—freedom—popular government—that elusive conception 'democracy,' were being evaluated." When Vanier read of Lincoln's assassination, he later recalled that he "felt for the man; his loss was dramatic and unacceptable. It made me reassess everything he had done. . . . Simultaneously, I won and lost my struggle to criticise the man."[34]

ALSC press releases, however, glossed over the complexities of Vanier's essay, portraying it as a straight-forward celebration of Lincoln by a young foreigner. American press reports on Vanier's visit to the United States, which included a trip to Illinois and an award ceremony in Washington, were similarly banal. Rather than explaining what Lincoln meant to this young West Indian, they detailed his encounters with comic books and baseball at Wrigley Field. "Teen testifies to universal Lincoln love" read a headline in the *Chicago Tribune*. This was no doubt the intention of the USIA, which feared that the whole episode might somehow expose the racial fault-line at home (USIA memos described Vanier, variously, as "a negro," "colored," and "by race from India"; in truth, his racial background reflected the full diversity of the region from which he came). In the charged context of the civil rights movement, Vanier's trip had the potential to turn into a public diplomacy disaster, not unlike the earlier international fallout from the racial discrimination that confronted visiting diplomats from the Caribbean and Africa. The USIA went to great lengths to ensure that Vanier returned to the West Indies with a positive image of the United States, even arranging a visit for the young student with an African American role model, Ralph Bunche, at the United Nations. So too did the propaganda agency seek to avoid controversy at home when it placed Vanier in the home of a "typical middle class colored family" during his visit to Chicago.[35]

These efforts paid off, for racial issues are notable for their absence in contemporary accounts of Vanier's trip. Indeed, USIA officials considered sidestepping racial controversy throughout the sesquicentennial campaign one of their greatest achievements. "Polishing up his greatness this year has not brought Little Rock to mind among West Indians, as I secretly feared it might," one USIS agent in Kingston, Jamaica reported, "as much as it has revealed a deep American concern of long standing for justice and fairness to all, as exemplified by the one American hero who most nearly approaches sainthood."[36] When compared to the Civil War centennial (1961–65), which became ensnared in sectional politics and the civil rights movement, this was no small accomplishment.[37]

The Lincoln sesquicentennial, of course, did not solve all of the United States' image problems, which ultimately were rooted in domestic and foreign policies over which American propagandists had little control. It is revealing that the USIA considered the negative accomplishment of avoiding racial controversy as a triumph. Yet, relative to other public diplomacy operations of its time, the sesquicentennial stacks up rather well. Voice of America re-aired its Lincoln programs due to popular demand; USIS agents in the field reported unprecedented interest in the United States; articles celebrating Lincoln appeared in newspapers and journals around the globe. Lincoln's "house divided" theme became shorthand for the struggle between "Soviet slavery" and "American freedom," a point that Willy Brandt picked up on in his visit to Springfield during the sesquicentennial. As Richard Current, the Civil War historian and USIA lecturer in India, put it, "In the present 'cold war,' we have one very valuable asset that the Russians do not: we have an Abraham Lincoln." The final report of the ALSC boasted that Lincoln's "image as the symbol of the free man grows in the hearts of people the world over . . . the name 'Lincoln' is almost as familiar to the schoolboy in Calcutta as it is to the one in Des Moines, Iowa."[38]

An irony of Lincoln's international celebrity is that it has been both an asset and liability to American propagandists. In their projections of the sixteenth president, American officials have found receptive audiences around the globe. Yet Lincoln's fame, which often has preceded public diplomacy initiatives, has enabled foreign peoples to counter American propaganda with their own interpretation of the American president. This paradox helps to explain why American officials have shied away from defining Lincoln's legacy and meaning. In almost all cases, American propaganda has emphasized the safe theme of the self-made man or reduced him to platitudes so broad and general that few could contest them. This approach has broadened the appeal of Lincoln's image, but necessarily has mitigated its utility as an instrument of public diplomacy.

Of course, it is impossible to measure the extent to which Lincoln's global celebrity is a result of American activities such as those during the sesquicentennial. But what is clear is that the promotion of Lincoln abroad has helped make him a recurrent symbol in international relations and public diplomacy. It is in part because the United States has promoted Lincoln that peoples and statesmen in other countries have pointed to him to justify their actions or to condemn those of the United States. Such invocations of Lincoln have more to do with the reality of American power than they do with the man himself. It is Lincoln's peculiar international legacy both to personify the rising United States and to serve as the standard to judge how his successors have since deployed its power.

Notes

1. *The Washington Post*, November 19, 2008; Doris Kearns Goodwin, *Team of Rivals: The Political Genius of Abraham Lincoln* (New York: Simon and Schuster, 2005).

2. David W. Blight, "The Theft of Lincoln in Scholarship, Politics, and Public Memory," in Eric Foner, ed., *Our Lincoln: New Perspectives on Lincoln and His World* (New York: W.W. Norton, 2008), 269–82; *Newsweek*, August 14, 2006; *Harper's Magazine*, February 12, 2008.

3. Hughes' comments can be found at www.state.gove/r/us/2005/55934.htm.

4. Bush's second inaugural can be found in *The Washington Post*, January 21, 2005.

5. http://usembassymalaysia.org.my/lincoln/KLCity.htm accessed July 7, 2009.

6. *Chicago Tribune*, October 30, 2007.

7. State Department official quoted in *Lincoln Lore*, no. 1463 (January 1960).

8. This is the case for the 1990 edition. United States Information Agency, *An Outline of American History* (Washington, DC: United States Information Agency, 1990).

9. See, for example, Michael Vorenberg's discussion of John Bigelow's activities in Paris in this book.

10. Lord Charnwood, *Abraham Lincoln* (London: Echo Library, 2007, reprint from 1916), 287; Charles G. Leland, *Abraham Lincoln* (London: Marcus Ward & Co., 1879).

11. For Lincoln's legacy within the United States, see Merrill D. Peterson, *Lincoln in American Memory* (New York: Oxford University Press, 1995); Barry Schwartz, *Abraham Lincoln and the Forge of National Memory* (Chicago: University of Chicago Press, 2003); Blight, "The Theft of Lincoln in Scholarship, Politics, and Public Memory."

12. Robert Reed to Librarian of the Bodleian, March 28, 1931, enclosed in Bodleian's copy of John G. Nicolay, *A Short Life of Abraham Lincoln* (London: T. Werner Laurie, Ltd., 1902).

13. Browder quoted in Peterson, *Lincoln in American Memory*, 319. For the Abraham Lincoln Brigade, see Peter N. Carroll, *The Odyssey of the Abraham Lincoln Brigade: Americans in the Spanish Civil War* (Stanford, CA: Stanford University Press, 1994).

14. Quoted in Francis P. Prucha, *The Great Father: The United States Government and the American Indians* (Lincoln: University of Nebraska Press, 1984), 704–5. For American educators in the Philippines, see Glenn Anthony May, *Social Engineering in the Philippines: The Aims, Execution, and Impact of American Colonial Policy, 1900–1913* (Westport, CT: Greenwood Pub Group, 1980).

15. Horace E. Scudder, *A History of the United States of America for the Use of Beginners* (New York: Taintor Brothers & Co., 1890), 222–23; James Baldwin, *Barnes's Elementary History of the United States Told in Biographies* (New York: American Book Co., 1903), 312–31. For an analysis of textbooks in this period, see Ruth M. Elson, *Guardians of Tradition: American Schoolbooks of the Nineteenth Century* (Lincoln: University of Nebraska Press, 1964).

16. Jeffrey Ostler, *The Plains Sioux and U.S. Colonialism from Lewis and Clark to Wounded Knee* (Cambridge, MA: Cambridge University Press, 2004).

17. Daniel B. Schirmer and Stephen Rosskamm Shalom, eds., *The Philippines Reader: A History of Colonialism, Neocolonialism, Dictatorship, and Resistance* (Cambridge, MA: South End Press, 1987), 29–31.

18. Stanley Karnow, *In Our Image: America's Empire in the Philippines* (New York: Random House, 1989), 338–39.

19. For example, a London publishing house reprinted an abridged version of Hay and Nicolay in 1902. See John G. Nicolay, *A Short Life of Abraham Lincoln* (London: T. Werner Laurie, Ltd., 1902).

20. A good place to start on these themes is Ian Tyrrell, *Transnational Nation: United States History in Global Perspective since 1789* (Basingstoke: Palgrave Macmillan, 2007), 95–117; Emily Rosenberg, *Spreading the American Dream: American Economic and Cultural Expansion, 1890–1945* (New York: Hill and Wang, 1982); Alfred E. Eckes and Thomas W. Zeiler, *Globalization and the American Century* (Cambridge: Cambridge University Press, 2003).

21. See the discussion of this point in chapter 1 of this book.

22. Nicholas J. Cull, *The Cold War and the United States Information Agency: American Propaganda and Public Diplomacy, 1945–1989* (Cambridge: Cambridge University Press, 2008), 151; Laura Belmonte, *Selling the American Way: U.S. Propaganda and the Cold War* (Philadelphia: University of Pennsylvania Press, 2008); Frank Ninkovich, *The Diplomacy of Ideas: U.S. Foreign Policy and Cultural Relations, 1938–1950* (Cambridge: Cambridge University Press, 1981).

23. See the press clippings in U.S. Lincoln Sesquicentennial Commission Office of the Research Director Records, 1957–1960, Box 35, Folder 1, Library of Congress, Washington, DC (hereafter USLSC Records, LoC).

24. Richard M. Fried, *The Russians Are Coming! The Russians Are Coming!: Pageantry and Patriotism in Cold-War America* (New York: Oxford University Press, 1998), 119–22.

25. Dulles quoted in Cary Fraser, "Crossing the Color Line in Little Rock: The Eisenhower Administration and the Dilemma of Race for U.S. Foreign Policy," *Diplomatic History* 24:2 (Spring 2000), 233–64; Mary Dudziak, *Cold War Civil Rights: Race and the Image of American Democracy* (Princeton, NJ: Princeton University Press, 2002), 115–51; Thomas Borstelmann, *The Cold War and the Color Line: American Race Relations in the Global Arena* (Cambridge, MA: Harvard University Press, 2003), 104. Routt to Child, November 14, 1958, Box 32, USIA Folder, Lincoln Sesquicentennial Commission Files, RG148, NARA II (hereafter LSC Files, NARA II).

26. Executive Director Report, January 24, 1959, Box 36, USLSC Records, LoC.

27. The preceding two paragraphs draw on the country by country reports from the USIA in Box 14, LSC Files, NARA II; information on the People to People program can be found in Box 25, People to People Folder, LSC Files, NARA II.

28. USIS Madras press release, January 4, 1959, Box 16, India Folder, LSC Files, NARA II.

29. Baringer to Child, January 13, 1959, Box 32, USIA Folder, LSC Files, NARA II.

30. For the original sound recording, see Abraham Lincoln Sesquicentennial Commission, *In Search of Lincoln*, RG 148, Motion Picture, Sound, and Video Records Section, Special Media Archives Services Division (NWCS-M), NARA II. A copy of the text can be found in Box 32, USIA Folder, LSC Files, NARA II.

31. The USIA's relationships with private enterprise are much commented upon in recent studies. See H-Diplo Roundtable review of Nicholas Cull, *The Cold War and the United States Information Agency*, Volume XI, No. 6, November 13, 2009.

32. Richard N. Current, "Through India with Abraham Lincoln," *Lincoln Herald* 62 (Winter 1960), 161–65; *Lincoln Lore* no. 1463 (January 1960); Morocco Folder, Box 18, LSC Files, NARA II.

33. Christopher Vanier, *Caribbean Chemistry: Tales from St Kitts* (Kingston upon Thames: Kingston University Press, 2009), 307.

34. Vanier, *Caribbean Chemistry*, 321–22.

35. For Vanier and the essay competition, see Box 18, USIA Essay Contest Folder, LSC Files, NARA II; *Chicago Tribune*, August 15, 1959. For USIA concerns about racial controversy, see "Memo," July 28, 1959; "USIS report from Port of Spain," July 15, 1959; Dunlap to Walton, July 10, 1959; all in Box 18, USIA Essay Contest Folder, LSC Files, NARA II. See also, *The Lincoln Sesquicentennial Intelligencer* Vol. 1, No. 4 (September 1959); *Ebony*, February 1960, 104–8.

36. Noonan to Fisher, May 28, 1959, Box 18, USIA Essay Contest Folder, LSC Files, NARA II.

37. For the cantankerous Civil War centennial, see Robert J. Cook, *Troubled Commemoration: The American Civil War Centennial, 1961–1965* (Baton Rouge: Louisiana State University Press, 2007).

38. Thomas F. Schwartz, "Lincoln and the Cold War," *Abraham Lincoln Association Newsletter* 6:1 (Spring 2004); Richard N. Current, "Through India with Abraham Lincoln," *Lincoln Herald* 62 (Winter 1960), 161–65; *Abraham Lincoln Sesquicentennial Commission: Final Report* (Washington, DC: U.S. Government Printing Office, 1960), 100–26.

Foreign Language Biographies of Lincoln

George Scratcherd

A full assessment of the contours of Lincoln's global presence and influence requires some means of empirical measurement. To that end, this appendix quantifies foreign biographies of Lincoln based on various library catalogues, union library catalogues, and bibliographies, especially WorldCat and the appendix of foreign language works in Jay Monaghan's *Lincoln Bibliography, 1839–1939*.[1] Using a broad definition of biographical works, this research reveals 654 works in 53 foreign languages. While this does not represent a definitive list of foreign language biographies, nor conclusively demonstrate which languages have produced the most books on Lincoln, it provides an indication of their probable numbers and presents a general overview of trends, both within and across nations.

It is surprising that Chinese languages and dialects might constitute the most numerous of foreign language lives. The research conducted found 120 distinct Chinese biographies, compared to 90 in German, 75 in Spanish, and 63 in French. The predominance of Chinese literature on Lincoln is a recent phenomenon—85 editions of Chinese biographies have been published since 1980, 43 of them since 2000. By contrast the greatest concentration of German biographies was published in the years immediately following Lincoln's assassination. The Chinese figure may be slightly misleading as 50 are translations and 28 seem to be intended for juvenile audiences. However, the number of biographies in other languages is also inflated by translations. Of the 90 German biographies 39 are translations, as are 36 of those in Spanish. If only original biographies focused specifically on Lincoln and written for adult audiences are included, then Chinese works stand-out less. Of such works 46 are in Chinese, 47 in French, 42 in German, 27 in Japanese, and 19 in Spanish.

The surge in Chinese lives of Lincoln in recent decades is no doubt due to China's increasing openness and contact with the United States. It might also be that Lincoln has a particular significance in China because he defeated secession and maintained the Union—acts which raise obvious parallels to the current situations Chinese leaders face in Taiwan and Tibet (a point explored in De-min Tao's essay in this volume).[2] However, a large proportion of the biographies in Chinese have had editions published in Taiwan. Forty-five editions of Lincoln biographies have been published there, compared to 96 in mainland China. It seems that analogies to Taiwan can only partially explain Lincoln's recent influence in Chinese contexts. The traction of the American president in other national and historical contexts might provide a further explanation for his presence in contemporary China: Lincoln's image has had its greatest political potency in places where the liberal and democratic values he embodies have been most contested (a point examined in chapter one of this volume).[3]

Numerous foreign-language biographical works about Lincoln followed in the wake of his death, with 65 works published in 1865 and 1866. The large production of studies in these years was principally driven by works in German and French, many of which were published letters, speeches, orations, and eulogies containing biographical sketches of Lincoln. By the 1870s this interest had diminished, but since the turn of the twentieth century foreign language biographies have been produced with increasing frequency right up to recent times, especially since 2000. Peaks in the numbers published coincide with the centennial and sesquicentennial of Lincoln's birth. A spate of publications also appeared in 1925, many of which were translations of Emanuel Hertz's essay *Abraham Lincoln: The Seer*, which portrayed Lincoln as a divinely-inspired prophet.[4] While Chinese biographies closely mirror the global growth in Lincoln studies in recent decades, German language biographies have not. There has been a small but steady production of biographies in German each decade. Until the mid-twentieth century, their publication also closely followed the pattern of all foreign language works, with peaks in 1865–66, 1909 and 1925 (that being said, no less than three original German biographies of Lincoln appeared in the bicentennial year of 2009).

Spanish-language works mostly have been published outside Spain. Nineteen editions have been published in Spain, 19 in the United States, and 41 in Latin America. Similarly, 16 of 22 editions of Portuguese works have been published in Brazil. Judged by this measure, Lincoln is a more visible figure in Latin America than in the Iberian Peninsula. Spanish biographical works have also been a predominantly late-twentieth century phenomenon, more like Chinese than German in this respect. Indeed, works in Spanish have closely followed the trend of all foreign works in the second half of the twentieth century, especially the surge in biographic works since 2000. Incidentally, only 19 of the 75 Spanish language works are original biographies: 36 are translations, 19 are for juvenile audiences, and 18 are lives of Lincoln in biographical compilations, works of the "Great Americans" genre.

It has often been noted that there have been comparatively few recent French biographies of Lincoln. Indeed, if one discounts translations, biographies for juvenile audiences and biographical compilations, there have only been 6 original French biographies of Lincoln in the second half of the twentieth century. If one includes these categories, there have been 16, 7 of which are translations. It is true that the publication of biographies of Lincoln in French has been slow since the 1860s, when there were numerous works, many of which were published letters, speeches, orations, and eulogies containing biographical sketches. Thirty of the 63 catalogued French biographies of Lincoln were published in the 1860s. This lends credence to the view advanced in Michael Vorenberg's essay in this volume that the influence of Lincoln waned in France with the rise of the Third Republic.[5]

Of the 654 biographies catalogued, 251 seem to be translations. Some works have been particularly popular and have been frequently translated into numerous languages. Perhaps the most translated is Emil Ludwig's controversial German biography *Abraham Lincoln* (1930) which was suppressed by Hitler: it has been translated 18 times into 11 different languages (Ludwig's study is discussed in Jörg Nagler's essay in this volume).[6] Emanuel Hertz's essay *Abraham Lincoln: The Seer* has been translated 16 times into 12 different languages. Biographies by Benjamin Platt Thomas, Carl Sandburg, and Dale Carnegie have all been translated numerous times, into numerous languages.[7] Among the biographies translated into Chinese are Ludwig's (8 different translations), Carnegie's (6) and Sandburg's (4). Given that most of these have been published since 2000, it may be surprising that so many are translations of books from the first half of the previous century, and in the case of Ludwig's biography, from a non-English work. This may be because these works were no longer under copyright.

Another barometer for gauging Lincoln's influence is to compare the number of foreign language biographies listed by WorldCat for a selection of other notable American leaders. The following totals are based solely on WorldCat and are therefore not comprehensive, but since they are drawn from a single catalogue they are broadly comparable. The fairer comparison is between biographies published since 1970, when all of these subjects had passed into history. This evidence strongly suggests that Lincoln has had great global influence even when compared to other great Americans of very recent memory.

	Abraham Lincoln	George Washington	Thomas Jefferson	Franklin D. Roosevelt	John F. Kennedy	Martin Luther King Jr.
All entries	646	466	185	294	344	220
Since 1970	309	210	89	160	228	188

It is difficult to empirically measure Lincoln's global influence. How has his legacy varied between different countries? How has his influence compared with that of other American leaders? Biographies alone cannot provide a carefully calibrated measure of visibility, let alone impact or influence. The figures presented here do not tell us how many copies were sold, who bought them, how widely they circulated, and what status they enjoyed. Nonetheless, these totals do provide a broad measure of pulses of interest in Lincoln around the globe. Biographies have been published in languages as diverse as Gujarati, Hawaiian, Indonesian, Siouan, Slovak, Uighur, Welsh, and many others. Lincoln is a truly global figure, and his influence surpasses that of most American historical figures.

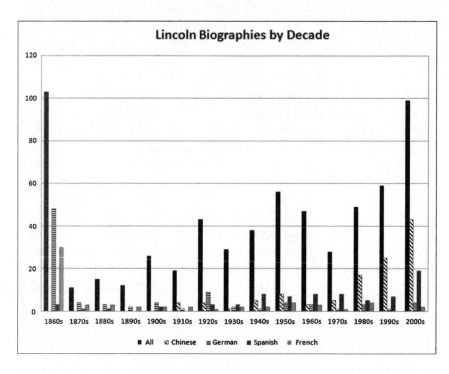

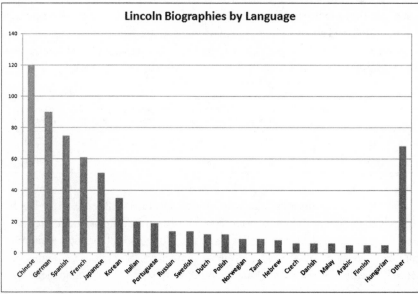

Notes

1. Jay Monaghan, *Lincoln Bibliography, 1839–1939*, 2 vols. (Springfield, Ill: Illinois State Historical Library, 1943–1945).

2. See chapter 13.

3. See chapter 1.

4. Emanuel Hertz, *Abraham Lincoln: The Seer* (New York[?]: 1925). Hertz was a Jewish Austrian immigrant, a leading Lincoln scholar, and collector of Lincolniana. *Abraham Lincoln: The Seer* was originally a WOR radio broadcast on February 12, 1925.

5. See chapter 5.

6. Emil Ludwig, *Abraham Lincoln* (London: G.P. Putnam's Sons, 1930). See chapter 14.

7. Benjamin Platt Thomas, *Abraham Lincoln: A Biography* (New York: Knopf, 1952); Carl Sandburg, *Abraham Lincoln: The Prairie Years* (New York: Harcourt, Brace & Co., 1926); *Abraham Lincoln: The War Years* (New York: Harcourt, Brace & Co., 1939); Dale Carnegie, *Lincoln the Unknown* (New York: Century Co. 1932).

{ Contributors }

Eugenio F. Biagini is a Fellow of Sidney Sussex College and Reader in Modern British and European History at the University of Cambridge. His research interests include Britain and Ireland since the 1860s, Italy in the age of the Risorgimento, and democracy, liberalism and republicanism in the nineteenth and twentieth centuries. His most recent publication is *Giuseppe Mazzini and the Globalization of Democratic Nationalism 1830–1920* (editor, with C. A. Bayly, 2008).

David W. Blight teaches American history at Yale and is the author of *Race and Reunion: The Civil War in American Memory*, the essay, "The Theft of Lincoln in Scholarship, Politics and Memory," and the forthcoming book *Fivescore Years Ago: Searching for America at the Civil War Centennial*. He is at work on a new biography of Frederick Douglass.

Carolyn P. Boyd is Professor of History at the University of California, Irvine. A specialist in the history of modern Spain, she is currently researching the cultural politics of nationalism, national identities, and history and memory in the nineteenth and twentieth centuries. Her books include *Praetorian Politics in Liberal Spain* (1974), *Historia Patria: Politics, History and National Identity in Spain, 1875–1975* (1997), and an edited volume, *Religión y política en la España contemporánea* (2007).

Richard Carwardine, Fellow of the British Academy and formerly Rhodes Professor of American History at the University of Oxford, is President of Corpus Christi College, Oxford. His research focuses on American politics and religion in the nineteenth century. His publications include *Transatlantic Revivalism: Popular Evangelicalism in Britain and America 1790–1865* (1978) and *Evangelicals and Politics in Antebellum America* (1993). His study of Abraham Lincoln won the Lincoln Prize in 2004 and was subsequently published in the United States as *Lincoln: A Life of Purpose and Power* (2006).

Kevin Gaines is the Robert Hayden Collegiate Professor of History and Afroamerican and African Studies, College of Literature, Science and the Arts, at the University of Michigan. He researches U.S. and African American intellectual and cultural history. His most recent book is *American Africans in Ghana: Black Expatriates and the Civil Rights Era* (2006). He is a past president of the American Studies Association (2009–10).

Lawrence Goldman is Fellow and Tutor in History at St. Peter's College, University of Oxford. He works on Victorian Britain and transatlantic social and intellectual movements in the nineteenth century. His publications include *Dons and Workers: Oxford and Adult Education Since 1850* (1995) and *Science, Reform, and Politics in Victorian Britain: The Social Science Association 1857–1886* (2002). He has been Editor of *The Oxford Dictionary of National Biography* since its publication in 2004.

Harold Holzer is Senior Vice President for External Affairs at The Metropolitan Museum of Art; served as co-chairman of the Lincoln Bicentennial Commission; and now chairs the Lincoln Bicentennial Foundation. A leading authority on the political culture of the Civil War Era, he has authored, co-authored, or edited thirty-six books, including *Lincoln and Cooper Union: The Speech That Made Abraham Lincoln President*, which earned a 2005 Lincoln Prize. He was awarded the National Humanities Medal by the President of the United States in 2008.

Kevin Kenny is Professor of History at Boston College. His research focuses on American immigration and on the transatlantic dimensions of popular protest. His books include *Making Sense of the Molly Maguires* (1998), *The American Irish: A History* (2000), *Peaceable Kingdom Lost: The Paxton Boys and the Destruction of William Penn's Holy Experiment* (2009), and (as editor) *Ireland and the British Empire: The Oxford History of the British Empire Companion Series* (2004).

Vinay Lal teaches history at UCLA. He writes widely on Indian history, Gandhi, popular culture and cinema, the Indian diaspora, global politics, contemporary American politics, and the politics of knowledge systems. His many books include *Empire of Knowledge* (2002), *The History of History: Politics and Scholarship in Modern India* (2003), *Of Cricket, Guinness and Gandhi: Essays on Indian History and Culture* (2005), *The Other Indians: A Cultural and Political History of South Asians in America* (2008), and (as editor) *Political Hinduism* (2009).

Nicola Miller is Professor of Latin American History at University College London. She works on the intellectual, cultural, and international history of the region. She is the author of *Soviet Relations with Latin America, 1959–1987* (1989), *In the Shadow of the State: Intellectuals and the Quest for National Identity in Spanish America* (1999), and *Reinventing Modernity in Latin America: Intellectuals Imagine the Future* (2008). She is a co-fundholder of the AHRC-funded project on "Images of the United States," the findings of which will be published as *America Imagined: Explaining the United States in Nineteenth-Century Europe and Latin America.*

Kenneth O. Morgan (Lord Morgan), Fellow of the British Academy, is an Honorary Fellow of The Queen's and Oriel Colleges, University of Oxford. He is the author of many works including a history of post-war Britain, *The People's Peace* (1989), and biographies of Lloyd George (1974), Keir Hardie (1975), James Callaghan (1997), and Michael Foot (2007). He is editor of *Oxford Illustrated History of Britain* (new ed., 2008). A former Vice-Chancellor of the University of Wales, in 2000 he was made a life peer as Baron Morgan of Aberdyfi.

Jörg Nagler is Professor of North American History at Friedrich Schiller University in Jena. He has written extensively on nineteenth and twentieth-century U.S. history, with a particular focus on war and society. He is interested in comparative history, the relationship between Germany and the United States, and the transnational significance of the American Civil War. His publications include *Frémont contra Lincoln* (1984), *On the Road to Total War: The American Civil War and the German Wars of Unification, 1861–1871* (3rd ed. 2002), and a biography of Lincoln in German (2009).

George Scratcherd is a D.Phil. candidate in American history at Christ Church, University of Oxford. His research explores the experience and roles of African American churchwomen in the post-Civil War South.

Jay Sexton is University Lecturer and Tutorial Fellow in American History at Corpus Christi College, University of Oxford. His research focuses on nineteenth-century U.S. foreign relations, the nineteenth-century global economy, and Anglo-American relations. He is the author of *Debtor Diplomacy: Finance and American Foreign Relations in the Civil War Era, 1837–1873* (2005) and *The Monroe Doctrine: Empire and Nation in Nineteenth-Century America* (2011).

Adam I. P. Smith is Senior Lecturer in American History at University College London. He researches mid-nineteenth century U.S. political culture, nationalism, and political mobilization. He is the author of *No Party Now: Politics in the Civil War North* (2006) and *The American Civil War* (2007). He is exploring British images of the United States as part of an Arts and Humanities Research Council project, "Images of America."

De-min Tao is Professor at Kansai University, Osaka, and founding President of the Society for Cultural Interaction in East Asia. As a specialist in Japanese Sinology and East Asian international history, he has published *A Study of the Kaitokudo Neo-Confucianism* (1994), *Meiji Sinologists and China* (2007), *New Horizons in the Study of Modern Sino-Japanese Relations* (2008), *Naito Konan's Collection of Calligraphic and Pictorial Works of the Late Qing Celebrities* (2009), and *The Transformation of Public Welfare Thought in East Asia* (2009).

Michael Vorenberg is Associate Professor of History at Brown University. He specializes in legal and constitutional history, especially in the era of the American Civil War and Reconstruction. He is the author of *Final Freedom: The Civil War, the Abolition of Slavery, and the Thirteenth Amendment* (2001) and *The Emancipation Proclamation: A Brief History with Documents* (2010). Currently he is at work on a study of the impact of the Civil War on American citizenship.

{ INDEX }

(Numbers in italics refer to illustrations)